THE

WOMANSPIRIT

SOURCEBOOK

A CATALOG OF BOOKS,

PERIODICALS, MUSIC,

CALENDARS & TAROT CARDS,

ORGANIZATIONS, VIDEO &

AUDIO TAPES, BOOKSTORES,

INTERVIEWS, MEDITATIONS,

ART

THE

WOMANSPIRIT

SOURCEBOOK

BY PATRICE WYNNE

1817

Harper & Row, Publishers, San Francisco
Cambridge, Hagerstown, New York, Philadelphia, Washington
London, Mexico City, São Paulo, Singapore, Sydney

FIRST EDITION

Designers: Tia Stoller and Donna Anderson, Stoller Design, San Francisco
            Border illustrations by Sandra Kunz and Tia Stoller.

Cover design: Phyllis Jane Rose

Cover art: Leslie Bowman

For a full-color poster of the cover painting, write
At the Foot of the Mountain
2000 South 5th Street
Minneapolis, MN 55454
Or call (612) 375-9487

ISBN: 0-06-250982-9
Library of Congress Catalog No.: 87-45201

88   89   90   91   MOY   10   9   8   7   6   5   4   3   2   1

The Womanspirit Sourcebook

is lovingly dedicated in service to Gaia,

the source of life, and to our future.

ACKNOWLEDGMENTS

To my mother, Gloria Bertonis, and my grandmother, Catherine Bernatonis, who have loved and encouraged me from the beginning.

To the women of Gaia—Mary Schmidt, Donna Ferina, Leslie Gardner-Gustufson, Sue Beard, and Elena Berliner—for "holding up the temple" of Gaia, and for keeping our business strong and holy, laughter and beauty-filled, freeing me to dedicate myself to the creation of the Sourcebook.

To the women in my community who have supported, inspired, provoked, sustained, and blessed me during the creation of the Sourcebook. At one particularly difficult stage I invited a group of women to "midwife" me to the next phase. Each of these women brought altar gifts to my home, symbols of the wisdom carried within, but which I had lost sight of in the creative process. I am grateful for a loving community of spiritual sisters in my life.

To the many women who have generously contributed reviews, artwork, interviews, and feature articles. And especially to those women whose work, due to the limitations of space, time, and resources, I was unable to include in this first edition of the Sourcebook, I offer my deepest gratitude.

To the people of Harper & Row, especially Yvonne Keller, Jan Johnson, John Loudon, and Clayton Carlson for their support of the vision behind the Sourcebook.

To Tia Stoller for bringing laughter and a fresh creative spirit to the final stages of the book production.

And to my partner, Eric Joost, for his strong, nurturing presence in my life and for the earth, air, fire, and water of his love.

**THE WOMANSPIRIT
SOURCEBOOK**

C O N T E N T S

CALL

Alla Renée Bozarth

There is a new sound

of roaring voices in the deep

and light-shattered rushes in the heavens;

the mountains are coming alive,

the fire-kindled mountains moving again

to reshape the earth.

It is we sleeping women

waking up in a darkened world,

cutting the chains from off our bodies

with our teeth, stretching our lives

over the slow earth,

seeing, moving, breathing in the vigor

that commands us to make all things new.

It has been said that while the women sleep

the earth shall sleep.

But listen! We are waking up and rising,

and soon our sister will know her strength.

The earth-moving day is here.

We women wake to move in fire.

The earth shall be remade.

From Alla Renée Bozarth, *Gynergy*, Wisdom House Press, 1978.

THE WOMANSPIRIT
SOURCEBOOK

INTRODUCTION

WOMANSPIRIT: A SPIRITUALITY
FOR OUR TIMES

Held as a prayer in the wombs of our ancestors, feminine spirituality is reemerging as a healing power in our lives. From a small group of pioneers on the fringes of the contemporary women's movement, we have grown since the early 1970s to a worldwide community of people engaged in the transformation of ourselves and our society. The feminine, awakening in the hearts and minds of people everywhere today, is guiding us in restoring spiritual, ecological, and political balance on Earth, for feminine consciousness knows that all of life is unified in a great unbroken circle. Cooperation, trust, wholeness, nurturance, synergistic power, and authentic love—for ourselves and for all of Creation—form the basis for our actions in a spiritual feminine world.

Feminine spirituality is not the exclusive domain of women. The feminine is an active, sacred principle embedded in human existence. There are many like-minded and like-hearted men who share women's spiritual awareness and who are engaged in positive personal and global transformation. Yet, the task is different for women and for men. Each of us has been shaped by the powers and oppressions, the ways of perceiving, and the ways of deceiving that are part of our gender socialization in a patriarchal world. The task, then, is to discover what lies beneath our role identity as women and men, to get to the sacred core of feminine and masculine powers, and as women and men to work together in partnership for the spiritual evolution of our endangered planet.

The global awakening of spiritual feminine consciousness in women, Womanspirit, is a movement whose time has come and whose effects are far-reaching. In healing rituals and seasonal gatherings, in workplaces and kitchens of friends, in group meditations and houses of prayer, in groves of trees and under the stars, women are gathering to shape a new reality. Unfolding in the great body of women's art and story, music and ritual, community and celebration, this new reality affirms our knowledge as women of spirit power and vision. Generation to generation, through ordinary acts of courage and creation, among women of different races, cultures, and religious beliefs, we are once again remembering and celebrating who we are.

We are the Visionkeepers

>   of a deep and abiding spiritual heritage that honors the sacredness

>   of life and the integrity of all life forms

We are the Guardians

>   of a rich body of myths and symbols, powers and knowings,

>   stories and traditions that honor the cycles

>   of birth, growth, aging, and death

We are the Creators

>   of a New Earth upon which the spiritual values

>   of women shall be fully woven into the fabric of our everyday lives.

We are the Weavers

>   of ancient and new patterns of living in kinship with Nature, for the

>   Earth is in us and we are in Her

Women of spirit are visible everywhere today. We carry the message that our suffering and the Earth's suffering are one. As we free the

"There are women everywhere with fragments Gather fragments, weave and mend When we learn to come together We are whole."

Anne Cameron
Daughters of Copper Woman

". . . because I know I am made from this earth, as my mother's hands were made from this earth, as her dreams came from this earth and all that I know . . . speaks to me through this earth and I long to tell you, you who are earth too, and listen as we speak to each other of what we know: the light is in us."

Susan Griffin
Woman and Nature

"The image of the Goddess inspires women to see ourselves as divine, our bodies as sacred, the changing phases of our lives as holy, our aggression as healthy, our anger as purifying, and our power to nurture and to create—but also to limit and destroy when necessary—as the very force that sustains life."

Starhawk
The Spiral Dance

immense reservoirs of compassion, love, wisdom, and strength within us, we help enable this aching planet and all people to thrive. Womanspirit, then, is a way of living in that delicately balanced place between full-hearted awareness of the military, ecological, and spiritual crises that afflict us and full-bodied immersion in our own natural powers of healing and renewal. Linked in common purpose with global movements for peace and social justice, personal transformation and ecological balance, our spirituality sustains our faith that the destructive course of humanity can be altered.

Women's spirituality values what is deeply and soulfully nourishing to the preservation of life. The recognition that we have adapted ourselves to living in a masculine world while losing our connection to the feminine has led many women to journey, like the Sumerian Goddess Inanna, to the depths of the Great Below. Often, a great grief overwhelms us when we discover how little we have loved and nourished our woman-selves. Patterns of addiction to food, love, alcohol, drugs, and work are symptoms of abandonment of the feminine, in ourselves and by our culture.

We are questing, women of this age, for a world of aliveness in a dying patriarchal world. Our quest leads us to the wealth of Goddess-, woman-, and Earth-honoring spiritual traditions, long suppressed by patriarchal mind, that are part of our inheritance as a human family. The return of the feminine, as imaged in the Goddess, is expressed in the hearts of all peoples seeking unity rather than separation, cooperation rather than domination, and a celebration of the sacred wisdom of body, Earth, and spirit. And how we long for a passionate, inclusive, and awakened spirituality!

Gaia and Grandmother Earth, the Feminine Face of God and the Goddess of Ten Thousand Names, the Shekhinah, the Womb of Creation, the Black Madonna, Changing Woman, Kuan Yin . . . . Her myriad names mirror the fundamental unity of religious teachings. She is found in all world religions. Her many forms reflect the infinite diversity of life, for She is of all races, all cultures, all creatures of the Earth. Spiritual and religious traditions, when shaped by the feminine principle, affirm the cyclical phases of our lives and the wisdom each phase brings, the sacredness of our bodies and the body of the Earth.

As each woman realizes her power, she transforms the world. Women of spirit, we are coming together, for the future of our Kin: the Earth's peoples, the hungry and the aged, the forgotten ones, the world's children, the family of the trees, flowers, and seeds. Women of spirit, we are engaged in transforming the human legacy. For our wondrous accomplishments and our stunning failures, the depths of our secret longings, our foolish notions and our collective wisdom, all that is known contained in each cell, the ongoing flow of life, the gift of Creation, ours to cherish and to preserve, for all our Kin we take our power in shaping a New Earth.

"She is slowly finding us and we are quietly everywhere."

Merlin Stone
Bloomington Festival and
Spirituality Conference

"The expression of women's spiritual quest is integrally related to the telling of women's stories. If women's stories are not told, the depth of women's souls will not be known."

Carol P. Christ
Diving Deep and Surfacing:
Women Writers on Spiritual
Quest

"Women's spirituality is a world-wide movement of womanenergy and vision whose work is the transformation of our selves and our society."

Woman of Power Magazine,
Premier Issue

"Through ritual moments and countless meditations, through absorbing the sacred myths of our prepatriarchal foremothers and passing them on to my daughter, through experiencing in my own mother/daughter mind and body the mysteries celebrated in the ancient rites, I have come to know, to feel, oneness with all the millions of women who have lived, who live, who will live. I contain those millions. Each of us does. Every moment. Such a power cannot be stopped."

Charlene Spretnak
The Politics of Women's
Spirituality

"For each of us as women, there is a deep place within, where hidden and growing our true spirit rises. . . . Within these deep places, each one holds an incredible reserve of creativity and power, of unexamined and unrecorded emotion and feeling. The woman's place of power within each of us is neither white nor surface; it is dark, it is ancient, and it is deep."

Audre Lorde
Uses of the Erotic as Power

"The bodhisattva can hear the music of the spheres and understand the language of the birds; but, by the same sensitivity to the web of life, he or she hears also the cries of torment from the deepest levels of hell. All is registered in the 'boundless heart' of the bodhisattva. Through our deepest and innermost responses to our world—to hunger and torture and the threat of annihilation—we touch that boundless heart. It is the web we have woven as interconnected system—or as synapses in the mind of God."

Joanna Macy
Despair and Personal Power in the Nuclear Age

"The return of the Goddess implies a return of her many priestesses—powerful female transmitters of the energy of the 'feminine' ray. All over the world women are being 'tapped' with this power and beginning to manifest the Goddess in their work and daily lives. Men who respect and respond to this energy are also feeling the power of the feminine."

Vicki Noble
Motherpeace: The Way to the Goddess through Myth, Art, And Tarot

"i found god in myself & i loved her fiercely."

Ntozake Shange
For Colored Girls Who Have Considered Suicide/When the Rainbow Is Enuf

"The feminine principle is more than just having feelings and being a nurturer; it is the fabric of society, setting the moral and ethical values of the culture. The return of the feminine principle will change the course of history—our priorities, values, and the way we live in the Earth."

Charlotte Kelley
Women's Alliance

"The Kaballah teaches us that . . . one of the causes of galut (exile) is the alienation of the masculine from the feminine in God, the alienation of God from the Shechinah. . . . Now that the masculine and feminine have been torn asunder and the feminine dismembered and banished, both from the discourse about divinity and

from the human community, a tikkun, a 'reparation,' is obligatory (a mitzvah). When the masculine and feminine aspect of God have been reunited and the feminine aspect of humanity has been returned from exile . . . the world will be repaired."

Rita M. Gross
Womanspirit Rising:
A Feminist Reader in Religion

"We are all the creation makers and a new world is awaiting creation. Follow your own path and discover your own women's wisdom within the larger wisdom that we all share."

Hallie Austen Iglehart
Womanspirit: A Guide to Women's Wisdom

"Let us note and celebrate the fact that 'woman-spirit' rising is a global phenomenon in our time. Everywhere women are on the move. What is coming into view now, on a worldwide scale, is the incredible collective power of women, so that anyone who has eyes to see can glimpse the power and strength of women's full humanity."

Beverly Harrison

P R E F A C E

ABOUT THE
WOMANSPIRIT SOURCEBOOK

———

In the spring of 1985 I placed a call to John Loudon, senior editor at Harper & Row, seeking information on a book they were about to release. It was a question any staff member could have answered, so it must have seemed odd that I would ask for him, but he was the only staff person I knew there. "Why do you want to know?" he asked me.

I told him about my catalogue company, which specialized in women's spiritual resources with an emphasis on Goddess spirituality. "That's interesting," he commented. "Harper & Row has been wanting to publish a similar catalogue of book and tape reviews." "I'll write it," I replied, without a moment's hesitation. "But it will include more than books and tapes. There will be art and music, rituals and stories, interviews and quotes. It will be alive with the beauty and power and diversity of a movement that is empowering the lives of so many women today."

It was a remarkable experience, for as I described the book to John I had a crystal-clear picture of the contents of the book. I could even see the colors of the book's cover. It was as if the Sourcebook already existed and was describing itself to me exactly the way it would potentially exist in the world. Now, this concept is very strange to a patriarchal worldview where communication, if it takes place at all, can only happen between humans. But the truth is that in a Universe alive with meaning and mystery, books ask to be written because the time has come for the message they contain.

In gathering the material for *The Womanspirit Sourcebook*, I simply asked the question, "What are the resources emerging from the contemporary women's spirituality movement that are guiding and inspiring the spiritual empowerment of women and the feminine principle"? That question led me to the people and places, groups and publications, images and creations that form the body of *The Womanspirit Sourcebook*. The reviews of the resources listed in the Sourcebook were contributed by women from around the country. The biographies of these women appear at the back of the book and their initials follow each review.

Women and men from many spiritual/religious traditions are represented in these pages—women who worship the Goddess, women whose spirituality is firmly rooted in feminism and women who do not identify as feminists, followers of New Age thinking, male friends and supporters, Protestant ministers and Catholic nuns, Pagan people and Biblical feminists, Lesbian, Jewish, Black, and Buddhist women, Christian women and Native American sisters. Though our paths may differ, we are linked by our faith in the sacredness of life, by our love of the Earth—the active, engaged love needed to sustain life at this perilous juncture in human evolution—and by our commitment to heal and bring forth the feminine spirit in ourselves and in our culture.

The Womanspirit Sourcebook is offered to you, with love, that you may discover your own unique role in bringing about a more just, loving, and compassionate world. Use it as a source of inspiration as you take your place in the community of planetary healers and let your voice be heard in the shaping of our world.

Patrice Wynne
Berkeley, California

**THE WOMANSPIRIT
SOURCEBOOK**

O R D E R I N G

I N F O R M A T I O N

The Womanspirit Sourcebook was created to provide you with access to the wealth of Earth-healing, feminine and feminist spiritual resources. Many of these resources have been produced by small businesses owned by women, by self-employed women, and by alternative organizations dedicated to the healing and renewal of our culture. Wherever possible, ordering information is provided in the Sourcebook. Besides the mail-order information provided after each review, many of the Sourcebook resources can be purchased through your local bookstore. Your support of the artists and businesses found in the Sourcebook will enable their efforts to grow and prosper.

Although every attempt was made to verify resource prices, descriptions, and availability at time of publication, the author and publisher make no guarantee of resource information provided in the Sourcebook. We regret any inconvenience this may cause you.

THE GAIA CATALOGUE COMPANY: Income from The Gaia Catalogue (formerly The Womanspirit Catalogue) has provided funds for The Womanspirit Sourcebook Project. To receive our current catalogue and be placed on the mailing list, send $3.00. Your support of our work makes possible future editions of The Womanspirit Sourcebook.
PRICES: Prices quoted include postage and handling but do *not* include tax. Please add appropriate state sales tax with your order. Prices are subject to change. Contact each supplier before ordering.
CORRESPONDENCE: Due to the scope of The Womanspirit Sourcebook Project, individual requests for personal information cannot be

answered. We welcome your comments and contributions to future editions of the Sourcebook.

Write:
The Gaia Catalogue Company
1400 Shattuck Avenue, #10
Shattuck Commons
North Berkeley, CA 94709
(415) 548-4172
Please include a self-addressed stamped envelope (SASE) with all correspondence.

For easy reference, I have listed the most frequently appearing sources for materials here, rather than repeat them throughout the text.

Harper & Row, Publishers
Keystone Industrial Park
Scranton, PA 18512
(800) 242-7737

Random House
400 Hahn Rd.
Westminster, MD 21157
(800) 638-6460

Beacon Press
25 Beacon Street
Boston, MA 02108
(617) 683-1570

Ladyslipper
P.O. Box 3130
Durham, NC 27705
(919) 683-1570

Flying Fish Records
1304 W. Schubert
Chicago, IL 60614
(312) 528-5455

Redwood Records
6400 Hollis Street
Emeryville, CA 94608
(415) 428-9191

Olivia Records
4400 Market St.
Oakland, CA 94608
(415) 655-0364

THE
WEAVERS OF
LANGUAGE:

BOOK RESOURCES

**THE WOMANSPIRIT
SOURCEBOOK**

BOOK
RESOURCES

A WEAVE OF WOMEN
E. M. BRONER

Empowerment, through the agency of a community of women. Retelling the past in our own voices, remaking the ritual with our own prayers, restructuring our lives with our own hands . . . this is the gift of vision in *A Weave of Women*. Set in Jerusalem, the sacred city of the Jewish people, the book shows women coming together to share and rebirth their lives. Storytelling is one of the most inspiring modes of spiritual power that women possess, the recounting of our own experience, the witnessing we do for each other, filling in the silent abyss with the body and song of ourselves. In this we find and define what is God, what is spirit, what is truth. Esther Broner continues to be an important voice in this process. May she continue to be blessed with the gift of tale. LG

Indiana University Press, 1985, 295 pgs. Available from Indiana University Press, 10th and Morton Sts., Bloomington, IN 47405, (812) 335-6804 ($11.45 ppd.).

A WOMAN LIKE YOU: LIFE STORIES OF WOMEN RECOVERING FROM ALCOHOLISM AND ADDICTION
RACHEL V.

Rachel V., a pseudonym for a well-known spiritual feminist writer and a recovering alcoholic, has drawn together a body of firsthand testimony by women who, as members of Alcoholics Anonymous, are recovering from addiction. Women of different races, sexual orientations, and socioeconomic classes (including a nun, an international lawyer, a wilderness guide, a doctor, a teenage drug dealer, a "proper matron")

share their pain, struggles, losses, and triumphs in arresting their disease and reclaiming their self-worth. As Dr. LeClair Bissell notes in her introduction, the social stigma of women's addiction often leads to denial and self-hatred, which work against recognition and treatment of the disease. The courageous voices of these women will inspire any woman attempting to alter destructive patterns and to love herself into well-being. *A Woman Like You* also features an invaluable resource section and an adaptation of the Twelve Steps to reflect inclusive God language. PW

Harper & Row, 1985, 223 pgs. Available from Harper & Row ($17.45 ppd.).

A WRINKLE IN TIME
MADELEINE L'ENGLE

I first read this delightful and thought-provoking children's book in sixth grade. Two decades later, I continue to find it a source of joy and inspiration. A unique blend of science fiction, mysticism, and fantasy, *A Wrinkle in Time* offers a compelling vision of faith. L'Engle, an Episcopalian laywoman, has authored numerous children's books and a series of personal journals. This book is a marvelous initiation into her writings. RK

Dell, 1982, 224 pgs.

ADDICTION TO PERFECTION: THE STILL UNRAVISHED BRIDE
MARION WOODMAN

"Our society has murdered the Great Mother, the inner life that feeds the spirit. As Jung has pointed out, we are so busy doing and achieving that we have lost touch with our inner life. No other era has so totally divorced outer reality from inner reality, the matrix of which is the Great Mother. Never before have we been so cut off from the wisdom of nature and the wisdom of our own instincts. What do we have left? The goddess at the center of our culture is the negative mother, one who would dash her baby's brains out and sacrifice love to power. She is Shakespeare's Lady Macbeth. She is not to be confused with the Black Madonna in Christian mythology who lives through our dark, uncanny, instinctual nature and who can, if she is to be given the chance, bring her healing to our despair. Through her, our divine child can be born."

In this, her second book, Jungian analyst Marion Woodman connects addictive behavior to a patriarchal society that emphasizes perfection. Those of us who are father's daughters are particularly vulnerable to addictive behavior in our quest to please. To heal ourselves we must face our own "dark, uncanny, instinctual nature," the dark goddess who is cut off from her feminine instincts. Woodman believes the way to maturity for women is through our bodies, where we may become truly virgins, women-unto-ourselves. MS

Inner City Books, 1982, 204 pgs. Available from The Gaia Catalogue Company ($13.50 ppd.).

ALL GOD'S CHILDREN NEED TRAVELING SHOES
MAYA ANGELOU

All God's Children Need Traveling Shoes is the fifth in a series of autobiographies that Angelou began writing in 1970. During the early 1960s, the era she chronicles here, Maya Angelou is a black American woman seeking her African roots. An accomplished singer, dancer, actress, journalist, Angelou has moved from Cairo, Egypt, where she was the first woman editor of an Arab newspaper, to Ghana with her teenage son, Guy. When Guy almost dies in a car accident, Angelou begins to realize the importance of home, a theme she carries throughout the book. *All*

God's Children proves, like the volumes before it, that for Maya Angelou the personal is always the political. Anyone who has ever sought the comfort of family, purpose, or place will be nurtured and uplifted by her story. (Contributed by Evelyn White. This review was originally published in the *San Francisco Chronicle/Examiner.*)

Random House, 1986, 208 pgs. Available from Random House ($4.95 ppd.).

ALL WE'RE MEANT TO BE: BIBLICAL FEMINISM FOR TODAY
LETHA DAWSON SCANZONI AND NANCY HARDESTY

The basic textbook of biblical (or evangelical) feminism, now updated and expanded. Scanzoni and Hardesty combined their backgrounds in sociology and history to produce the 1974 book that helped launch the biblical feminist movement in the United States and Canada. Scholarly and meticulously documented, lauded and hated, this book sets out to answer questions frequently asked by women and men about Christianity and feminism. VH

Abingdon, 1986, 272 pgs. Available from Daughters of Sarah, 3801 N. Keeler, Dept. 1114, Chicago, IL 60641, (312) 736-3399 ($14 ppd.).

ALONE OF ALL HER SEX: THE MYTH AND CULT OF THE VIRGIN MARY
MARINA WARNER

Written by a feminist who was once a convent schoolgirl, this book is the place to start for an understanding of the profoundly ambivalent figure of the Virgin Mary. Warner clarifies the ways in which Mary embodies ancient, indestructible memories of female power and sacredness, and how at the same time she has been subjected to a steady barrage of misogynist projection. In successive sections, Mary appears as Virgin,

Queen, Bride, Mother, and Intercessor; Warner amplifies the historical and cultural influences that shaped these ideals and shows the impact they have had on Mary's devotees. JIS

Alfred A. Knopf, 1976, 419 pgs. Available from Random House ($11.95 ppd.).

ALWAYS COMING HOME
URSULA K. LE GUIN

"As I go along getting old, as I get yinner every day, the need for my own tongue grows more, becomes hunger—and I eat mushrooms, I eat earthworms, I eat thunder to fill that hunger for a word of my own, a language I, this old woman, can speak with all my heart."

Always Coming Home is a book of imagination, insight, and hope that, in sheer breadth of vision, is unlike any other ever written. The book (and its companion audio cassette tape) is simultaneously a novel, an anthropological study, and a vast collection of poems, myths, ceremonies, recipes, wordplays, gossip, romance, technology, meditations, birth and death songs, poetry, drama, and music. Le Guin has envisioned the kind of world we might create if we truly integrated the wisdom of pacifistic, woman, and Earth-honoring traditions into the totality of our culture. Working with Le Guin, Margaret Chodos has illustrated the book with a hundred drawings of plants, animals, artifacts; and composer Todd Barton has created original music and beautiful recordings of love songs, rituals, and poetry. AR

Harper & Row, 1985, 523 pgs. Available from Harper & Row ($26.50 ppd. includes book and audio cassette).

AN INTERRUPTED LIFE: THE DIARIES OF ETTY HILLESUM 1941–1943
ETTY HILLESUM

These autobiographical writings chart the spiritual journey of a young Dutch Jew during the two years prior to her death at Auschwitz in 1943. In that time she develops a sense of her own strengths and a clarity of purpose expressed in words that continue to speak directly to contemporary spiritual searchers. She begins to write as an insecure woman of twenty-seven, looking to others, especially men, for her sense of self-worth. Yet, by the end of her life, she has developed her own voice and a personal understanding of the events that have overtaken her. As she corresponds with herself in her diaries she also addresses an outward divinity. Implicit in her words is the inextricable link between the two:

" . . . somewhere inside me the jasmine continues to blossom undisturbed, just as profusely and delicately as it ever did. . . . And I shall bring You all the flowers I shall meet on my way, and truly there are many of those. I shall try to make You at home always." LG

Washington Square Press, 1981, 281 pgs. Available from Washington Square Press, 200 Old Tappan Rd., Old Tappan, NJ 07675, (201) 767-5937 ($5.50 ppd.).

AN OUTBREAK OF PEACE
SARAH PIRTLE

Sarah Pirtle is a core member of the national Interhelp network and founder of Arts Resources for Cooperation. Her musical recording *Two Hands Hold the Earth* was named one of the best children's recordings of 1985 by the American Library Association (see listing on page 157). The publication of *An Outbreak of Peace* fulfills her personal goal of creating a feminist novel for teenagers that addresses the key issue of peace in our lifetime. The story takes place in a New England town where thirteen-year-old Cassie and her best friends enlist the entire community in declaring "an outbreak of peace." There are three strong role models in the novel, three women in their forties: Cassie's mother, who is Polish American, a sculptor who is Japanese American, and a photographer and professor who is Afro-American. The book portrays friends supporting one another and characters addressing and interrupting racism. Written with the aid and guidance of young people and illustrated by artists eight to twenty years old, *An Outbreak of Peace* will inspire hope and empowerment in readers of any age. PW

New Society Publishers, 1987, 285 pgs. Available from New Society Publishers, Box 582, Santa Cruz, CA 95061, (408) 458-1191 ($11.45 ppd.). Note: New Society Publishers publishes books and other resources that teach skills in creating a more peaceful and just world through non-violent action. A free catalogue of "Books to Build A New Society" is available upon request.

ANCIENT ART AND RITUAL
JANE ELLEN HARRISON

In *Ancient Art and Ritual*, Jane Ellen Harrison (1850–1928) takes us on a theoretical journey to the origins of ritual. Harrison describes the evolution of ritual from the magical dances of primeval groups, through its development into a form of collective worship of the natural world, and on to its perversion and later demise at the hands of patriarchal rulers. She illustrates for us the emergence of art from ritual and the intimate relationship between the two, concluding with a number of valuable theoretical aesthetic insights. Implicit in Harrison's discussion is her awareness that humanity has a "real and recurrent need" for sacred ritual to express our reverence for life. She further emphasizes that

art functions "to feed and nurture the imagination and spirit, and thereby enhance and invigorate the whole of human life," an important reminder in this age of the intellect. AM

Henry Holt & Co., 1913, 256 pgs. This book is now out of print but can be found in many libraries.

ANCIENT MIRRORS OF WOMANHOOD: A TREASURY OF GODDESS AND HEROINE LORE FROM AROUND THE WORLD
MERLIN STONE

A collection of Goddess stories written in both poetic and prose narrative, *Ancient Mirrors* recovers for our times the nearly lost heritage of courageous, wise, and powerful women that flourished centuries ago. It includes rare material from a wide range of cultures: Africa, China, Mexico, the Americas, Scandinavia, Australia, Polynesia, India, Japan, Greece, and more. Like Merlin Stone's previous book *When God Was a Woman* (see listing on page 99), this work deepens our understanding of the pervasive, enduring, and powerful presence of the Goddess throughout human culture. An excellent sourcebook. PW

Beacon Press, 1984, 425 pgs. Available from The Gaia Catalogue Company ($13.45 ppd.).

THE MYTH OF CHANGING WOMAN

MERLIN STONE

Although Changing Woman is regarded as an anthropomorphic figure, the beliefs and customs associated with Her allow us to understand that She is the processes of Nature. This Navajo concept of female deity may well be compared to the accounts of Nu Kwa and Mother Nature (Tao). The extremely important Navajo concept of walking in The Trail of Beauty certainly brings the concept of Tao (The Way) to the mind of any student of spiritual thought.

Creator of the Navajo people, Changing Woman, Estsan Atlehi, is the Mother of All. She is the Holy Woman who brings each season, Mother Earth who is the seasons, Iyatiku who Brings All Life, Mother Nature in all that She unfolds.

Some say that She was born at the foot of the Mountain Around Which Moving Was Done, born on a bed of flowers, a delicate rainbow arching as coverlet over Her infant body. From Her body grew the four mountains of the compass points, the mountains that mark the East and West, the mountains that mark the North and South. This day of birth was a day of joy, a day of brilliance and thus the memory of it is kept in the ever joyous song of The Blessing Way. For if Changing Woman had not been born, She would not have rubbed the skin of Her perfect body—and in this way brought forth the Navajo people.

It is Changing Woman who teaches the flow of life, the restlessness of the sand as it flies with the wind, the wisdom of the ancient rocks that never leave their home, the pleasure of the tiny sapling that had risen through them. So it is into the House of Changing Woman that each young girl enters, as her blood begins to flow with the moon, as she passes into womanhood.

It is Changing Woman who teaches the cycles, the constant round of hot and cold, of birth and dying, of youth and aging, of seedling to corn, of corn to seedling kernel, of day to night, of night to day, of waxing moon to waning moon—and thus She gave the sacred songs that help to ease all in their passage. For is it not Changing Woman who each year sleeps beneath the blanket of snow as Grandmother who walks with a turquoise cane, but then each year awakes with the flowers of Spring, awakes as the young Mother of us all?

It is to Changing Woman that we look as we search for the wisdom of life. While some may believe that they can defy Changing Woman's patterns to make their own, wise people know that this cannot be done, for to try to change the ways of Changing Woman, is to destroy all life. But those who understand the ways of Changing Woman, forever walk The Trail of Beauty.

From Merlin Stone, *Ancient Mirrors of Womanhood*, Beacon Press, 1979.

Ceremonial Basket © Kathleen Curtis, 1985. Raffia, fiber flex, and Earth, 16″ × 12″ × 6″. Photo by Carolyn Brown. Ceremonial art available for sale from the artist. Write: Kathleen Curtis, P.O. Box 10, Truckee, CA 95734.

ANNIE AND THE OLD ONE

MISKA MILES, WITH ILLUSTRATIONS BY PETER PARNALL

This poignant story of Annie and her dying grandmother (the Old One) is set in the world of the Navajo Indians. The Old One understands that all things return to Earth. She gathers the family together and allows each of them to select a special object from her possessions. She tells them that once the rug currently on her loom is completed, her time on Earth is completed. Annie cannot imagine her world without the Old One. She plots to stop the weaving and so, she hopes, to prevent the inevitable loss of the Old One. Her grandmother's loving patience helps her to understand that time cannot be held back and to accept the natural rhythms of life and death. A fine book for helping children understand the aging and dying process. (Contributed by Jane Potter, publisher of *A Child's Garden Catalogue: Life-Affirming Books for Children to Grow With*.)

Little, Brown & Co, 1971, 44 pgs. Available from A Child's Garden, 920 St. Helena Ave., Santa Rosa, CA 95404 ($7.95 ppd.).

ANOTHER MOTHER TONGUE: GAY WORDS, GAY WORLDS

JUDY GRAHN

A powerful, courageous, and landmark book, *Another Mother Tongue* reclaims the heritage of lesbian and gay people over time and around the world, as shamans, healers, sacred figures, priestesses, and ceremonial dykes. By chronicling the contributions made to culture by this 10-percent minority, Grahn provides historical substantiation to lesbian and gay pride and demonstrates the role of lesbians and gays in healing and shaping culture. Her own story, woven throughout the text, provides the reader with the living, loving, and at times painful reality of a con-

temporary lesbian's spiritual journey. CS

"Had I been born into a tribal society as were my European genetic ancestors, I believe I would have been the European equivalent of a shaman: a hag, a wisewoman, a sorcerer, a dervish, a runic bard, a warrior/priest, a wiccan-woman. Born into an American white Protestant family in a modern industrial democratic state I became, instead, a very purposeful Lesbian poet. It has become clear to me that I am some kind of modern ceremonial dyke. I think there are in our country hundreds of thousands of such people, as well as hundreds of thousands of ceremonial faggots, and many varied avenues to these traditional Gay offices."

Beacon Press, 1984, 324 pgs. Available from Beacon Press ($11.95 ppd.).

ARTEMIS SPEAKS: V.B.A.C. AND NATURAL CHILDBIRTH INFORMATION

NAN KOEHLER

This book, though written for women preparing to have a vaginal birth after cesareans (VBAC), is immensely useful for any birthing woman. Nan Koehler is a holistic educator, birth attendant, herbalist, writer, biologist, wife and mother of five. In *Artemis Speaks* she has compiled a mass of information on the emotional/spiritual aspects of pregnancy and birth for women. The book includes first-person accounts of VBAC women, articles on infant, self-, and family care gathered from a wide range of sources, practical resources, an index of plants and herbs, and words of wisdom to empower women and their families in becoming choice-makers about birth. Nan's faith in the experience

of birth as a rite of passage is as constant as the moon goddess, Artemis. PW

Jerald R. Brown, Inc., 1985, 575 pgs. Available from Paul Armitage Sales, 17440 Taylor Ln. Occidental, CA 95465 ($16.95 ppd.).

THE AVEBURY CYCLE

MICHAEL DAMES

See listing on page 82. PW

Thames & Hudson, London, 1977, 240 pgs.

BECOMING WOMAN: THE QUEST FOR WHOLENESS IN FEMALE EXPERIENCE

PENELOPE WASHBOURN

Becoming Woman explores the personal and spiritual questions implicit in the female life cycle. Washbourn examines critical turning points in a woman's life—the onset of menstruation, leaving home, marriage, and pregnancy. Drawing on cross-cultural insights, contemporary psychology, and her own personal experiences, Washbourn shows how each passage presents an opportunity for growth and wholeness in the formation of women's personal and spiritual identity. RK

Harper & Row, 1977, 174 pgs. Available from Harper & Row ($9.95 ppd.).

BEYOND GOD THE FATHER: TOWARD A PHILOSOPHY OF WOMEN'S LIBERATION

MARY DALY

"The cutting away of this phallocentric value system in its various incarnations amounts also to a kind of "exorcism" that essentially must be done by women, who are in a position to experience the demonic destructiveness of the super-phallic society in our own being. The 'mach-

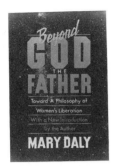

ismo' ethos that has the human psyche in its grip creates a web of projections, introjections, and self-fulfilling prophecies. It fosters a basic alienation within the psyche—a failure to lay claim to that part of the psyche that is then projected onto "the Other." It is essentially demonic in that it cuts off the power of human becoming."

For anyone who cares about feminist spirituality, Mary Daly's writing is essential. This early work is angry: a devastating analysis of how patriarchal religion has functioned as an integral part of women's oppression, written by someone deeply familiar with its history and doctrines. The book is also hopeful: the articulation of women's experience as liberating truth, creating a "sisterhood as cosmic covenant." RK

Beacon Press, 1985, 225 pgs. Available from Beacon Press ($10.95 ppd.).

BEYOND POWER: ON WOMEN, MEN AND MORALS
MARILYN FRENCH

The spiritual heart of *Beyond Power* is its analysis of the effects of patriarchy—on women, on men, and on our social institutions. French paints a devastating portrait of women's condition under patriarchy. Patriarchy has constricted men too, says French, often in ways that are nearly as destructive. As for our social institutions, French demon-

strates in detail how the patriarchal morality (power-as-control) has twisted them all horribly. Her presentation of the feminist alternative is in many ways the high point of the book. Here is its essence:

"The only true revolution against patriarchy is one which removes the idea of power from its central position, and replaces it with the idea of pleasure. Despite the contempt in which this quality has been held for several millennia, pleasure, felicity—in its largest and deepest sense—is actually the highest human good. . . . Power-to primarily increases pleasure, and power-over primarily increases pain. . . . To restore pleasure to centrality requires restoring the body, and therefore nature, to value. . . . "

How can we do away with the patriarchal morality of power-as-control? Wisely, perhaps, French doesn't offer one definitive answer, but several partial ones. She urges us not to identify goodness with powerlessness. She urges us to use our power in the public world "as a means to noncontrolling well-being." And she urges us to live "with an eye to delight rather than domination." (Excerpted from a previously published review contributed by a friend and supporter of *The Womanspirit Sourcebook*.)

Ballantine Books, 1985, 640 pgs. Available from The Gaia Catalogue Company ($13.45 ppd.).

BEYOND SEX ROLES: A GUIDE FOR THE STUDY OF FEMALE ROLES IN THE BIBLE
GILBERT G. BILEZIKIAN

A thorough, well-organized study of women's roles as pictured in the Bible by a scholar with a high view of women and of Scripture. Bilezikian shows that we are called to live in equality and partnership, then challenges the Church to deliberate pro-

grams of depatriarchalization. VH

Baker, 1985, 264 pgs. Available from Daughters of Sarah, 3801 N. Keeler, Dept. 1114, Chicago, IL 60641, (312) 736–3399 ($11 ppd.).

BEYOND THE CURSE: WOMEN CALLED TO MINISTRY
AIDA BESANCON SPENCER

An inquiry into Old Testament references, rabbinic and Greek culture, and New Testament times with reference to "woman's place," the ordination of women, the gender of God, and Jesus' teachings and attitudes, with special focus on problematic passages (for example, 1 Timothy 2:11). In an afterward, the author's husband describes his personal journey as the spouse of an ordained Presbyterian minister. VH

Thomas Nelson, 1985, 223 pgs. Available from Daughters of Sarah, 3801 N. Keeler, Dept. 1114, Chicago, IL 60641, (312) 736–3399 ($12 ppd.).

THE BIRTH PROJECT
JUDY CHICAGO

See listing on page 92. MG

Doubleday, 1985, 231 pgs.

BLACK WOMEN IN ANTIQUITY
IVAN VAN SERTIMA, ED.

"The Egyptians believed that the Nile began with Isis' tears splashing from the heavens as she mourned her murdered husband Osiris. They believed, too, that she resurrected him at great sacrifice and, thus, initiated the whole concept of resurrection. Osiris is, indeed, the first of a long line of resurrected gods: Tamuz (Babylonian and Assyrian), Mithras (Persia), Balder (Norwegian), Dionysius (Greek), Bacchus (Rome), and Christ. The Egyptians also be-

lieved that Isis' tears became more profuse in certain seasons, causing the Nile to overflow and nourish the soil. So important was her first tear in creating the river, that even today, Egypt observes a holiday in mid-June, "The Night of the Drop."

(Eloise McKinney-Johnson, "Egypt's Isis: The Original Black Madonna".)

This illustrated book contains rare, scholarly, and stimulating essays on the black queens, goddesses, warriors, and madonnas of antiquity and their leading role in the history and development of civilizations throughout the world. Essays include: "Egypt's Isis: The Original Black Madonna," "African Goddesses: Mothers of Civilizations," "The Image of Women in African Cave Art," and "African Women in Early Europe." PW

Journal of African Civilizations, 1984, 159 pgs. Note: The Journal of African Civilizations is dedicated to providing a different historical perspective within which to view the ancestor of the African-American and the achievement and potential of black peoples the world over. It celebrates black genius, Africa's role in the world's great civilizations, and African contributions in the arts, religions, and sciences of human culture. Twelve special issues are available from the publisher; each issue contains essays on the contributions of black women and historical information on the venerated black madonnas of the world. For a list of titles and ordering information, write: Ivan Van Sertima, Editor, Journal of African Civilizations, African Studies Department, Beck Hall, Rutgers University, New Brunswick, NJ 08903.

BODHISATTVA OF COMPASSION: THE MYSTICAL TRADITION OF KUAN YIN
JOHN BLOFELD

"*. . . With your mind you make everything empty. There's nothing there you say. . . . Then you say, ah but there is something. Look, there's the sea and the moon has risen—full, round, white. . . . You stare at the moon a long, long time, feeling calm, happy. Then the moon gets smaller, but brighter and brighter till you see it as a pearl or a seed so bright you can only just bear to look at it. The pearl starts to grow and, before you know what's happened, it is Kuan Yin Herself standing up against the sky, all dressed in gleaming white and with Her feet resting on a lotus that floats on the waves. . . . She smiles at you—such a lovely smile. She's so glad to see you that tears of happiness sparkle in Her eyes. If you keep your mind calm by just whispering Her name and not trying too hard, She will stay a long, long time.*" (an elderly Buddhist nun in quangdong speaking with author Blofeld)

At the moment, this book is the best single source on Guanyin (Kuan Yin), the embodiment of centered and courageous compassion, with whom many contemporary women are finding a deep connection. Blofeld combines information on the historical evolution of this archetype and her iconography with a highly personal account of his own relationship with her. His sometimes precious style and androcentrism are offset by his firsthand accounts of devotional practices to the Great Mother of most of Buddhist Asia. JIS

Shambhala, 1978, 158 pgs. Available from The Gaia Catalogue Company ($12.45 ppd.)

THE BOOK OF QUALITIES
J. RUTH GENDLER

"*Courage looks you straight in the eye. She is not impressed with powertrippers, and she knows first aid. Courage is not afraid to weep, and she is not afraid to pray, even when she is not sure who she is praying to. When she walks it is clear she has made the journey from loneliness to solitude. The people who told me she was stern were not lying; they just forgot to mention that she was kind.*"

J. Ruth Gendler describes herself as a Jewish Buddhist who loves Sufi poetry and believes in the Goddess. In *The Book of Qualities* Ruth has transformed seventy-four emotional qualities into human characters recognizable from the theatre of life. Meet Devotion: "She braids her grandmother's hair with an antique comb"; Sensuality: "She thinks with her body"; Ecstasy: "He loves the drum and the flute and the dark winter moon"; Integrity: "She makes ritual vessels for the local temple." Like a good friend, the qualities mirror our strengths and whimsies, our fantasies and complexities, our very basic humanity and most divine nature. PW

Harper & Row, 1987, 101 pgs. Available from The Gaia Catalogue Company ($8.45 ppd.).

THE BOOK OF THE GODDESS: PAST AND PRESENT
CARL OLSON, ED.

A collection of scholarly articles on various avatars of the Goddess from around the world includes Ishtar, Isis and Hathor, the Greek and Roman mother goddess, the Hebrew Goddess, Black Madonna, Kali and other Indian goddesses, Kuan Yin and Amaterasu, Oshun, and North American goddesses. This book is an excellent resource for students of "The Goddess of Ten Thousand Names" as she appears in the world religions. JIS

Crossroad, 1986, 261 pgs. Available from Harper & Row ($11.95 ppd.).

Braided Streams: Esther and a Woman's Way of Growing

Marjory Zoet Bankson

Bankson uses the biblical story of Queen Esther as a woman's tale of spiritual development, weaves this story with her own and that of U.S. women, and invites women readers to journal on their own "streams." The book challenges women to gather together in small groups to discover their commonality; claim their bodies; integrate work, sexuality, spirituality; and celebrate womanhood. A powerful tool for Christian women seeking feminist stories of their biblical foremothers. An audio tape is also available for women who prefer the spoken word as a means of learning stories. PB

LuraMedia, 1985, 179 pgs. Available from LuraMedia, P.O. Box 261668, San Diego, CA 92126, (619) 578-1586 (book $9.95 ppd./tape $10 ppd.).

Cakes for the Queen of Heaven

Shirley A. Ranck

Cakes for the Queen of Heaven is a curriculum in feminist thealogy (from the Greek *thea* meaning goddess), recommended for educators, women's groups, women's studies programs, schools, churches, and workshop facilitators. The program is designed to help women explore and reclaim female religious history and its meaning in their lives. Ten sessions, each approximately two hours in length, cover topics including ancient Goddess religion and imagery, mother-daughter myths and relationships, reclaiming our bodies, contemporary routes to female spirituality, and more. A full range of educational resources (readings, visual images, learning activities, discussion guides, songs, and simple rituals) is included in the program package. PW

Unitarian Universalist Association, Department of Religious Education, *1986. Available from Unitarian Universalist Association, Department of Religious Education, 25 Beacon St., Boston, MA 02108, (617) 742-2100 ($54.25 ppd.).*

Cassandra: A Novel and Four Essays

Christa Wolf (Trans. Jan Van Heurck)

Cassandra, daughter of King Priam of Troy, was persecuted for her gift of accurately foreseeing the future. German author Christa Wolf clearly has been touched by the spirit of Cassandra. At last Cassandra is able to tell her story of the fall of Troy and the end of an epoch. *Cassandra*, the book, is the author's story of her journey to find Cassandra—her travels through Greece, reflections on the relevance of Cassandra, and the parallels to the present moment. As women, we each carry the foreknowledge that speaks through Cassandra. Wolf encourages women to trust in the sanity of their voices about nuclear energy, war, and the environment. AG

Farrar, Straus & Giroux, 1984, 320 pgs. Available from Harper & Row ($19.45 ppd.).

Celebrations of Biblical Women's Stories—Tears, Milk and Honey

Martha Ann Kirk, with music by Colleen Fulmer

Sister Martha Ann Kirk is a peace and justice educator, a ritualist, a dancer, and an artist. In her book, a collection of rituals based on the lives of ten biblical women, she brings these perspectives together. She extensively develops feminine images of God and uses the arts as a way of engaging the whole person in experiencing these stories. Includes rituals, dramatic stories, music, songs, dances, and prayers. An excellent resource for women who live out of a feminist biblical perspective. PW

Sheed & Ward, 1987, 150 pgs. Available from Sheed & Ward, P.O. Box 414292, Kansas City, MO 64141-0281, (800) 333-7373 ($12.45 ppd.).

Celebrations of Daughterhood: Poetry for Young Girls

Suellen M. Fast

"The Mother Earth belongs to the Beloved Daughters / who sing / the mirthful songs of fire, air, earth, and water / that bring / the birth of longed-for Daughters / who become / Amazing Queens / singing mirthfully along for the springing of more / beloved Daughters / to be born upon / the Loving Mother Earth."

The stories and myths a young girl hears as she develops greatly affect her self-image and self-esteem. To fill a need for visual and poetic images of the Goddess and female-empowered archetypes for girl readers, Suellen Fast began writing and publishing books for young girls. *Celebrations of Daughterhood*, Fast's first book, is a rich treasury of poems and short rhymes for remembering our sisterhood and our significance as

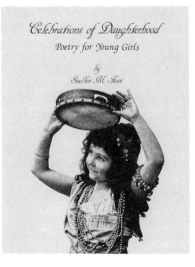

Celebrations of Daughterhood
Poetry for Young Girls
by
Suellen M. Fast

Daughters of the Earth. Highly recommended, *Celebrations* is filled with heartwarming verses that will evoke positive images of the divine feminine in our daughters, our young friends, ourselves. PW

Daughter Culture Publications, 1985, 61 pgs. Available from The Gaia Catalogue Company ($9.50 ppd.).

THE CHALICE AND THE BLADE: OUR HISTORY, OUR FUTURE
RIANE EISLER

Ten years of research have gone into this epochal work by international feminist, futurist, and peace activist Riane Eisler. Eisler presents prehistoric discoveries in a richly woven tapestry of art, philosophy, religion, social science, and history. The book begins with convincing evidence that the prepatriarchal era, a period of partnership between women, men, and nature, veered off on a bloody five-thousand-year dominator detour. Eisler sheds light on the amazing realities behind the legends of Atlantis and other "mythical" cultures, on the central role of women as builders of human civilization, and on the partnership teachings of Jesus and other gentle prophets as indicated by suppressed gnostic scriptures. Her research illuminates why human progress has until now been offset by cyclic regression to brutality and tyranny and provides a compelling portrait of evolutionary possibilities as humanity hovers on the brink of rad-

ical transformation. Most important, *The Chalice and the Blade* points to concrete ways we can work together toward a breakthrough in our own evolution—and a new era of world peace, which Eisler names "gylany." For everyone seeking a new worldview adequate to address the challenges we face, this book is enormously significant—politically, ethically, spiritually.

Harper & Row, 1987, 261 pgs. Available from Harper & Row ($18.95 ppd.).

THE CHANGING OF THE GODS: FEMINISM AND THE END OF TRADITIONAL RELIGIONS
NAOMI R. GOLDENBERG

One of the earlier books on feminist spirituality (now out of print), this book remains an excellent introduction to the feminist spirituality movement. Goldenberg, a psychologist of religion, critically analyzes the impact Jung, Freud, and "father/son/oedipal" religions have on women's development. She predicts that major psychological/cultural changes will occur when women regard themselves as "images of divinity." Ruthless in her condemnation of sexist religions, Goldenberg suggests as alternatives Greek goddess mythology, tarot, Wicca, Jungian psychology, dream interpretation, and mysticism.

"We must re-evaluate all female images that have been despised by previous generations of male scholars.

Behind every witch, dragoness, and temptress there is a vision of female power—power that society is ready now to understand and perhaps, to embrace." GB

Beacon Press, 1979, 152 pgs. Available from Beacon Press ($9.45 ppd.).

CHANGING WOMAN AND HER SISTERS
SHEILA MOON

This book introduces the reader to the rich world of female deities within the Navajo and Pueblo cultures. These deities—First Woman, Changing-Bear-Maiden, Snapping Vagina, Spider Woman, Changing Woman, Snake Woman—are then related to various facets of our inner and outer life. Dreams, symbols, healing rituals, folktales, chants, words of magic, rites of passage, and archetypal energies are examined in both their healthy and disorderly functioning. Sheila Moon, poet, therapist, philosopher, has woven her spiritual commitment to the Earth and Creation into the teachings found within this book. RF

Guild for Psychological Studies, 1985, 200 pgs. Available from Guild for Psychological Studies, 2230 Divisadero St., San Francisco, CA 94115, (415) 931-0647 ($12.50 ppd.).

CHASM OF FIRE: A WOMAN'S EXPERIENCE OF LIBERATION THROUGH THE TEACHINGS OF A SUFI MASTER
IRINA TWEEDIE

Distraught by her husband's early death and seeking solace and meaning in her life, Irina Tweedie found her way to a Sufi teacher in India who showed her the path to spiritual liberation. Tweedie's growing calm, inner awakening, and her enthrallment with and complete surrender to her Indian male guru sharply contrast with her social and psychological distance from and disdain toward her Indian surroundings and the people who welcome her into their midst. This account raises some broader political questions. Is spiritual or inner liberation simply an esoteric exercise divorced from our everyday social relations? Can we truly awaken ourselves without freeing our minds and our behavior from the controlling effects of patriarchy, racism, and class privilege? AB

Element Books, 1985, 206 pgs. Available from Dawn Horse Book Depot, P.O. Box 15260, Seattle, WA 98115, (800) 843-1170 ($13.70 ppd.).

THE COLOR PURPLE
ALICE WALKER

"She say, My first step from the old white man was trees. Then air. Then birds. Then other people. But one day when I was sitting quiet and feeling like a motherless child, which I was, it come to me: that feeling of being part of everything, not separate at all. I knew that if I cut a tree, my arm would bleed. And I laughed and I cried and I run all around the house. I knew just what it was. In fact, when it happen, you can't miss it. It sort of like you know what, she say, grinning and rubbing high up on my thigh . . . 'Here's the thing,' say Shug. 'The thing I believe. God is inside you and inside everybody else. You come into the world with God. But only them that search for it inside find it.' "

It is difficult to think of a modern novel that has touched more people more deeply than *The Color Purple*, the wondrous, heartrending, life-affirming story of a southern black woman's spiritual transformation through the very matter of her life. Celie tells her story through letters. She begins as a young girl by addressing them to God, who is "big and old and tall and graybearded and white." When, in the midst of incredible adversity, she turns her back on this God—"If he ever listened to poor colored women the world would be a different place, I can tell you"— she writes to her beloved sister Nettie, who has gone to Africa as a missionary. In holding fast to her vision that human love is the thing that matters, she comes to a profound new understanding of God, addressing her last letter: "Dear God. Dear stars, dear trees, dear sky, dear peoples. Dear Everything. Dear God." The book is dedicated to the Spirit and ends with an Amen, as any prayer should. JIS

Harcourt Brace Jovanovich, 1982, 295 pgs.

CONFESSIONS OF MADAME PSYCHE
DOROTHY BRYANT

Dorothy Bryant is a writer of consummate skill, and *Confessions of Madame Psyche* is a novel of unsurpassed beauty and sensitivity. I believe this story of a woman's spiritual quest may be the finest work of spiritual fiction available today. As Madame Psyche travels her sometimes devastating life path, the path of the mystic, she sweeps the reader along with her. She is vulnerable, candid, and overwhelmingly humble. Her spirit soars, and I find that the wisdom she gains stayed with me, turning up unexpectedly to guide me in my life long after I read her story. This novel explores powerful themes, like deception, glamor, disillusionment, racial bigotry, social conscience, and, perhaps most important of all, persistence and joy in the face of terrible adversity. AM

Ata Books, 1986, 376 pgs. Available from The Gaia Catalogue Company ($13.45 ppd.).

CONSCIOUS CONCEPTION: ELEMENTAL JOURNEY THROUGH THE LABYRINTH OF SEXUALITY

JEANNINE PARVATI BAKER, FREDERICK BAKER, AND TAMARA SLAYTON

Jeannine Parvati Baker is a leading teacher and writer in the women's health and conscious birth movement. Her work seeks to move our society away from the patriarchal success/failure model of reproduction to a feminist/spiritual vision of sexuality and reproduction as sacred experience. *Conscious Conception* is drawn from fifteen years of her work with women and men seeking a clearer communion with their reproductive cycles. The book is designed to assist readers in trusting and appreciating their reproductive cycles as a means of soul making and spiritual development. "Reclaiming the fertile body, the rich, fecund messages coming forth with each turn of the cycle and aligning ourselves with the larger family within which we all actually reside, is the beginning of conscious conception," writes Baker. "Just as Demeter searched for her daughter, Persephone, we too are moving into the source each time we acknowledge our bodies' rich information; the data-giving depth of our own tissue. . . . Conscious conception is pro-life and pro-choice: the process of conscious conception involves seeing all the possibilities— not just the either/or choices." The book is designed around the primal elements earth, water, fire, air, and ether. At the end of the elemental sections are rituals for each element emphasizing a particular aspect of the conception experience. PW

Freestone Publishing Co. with North Atlantic Books, 1987, 411 pgs. Available from Freestone Publishing Co., P.O. Box 398, Monroe, UT 84754, (801) 527-3738 ($18.95 ppd.).

THE CRONE: WOMAN OF AGE, WISDOM, AND POWER

BARBARA G. WALKER

A fascinating journey through time, back to the origins of the suppression of the feminine in religion, science, politics, mythology, and psychology. Walker is irreverent, incisive, demanding, and merciless in her critique of this culture's outcasting of the Wise Woman or Crone. She redefines older women as towers of strength, courage, and life wisdom, Walker herself looks like the sweet-faced old lady one encounters in all the respectable places. You might even find her at the Morristown, New Jersey, Free Library, where she has displayed her collection of handmade doll costumes. Walker, who many consider a zealous feminist scholar, is also a world authority on knitting. The Crone wears many faces. GB

Harper & Row, 1985, 191 pgs. Available from The Gaia Catalogue Company ($16.45 ppd. cloth, $10.45 ppd. paper).

O L D   W O M A N ' S   H A N D S

Barbara Mor

an old woman's hand

is the thinnest hand in the world

it is as hollow

and tearless

as bird bones

it has grown flesh

held the sun

passed on

it has clutched the sinews

of trees

and let go

hunger has chewed it

dogs bite it

it has sewn up the eyelids

of years, of stars

it is as brittle

as gray branches underfoot

knowing, from that distance,

gods' shadows

and older than crying

almost older than death

an old woman's hand

is the first hand

of earth

and the last reaching out

as your night descends

when it comes to you

touch it

stroke the bones

in which time

    lizards

    canyon veins

    primeval birds

have flown

Barbara Mor is a poet, a writer, and a mother living in Arizona. She is the coauthor, with Monika Sjöö, of *The Great Cosmic Mother* (Harper & Row, 1987). This poem was originally published in *Crow Call*, Summer 1978, Taos, New Mexico.

THE CRONE'S BOOK OF WORDS
VALERIE WORTH

In every person the Goddess exists in her three aspects: Maiden, Mother, Crone. The Crone stands at the crossroads of death and rebirth, question and decision, confusion and direction. This book is a collection of poetry, rituals, and spells to invoke the Crone's wisdom for guidance, protection, and power based on the fundamental premises of Witchcraft: that words themselves have power in our inner reality and outer experience and that all positive ritual forms, ancient and new, spring from the same source in humanity—the desire to create meaning. PW

Lewellyn Publications, 1986, 155 pgs. Available from Lewellyn Publications, P.O. Box 64383-J, St. Paul, MN 55164, (800) THE MOON ($8.45 ppd.).

CRYSTAL ENLIGHTENMENT: TRANSFORMING PROPERTIES OF CRYSTALS AND HEALING STONES
KATRINA RAPHAEL

Crystals and gemstones are particularly attuned to a feminine healing model as they require deep listening to receive their full positive benefit. In the preface to *Crystal Enlightenment*, Katrina Raphael describes the process of sitting in meditation with crystals in order to receive the crystals' wisdom. She believes that crystals can transform our consciousness and contribute to the evolution of the planet. Written with respect and love for these gifts of the mineral world, the book includes chapters on the physical and esoteric properties of crystals, attunement/meditation with crystals, crystal healing layouts, stones within the quartz family, charts, and resource information. Unlike many other books on the subject that are either oversimplified or written for the scientific community, this book is accessible to anyone interested in becoming a student of the

crystals' healing powers. The book is organized to be used as a resource guide. PW

Aurora Press, 1985, 171 pgs. Available from The Gaia Catalogue Company ($11.45 ppd.).

CRYSTAL VISIONS: NINE MEDITATIONS FOR PERSONAL AND PLANETARY PEACE
DIANE MARIECHILD

Inspired by her work with Dhyani Ywahoo, a Lineage Holder of the Tsalagi (Cherokee Nation), and her studies in Tibetan Buddhism, Diane Mariechild offers a series of meditations designed to rekindle our connection with family, friends, Earth, and the child within. Following each meditation are blank pages to be used as a process journal. Includes material on the symbolism and use of crystals and explanatory notes on basic Buddhist principles and practices. PW

Crossing Press, 1985, 125 pgs. Available from Crossing Press, P.O. Box 1048, Freedom, CA 95019, (408) 722-0711 ($7.95 ppd.).

THE CULT OF THE BLACK VIRGIN
EAN BEGG

Begg, a Jungian analyst and former Dominican friar, explores the origin and significance of the "black" or "dark" images of the Madonna popular throughout Europe and the Americas. Derived from Pagan traditions, these black virgins express powerful female sexuality, the underworld, and Nature wisdom, standing in stark contrast to Christian ideals of maidenhood and tender maternity. This thorough exploration of a rarely examined aspect of Christian worship includes a valuable listing of Black Virgin worship sites in Europe and the Americas. PW

Routledge & Kegan Paul, 1985, 288 pgs. Available from Routledge & Ke-

gan Paul, 29 W. 35th St., New York, NY 10001, (212) 244-3336 ($14.45 ppd.).

DAILY AFFIRMATIONS: FOR ADULT CHILDREN OF ALCOHOLICS
ROKELLE LERNER

"If I am powerless over my compulsiveness, I can seek help. I don't have to do it myself. There is no secret that is so dark and repulsive that it can't be faced. Others have done it, and I will too. Emerging from isolation, I take my place on this earth with pride and dignity."

There are many affirmation books that address the need for daily support in recovering from compulsive patterns. This book is one that seems particularly suited to a Womanspirit reader: the affirmations holistically address women's spiritual/emotional/ sexual needs, an absence of God references allows the reader to affirm deity on her own terms, and the illustrations portray positive, powerful, and sensuous female images. PW

Health Communications, Inc., 1985, 372 pgs. Available from The Gaia Catalogue Company ($8.45 ppd.).

Daily Affirmations
For Adult Children of Alcoholics

DANCING IN THE LIGHT
SHIRLEY MACLAINE

While autobiographies of the famous are fairly commonplace, MacLaine's writings are radically different and refreshing as she involves the public on a deeply personal level in her quest for spiritual understanding. This book, the fourth of the series, begins at her fiftieth birthday party, attended by thousands of friends and well-wishers in New York. The outpouring of love that she receives leads to a period of self-reflection during which she explores her relationships with her daughter, parents, lover, audiences, and spirit guides. The lessons she learns from a volatile Russian lover who maintains that "love and respect are not coexistent human emotions" are especially relevant to women involved in abusive relationships. The second half of the book explains her philosophy of reincarnation, karma, past life regressions, spirit guides, and the nature of consciousness. GB

Bantam, 1985, 421 pgs. Available from Random House ($5.50 ppd.).

SELF-REFLECTION, LOVE, AND THE UNIVERSE: AN INTERVIEW WITH SHIRLEY MACLAINE

BY GLORIA STEINEM

Shirley MacLaine's many visible lives (actress, political activist, singer, dancer, world traveler, writer of her own autobiography) have been attracting acclaim for more than thirty years. Now her spiritual quest and discovery of invisible lives through a belief in reincarnation (which she first wrote about in Out on a Limb *and now in* Dancing in the Light, *both published by Bantam) have found a resonance in millions of readers who are also searching for some personal spirituality, or just a sense of continuity of life. These words were spoken during a relaxed afternoon in her living room.*

Gloria Steinem

It's fascinating to me that so many intellectual liberals know more about what to do with the rest of the world than they know about what to do with themselves. And they feel self-centered, self-indulgent, and arrogant if they spend time looking at who they really are. Being that way, I learned that all my social and political views finally got back to one basic principle: What did I think of myself? It all starts with self-reflection. Then you can know and empathize more profoundly with someone else.

This whole spiritual philosophy is based on learning to trust more the intuitive energy—the right side of your brain, the sensitive, soul-seeking energy—instead of only the intellectual, left-brain, mind-speaking energy. To balance the two is the goal. What this really is, then, is the ultimate sense of androgyny, where the male and female aspects of oneself come together. When you start to operate and function on these kinds of spiritual principles, you walk around with a different center and balanced feeling about yourself. And you literally then start to exude a higher frequency of understanding, a higher frequency of peace, and a higher frequency of light, you might say. People who are centered in their own sense of self are drawing in universal energy that I think is harmoniously perfect and that ultimately one can shed on others.

I think everything that I'm doing and every person in my life is a mirror to what I haven't yet seen about myself. In other words, *all* of this is about self. And the reason that now is the time for a feminist understanding and a feminine thrust is that this is the age of female energy. I had to get in touch with my feminine energy much later in my life than some women. I never really felt that I was a second-class citizen. I had a little bit of the dominating authoritarian father stuff, but frankly, I identified with my father. I was always very comfortable with being outspoken and aggressive about what I wanted. The most hospitable part of feminism starts with self, whether you're a man or a woman! It's that recognition that you are essentially a spiritual being who is a balance of male and female.

This significant difference between what I'm saying and what organized religion is saying is that evil is not an outside force. Evil is an inside conception. That eliminates authoritarian reverence. I agree with the traditional church concept that the more souls there are in a room collectively feeling something, the more powerful that energy is. But the requirement for the church to be the arbiter between people and God is where I feel the church is being a bit too secular. I think each of us is the arbiter between ourselves and our own God. And I agree with what Alice Walker said, the *we* make God in our own image.

It's this addiction to victimization that we need to break because that can be as severe as the addiction to power. Breaking the addiction to powerlessness is every bit as painful as breaking the addiction to dope.

But what starts to happen when you begin to use these spiritual techniques is that you usually have a kind of a breakthrough in sorrow. You just forgive yourself for making yourself a victim, for putting yourself through all that. You forgive yourself for victimizing someone else because you felt they might get you first if you didn't. So that whole kind of theological sense of forgiveness is really true. Once that breakthrough happens and all that pain kind of washes away, you're totally vulnerable, which is totally wise, totally open. And once you're totally open, this universal force can come through.

There are really only two emotions, I think. There is love and there is fear, and everything else comes from that. Love is an understanding that you are part of everything. So you're walking around in your life feeling that <u>that</u> is the ultimate love—love of self and God and love of all the other people who are playing characters in our lives. And fear comes from the feeling that there may indeed not be any God there, which is really the feeling that there is no self there. So fear is really based on this feeling of self-abandonment.

©Gloria Steinem. December, 1985. Reprinted from *Ms. Magazine* with permission.

"Deva is the ancient word for shining light or guardian angel. Humans as well as all aspects of nature are helped and surrounded by these spirits. The images portrayed have been inspired from the devic kingdom to encourage and renew the connection between humans and

The Moon Deva
© Azra Simonetti, 1986. Oil on canvas, 16" × 14".

the angels of earth. It is hoped that this oneness will help create harmony and reverence for the earth and her creatures." From the notecard series, Deva Cards. Available from the artist: Azra Simonetti, 20 Franklin St., Montpelier, VT 05602.

DAUGHTERS OF COPPER WOMAN
ANNE CAMERON

Anne Cameron weaves and mends the scattered fragments of history and myth into an uplifting story of the Sisterhood that is as old as the Earth herself. The tale begins with Copper Woman, her creation Snot Boy, and the birthing of human beings. We are led into the world of the Northwest Coast Indians of North America, the beauty of their ways, and the strength the women carry. The story is told to Cameron by the few remaining women who carry the memory of what has come to pass. This book touches the heart and enlivens the spirit. Recommended as a gift for a young girl's coming of age. Royalties given to the people of the Ahousat tribe. AG

Press Gang Publishers, 1985, 150 pgs. Available from The Gaia Catalogue Company ($11.00 ppd.).

THE FACE OF OLD WOMAN

Anne Cameron

Old Woman is watching

Watching over you

 in the darkness of the storm

 she is watching

 watching over you

 weave and mend

 weave and mend

Old Woman is watching

 watching over you

with her bones become a loom

 she is weaving

 watching over us

 weave and mend

golden circle

weave and mend

sacred sisters

weave and mend

I have been searching

lost

alone

I have been searching

for so many years

I have been searching

Old Woman

and I find her

in

mySelf

From Anne Cameron, *Daughters of Copper Woman*, Press Gang Publishers, 1981.

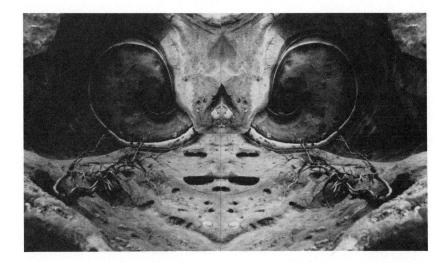

The Owl Goddess
© Maureen
Murdock, 1985.
Black-and-white
photograph, 11"
× 14".

"The Owl Goddess represents that aspect of Mother Earth that sees clearly in the dark the connecting web of all life. She invites us to open ourselves to vision. The Owl Goddess has inspired a photographic series on the goddess of today entitled 'In Service of the Goddess: A Photo Essay on Contemporary Women.' In this portrait/interview series, women speak out about their personal relationship to the goddess and what part she plays in their lives and work" (Maureen Murdock). For information on the photo essay "In Service of the Goddess" and photographs available for sale by the artist write: Maureen Murdock, 121 Wavecrest Ave., Venice, CA 90291.

DEAREST GODDESS: TRANSLATIONS FROM LATVIAN FOLK POETRY
ESO BENJAMINS, TRANSLATOR/ PUBLISHER

"Though we are not sisters we call ourselves sisters. It makes some people mad. It makes the Dearest Goddess glad."

For thousands of years in agrarian Latvia the women created songs and poems to their "Dearest Goddess" while working together. Scholars have collected over one million of these poems. The author, a native-born Latvian poet and writer, gathered and translated Goddess poems over a thirty-year period. These are not prayers, but brief conversations the women have with the Goddess about love, friendships, work, and life's poignant moments. PW

Current Nine Publishing, 1985, 115 pgs. Available from Current Nine Publishing, P.O. Box 6089, Arlington, VA 22206 ($9.45).

DESCENT TO THE GODDESS: A WAY OF INITIATION FOR WOMEN
SYLVIA BRINTON PERERA

"The return of the Goddess for renewal in a Feminine sourceground and spirit, is a vitally important aspect of modern women's quest for

wholeness. We women who have succeeded in the world are usually 'daughters of the father'—that is, well adapted to a masculine-oriented society—and have repudiated our own full feminine instincts and energy patterns, just as the culture has maimed or derogated most of them. We need to return to and redeem what the patriarchy has often seen only as dangerous threat and called terrible mother, dragon, or witch."

In Sumerian myth, Inanna, the Queen of Heaven, descends to the underworld to confront her dark sister Ereshkigal; there she dies and is reborn, returning to the world above. Perera, a Jungian analyst, explores this archetypal story through the experiences of her analysands, creating what she calls a way of initiation for women. Less burdened with a restricted image of the feminine than most Jungian writers, she offers many valuable insights on Inanna as a daughter of the patriarchy, Ereshkigal as the feminine matrix of Nature, and the night sea journey of suffering and transformation. In Perera's writing there is the welcome sense of someone who has truly experienced the process of psychological integration as spiritual quest. JIS

Inner City Books, 1981, 112 pgs. Available from The Gaia Catalogue Company ($11.50 ppd.).

DESPAIR AND PERSONAL POWER IN THE NUCLEAR AGE

JOANNA ROGERS MACY

A powerful and compassionate sourcebook for directly confronting our psychological and spiritual responses to the looming threat of nuclear holocaust and ecological disaster. The book provides a system to guide and support us in unblocking our feelings, connecting with one another, and transforming our deepest fears into action, both alone and with others. Includes empowerment rituals, affirmations of commitment, and a valuable section on responding to children and young people's living in the nuclear age. PW

New Society Publishers, 1983, 180 pgs. Available from The Gaia Catalogue Company ($12.45 ppd.).

LEARNING TO SEE EACH OTHER: THE FOUR ABODES MEDITATION

JOANNA ROGERS MACY

This exercise is derived from the Buddhist practice known as the Brahmaviharas, or the Four Abodes of the Buddha, which are lovingkindness, compassion, joy in the joy of others, and equanimity. Adapted for use in a social context, it helps us to see each other more truly and experience the depths of our interconnections.

In workshops I offer this as a guided meditation, with participants sitting in pairs facing each other. At its close I encourage them to proceed to use it, or any portion they like, as they go about the business of their daily lives. It is an excellent antidote to boredom, when our mind is idling and our eye falls on another person, say on the subway or waiting in line at the check-out counter. It charges that idle movement with beauty and discovery. It also is useful when dealing with people we are tempted to dislike or disregard, for it breaks open our accustomed ways of viewing them. When used like this, as a meditation-in-action, one does not, of course gaze long and deeply into the other's eyes, as in the guided exercise. A seemingly casual glance is enough, or the simple exchange of buying stamps or toothpaste—any occasion, in other words, that permits us to be present to another human being.

The guided, group form goes like this.

Sit in pairs. Face each other. Stay silent. Take a couple of deep breaths, centering yourself and exhaling tension. Look into each other's eyes. If you feel discomfort or an urge to laugh or look away, just note that embarrassment with patience and gentleness toward yourself and come back, when you can, to your partner's eyes. You may never see this person again: the opportunity to behold the uniqueness of this particular human being is given to you now.

As you look into this being's eyes, let yourself become aware of the powers that are there . . . open yourself to awareness of the gifts and strengths and the potentialities in this being . . . Behind those eyes are unmeasured reserves of ingenuity and endurance, of wit and wisdom. There are gifts there, of which this person him/her-

self is unaware. Consider what these untapped powers can do for the healing of our planet and the relishing of our common life . . . As you consider that, let yourself become aware of your desire that this person be free from fear . . . Let yourself experience how much you want this being to be free from hatred . . . and free from greed . . . and free from sorrow . . . and the causes of suffering . . . Know that what you are now experiencing is the great lovingkindness . . . It is good for building a world.

Now, as you look into those eyes, let yourself become aware of the pain that is there. There are sorrows accumulated in that life's journey . . . There are failures and losses, griefs and disappointments beyond telling . . . Let yourself open to them, open to that pain . . . to hurts that this person may never have shared with another being . . . What you are now experiencing is the great compassion. It is good for the healing of our world.

As you look into those eyes, open to the thought of how good it would be to make common cause . . . Consider how ready you might be to work together . . . to take risks in a joint venture . . . Imagine the zest of that, the excitement and laughter of engaging on a common project . . . acting boldly and trusting each other . . . As you open to that possibility, what you open to is the great wealth: the pleasure in each other's powers, the joy in each other's joy.

Lastly now, let your awareness drop deep, deep within you like a stone, sinking below the level of what words or acts can express . . . Breathe deep and quiet . . . Open your consciousness to the deep web of relationship that underlies and interweaves all experiencing, all knowing . . . It is the web of life in which you have taken being and in which you are supported . . . out of that vast web you cannot fall . . . no stupidity or failure, no personal inadequacy, can sever you from that living web, for that is what you are . . . and what has brought you into being . . . feel the assurance of that knowledge. Feel the great peace . . . rest in it . . . Out of that great peace, we can venture everything. We can trust. We can act.

From Joanna Rogers Macy, *Despair and Personal Power in the Nuclear Age,* New Society Publishers, 1983.

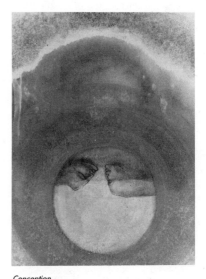

Conception
© Deborah Koff-Chapin, 1984.
Touch drawing.
For more information about the artist's work see page xx.

THE DINNER PARTY: A SYMBOL OF OUR HERITAGE
JUDY CHICAGO

See listing on page 92.

Anchor Press/Doubleday, 1979, 225 pgs.

THE DIVINE FEMININE: THE BIBLICAL IMAGERY OF GOD AS FEMALE
VIRGINIA RAMEY MOLLENKOTT

A discussion of problems inherent in describing God with exclusively male images and pronouns, along with a survey of Scripture's female God imagery: nursing mother, midwife, mother pelican, mother eagle, Dame Wisdom. The author, a member of the Inclusive Language Lectionary Committee of the National Council of Churches, provides practical suggestions on how to use inclusive language in prayer and worship. VH

Crossroad, 1983, 128 pgs. Available from Harper & Row ($9.95 ppd.).

DIVING DEEP AND SURFACING: WOMEN WRITERS ON SPIRITUAL QUEST
CAROL P. CHRIST

"Women's rituals create a space in which women's visions of power can be experienced and healing of ancient pains can occur. By enabling women to recognize the grounding of their lives in the ground of being, women's spiritual quest gives women the strength to create alternatives to personal relationships and social institutions where women's value is not recognized. Women's spiritual quest thus is not an alternative to women's social quest, but rather is one dimension of the larger quest women have embarked upon to create a new world."

Carol Christ is a deep and passionate writer, a scholar of religions, and a spiritual feminist educator who has

stimulated and inspired women students (including the author) for a decade. In this landmark book, originally published in 1980, she articulates the stages of women's spiritual quest (nothingness, awakening, insight, new naming) and suggests the works of five women writers (Kate Chopin, Margaret Atwood, Doris Lessing, Adrienne Rich, Ntozake Shange) as a way of naming the essential sacredness of our spiritual experiences. *Diving Deep* is an affirmation of the many layers of female knowings and a book to return to as an ongoing source of spiritual sustenance. PW

Beacon Press, 1986, 159 pgs. Available from The Gaia Catalogue Company ($10.45 ppd.).

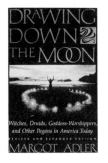

DRAWING DOWN THE MOON: WITCHES, DRUIDS, GODDESS-WORSHIPPERS, AND OTHER PAGANS IN AMERICA TODAY
MARGOT ADLER

A comprehensive guidebook and intelligent study of the neo-Pagan movement today. Adler, a reporter for National Public Radio and herself a priestess in a coven, corresponded with hundreds of people and participated in many covens and ritual groups throughout the United States to gather her material. She presents the historical roots of the movement, the origins of various traditions, and examines the religious experiences, beliefs, and practices of contemporary Pagans. Includes resource list-

ings, photographs, a list of publications, organizations, and examples of rituals. A must for anyone wishing to sort through the distortions and fears surrounding the Pagan religion. PW

Beacon Press, 1986, 608 pgs. Available from The Gaia Catalogue Company ($16.95 ppd.).

DREAMING THE DARK: MAGIC, SEX AND POLITICS
STARHAWK

"To work magic, we begin by making new metaphors. Without negating the light we reclaim the dark, the fertile earth where the hidden seed lies unfolding, the unseen power that rises within us, the dark sacred human flesh, the depths of the ocean, the night—when our senses question, we reclaim all the lost parts of ourselves we have shoved down into the dark; instead of enlightenment we begin to speak of deepening."

In *Dreaming the Dark* Starhawk examines the conflicts present in society and within ourselves and names the power within us to "bend" or alter the apocalyptic route that our planet seems to be traveling. The subtitle of the book, *Magic, Sex and Politics*, is quite deliberate. Starhawk identifies the cultural bias against aspects of our lives considered negative; she delves into the dark aspects of Nature and examines what societal influences have caused us to fear them. Starhawk reacquaints us with sex as the basic element of the Old Religions and the ancients' acknowledgment of the death, birth, and rebirth cycles. The Goddess is sex, for in many traditions all life begins and ends with her. Sex and magic cannot be separated, just as politics cannot be separated from spirituality and just as sex cannot be separated from politics. Contains three appendixes: a historical overview of the Witch persecutions, a practical guide for group work, and a collection of chants that Starhawk has introduced to many groups and that have by now become famous. PCC

Beacon Press, 1982, 242 pgs. Available from The Gaia Catalogue Company ($11.45 ppd.).

Drawing © Sudie Rakusin, 1987. From *Dreams and Shadows: a journal.*

DREAMS AND SHADOWS: A JOURNAL
SUDIE RAKUSIN

Sudie Rakusin's images have been published in *Woman of Power* magazine, on the cover of *Hear the Silence*, and in the Syracuse Cultural Workers' 1988 "Carry It On" Peace Calendar. *Dreams and Shadows* is Sudie's second self-published book/journal. This is feminist visionary art at its best—imaging the Goddess within each woman, calling forth our divine powers, sparking and igniting our visions of a new culture. Illustrated with fifty original drawings, many never before published, the journal provides ample space to keep your own dreams and shadows. First edition printed in limited numbers. PW

Sudie Rakusin/Journal, 1984, 224 pgs. Available directly from the artist: Sudie Rakusin/Journal, P.O. Box 88, Brooke, VA 22430 ($19.95 ppd.).

DREAMSPEAKER
CAM HUBERT

In this award-winning novel by the author of *Daughters of Copper Woman*, a severely disturbed boy finds through friendship the love, spiritual guidance, and courage to overcome the haunting inner terror that threatens to destroy him. The relationship between Peter, Grandfather Dreamspeaker, and his mute companion, He Who Would Sing, is an account of the powerful healing love that men of three generations can share with one another. This is an important book for helping us to envision more clearly what loving relationships among men might be like—and to help each of us more readily bring such possibilities into being. MLK

Avon Books, 1978, 122 pgs. Available from Avon Books, 959 Eighth Ave., New York, NY 10019 ($4.45 ppd.).

EARTH FESTIVALS, EARTH WISDOM, SACRED LAND, SACRED SEX— RAPTURE OF THE DEEP
DOLORES LACHAPPELLE

In *Earth Wisdom*, Dolores LaChappelle builds on the foundation established in *Earth Festivals*, a book she coauthored with Janet Bourque in 1977 (now out of print). In *Earth Festivals*, LaChapelle's intention is to bring her readers into a living, sacred relationship with the Earth. To accomplish this she artfully plots the cycle of the seasons, drawing from the ancient Native American traditions. The result is a beautiful blend of ecology and ritual practices. *Earth Wisdom* moves away from the ritual structure and explores the relationship between Nature and human consciousness in literature. She draws us more deeply into the new ecology, delineating the potential for spiritual transcendence within the immanent divinity of Nature. LaChapelle's latest book, *Sacred Land,*

Sacred Sex: Rapture of the Deep, explores radical questions about the relationship of the natural world and human sexuality and provides rituals to "once again become part of the sacramental-energy-exchange of all life." AM

Finn Hill Arts, 1977, 96 pgs.

EARTH MAGIC: A DIANIC BOOK OF SHADOWS
MARION WEINSTEIN

Long out of print and recently reissued, *Earth Magic* is designed to be used as an adjunct to *Positive Magic*, Weinstein's popular book on the Craft (see listing on page xx). Once again, the author has given us a non-dogmatic, humorous, and practical guidebook for applying magical principles to everyday life for the positive benefit of all. Includes chapters on tools, coven work, the holidays, moon work, protective shields, community service, and advanced magical techniques. PW

Phoenix, 1986, 101 pgs. Available from Phoenix Publishing, P.O. Box 10, Custer, WA 98240 ($7.95 ppd.).

EARTH SONGS: A BOOK OF AFFIRMATIONS MOONFLOWER: A BOOK OF AFFIRMATIONS WATERSPIRIT: A BOOK OF AFFIRMATIONS
IRENE ZAHAVA, ED.

Each page of these notebook/journals features a woman-honoring poem or affirmation, drawn from a variety of cultural and spiritual traditions. A delightful way to record dreams and intentions, to affirm ourselves, to remember the Goddess within. PW

Crossing Press, 1984/1987/1988/, 128 pgs. Available from The Gaia Catalogue Company ($5.95 ppd. each).

EARTH WITCH
ANNE CAMERON

This collection of erotic love poetry, and one extraordinary short story, celebrates the author's love of women and her specific desire to name the experience of women's lovemaking. Cameron communicates honestly and sensuously the joy and sometimes the pain she feels as a woman who loves the spirit-mind-body of another woman. The range, intensity, and bold love of this book together create an autobiographic image of one of the most forthright authors of our era. MLK

Harbour Publishing, 1985, 51 pgs. Available from Harbour Publishing, Box 219, Madeira Park, BC, Canada V0N 2H0 ($7.45 ppd.).

EDUCATING THE NEW JEWISH WOMAN: A DYNAMIC APPROACH
DR. IRENE FINE

This book by Dr. Irene Fine, Ph.D. renewed my internal identification as a Jewish woman, and it made me feel beautiful about it. Dr. Fine gives women's classes in continuing Jewish education in San Diego (see listing on page xx). She includes classes in prepatriarchal goddesses, in the great heroines of the Old Testament and how their lives relate to ours today, God-wrestling and the birth of female theology, and new writing in Jewish feminist literature. This is an excellent guidebook for women interested in reidentifying with Judaism from a fresh and healthier perspective, for women (or men for that matter) interested in learning how other women might experience the messages of Judaism. The following is the beginning of a midrash by

Betsy Arnold, a member of one of Dr. Fine's classes:

"When God was young, She used to play in the void, dancing until Her skirts flew wide around Her and mists and winds twirling with Her screamed with delight. One day, as She was leaping and prancing about, a small seed bounced out of Her pocket. Instantly the winds grabbed it and began to play with it, tossing it among them. Just as quickly, God rescued Her seed and held it close against Her breast. It was so tiny that it stayed comfortably on one strand of Her silken hair and so fragile that it shuddered in the wake of Her breath. Now as God looked at this seed in Her hand, She made a decision. "Grow," She directed the seed. "Stay here and grow. Nothing will disturb you, for you are part of Me, and I am the Sovereign of everything."

Women's Institute for Continuing Jewish Education, 1985, 120 pgs. (For ordering info. see listing for Taking the Fruit, page 91.) (Contributed by Elizabeth Gips, Changes Radio. For free catalogue of cassette interviews by spiritual teachers send SASE to Elizabeth Gips % Changes Radio, P.O. Box 7305, Santa Cruz, CA 95061.)

ELSA: I COME WITH MY SONGS, THE AUTOBIOGRAPHY OF ELSA GIDLOW
ELSA GIDLOW

"Let none speak sadly of October, / I, Elsa, in the peak of years, / Say this; I have loved all seasons."

Elsa Gidlow was the "Poet-Warrior" (Ella Young) and "quietly achieved mystic" (Kenneth Rexroth) whom millions came to know through her many poetry volumes, essays, and the film *Word Is Out*. Elsa was born *avant-garde*. She was North America's first published writer of a lesbian

poetry volume (1923), a radical feminist of the "first wave," a protest poet attacked by McCarthyites, a member of San Francisco's bohemian, psychedelic, New Age, and women's spirituality circles. *Elsa* is the magnificent "portrait of the artist as an old woman" and enduring *esprit libre*, who moves us to forge ahead with our own lives, to be all that we can be. (Contributed by Celeste West, Publisher/Booklegger Press.)

Booklegger Press, 1986, 422 pgs. Available in women's bookstores or directly from the publisher: Booklegger Press, 555 29th St., San Francisco, CA 94131 ($12.95 ppd. paper, $19.95 ppd. cloth).

Photomythology
Series, *Poet-
Warrior, Elsa
Gidlow*
© Marcelina
Martin, 1985.

*"Today's world calls
each of us to become
a shaman, the one
who in pre-
industrial/earth-
oriented societies
was the focus for
strengthening the
collective psyche.
Shamanism was, in
fact, the beginning
of art. The shaman
gave shape and
portrayed both inner
spirits and collective
mythologies. She
identified herself
with these images,
recognizing and
using them as an
energy force. She
transformed the
chaotic mythologies
by interpreting them
artistically. In
similarly reviving
our birthright as
artists, we regain
control of the power
of our psychic
imagery."*
(Marcelina Martin).

EMBROIDERING OUR HERITAGE: THE DINNER PARTY NEEDLEWORK

JUDY CHICAGO WITH SUSAN HILL

See listing on page 92.

Anchor Books, 1980, 287 pgs.

EVE: THE HISTORY OF AN IDEA

JOHN A. PHILLIPS

Phillips's thesis is that the biblical creation story carried forward the death of the Mother Goddess at the hands of the worshipers of the Father God and her rebirth as a first woman upon whom man's fear of the Goddess were projected. The myth of Eve, very much alive in the psychology, laws, religious life, and social structures of the Western world, must be scrutinized to remove its debilitating effect on society. An insightful examination of the key themes of the Eve myth supplemented with art reproductions from many historical periods. PW

Harper & Row, 1984, 200 pgs. Available from Harper & Row ($9.95 ppd.).

THE FEMININE DIMENSION OF THE DIVINE

JOAN CHAMBERLAIN ENGELSMAN

In this scholarly work, Engelsman traces the expression and repression of the feminine dimension of the divine, moving from Demeter and Isis of the Hellenistic world to the Mar-iology of the early Christian era. Drawing from Jungian notions of archetypes and the collective unconscious, she explores the ways in which the repression of the feminine occurs and the ways in which feminine archetypes resurface, often in distorted or disguised forms. For Christian feminists, her examination of Wisdom and Sophia—and their relationship to Christ imagery—is particularly illuminating. RK

Westminster Press, 1979, 203 pgs. Available from Daughters of Sarah, 3801 N. Keeler, Dept. 1114, Chicago, IL 60641, (312) 736-3399 ($9 ppd.).

THE FEMINIST MYSTIC AND OTHER ESSAYS ON WOMAN AND SPIRITUALITY

MARY E. GILES, ED.

"A woman's spiritual quest in God the Mother awakens her to forces of energy within herself, yet larger than self, transcending self, deeply connecting her with the cyclic movements of creation and personally with her foremothers whose energies still surge through her body, her Tree of Life. The tree and moon are two of many female symbols in the world of ordinary, daily sensory experience by which the Mother Spirit is manifest in the goodness of creation. When we pray through our bodies we energize our will to transform and be transformed within our rhythmic changes and seasons. To do so is to acknowledge and affirm our nature explicitly and to glorify God the Mother by our very womanhood" (Meinrad Craighead, "Immanent Mother").

This anthology of Christian feminist writing covers Teresa of Avila and Catherine of Siena, apophatic mysticism, God the Mother, aloneness and relationship, contemplative experience, sexuality, and Simone Weil. Women working to create a feminist presence within the Church and an affirming Christian spirituality will find much nourishment in these essays. The editor, Mary E. Giles, is the founding editor of *Studia Mystica*, a quarterly journal of mysticism and the arts. Other contributors to *The Feminist Mystic* include Meinrad Craighead, Margaret R. Miles, Wendy M. Wright, Dorothy H. Donnelly, and Kathryn Hohlwein. JIS

Crossroad, 1982, 158 pgs. Available from Harper & Row ($11.95 ppd.).

FEMINIST SPIRITUALITY AND THE FEMININE DIVINE: AN ANNOTATED BIBLIOGRAPHY

ANNE CARSON

Consists of seven hundred annotated listings of works relating to feminist spirituality (primarily books, periodicals, and newspaper articles), including many rare, out-of-print, and difficult to find references. The author, a librarian at Cornell University, has been researching feminist spirituality for five years. An excellent research tool that should be stocked in every university and community library. PW

Crossing Press, 1986, 139 pgs. Available from The Gaia Catalogue Company ($14.45 ppd.).

THE FLAME BEARERS

KIM CHERNIN

In her first novel, Kim Chernin tells a haunting tale of a contemporary spiritual quest. Her story depicts a close-knit family struggling with complex family relationships while immersed in a hereditary mystical tradition that compels them forward from its roots in the deep, prepatriarchal past. As she unfolds the story of this tradition, Chernin spins a web of suspense that holds the reader while her characters come to grips with destiny. Chernin uses a theme that penetrates the hearts and minds of many questing women: The dream of an ancient goddess-centered sect, carefully preserved throughout the ages, and bearing the flame of woman-wisdom to guide us into the future. With her earlier works of poetry and nonfiction, particularly *The Obsession: Reflections on the Tyranny of Slenderness*, Chernin established her reputation as a feminist writer addressing critical themes in the lives of many contemporary women. *The Flame Bearers* exhibits yet another facet of her talent. I thank Kim Chernin for bringing such courageous and memorable works to us. AM

Random House, 1986, 276 pgs. Available from Harper & Row ($8.95 ppd.).

FLIGHT OF THE SEVENTH MOON: THE TEACHING OF THE SHIELDS
LYNN V. ANDREWS

See listing on page 55.

Harper & Row, 1984, 203 pgs.

THE GNOSTIC GOSPELS
ELAINE PAGELS

Gnosticism flourished during Christianity's first centuries, though it was declared heretical by the Church and driven underground. Ironically, it is exactly those elements most vehemently condemned by orthodox Christianity that capture our imagination today. *Gnosis* means knowing in the sense of insight or intuition. Gnostic doctrine differs from orthodoxy in its belief in the identity of the self and the divine, its emphasis on illusion and enlightenment rather than sin and repentance, its portrayal of Jesus as guide to spiritual understanding rather than savior from sin, its celebration of the feminine divine, and its general insistence on the equality of women, particularly in the religious hierarchy. In this lucid book, Pagels explores Gnostic doctrine and compares it with orthodox Christianity; readers may be par-

ticularly interested in the chapter entitled "God the Father/God the Mother." While there is much to refresh us here, we should remember that Gnosticism could also embrace such unappealing doctrines as the material world as a vile trap from which the spirit must extricate itself. Nonetheless, this book is an excellent introduction to the subject of Gnosticism. JIS

Random House, 1979, 214 pgs. Available from Random House ($4.95 ppd.).

GOD AND THE RHETORIC OF SEXUALITY
PHYLLIS TRIBLE

Superb literary study of diverse, often neglected, biblical traditions from the standpoint of rhetorical criticism. Trible, a professor of the Old Testament at Union Seminary (New York), explores female imagery of God along with other issues of gender and sexuality in this early, profound, and ground-breaking work. VH

Fortress Press, 1978, 228 pgs. Available from Fortress Press, 2900 Queen St., Philadelphia, PA 19129, (800) 367-8737 ($10.39 ppd.).

GOD THE MOTHER: THE CREATRESS AND GIVER OF LIFE
LAWRENCE DURDIN-ROBERTSON

Lawrence Durdin-Robertson is an Irish scholar of Goddess religion and the founder, together with his wife, Anna, and daughter, Olivia, of the Fellowship of Isis, an international organization dedicated to the furthering of Goddess practice and study. Durdin-Robertson is a prolific writer and researcher. His self-published works, which include books, liturgies, manuals, and calendars related to Goddess religion, are available through Cesara Publications. *God the Mother*, Durdin-Robertson's most recent work, examines the origins, history, and implications of

Goddess religion and the attempts made by patriarchal religions to obliterate her worship. The book encompasses a multitude of eras and religious traditions, including modern-day spiritual feminism, to show the pervasiveness of Goddess worship throughout times and cultures. Includes an index and bibliography. PW

Cesara Publications, 1986, 86 pgs. For a complete list of Cesara Publications titles write: Clonegal Castle, Enniscorthy, Ireland.

GOD'S WORD TO WOMEN
KATHERINE C. BUSHNELL

One hundred studies—detailed, carefully reasoned, and imaginative—of biblical references to women. Concerned about the low opinion of women generally held by male commentators and expositors, Bushnell set out to suggest new hermeneutical possibilities for traditional "antiwoman passages." Originally published in 1912, this is a fervid, at times quaint, pioneering attempt to improve the status and treatment of women among decidedly conservative church people. VH

GWW Publishers, 1984, 402 pgs. This 1984 edition is a reprint of the original. Available from Daughters of Sarah, 3801 N. Keeler, Dept. 1114, Chicago, IL 60641, (312) 736-3399 ($9 ppd.).

THE GODDESS: MYTHOLOGICAL IMAGES OF THE FEMININE
CHRISTINE DOWNING

Christine Downing courageously enters the archetypal labyrinth of the goddesses of archaic and classical Greece, revealing their relevance to contemporary women in both their repressive aspects and healing potentiality. Thus, for example, while Athena points to how our creativity may be distorted by the power of the father in our imagination, she is also the prototype of the artistically creative woman who imparts soul into the work of the world. The combination of serious scholarship and personal revelation by Downing makes this book intellectually and emotionally compelling reading. PW

Crossroad, 1981, 250 pgs. Available from The Gaia Catalogue Company ($11.45 ppd.).

THE GODDESS OBSCURED: TRANSFORMATION OF THE GRAIN PROTECTRESS FROM GODDESS TO SAINT

PAMELA BERGER

As late as the fifth century A.D. the grain protectress was worshiped throughout the agrarian cultures of western Europe. In *The Goddess Obscured*, art historian Pamela Berger describes these cultures and the techniques used by early Christian fathers to discredit their earth goddess, known cross-culturally as Ceres, Cybele, Astarte, and Terra Mater. Berger uses archaeology, folklore, and art reproductions to show how the mythic elements of the Goddess were assimilated into the lives of Catholic saints and the Virgin Mary. A scholarly work that provides valuable documentation of the feminine in Christianity. GB

Beacon Press, 1985, 173 pgs. Available from Beacon Press ($13.45 ppd.).

GODDESSES

MAYUMI ODA

The vitality, fullness, and inner strength of women is illuminated in these thirty original color portraits of goddesses by internationally acclaimed Japanese artist Mayumi Oda. Accompanying prose by Mayumi tells a personal story of each goddess drawn from her Buddhist childhood in Japan. PW

Volcano Press, 1988, 78 pgs. Available from The Gaia Catalogue Company ($15.95 ppd.).

GODDESS COMING TO YOU: CAN YOU COME TO HER?

MAYUMI ODA

Mayumi Oda is an internationally acclaimed silk-screen artist, and one of the first contemporary woman artists to image the feminine principle as goddess. Her art transforms the stern masculine heroes found in Buddhist and Japanese religious myths into lively goddess portraits of the free-spirited female self. Born on June 2, 1941, in a suburb of Tokyo, Mayumi graduated from the Tokyo University of Fine Arts in 1966 and soon thereafter moved to New York. Here, immersed in the world of Vietnam activism and the New York modern art scene, she struggled to find an artistic expression that reflected herself as a Japanese woman of spirit and power. In the following autobiography, first published as a retrospective to an exhibit of her art at the Institute of Culture and Communication in Honolulu, Mayumi describes her spiritual artistic quest for the Goddess.

My past doesn't seem to exist behind me but here with me creating the present. I was born in the middle of World War II, on the edge of Tokyo. My earliest memory is having a tantrum in my crib, being very, very angry. Huddled under the dim light, we listened to the news of the bombing in Tokyo. Sometimes air-raid sirens filled our town as well. I wanted to be somewhere else, where it was peaceful.

Across the river in a little wood, there was a Shinto shrine, which guarded the people of my town. Children of age three, five, and seven went there in November to report their growth and be blessed with future prosperity. I must have been seven years old. My grandmother finished sewing a kimono for me. My uncle, who had just returned from Java, cut my hair, my bang straight on my forehead, telling me that I would be a beautiful woman when I grew up. My mother tied the wide, pink silk bow that covered my whole, small head. All dressed up, feeling solemn, we walked to the shrine. The high-pitched note of the *sho* flute filled the shrine's grounds. Children in special dress waited their turn to be blessed. The priest shook the green branch of the sakaki tree over my head a few time to brush off the evil spirits and purify me. Bending my head down, all I could see was the red hakama, the long culotte skirts of the girls who served at the shrine. But in the dim light, deep behind the center of the altar, I saw the small, round mirror on the cloud-shaped pedestal that I knew was the Sun Goddess. I asked her to help me, though I did not know exactly for what.

My mother had wanted to be an artist, and she taught me the joy of creativity. She made the great effort necessary to buy materials for me and send me to art lessons. When I was eleven years old, she took me to see Siko Munakata's woodblock exhibition, where I saw his Ten Disciples of the Buddha. My mother transmitted her love of art to me by holding my hand and going over each print. She was still young and beautiful, and her full white face seemed to resemble Munakata's Kannon Bodhisattva. She then took me to the cafeteria and bought me vanilla ice cream. Licking the silver spoon, I dreamed about my adult life as an artist and made a vow that I would make my mother happy.

Mayumi Oda.
Photo © The
Chronicle/Chris
Stewart, 1981.

My father was a Zen Buddhist and historian. At the dinner table, he would give me the teachings of Zen. To him the most important thing was concentration. He often told a story about Tozan, a very well-known monk, who was asked, "What is Buddha?" Tozan, who happened to be weighing hemp, answered, "Three pounds of hemp." As a child I didn't understand what it meant, and it is still quite a difficult koan or Zen riddle. But that was my father's teaching. He said, "Concentrate. Be here now." That's it.

Becoming an artist was never a decision for me. I had loved to draw since I was very small and simply never stopped. Both my parents supported my interest. So I went to art college.

Right after entering, I met John Nathan, an American studying Japanese literature at Tokyo University. We married soon after. He was translating Japanese novels, and I read with him. In turn, he taught me about American literature. We inspired each other.

Not knowing what to express, I was miserable in art college. I knew already how to draw, so I studied mostly fabric dyeing and designing. The school was connected to museums, so we saw a lot of old lacquer ware, kimonos, Noh costumes, and ceramics. The

"I do not think of myself as a feminist but I believe in the strength and vitality of the female. We are creators and our maternity comes out of a universal womb."
(Mayumi Oda,
Goddesses, *Volcano Press, 1988*).

Wind Goddess
© Mayumi Oda, 1977. Silk-screened on rice paper, 26" × 38".

only thing I learned at college was to love the freedom and flexibility of Japanese design.

After we graduated from the University in the mid-sixties, we moved to New York. The heavy clouds of the Vietnam War were hanging over us. John wrote a column called "Notes from the Underground" in the *Evergreen Review*. Allen Ginsberg and flower children, Timothy Leary and his psychedelic light show, movements to legalize abortion and pornography were filling my life. I met many artists, some of whose names were familiar to me before I came to America. Mark Rothko and Willem de Kooning were the most powerful I met. De Kooning's paintings were so violent, so full of raw passions, that when I was in his studio surrounded by them, I could not breathe. Rothko told me that he often read Shakespeare. Later, when I heard about his suicide, I understood what he had meant: his paintings were so intensely sad and burdened. I knew right away that I could not be a painter like them. I said to myself, "I am small," "I am Japanese." I kept questioning myself: "What is my art?"

I got pregnant in the midst of this. My quest for the goddesses began. I had a strong urge to create large-breasted female figures. I was working in etching, and from the black aquatinted background, goddesses started to emerge like Hesiod's description of the birth of Gaea: "There was chaos, vast and dark. Then Gaea appeared, the deep-breasted Earth." Sometimes my goddesses burst from the sea like Venus: sometimes they floated in the night sky.

I had my first son Zachary in 1967. Then we moved to Cambridge, Massachusetts, where I encountered student strikes and the birth of women's liberation. Everybody was for social change. It was a confusing but exciting time. I had my second son Jeremiah in 1970. Between taking care of two children and the house, I had very little time to create. I felt like I was going to lose myself. Out of desperation, my art became a survival force. Without creating art, I wouldn't be myself. The children forced me to see who I was. Being an artist wasn't a luxury anymore. I needed to see myself as positive, strong. Through creating goddesses, I became stronger. I never thought that my art should be "pretty," "beautiful," or "well-balanced." Art was a means for my survival. Through my creative process, I have been creating myself. Goddesses are projections of myself and who I want to be. Each picture represents a stage of my own development, the influences I was feeling and the events that were going on around me.

I made my goddesses to explore Japanese traditional design, which is so free, extravagant, and sometimes even wild. Goddesses started to play in the flowering fields of kimono brocade and swim in oceans of Hokusai waves. My free female figures brought old designs into the present.

The urge to know myself became stronger, and I read a lot of books on psychology, spirituality, and feminism. I realized that my upbringing as a Buddhist was very important to me. I started reading about Buddhism with fresh eyes, reading for myself, not because my father was forcing me to. Being in America, in a different culture, helped me to see my Japanese tradition. It was like opening the door of a treasure house, filled with wonderful gifts.

Back in Japan in 1978, I started to practice *zazen* meditation. Dogen Zenji, the founder of Sōtō Zen in Japan, says that you sit *zazen* in order to know yourself. In the lotus position, in the same spot sometimes for as long as seven days, you invest your whole body and mind. Your mind becomes a screen on which you observe your thoughts and emotions, your longing and your despair, as they filter through. For a long time I no longer painted goddesses. I did self-portraits.

In 1979, I moved to Muir Beach, California, five miles north of the Golden Gate Bridge and right next door to the Green Gulch Zen Center Farm. The first time I saw the farm from Route 1, nestled in the bosom of the gentle, sloping hills, it reminded me of the traditional Chinese painting of paradise. Tracing its way from its source at Mt. Tamalpais—the sacred healing ground of the Miwok Indians—the Red-wood River runs through the Green Gulch fields, watering vegetables and flowers, and then empties into the Pacific Ocean. Under the morning fog, kale, broccoli, and spinach reflect the turquoise blue of the sea. Dewdrops on their leaves look as if a crystal rosary had been scattered over them. Cauliflower looks like white coral. I love to sketch lettuces and purple cabbage spreading their leaves open like the mandala of the Buddha fields, revealing the mystery of creation. Even when I feel sad and tired, the unfolding shape of these vegetables gives me energy to create. I live in the alder grove on the edge of this fertile gulch, the image of the maternal universe. I named my house "Spirit of the Valley" from the poem in *Tao Te Ching*:

The spirit of the valley never dies.

It is called the mysterious female.

Gateway of the creating force.

It flows continuously.

Use will never drain it.

Goddess Coming to You; Can You Come to Her?
© Mayumi Oda, 1976. Silk-screened on rice paper, 24" × 33".

"Repeating the name of Kannon Bosatsu (Avalokiteshvara Bodhisattva) hundreds and thousands of times, people eventually get in touch with their own source of energy and compassionate self. This is the simplest, probably the most powerful Buddhist practice. Kannon Bodhisattva is liberating universal energy, and your belief in her makes you a Kannon goddess." (Mayumi Oda, Goddesses, *Volcano Press, 1988*).

Mayumi Oda can be contacted ℅ Editions Gaia, P.O. Box 310 Star Route, Sausalito, CA 94965. Her silk-screen goddess notecards and fabric goddess images are available through The Gaia Catalogue Company or by writing directly to her.

THE GODDESSES AND GODS OF OLD EUROPE: MYTHS AND CULT IMAGES
MARIJA GIMBUTAS

"The 'Fertility Goddess' or 'Mother Goddess' is a more complex image than most people think. She was not only the Mother Goddess who commands fertility, or the Lady of the Beasts who governs the fecundity of animals and all wild nature, or the frightening Mother Terrible, but a composite image with traits accumulated from both the pre-agricultural and agricultural eras. During the latter she became essentially a Goddess of Regeneration, i.e., a Moon Goddess, product of a sedentary, matrilinear community, encompassing the archetypal unity and multiplicity of fertility, and at the same time she was the wielder of the destructive powers of nature. Feminine nature, like the moon, is light as well as dark."

Archaeologist Marija Gimbutas has forever changed our understanding of mythology and history with this landmark work on the Goddess religion and matristic cultures of prepatriarchal Old Europe. Professor Gimbutas introduces us to the great civilizations of the Neolithic and Copper Age, who developed agriculture, invented metallurgy, created art of beauty and sophistication, maintained vast trade networks, and flourished in abundance and peace. What linked these gynocentric societies was a common belief in the Goddess,

and Gimbutas focuses on the rich variety of this tradition. From the "Lady Bird" figurines that sat on home altars to the complex symbolism of sacred vase painting, from elaborate communal temples to the mysterious cave sanctuaries, the book's copious illustrations and careful scholarship bring this most fundamental aspect of our heritage beautifully to life. JIS

University of California Press, 1982, 304 pgs. Available from The Gaia Catalogue Company ($17.45 ppd.).

GODDESSES IN EVERYWOMAN: A NEW PSYCHOLOGY OF WOMEN
JEAN SHINODA BOLEN

Using the seven major goddesses of classical Greece, Jungian psychiatrist Jean Bolen weaves a complex, thorough psychology whereby women may understand the powerful patterns responsible for shaping our inner and outer reality. Where Jean diverges from traditional Jungian psychology is in her recognition that all of the goddesses are potentially present in everywoman. Essential to this psychology is the element of choice: we are invited to recognize, choose, and cultivate the goddess qualities needed to become better heroines on our own life journeys. RF

Harper & Row, 1984, 334 pgs. Available from The Gaia Catalogue Company ($9.45 ppd.).

THE GREAT COSMIC MOTHER: REDISCOVERING THE RELIGION OF THE EARTH
MONICA SJÖÖ AND BARBARA MOR

What Barbara G. Walker did in dictionary form in *The Woman's Encyclopedia of Myths and Secrets*, Sjöö and Mor have done through historical narrative in *The Great Cosmic Mother*. They show that the religion of the Goddess, the religious view of all humanity for two hundred thou-

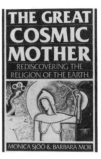

sand years, has been displaced by patriarchal, sky-God religions for only the last five thousand years. In prose and images, they recreate the full picture of the Goddess religion— tied into the fertility of the Earth, the phases of the moon, the seasons, female creativity, the cycles of women's bodies. They argue powerfully that patriarchy is destroying and reversing the living system that has sustained humankind. If we are to survive we must recover our matriarchal roots in humanity's longstanding religious tradition. Monica Sjöö is a Norwegian artist, well known throughout Europe as an artist and theoretician of the Goddess religion's reemergence as a religious/political movement. Barbara Mor is an American poet and writer living in Arizona. Both women are mothers. PW

Harper & Row, 1987, 416 pgs. Available from The Gaia Catalogue Company ($18.95 ppd.).

GREEN PARADISE LOST
ELIZABETH DODSON GRAY

Dodson Gray fuses spiritual, feminist, and ecological values, guiding the reader toward a reimaging of the relationship between humanity and creation. She explores the psychosexual roots of our Western imaging of Nature, showing how the hierarchical patterns in male-female relationships find parallels in man's (sic) treatment of "mother Nature." Dodson Gray has gathered an amazing variety of resources into this feminist/ecological conversation—including the works of Karen Horney, Ernest Becker, May Sarton, and Fritjof Capra. RK

Roundtable Press, 1981, 166 pgs. Available from Roundtable Press, 4 Linden Sq., Wellesley, MA 02181, (617) 235-5320 ($9.64 ppd.).

GREEN POLITICS: THE GLOBAL PROMISE

CHARLENE SPRETNAK AND FRITJOF CAPRA

Green politics is one of the most promising political movements to emerge in the last half of the twentieth century. The first major book on the Green movement available in this country, *Green Politics* is a clear account of the origins of the Green movement in West Germany and an assessment of the application of Green idea to U.S. politics. Green values are in alignment with women's spirituality: ecological wisdom, sexual equality, nonviolence, social responsibility, grassroots democracy, an economic system in which people have significant control of their lives, and peacekeeping and world security measures based on a cooperative world order. *Green Politics* explores these values in depth. (See also listings for *The Spiritual Dimension of Green Politics*, page 87, and Committees of Correspondence, page 184.) PW

Bear & Company, 1986, 245 pgs. Available from The Gaia Catalogue Company ($10.45 ppd.).

GYN/ECOLOGY: THE METAETHICS OF RADICAL FEMINISM

MARY DALY

In this later work, Daly has become a voice unique in English literature. Her writing is passionate, brilliant, exhausting, playful, exasperating, uncompromising; for many readers, *Gyn/Ecology* is one of those rare books that absolutely and forever changes one's understanding of the world. Daly weaves back and forth between two realms: the foreground of patriarchy as ontological evil, and its horrendous effects on women; and the deep ground of sparking and spinning, of women's elemental energy unleashed. To name what has so deliberately remained unnamed, she has created a whole new language, reclaiming titles like Spinster and Nag, inventing new terms such as *sadospirituality* and *Crone-ology*, written in such a torrent of pure energy that all the reader can do is grab her snorkel and dive in. JIS

Beacon Press, 1978, 485 pgs. Available from Beacon Press ($12.95 ppd.).

HADEWIJCH: THE COMPLETE WORKS

MOTHER COLOMBIA HART, O.S.B. (TRANSLATION AND INTRODUCTION)

Like that of so many spiritual women throughout history, the life of Hadewijch, a Flemish Catholic mystic of the thirteenth century, has been largely hidden from view. Her writings, a gift of visionary mysticism and literary genius, reemerged from oblivion only in the late nineteenth century. Hadewijch was a spiritual leader of the radical women's movement of her day, the Beguines, who dedicated themselves to a life of spirituality without taking the veil or vows of chastity. The Beguines sought not cloistered, church-governed lives, but active, spiritually committed, self-governed lives of work, study, and teaching. Nearly all

Hadewijch's poetry and prose writings were directed to her Beguine sisters, some of whom eventually rebelled from her unremittingly high standards. Her medieval Christology and asceticism may present some difficulties to the feminist reader. This collection of her works can serve as an introduction to her mystical vision but requires a more feminist interpretation. PW

Paulist Press, 1980, 412 pgs. Available from Paulist Press, 997 MacArthur Blvd., Mahwah, NJ 07430, (201) 825-7300 ($11.95 ppd.).

THE HANDMAID'S TALE

MARGARET ATWOOD

A satirical novel about a monotheocracy (based literally on the Book of Genesis) as told through the eyes of the handmaid Ofglen. Atwood has created a bone-chilling nightmare of a male-dominated society that dehumanizes both the women and the men who seek to control them. Ironically, all of the seemingly bizarre events in the book have already taken place somewhere in the world, according to Atwood. An important work for understanding the threat to religious and personal freedom posed by the religious right. GB

Houghton Mifflin, 1986, 240 pgs. Available from The Gaia Catalogue Company ($6.45 ppd.).

HEAR THE SILENCE: STORIES OF MYTH, MAGIC, AND RENEWAL

IRENE ZAHAVA, ED.

Writes Irene Zahava: "I wanted this book to convey a sense of the innumerable ways spiritual awareness operates in our lives—even if those aren't the words we use to describe our own experiences. . . . All of them, I feel, have the potential to reveal another truth; one which lies just beyond the surface of our daily lives. It is what you learn when you listen for—and hear—the silence."

This rare collection of spirited short stories includes works by women writers well known in the Womanspirit movement: Anne Cameron, Merlin Stone, Deena Metzger, Judy Grahn, Ursula Le Guin, Kitty Tsui, Sandy Boucher, Judith Stein, and others. Tales of lovers and beings from other planets, basket weavers and bus drivers, meditators and dragon women. Read and let your imagination soar. PW

Crossing Press, 1986, 194 pgs. Available from The Gaia Catalogue Company ($10.45 ppd.).

THE HEBREW GODDESS
RAPHAEL PATAI

Raphael Patai was one of the first to uncover the existence of the ubiquitous Goddess in Judaism. He examines Asherah, Astarte, and Anat in biblical literature and shows how the Goddess has continued to play a role in Jewish theology throughout Jewish history. His work provides women with positive materials to build and link up their Jewish and female selves. Patai shows how the Goddess, although banished to the dark side of the moon, has retained her powers in the imagination of the Jewish people. LG

Avon, 1978, 349 pgs. This book is out of print, but it's worth requesting a library search to find it!

THE HOLY BOOK OF WOMEN'S MYSTERIES, VOLUME 1
THE HOLY BOOK OF WOMEN'S MYSTERIES, VOLUME 2
Z. BUDAPEST

In *The Holy Book of Women's Mysteries*, Z. Budapest describes the Pagan teachings handed down from her mother to her, as well as what she has learned as a priestess in the contemporary Craft. Throughout both volumes, she expresses a deep and enduring reverence for the Goddess. When my daughter Kristin was

twelve, I handed her *The Feminist Book of Lights and Shadows*, now published as *The Holy Book of Women's Mysteries, Part 1*, to help her learn to use the tarot. This book, worn and aged, had served me well as I learned to read the tarot. Each tarot image Budapest defines for us is sheer liberation—liberation from abstractions, from clutter, and mostly from patriarchal thinking. Her words are like mantras, working on our minds at many levels. I shared *The Holy Book of Women's Mysteries* with Kristin confident that she would glean from it the essence of "wimmin's spirituality" as well. I was not wrong. Over the past five years, the book has spent as much time with her as it has on my shelf. It is now as covered with ice cream spills as it is with coffee spills and candle drips. Many times we have used the ideas expressed so simply and truthfully in this work as starting points for sharing our experiences and our political views. I hope many generations of mothers and daughters to come will derive the benefits from this work that we have. AM

Wingbow Press, 1986 revised editions, Volume 1, 136 pgs; Volume 2, 223 pgs. Available at local feminist and metaphysical bookstores.

HUNGER AND DREAMS: THE ALASKAN WOMEN'S ANTHOLOGY
PATRICIA MONAGHAN, ED.

"Spirit Woman will rise from these furrows. / She burns like fireweed. / She is strong as seal gut. / She is plump as salmonberries. / 'Here is the map,' she will say and wind her hair into rings of tree." (Joanne Townsend, "Leavetaking").

Most of the writers and/or characters in this anthology of poems and stories have struggled with a harsh and beautiful environment, oppressive social conditions, or both. In the process these women have learned much about their own strength, the strength

Arctic Madonna. Photo by Fred Belcher commemorates the October 1986 tour across the Soviet Union by the Alaska Performing Artists for Peace. Posters are available for $23.00 ppd. Write: CAMA–I, 1991 Hughes Way, Juneau, AK 99801 (907) 789-0449

of kinship, and the strength of Spirit Woman, to whom many appeal. The writing is consistently good, and the anthology presents an impressive picture of the Alaskan land and character shaping one another. LY

Fireweed Press, 1983, 109 pgs. Available from Fireweed Press, P.O. Box 83970, Fairbanks, AK 99701 ($9.45 ppd.).

HYGIEIA: A WOMAN'S HERBAL
JEANNINE PARVATI

Hygieia is presented as though the writer and reader were sitting over a cup of herbal tea. Jeannine, an herbalist and practicing midwife, interweaves women's spirituality and holistic health in a warm, generous fashion. Each herb is respected as a gift from the Mother, a plant ally in the journey toward female health. In a very practical fashion the book assists women in reconnecting the cycles and phases of our lives with the Earth's—the missing gnosis of woman as herbalist/healer. Includes herbal recipes for resanctifying the bleeding time, personal stories, medications for conception, ritual, mythology, and traditional lore from a variety of cultures, and a glossary of mythological, feminist, and gynecological terms. A truly feminine book, beautifully conceived and designed. RF

Freestone Publishing, 1978, 276 pgs. Available from The Gaia Catalogue Company ($14.50 ppd.).

THE I CHING OF THE GODDESS
BARBARA G. WALKER

This is the fourth book by Walker, whose previous works *The Woman's Encyclopedia of Myths and Secrets* and *The Crone* are best-sellers in the Women's spirituality movement. Here she applies her prolific re-

search skills to unearthing the matristic and prepatriarchal origins of the Chinese I Ching, one of the early systems of divination and understanding that grew out of the original Mother Goddess religion. The I Ching is best known in its commonly used King Wen arrangement. Walker sheds light on the lesser-known but more systematic and balanced Fu

Hsi arrangement. Walker reveals here the matristic origins of the Fu Hsi pattern, demonstrates its overall logic as a binary notation system, and offers fresh commentary on the hexagrams. She invites women to reclaim the I Ching, returning to the simplicity and consistency of the Fu Hsi pattern, as a source of guidance in these times of crucial planetary change. PW

Harper & Row, 1986, 113 pgs. Available from Harper & Row Publishers ($14.45 ppd.).

I SEND A VOICE
EVELYN EATON

In her youth, Eaton was involved with the Theosophists' Order of the Golden Dawn in Great Britain. Years later, severe illness led her to an indigenous healer and her eventual study with the Paiute Indians. This book tells of her efforts to bridge the Indian worldview and white consciousness and her ostracization by both her own people and the Indian culture. She eventually became a Medicine Woman in the Sweat Lodge tradition charged with the task of carrying the insights of Native American religion to non-Indians. DLP

Theosophical Publishing House/ Quest Books, 1978, 178 pgs. Available from Quest Books, P.O. Box 270, Wheaton, IL 60189, (312) 665-0123 ($7.00 ppd.).

ILLUMINATIONS OF HILDEGARD OF BINGEN
MATTHEW FOX, O.P. (COMMENTARY)

Hildegard was one of the most remarkable figures of medieval Europe: abbess, theologian, prophet, scientist, author, composer, healer, and mystic. Like many strong women within a patriarchal system, she ambivalently expressed but actively lived her feminism. She was one of the most influential theologians in a movement within the Catholic tra-

dition that embraced a deep love of Nature, a belief in the sacredness of being, and an affirmation of creativity. Her many visions were written down and illustrated; this book is a collection of her mandalas, with commentary by theologian Matthew Fox. JIS

Bear & Company, 1985, 128 pgs. Available from The Gaia Catalogue Company ($16.45 ppd.).

Text by Hildegard of Bingen with commentary by Matthew Fox

IN A DIFFERENT VOICE
CAROL GILLIGAN

In this ground-breaking work, Gilligan examines women's development, identity formation, and moral decision making. She reveals that studies of human development frequently omit women, that women tend to see the world in terms of connectedness (and men in terms of autonomy), and that women and men seem to have differing modes of development and moral voices. "I wanted to ask men to listen to women's voices," Gilligan said in a January 1984 *Ms.* magazine interview. "I would really like to remap the whole domain of human development—the story we tell ourselves about the Nature of Man." Gilligan asserts that women's moral reasoning has become a political necessity for the preservation of the world. GB

Harvard University Press, 1982, 184 pgs. Available from The Gaia Catalogue Company ($8.95 ppd.).

INANNA, QUEEN OF HEAVEN AND EARTH: HER STORIES AND HYMNS FROM SUMER

DIANE WOLKSTEIN AND SAMUEL NOAH KRAMER

The myth of Inanna, the first goddess of recorded history, is considered by many to be the myth of our times. Her story describes the cyclical and depth dimension of contemporary women's spiritual quest, which often necessitates a journey to the underworld where we seek reunion with the buried, rejected feminine self. *Inanna, Queen of Heaven and Earth* is a living and vibrant translation of the Goddess's journey from youth through her marriage, the coming to queenly power, her descent to the underworld, and return. Scholarly comments are wisely saved until the end, allowing us to experience the story directly. Wolkstein has phrased the translation to keep the poetic and ritual flavor of the original while allowing the story to move along at a pace familiar to today's readers. PW

Harper & Row, 1983, 227 pgs. Available from The Gaia Catalogue Company ($10.45 ppd.).

THE INNER DANCE: A GUIDE TO PSYCHOLOGICAL AND SPIRITUAL UNFOLDING

DIANE MARIECHILD

The Inner Dance lays out clearly and precisely the steps each of us can take to know our life purpose and experience the joy of daily living. The book consists of simple exercises to be used alone, with a partner, or with a group that gently and lovingly enable participants to transform anger and let go of anxiety. It includes physical exercises to open and strengthen the body, meditations, visualizations, and rituals. What makes this book particularly useful is that the rituals can be used for a broader purpose such as planetary peace or specific issues such as fear of changing jobs or reducing stress. All of the exercises teach a fundamental spiritual truth that lies at the core of Diane Mariechild's teachings: everything in the universe exists within a relationship that is continually moving and changing. PW

Crossing Press, 1987, 180 pgs. Available from The Gaia Catalogue Company ($12.95 ppd.).

IN SEARCH OF OUR MOTHERS' GARDENS: WOMANIST PROSE

ALICE WALKER

"I notice that it is only when my mother is working in her flowers that she is radiant, almost to the point of being invisible—except as Creator: hand and eye. She is involved in work her soul must have. Ordering the universe in the image of her personal conception of Beauty. Her face, as she prepares the Art that is her gift, is a legacy of respect she leaves to me, for all that illuminates and cherishes life. She has handed down respect for the possibilities—and the will to grasp them. Guided by my heritage of a love of beauty and a respect for strength—in search of my mother's garden, I found my own. . . . And perhaps in Africa over two hundred years ago, there was just such a mother; perhaps she painted vivid and daring decorations in oranges and yellows and greens on the walls of her hut; perhaps she sang—in a voice like Roberta Flack's—sweetly over the compounds of her village; perhaps she wove the most stunning mats or told the most ingenious stories of all the village storytellers. Perhaps she was herself a poet—though only her daughter's name is signed to the poems that we know."

In her first collection of nonfiction, Walker explores the themes found in her prize-winning novel *The Color Purple*: compassion for the Earth, trust in humanity, and an abiding love of justice. Some of these essays are vintage Walker, dating from the 1967 civil rights movement; all are insightful, witty, deeply poignant, and self-revealing. In one of her greatest, Walker's exploration of the limitations of feminism leads to the creation of a new word, one that better articulates the innate strength, power, and audacity of black women: *womanist*. It is 'to feminist as purple is to lavender." GB

Harcourt Brace Jovanovich, 1983, 397 pgs. Available from The Gaia Catalogue Company ($8.45 ppd.).

JAGUAR WOMAN AND THE WISDOM OF THE BUTTERFLY TREE

LYNN V. ANDREWS

See listing on page 55.

Harper & Row, 1985, 194 pgs.

JAMBALAYA: THE NATURAL WOMAN'S BOOK OF PERSONAL CHARMS AND PRACTICAL RITUALS
LUISAH TEISH

Jambalaya is the story of a woman's reclamation of her personal and political spiritual power as a black female. Luisah Teish, dancer, storyteller, and priestess of the Yoruba goddess Oshun, takes the reader on an incredible journey through the brothels of New Orleans in the early 1800s up to her present-day experiences as a self-actualizing woman of color. A veritable feast of memorable characters and events, Afro-American spiritualism, traditional recast rites and charms, homespun recipes, invocations, affirmations, visualizations, and feminist spiritual rituals. Teish's writing style is engaging, her humor is contagious, and her passionate commitment to the spiritual, physical, and emotional health of the Sisterhood will inspire any reader. GB

Harper & Row, 1985, 268 pgs. Available from The Gaia Catalogue Company ($19.45 ppd. cloth, $11.45 ppd. paper).

PRACTICAL WISDOM: AN INTERVIEW WITH LUISAH TEISH

BY PATRICE WYNNE

"I was asked to lead a meditation at the National Black Women's Health Project. I took a deep breath and said, 'Mother, speak to the benefit of all.' And then this stuff came through me and it was said. Everybody loved it and women came up to me afterward and said, 'Can I have a copy of that?' I said, 'It's not written down,' and they said, 'Well, can you speak it into a tape?' I said, 'I don't know what I said,' and it was like, 'You just stand there and do that?' and the answer is yes. All you have to do is get your ego out of the way, stop being afraid you're gonna say the wrong thing or that you're going to encounter ridicule and just let Mama speak. She's most often right."

—Luisah Teish

Luisah Teish, Iwa L'orisha Oshun, is an initiated priestess of Oshun, the Yoruba goddess of love, art, and sensuality. She is the author of Jambalaya: The Natural Woman's Book of Personal Charms and Practical Rituals *(Harper & Row, 1985). Teish (her name means adventuresome spirit) is a dancer and storyteller performing ancient African and Afro-American tales with an emphasis on reclaiming their significance for contemporary women. A well-loved sister and spiritual guide, Teish has a sense of humor and audacious wisdom that cannot help but inspire those whose lives she touches. This interview took place in the kitchen of my home where Teish and I sat telling stories and savoring an artichoke frittata. Before leaving my home for the day she turned back and waved good-by to the spirits of the house.*

PW *What does an understanding of African-based spirituality offer Western culture?*

LT First we must recognize that there is nothing abnormal or freaky about African spirituality. African spirituality offers a view of Nature as alive and functioning, a reverence for woman, reconnecting to spirits without fear, rejection of the concept of the devil, real community, putting joyousness back into worship.

African spirituality says that getting up in the morning is worship, cooking your meals is worship, washing your body is worship, working in your garden is worship, sweeping your floor is worship, making love is an act of worship. Worship is every act done with integrity and love and the understanding that it is connected to the overall scheme of Nature. The tradition teaches the real dynamics of power and to trust that your own head, your own ovary, your own crown chakra is connected to the big, holy picture of God and Nature.

Christianity is discovering that not worshiping the Mother and not honoring the sacredness of women is killing the effectiveness of the tradition. African spirituality is a healing for this society's decay.

PW How is Mother worship transmitted in African culture?

LT Gelede, which is practiced up and down the west coast of Africa, is a celebration of the Mothers. Even in West African cultures where patriarchy has been adopted from incoming cultures, the Gelede festival is still held. Gelede recognizes that the Old Woman is greater than us, greater than the ancestors, is equal to the gods themselves. Woman was originally revered in Africa and by African peoples, but with more and more exposure to patriarchal tradition, we started to take the accent off of the feminine. But there can be no doubt that if you look at the folklore, and if you look at the practice, the Mother Goddess is of infinite importance.

PW How did you receive your deity?

LT For years I thought I was a child of Yemaya, the African Mother of the Sea who rules the house and has jurisdiction over the affairs of women. I had grown up being my mother's right hand. I had taken care of the children. I was old for my age. The one who wanted to be pretty, creative, and erotic, I kept suppressed inside because I lived in a society that told me a Black woman couldn't be nothing but a mule.

When I went for my first cowrie shell reading, the priest tried to discern my Orisha. [Orishas are the African personifications of the forces of nature. Each child is born under the guidance of an Orisha.] He asked, "Is it this one, is it that one, is it the other one?" and then he said, "Let me ask what I really think. Oshun, is this your child?" and she came back with a definite, "Yes, this is mine." And when he said, "You are the daughter of Oshun" I nearly fell out because the oracle was saying to me, "No matter what anybody else says, beauty and eroticism and creativity are your gifts from birth. You have a right and a responsibility to show that side of yourself." It totally changed my life to know I was a child of Oshun.

I had been laboring under a stereotype of Yemaya. When somebody says Great Mother, what you picture is a fat, Black woman with titties all over her (Isis of a thousand breasts), a million children sucking on her, eternal caretaker. You don't see physical beauty or fight. That's our secular stereotype. In reality, Yemaya is as beautiful as the shimmer of moonlight on the ocean. She is as rich as all those

Luisah Teish.
Photo © John
Williams Lund,
1985.

wonderful shells and coral and pearls on the ocean floor. We have a rogue of Yemaya who walks around in an apron and when she reaches down in her apron pocket, she comes out with a machete. Cause anybody messes with her or her kids, she goes into fighting.

Stereotype of gods and goddesses, daughters, do not hold. Just as Aphrodite got played down into this silly little girl, in a lot of circles among the uninitiated, if you ask somebody, "What is the goddess Oshun like?" they'll say, "Hm, Oshun is fickle, and kind of dizzy, and she sits around looking in the mirror all day and patting her face." That is a stereotype of Oshun. The mirror she's looking in is not as much about vanity as self-contemplation. And the rouge on her cheek comes from the blood of her enemies. She is not fickle, she is versatile.

We live in a culture where we want eroticism to be the missionary position between a repressed man and a repressed woman only for the sake of reproduction. And that is not Oshun.

PW How would our culture be different if Oshun was an active force?

LT Well, first of all we would be inundated with art, art up the yin yang. Every time you looked at a piece of paper you would be thinking, "How do I turn this into something beautiful?" To be in the realm of Oshun is to be very concerned about the affairs of women. You would have the quote unquote problem of being pansexual, of loving the feel of a whole lot of things. I've gotten into trouble with people because I have said I made love to a tomato. I remember one man who jumped up and made the sign of the cross on himself and said he was going to pray for me because I was a pervert. I mean, to take a tomato and rub it in the palms of your hands can feel very erotic if you're tuned in.

Discordant sounds drive the daughters of Oshun mad. To me there is music and orderly conversation, and everything else is madness. Now, the sound of a child calling is music, the sound of a leaf falling is music. The sounds of life are music. People being combative with each other is like a scratch on my brain. We are touchy, feely, always hugging and kissing, doing the stuff that this society does not like. We love bright colors. I've had people tell me, "You ought to dye that dress black. It's winter. Don't you know you can't wear orange and yellow in winter?" Well, of course I can!

We love the bathtub. At any given time, if Teish is out of whack and you want to do something for her, put me in a tub of water. This is medicine. You want to know what to do for me, take me to a stream or a river. You want to give me a gift, give me a beautiful rock. To have Oshun in our life in a day-to-day way would be for every act, including work, especially work, to be done in a celebratory fashion. The children of Oshun love pastry. We can be lured in with cream puffs and little cookies and fruit compote things.

PW But I noticed you gave them back to her. Your altar is filled with chocolate and jelly beans!

LT Right. You have to.

PW Why is ritual important?

LT We have a concept of *Ache. Ache* means power, not power to dominate anybody, but the power to run your body, to think, to create, just the power to be. Ritual is primarily done for the purpose of pulling *ache* from the universe, having guidance on how to use *ache*, and then to give that *ache* back to the universe. To circulate, renew, use, attract, and commune with power is the primary reason for all rituals. Ritual is stylized in order that it become a habit. If I am in the habit of getting up in the morning and drinking a glass of spring water as a ritual to Oshun I remember how precious that stuff is. Only 2 percent of the water on the Earth's surface is sweet water. The rest of it is ocean. She's a precious jewel. That's a ritual.

Ritual is also a way to build community. When we come together for rituals, there is the quiet, reverent contemplative part and then there is the joyous, jump up, sing and dance part. Our rituals at this point are going through some interesting transformations because during the slave era, the only way to practice our religion was to imitate Catholicism. The penalty for practicing African ways was death. We incorporated Catholicism into our practice, but we also kept the pageantry that Catholicism didn't have. Now we're coming into a place where a lot of us are judiciously removing certain Catholic elements. You know what I'm saying. None of my kids can walk around with bleeding Jesuses hanging from their necks. Those symbols have to go.

PW Your work restores the sacred to the ordinary objects we have around us. Spirituality then becomes accessible and immensely practical.

LT And that's the way it should be. Spirituality happened when the sun rose down by the river, with candles, oranges, honey, and people who felt like singing and talking to the Mother. It did not happen in million-dollar cathedrals from nine to ten o'clock A.M. with all of the high mucky-mucks in attendance.

When I was coming into this tradition I had an amazing discovery. I was learning and waiting for the great secret, and then one day it dawned on me—TADA!—that I've been doing the Great Secret. With this spirituality you can fix it up so that mopping your floor is a spiritual act. Washing your dishes can turn into an exquisite ritual. And I'm going to tell people about that one, because I'm not hot on washing dishes. With some music for the water spirits on the box, you in your kitchen drawing a sink full of dishwater to which has been added an ounce of river water, an ounce of ocean water, an ounce of rain water, and some lemon oil, the whole business of washing the family dishes becomes an opportunity to invoke for the health of every person in your household. You can draw from the energy of cleaning, which is what Yemaya does. Woman's work has been degraded and it never should have been. It's what preserves life. When you start to make your everyday work a ritual, you become re-empowered as queen of the manor.

PW   How can women re-empower themselves in the workplace?

LT   I will be quite honest with you. When I enter my house, the first thing I do is look at what everybody is going through. When I see what is not to my liking, I run through the house with herbs and water and invocations, and before it's over, what I want to be going on in my house is what's going on there. I got the power. Not these negatives that have creeped in here while I'm gone. Not all these funky thought forms. I say "Hey, get the hell out of my crib! Get out!" Unfortunately, often at work we find ourselves in a position where it's more difficult to do that. You walk in the office with a smudge pot, or even in some places with a stick of incense . . . well, it's not exactly welcomed.

You have to be a smart woman. One way for a woman to be smart in the office is to get herself the assignment of misting the plants. She can mist them with her own intention, and when they produce oxygen in that room, she'll get the kind of peace she needs. Business environments are very, very difficult because of stupid stuff that people have sitting in their head. The same applies to the educational system. Do you know how difficult it is to try to teach junior high school kids the miracles of visualizations? There was even a case in the southern United States, where a couple got sued for trying to teach self-esteem in the schools. So, we do have to transform the workplace. But when Sister comes home, it ought to be her chamber where she gets renewed and refreshed.

PW   Why are altars important?

LT   An altar is a perfect opportunity to express the Goddess within. Your altar is your personal signature. Here's a place where you need not be scared that you're gonna do it wrong. An altar can be made of anything that appeals to you. There are universals—like you want to mark the four directions, you want to make sure you have the elements of earth, air, fire, and water on the altar. Generally, when I build altars for specific rituals, I clean the space, smudge, and spray. I invoke the directions. I place a glass of water and a candle on the altar. Then, I call the spirits into the space and I say, "What do you want here?" Then I just do what they say.

Now what tickles me very much is people who say, "I'm not the slightest bit spiritual. I don't know how to build altars." And you walk in their living room and they have a lamp, a candle, some flowers sitting on a doily, a picture of grandma, the image of the ancestors. You see what I'm saying. All they need is a glass of water and a stick of incense and they've got an altar. People do subconscious altar building all the time. We call it interior decorating.

Once the ancestors decided I no longer needed a dining room and so the whole dining room turned into this incredible altar space. I had fabric canopied on the ceiling. I got seaweed from the ocean and made a serpent across the walls. There were shells and sand, driftwood and lickable rocks, dried plants and living plants and pictures of gods and goddesses everywhere. Folks would go in that room and be there for the longest while just touching and feeling and going on.

Altars don't cost a fortune. What it costs is creativity. Go down to the ocean, pick up some driftwood. If a stone yells at you, "take me home," do it. You see an unusual plant. Ask permission to break off a leaf. The Mother's marketplace does not require a lot of money. What it requires is walking in the environment in a sensitized manner and hearing who wants to go home with you to be placed on your altar. Of course, I'm a bad one to talk to because altars take me over. There is an altar in every room of my house and in some rooms, two. One day I'm going to make me a hat that has an altar on top of it.

PW Have women traditionally held positions of spiritual leadership within your tradition?

LT There are positions that are traditionally men's and positions that are traditionally women's. Unfortunately, a lot of the positions that existed for women in native Africa have been lost or diminished in this hemisphere. But in reality, our hierarchy is not based on sex. It's based on age. So that you may have a man running things who has been a priest eight years. A woman who has been a priestess ten years can come in and change his plans because it's based on wisdom in the tradition, not on gender.

The tradition has gone through several changes. We had what I call the originators—that is, the people in Africa who perceived the universe intuitively and devised a tradition in response to their environment. Then we have what's called the maintainers, those transported Africans who were in the slave trade, who remembered what they could under the conditions and blended it with what they encountered to create something to suit a new environment. Then you have the transformers, which is the generation that I belong to, where we've learned what the maintainers created. We are taking a look at what the originators created, and we are attempting to take the best from both groups of ancestors and transform that into something that is relevant to today and tomorrow.

Now among the transformers there have been two important changes. One occurred in the late sixties when we were rediscovering our heritage. Through political manipulation, not biological imperative (and I want my brothers and sisters to understand this) the idea of black macho was propagated throughout the black community. The Moynihan Report said that the Black man's problem was not political injustice but the position of the Black woman in the Black family.

That is a crock of untruth! If the black woman hadn't been strong, there would be no Black people in this country, period. But we went for the okydok and put macho in the tradition where it didn't exist in order to say, "Yea, we're like you." My people became ashamed of the matrifocality of Africa and started to negate the feminine in order to please the white man. Negating the feminine leads to destruction, death, and no regeneration. Those of us who love our spirituality had to eventually say "No, this is killing us. Let's take another look at what we had in the Motherland."

What we are now saying—and it's primarily women—is that all people, male and female, had important roles in the Motherland. There was the Women's Secret Society and the Men's Secret Society. We must reinstate and take pride in our spiritual roots. Science and our own knowledge tell us that human life began in Africa. We are the parents of humanity. We deserve the respect that that carries and the responsibility that that carries. That's real hard when you've been oppressed by somebody and in your search for truth find out that that somebody is your kin. Certain structures kill the spirituality, so we are re-examining our original structures that were built through the slave period so that we can take the best from both and create something for these times.

We are structured at this point on the African extended family. I am the mother of certain people who are studying with me for the priesthood. I have fathers in my house and I have mothers in my house. When we address each other, it is Ya and Baba, which is mother and father. The people I teach are my children. When I became initiated, I became sister, aunt, cousin to a whole lot of people that I haven't even met. I became a member of a family of thousands. Now I'm given certain things that will allow them to identify me. If I'm walking down the street in New York and somebody who is a member of my spiritual family sees me, if I'm properly dressed, they will know that they're kin to me. And it extends and it extends so that anybody I initiate becomes related to everybody who has been initiated before. Our kinship is based on the natural laws of relationship, not on child as property. You don't have to be born of the same blood to be kin. That is very important.

PW Are these rules or laws that govern personal responsibility within the tradition?

LT There are basic tenets of the tradition. You respect your elders. You observe high holy days and food taboos. Outside of that, the deity speaks directly to each person. As long as you are listening to your own deity, nobody can challenge you. There's an autonomy in the midst of the extended family relationship that is wonderful.

If you are listening to your Ita, your guidance, what you do will benefit the whole. I'll give you an example. Oya, the Goddess of the Winds of Change, told me she doesn't want me to wear a mask. Do not disguise yourself, she said. Do not pretend to be somebody that you are not. This puts me in a position where I have to be open and honest. It is that attitude that is the flavor and color of my book *Jambalaya*, which has been very freeing to a lot of people.

PW Would you tell us about your Mother's Day bouquet?

LT Well, my Mother's Day bouquet came from the women at the Woman Earth Feminist Peace Institute. It arrived with perfect timing.

*Mask of
Persephone in the
Underworld
© Jennifer Badger
Sultan, 1981.
Paper mache,
plaster bandage,
bones, acrylic.
18" high.*

I hurt my back, I was depressed and feeling overwhelmed. I cast the oracle and Shango, the Lord of the Flame, said to me that several members of my family were depressed. His orders were that we set up an altar for him and have a party. We get those kind of instructions from the oracles. "Wednesday, we want you to have a good time." I was so sluggish at the time, I could barely pull it together to build the altar for the party. Then here comes the flower man, with orange and yellow and red flowers and it was the perfect thing to get me started on the altar. The women sent it to me in recognition that I do a lot of mothering without getting any breaks. And I have gotten and am still getting all the worth in the world out of those flowers. I've taken the red flowers and put them in my hair. I've been bathing in the flowers, and the ones that are dried out I am going to put in a jar for potpourri. The stems will go in the compost or the green manure. Something sent to me with that much love and with such perfect timing carries healing energy. I'm not gonna waste one drop of it, not one drop!

We have to reeducate ourselves in the old ways. Think of the phrase, a useless weed. There is no such thing as a useless weed. There is only a blade of grass that we have not yet been educated about. Every leaf has its purpose.

Luisah Teish leads rituals and teaches classes throughout the country of African spirituality, dance, and storytelling. For booking inquiries write: Jodi Sager, P.O. Box 9725, Berkeley, CA 94709. All other correspondence send to: Harper & Row, Icehouse One-401, 151 Union St., San Francisco, CA 94111-1299.

JEWISH AND FEMALE:
A GUIDE AND SOURCEBOOK FOR
TODAY'S JEWISH WOMAN
SUSAN WEIDMAN SCHNEIDER

A vast compendium of essays, lists, and images concerning Jewish women. Several sections deal explicitly with spiritual concerns: prayer, spiritual leadership, liturgy, rituals for women's life cycles. Many others address related topics such as study, sexuality, body image, family life, aging, and self-esteem. This book can lead you to many other books, as well as films, organizations, support groups, and new ideas from which to expand your own resources. TDS

Simon & Schuster, 1984, 649 pgs.

JOAN OF ARC:
THE IMAGE OF FEMALE HEROISM
MARINA WARNER

As virgin, amazon, saint, or patriot, Joan of Arc remains one of the most compelling exemplars of female heroism, and this study makes fascinating reading. Part One is the biography of Jeanne la Pucelle, placing her in the cultural framework of her times, while Part Two concerns the mythology of Joan that sprang up in Catholic Europe after her martyrdom. Warner is particularly interesting in her analysis of the meaning behind Joan's cross-dressing, which led directly to her execution; on the other hand, she dismisses too quickly the theory that Joan had strong connections with paganism. JIS

Random House, 1982, 349 pgs. Available from Random House ($10.95 ppd.).

THE JOURNEY IS HOME

NELLE MORTON

Distinguished theologian and social activist Nelle Morton has been a mentor to a generation of spiritual feminists. In this collection of essays she traces her decades-long spiritual journey, which she says is "not so much a journey into space, but a journey into presence." Morton writes of "hearing women into Speech"—a phrase that has struck a responsive chord in many women's hearts. Written with passion and clarity, the book interweaves various themes in the struggle of faith and feminism and provides a brilliant analysis of language and metaphor. Morton searches for new symbols and images, reclaiming the Goddess as a positive metaphor. A book for feminist visionaries both in and outside the Church. RK

Beacon Press, 1985, 255 pgs. Available from Beacon Press ($10.95 ppd.).

JOURNAL JOTTINGS

NELLE MORTON

It was in 1971 that I received a totally new understanding of hearing. It came from the lips of a most ordinary woman in a workshop I was conducting in Illinois . . . The last day of the workshop, the woman, whose name I do not know, wandered off alone. As we gathered sometime later in small groups she started to talk in a hesitant, almost awkward manner. "I hurt," she began. "I hurt all over." She touched herself in various places before she added, "But I don't know where to begin to cry. I don't know how to cry." Hesitatingly she began to talk. Then she talked more and more. Her story took on fantastic coherence. When she reached a point of the most excruciating pain, no one moved. No one interrupted her. No one rushed to comfort her. No one cut her experience short. We simply sat. We sat in a powerful silence. The women clustered about the weeping one went with her to the deepest part of her life as if something so sacred was taking place they did not withdraw their presence or mar its visibility. Finally the woman, whose name I do not know, finished speaking. Tears flowed from her eyes in all directions. She spoke again: "You heard me. You heard me all the way." Her eyes narrowed then moved around the group again slowly as she said: "I have a strange feeling you heard me before I started. You heard me to my own story. You heard me to my own speech."

I filed this story away as a unique experience. But it happened again and again in other such small groups when we allowed the pain to reach its own depth, or as another woman told me later: "You went down all the way with me. Then you didn't smother me. You gave it space to shape itself. You gave it time to come full circle." It happened to me. Then I knew I had been experiencing something I have never experienced before. A complete reversal of the going logic. The woman was saying, and I had experienced, a depth hearing that takes place before speaking—a hearing that is more than acute listening. A hearing that is a direct transitive verb that evokes speech—new speech that has never been spoken before. The woman who gave me those words had indeed been heard to her own speech.

From Nelle Morton, *The Journey Is Home*, Beacon Press, 1985.

JULIAN OF NORWICH—SHOWINGS
RICHARD J. PAYNE, ED.

Fourteenth-century contemplative Julian of Norwich received sixteen "showings," or revelations of God's love, in a series of mystical visions when she was thirty-one years old. She experienced God directly as "Our Mother" and, from her experiences, developed a theology of the all-embracing, healing, and strengthening quality of God's love. This work, the first volume of the Classics of Western Spirituality series by Paulist Press, is a translation of her writings and includes an introduction to her life and works. Her writings have particular relevance to Catholics seeking to incorporate the feminine nature of God within the tradition. PW

Paulist Press, 1978, 369 pgs. Available from Paulist Press, 997 Mac-Arthur Blvd., Mahwah, NJ 07430, (201) 825-7300 ($10.95 ppd.).

KENYAN WOMAN HEROES AND THEIR MYSTICAL POWERS
REBEKA NJAU

Colonial scholars portray the African woman as a "beast of burden" and a "slave of man." Author Rebeka Njau found in the oral narratives of her people a different African woman: one who could own property, who was consulted before important decisions were made, and who held a position of spiritual and political leadership within the traditional religion. This book, a collection of folktales and modern fables, aids in correcting the distorted image of African women. It contains the biographies of ten Kenyan women, poets, seers, and women with spiritual leadership abilities. PW

Risk Publications, 1984, 151 pgs. Available from Risk Publications, P.O. Box 54898, Nairobi, Kenya (U.S. $10.00 ppd.).

THE KIN OF ATA ARE WAITING FOR YOU
DOROTHY BRYANT

A near-death experience transports the lead character of this extraordinary visionary novel into the land of Ata. Here he discovers a world far removed from his/our reality. For the Kin of Ata, the Dreamtime is the reality, the Source from which they derive guidance for their life. This book carries a vision of spiritual community guided by our kinship with the Earth and each other, the primacy of the Earth, and the wisdom derived from the unconscious as means to guide our lives. MLK

Moon Books/Random House, 1971, 220 pgs. Available from The Gaia Catalogue Company ($8.45 ppd.).

KNOWING WOMAN: A FEMININE PSYCHOLOGY
IRENE CLAREMONT DE CASTILLEJO

Castillejo, a Jungian analyst for twenty years, traces the development of feminine psychology from Jung's discussion of the anima/animus. She encourages women to make decisions based on the diffuse awareness that arises from the intuitive faculty. Castillejo's presentation is weakened by the limitations of traditional Jungian theory but the book has historical significance. Castillejo, along with M. Esther Harding, encouraged a generation of women to acknowledge and trust their inner female way of knowing. RF

Harper & Row, 1974, 188 pgs. Available from Harper & Row ($7.95 ppd.).

THE KUAN YIN BOOK OF CHANGES
DIANE STEIN

This book does for the I Ching what the women's decks have done for the tarot: provide a completely matristic context in which to consult the oracle. *The Kuan Yin Book of Changes*

is not a reconstruction of the female shamanistic roots of the I Ching, but rather an adaptation of the later patriarchal version. The symbol system is one that practitioners of women's spirituality will find rich and meaningful, with welcome correspondences to tarot, Wiccan, Hopi, and other traditions. Sometimes this has been at the expense of the traditional Chinese formulas, which, when entered intuitively and filtered through woman-loving eyes, can be deeply evocative; but as an antidote to their appalling sexism, this is a powerful re-visioning grounded in contemporary lesbian-feminist lives and dreams. JIS

Llewellyn Publications, 1985, 231 pgs. Available from Llewellyn Publications, P.O. Box 64383-J, St. Paul, MN 55164, (800) THE MOON ($14.45 ppd.).

THE LANGUAGE OF THE GODDESS: UNEARTHING THE HIDDEN SYMBOLS OF WESTERN CIVILIZATION
MARIJA GIMBUTAS

"V's, chevrons, zigzags, M's, meanders, streams, nets, and trilines are frequently repeated Old European symbols. However, in all the literature on neolithic and later ceramics they are considered to be just 'geo-

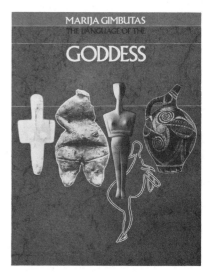

metric motifs'; the relationship between design and symbol was not suspected. It took me years of detective work to pin down the interrelationships between them all. The amazing repetition of symbolic associations through time and in all of Europe on pottery, figurines, and other cult objects has convinced me that they are much more than 'geometric motifs'; they must belong to an alphabet of the metaphysical. Further search for the links between these symbols and the image of a deity revealed that the "V" and chevron (double or triple "V") are the Bird Goddess' insignia, and that other symbols of this family are associated with her mysterious source of life, the life waters, and with her functions as Life-Giver."

Gimbutas's understanding and insight have ripened still further over the last few years since publication of her first work, *Goddesses and Gods of Old Europe* (see listing on page 32). The result is one of the most important books of our era. Gimbutas guides us through the wondrous world of the first religion, from its upper Paleolithic origins through its flourishing in the Neolithic, Copper, and Bronze Ages, to its incomplete destruction by Indo-European patriarchy and its partial survival right up to modern times. This book contains many new illustrations and a text resonant with the unique combination of unassailable scholarship and profound intuition that is the hallmark of Gimbutas's work. JIS

Alfred van der Marck Editions, 1988, 512 pgs. Available at select bookstores or by mail from The Gaia Catalogue Company ($42.95 ppd. hb.).

LAUGHTER OF APHRODITE: REFLECTIONS ON A JOURNEY TO THE GODDESS
CAROL P. CHRIST

This brilliant new book by one of our foremost Euro-American theologians

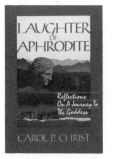

is strong and courageous, profound, beautiful, and loving all at once. Carol Christ shares with us her highly personal story of journeying away from the Father God of Hebrew and Christian traditions and toward the Goddess of the ancient past and challenging present. For Christ, the Goddess is a symbol of our love of all women and of all Nature. The book is a record of this scholar's dynamic confrontation with the established norms of theological thought in Western civilization. In Part I, Dialogues with God and Tradition, Christ discusses the interrelationship of "Women's Liberation and the Liberation of God"; how women as subjects and as spiritual leaders have been condemned as "Heretics and Outsiders" by Judaism and Christianity; how the God of the Hebrew Bible/Christian Old Testament is all too frequently depicted as "Holy Warrior" and why this conception does not serve us for planetary survival in the nuclear age. She forthrightly addresses the importance of opposing anti-Semitism in parts of both the Christian and also feminist traditions; and the essential significance of constructing "A Spirituality for Women." Part II, Journey to the Goddess, contains Christ's very popular keynote speech, "Why Women Need the Goddess"; an encyclopedic synopsis of ancient Goddess (pre)history; and the fascinating, sensuous narrative of the experience and symbolic meaning of Goddess rituals she created, wherein she learned the meaning of the laughter of Aphrodite. Part III contains her provocative and poignant reflections

on "Finitude, Death and Reverence for Life." This work is a major contribution to the progressive development of religious thought in our century. Carol Christ's lifelong commitment to Goddess spirituality serves as a model and inspiration for women and men who, by going deep inside and reconnecting to Nature at all levels, are committing themselves to building a spirituality for the future. MLK

Harper & Row, 1987, 238 pgs. Available from Harper & Row ($17.45 ppd.).

LESBIAN NUNS: BREAKING SILENCE
ROSEMARY CURB AND NANCY MANAHAN

With the publication of *Lesbian Nuns*, the centuries-long silence about the existence of lesbians in the convent has been publicly broken. Forty-nine women, many former nuns, some still in the convent, reveal the emotional process of honoring themselves as religious women and as sexual beings. Their reasons for entering, the conflict of leaving or staying, sexual experiences within the convent, and current spiritual definitions of themselves are some of the many issues these women describe with honesty and integrity. CS

Naiad Press, 1985, 383 pgs. Available from Naiad Press, P.O. Box 10543, Tallahassee, FL 32302 ($11.45 ppd.).

LIFE FORCE: THE PSYCHO-HISTORICAL RECOVERY OF THE SELF
JEAN HOUSTON

In this book, as in her intensive workshops, Jean Houston takes readers/participants through a series of body-mind exercises designed to resolve and heal their traumas of past and present and open them to evolutionary potentials barely thought possible before. A research psychologist, scholar of history, and weaver of stories and atmospheres, Houston has synthesized vast ages of history, prehistory, myth, and ritual into five initiation rites, beginning with birth and leading through childhood, adolescence, and maturity to what she calls the second maturity or the post-individual. While Houston does not interpret myth and ritual from a feminist perspective, her work, as exemplified by this book and her more recent *The Possible Human*, has the potential to take women deep into their own beings, shedding layers of cultural conditioning in the process and emerging stronger, more passionate, and more creative. CRS

Delacorte Press, 1980, 237 pgs.

LILY MONTAGU AND THE ADVANCEMENT OF LIBERAL JUDAISM: VISION TO VOCATION
ELLEN UMANSKY

This book and *Lily Montagu: Sermons, Addresses, Letters and Prayers* by the same author are the first and only works about Lily Montagu, the woman who founded Liberal Judaism in England and who served as pulpit rabbi of her own congregation from 1893 to her death in 1963. Lily believed that the best source of theology is one's own experience in everyday life. As a pacifist she committed herself to serving those overlooked in Jewish life. Her life achievements are remarkable and are finally made part of our official history through the courageous scholarship of Ellen Umansky. These books are invalu-

able not only for the contribution Lily has made to the history of Jewish women but also as an inspiration to reconstruct the lives of women whose stories have remained untold. LG

Edwin Mellen Press, 1985, 305 pgs. Available from Edwin Mellen Press, P.O. Box 450, Lewiston, NY 14092 ($49.95 ppd.).

LISTENING TO OUR BODIES: THE REBIRTH OF FEMININE WISDOM
STEPHANIE DEMETRAKOPOULOS

The author, a professor of women's studies at Michigan State University, names women's bodily experiences of birth, menstruation, defloration, sexuality, nursing, miscarriage, grief, menopause, aging, and death as stages of spiritual growth. Demetrakopoulos uses the word *body* in the broader sense, including bodies of thought and Mother Earth as our ground of being. She writes of a

uniquely feminine metaphysics, grounded in relatedness to the rhythms of our bodies, the cycles of Nature, and connectedness to the universe, as well as to each other, as mothers, daughters, sisters, grandmothers, friends. Her section on the "spiritual grief of rape" is compelling and timely. GB

Beacon Press, 1983, 256 pgs. Available from Beacon Press ($18.45 ppd.).

LIVING IN THE LIGHT: A GUIDE TO PERSONAL AND PLANETARY TRANSFORMATION
SHAKTI GAWAIN WITH LAUREL KING

Shakti Gawain, author of *Creative Visualization*, writes about complicated metaphysical concepts in an easily comprehensible, personal style. Like her first book, this work contains simple exercises for many areas of life: relationships, sexuality, children, work, money, health, and death. The book provides guidelines for confronting our belief systems, unblocking our energy, and trusting the intuitive power of the universe. The chapter entitled "The Male and Female Within" is especially useful for healing wounded male/female relationships. *Living in the Light* contains much that is of value for a woman becoming conscious: rituals for loving our bodies, transforming victim consciousness, validating our financial health, and developing the male principle within. "Living in the Light," an audio tape of Shakti Gawain discussing the principles presented in the book is also available. GB

Whatever Publishing, 1986, 199 pgs. Available from The Gaia Catalogue Company (Book, $10.45 ppd., Tape, $12.50 ppd.).

LISTENING TO THE INNER VOICE:
AN INTERVIEW WITH SHAKTI GAWAIN

―――――――――

BY PATRICE WYNNE

Shakti Gawain is the author of Creative Visualization *(Whatever Publishing, 1976), one of the best-selling books in the New Age market, and* Living in the Light *(Whatever Publishing, 1986), as well as a successful New Age teacher and businesswoman. I first met Shakti several years ago at a workshop she was facilitating. She struck me at that time as a woman who lives her life with a deep trust in her inner voice. This interview took place at her home along San Francisco Bay. As the sun was setting we sat in silence listening to the ocean waters gently lapping upon the shore.*

PW   *In talking with others about your new book* Living in the Light, *I've noticed that one of the questions that frequently comes up is, "Does she really live like that?" It seems to me that what is underneath the question is an awareness that while your book may appear to be deceptively simple, it is quite difficult to live our life as a mirror with the level of self-responsibility that requires of us.*

SG   The answer to the question is: Yes, I live like that.

PW   *Many of the practices that you are writing about and as you say, living, are intrinsic to women's spirituality. Do you consider yourself a feminist?*

SG   What is different about my life is that I was not brought up with the conventional traditional values of male dominance and female inferiority. I think the feminist movement basically arose out of the need for women to establish their sense of themselves. I didn't need to do that because my mother was a very successful professional woman. She was one of the first women in her field, city planning, a powerful woman, very capable in the world. Fortunately, I was taught I could do anything I wanted to do and that I was very bright and capable. I didn't need to establish my power and my sense of myself in that way. So, in answer to your question, no, I don't consider myself a feminist. I certainly support women in moving into their power, and I support women *and* men in breaking out of old

Shakti Gawain.
Photo © Russ
Fischella, 1985.

roles and expanding into a fuller expression of themselves.

PW You mentioned in your book you have a very strong inner male, so has it been necessary for you to get in touch with your female side.

SG I cultivated my ability to be in the world and to take care of myself. What I neglected in some senses is what you might call the more feminine energies. The traditional feminine role seems very beautiful and attractive to me because I didn't do it. I did an opposite thing of going out and becoming very successful in the world. I have always felt confident in myself in that realm, but less so in the other. I honor both the masculine and feminine energies. I feel the feminist movement is going in that direction, as well. They had to swing very far into one direction in order to establish an integration and a balance.

The way I explain it in my book, I don't see it in terms of men and women but rather that it is the male and the female within that needs healing and integration.

PW Could you explain the process of "backing yourself up"?

SG To me, that means trusting your feelings, trusting your intuitive sense, trusting your own truth and acting on it. You can think of it as the male energy backing up the female, acting on what you feel. Backing your feelings with action. If you feel something, saying it as opposed to blocking yourself by thinking "It is going to hurt somebody's feelings" or "It is going to sound stupid." Rather than depressing yourself or holding yourself back, supporting yourself. Being who you really are, saying what you really want to say. Asking for what you want. It is called assertion. In the best sense of the word, being yourself.

Since we actually have many different voices inside, what seems to be simple actually gets more complicated. There may be a voice that says, "This is really what I want to do and I can do it" and then there is another voice of fear and doubt that says, "I can't do it." I can say, "Trust your inner voice and act on it. You will always be right." Well, that is true, but what inner voice are we talking about? I am talking about the deepest, most knowing voice inside of you. If you always hear that voice and act on it you will always be doing exactly what you need to be doing with your life.

Since I wrote *Living in the Light* some of the most powerful work I am doing has to do with recognizing and dialoguing with the different subpersonalities within ourselves. When you begin to recognize the different voices that are speaking inside of you, you know which ones you want to choose to listen to at what time. I feel there is an absolute inner guiding voice but it is hard to get in touch with that voice because there are so many other voices speaking. I have learned to recognize that voice. When it is speaking I know it.

It is really a matter of listening to all the voices, recognizing where they come from and what their fears and needs are. Then let them sort it out.

PW   Like a committee . . .

SG   Exactly. I always thought I was one person and I couldn't figure out why I was so terribly inconsistent. Now I let them all have their say. They all need to be heard, and they all have a reason for existing. They are a part of the whole but unless they are felt and acknowledged they will be in conflict.

One of the things I have been working with is the concept of the disowned selves within us, that there are certain parts of us that are in charge of running the show, and other parts that are repressed and disowned. They are the ones we never want to hear from. So, we're out of balance, with some parts too much in control and other parts never getting expression.

PW   What practices can we do to get in touch with our disowned selves?

SG   I have been doing a technique called Voice Dialogue* where there is a facilitator who talks to the different voices in you. If I were going to facilitate you I would ask to speak to a particular voice inside of you and I would dialogue with that voice. The wonderful thing about this technique is that it is totally nonjudgmental. The facilitator listens to the different voices and just allows them to have their say, whereas in Gestalt, for instance, the two voices try to work something out between them. In Voice Dialogue you are not so much looking for a resolution as you are looking to allow all the parts to be heard fully. Over time the ones who have been in control begin to relax and let go and the ones who have been weak begin to gain power. In this way you get a fuller integration of your being.

This last year has been the most humbling of my life experiences so far. It has been a process of developing my spiritual self by getting in touch with the human and the animal part of me, the physical, primal, earthy part.

PW   Would you call that the Goddess energy?

SG   To me the Goddess is a combination of all of the energies, the heavenly and the earthy. Compared with most spiritual types I am very earthy, very practical, but even so, I denied my humanity. Our human part is difficult. That is where the pain is present, the neglected child. And that is exactly what I have been doing for the last six months. In my relationships certain patterns kept recurring so I finally had to be honest with myself by facing the depths of the old pain. This is a healing time for me. It is like going back to a newborn state.

PW   It seems that is one of our major tasks—to restructure the inner

*Created by Hal Stone and Siddra Winhelman. Their book *Embracing Our Selves* is available through DeVorss & Co., Box 550, Marina Del Rey, CA 90294, (213) 870-7478 ($13.50 ppd.).

patterns, so that we can function in more healthy, playful, loving ways.

SG The newborn expresses the essence of what my life seems to be now—going back to the child state, feeling all the child's feelings, returning to a place of total innocence but from a place of living wisdom. I see it as going back to the Garden of Eden. It is a completely open, childlike, spontaneous, deep place and yet with all the wisdom somehow present, too. I have a lot of moments like that now.

PW How do the conditions on the planet mirror the denial of the personal?

SG I think the Chernobyl disaster mirrors the level of denial that exists in this world, the denial of our power, our feelings, our fears. I felt Chernobyl very deeply. I was in Denver conducting a workshop and I had a powerful personal breakthrough. The first day of the workshop I didn't feel I had done much in the workshop and yet a lot was happening. At the end of the day I was meditating and I realized that though I didn't do anything I could feel people's lives were being transformed. On the surface it wasn't as if anything spectacular happened but I could feel on a deep level the changes that were going on.

When I was sitting in meditation my inner voice said, "You know, it is really time for you to acknowledge what a healing channel you are, that there isn't anything you *do*. It is your presence that catalyzes people to change. You need to stop *doing* and just *allow* that to be. The less you do, the less you are going to get in the way, and I need you to get out of the way and let me do what I am here to do."

The next day the workshop was so powerful people literally got healed. I was sitting there watching it happen. I came home with an intense experience of this power and then I heard about the nuclear disaster. At first I was stunned. How could something so awful happen on the planet and at the same time something so wonderful and incredible have taken place for me? And I thought, That is it, it is the power moving through, you either honor it or deny it. If you deny it, it is utterly catastrophic. That is what we are up against, the unconsciousness and the denial. You can't do it, you can't stop it, you have simply to allow it. Which is to own it, to recognize it and let it be.

When you put the power outside of yourself it boomerangs back on you. I think Chernobyl is a warning and an intense mirror to us. The main denial in the world is the denial of our feelings.

PW How is the world transformed?

SG To me, the world is transformed when we transform ourselves. If you are moved from within to do something, then it is going to have the power of the universe in it and it will be transformational. If you are doing it from your head, saying, "This is a problem, maybe if I do this . . . it will help," it is simply perpetuating the fear and it will have little real effect.

PW Do men and women have different tasks in the personal and planetary transformation we are undergoing?

SG There is a difference between men and women, in that culturally and historically it has been different. We have different programming that we are working through, which makes a difference. From the inside I think all beings are the same, and yet we have different bodies with their own history and their own development. On the level of form there are different things that we're each having to work with. Men have an incredible history of not being OK with being vulnerable, of having to always be in control, to look strong no matter how they feel. It's unmanly to have feelings, especially vulnerable feelings. The feminine, for men, is terrifying.

It hasn't been OK for women to be strong or powerful in the world. It is OK to be vulnerable, that is feminine, but it is not OK to be strong. According to that traditional programming, there is a great fear for women in being powerful. The inner voice says, "I will always be alone, no man will ever want to be with me, I will be abandoned, I will be alone, I will lose my femininity." We each have our own variation on that kind of conditioning. What I see happening in the world now is that the old male in each of us, which is the part that did not trust the feminine, that tries to control and suppress the feminine, the ego needing to keep control, has surrendered internally. The male is now coming forth from the feminine and supporting and expressing the female energies, which is his true role in each of us. This is being mirrored externally in that power is expressed more visibly and obviously through the feminine right now, because that is what is happening in each of us. The rise of women spiritual teachers in the world is a mirror of each of us turning to the feminine teacher within.

Shakti Gawain's books, audio tapes, and video tapes are available from The Gaia Catalogue Company. For information about Shakti Gawain's workshops, retreats, leader training programs, and products write: Shakti Center, P.O. Box 377, Mill Valley, CA 94942, or call (415) 383-1154.

LOST GODDESSES OF EARLY GREECE: A COLLECTION OF PRE-HELLENIC MYTHS

CHARLENE SPRETNAK

Throughout the millennia, until their perversion by the militaristic Indo-Europeans in classical Greece, the goddesses of Old Europe were revered as divine presence immanent in Nature. In reconstructing the lost fragments of pre-Hellenic goddess mythology for the first time in thirty-five hundred years, Charlene Spretnak illuminates one of the earliest chapters of Western religion and culture and provides us a body of ecologically wise stories from which to draw inspiration in our efforts to re-sanctify the Earth. Discover that

The Goddess Hera, from drawings of Minoan and Mycenaean seal rings and seal stones (1950 B.C.), by Patricia Reis for *Lost Goddesses of Early Greece* © 1978 by Charlene Spretnak.

Illustrations copyright © 1984 by Beacon Press. Reprinted by permission of Beacon Press.

"Our myths can imprison as well as inspire us. When they no longer reflect our deepest sense of who we are and who we can be, it is up to us to transform them by living our new vision, and sharing it with others. In doing this, we cleanse the

obstructions to the flow of the life force within us, tapping deep roots which nourish the whole in ways we may never even know." (Deborah Koff-Chapin, "Transforming the Myth", In Context magazine, Spring 1984).

Pandora actually gave gifts of pleasure and prosperity to humanity, that Hera's cyclical return each year was ritualized in the spring baths of Greek women, that Athena was the venerated, peaceful Cretan goddess of the arts. These stories, which read like poetic memory, are highly recommended for parents seeking female- and life-affirming myths for their daughters and for educators seeking to counterbalance the distorted patriarchal myths often presented in school curricula. Illustrated by Patricia Reis with line drawings of Minoan and Mycenaean seal rings, circa 1500 B.C. PW

Beacon Press, 1981, 132 pgs. Available from The Gaia Catalogue Company ($8.45 ppd.).

THE MYTH OF PANDORA

CHARLENE SPRETNAK

Earth-Mother had given the mortals life. This puzzled them greatly. They would stare curiously at one another, then turn away to forage for food. Slowly they found that hunger has many forms.

One morning the humans followed an unusually plump bear cub to a hillside covered with bushes that hung heavy with red berries. They began to feast at once, hardly aware of the tremors beginning beneath their feet. As the quaking increased, a chasm gaped at the crest of the hill. From it arose Pandora with Her earthen pithos [jar]. The mortals were paralyzed with fear but the Goddess drew them into Her aura.

I am Pandora, Giver of All Gifts. She lifted the lid from the large jar. From it she took a pomegranate, which became an apple, which became a lemon, which became a pear. I bring you flowering trees that bear fruit, gnarled trees hung with olives and this, the grapevine that will sustain you. She reached into the jar for a handful of seeds and sprinkled them over the hillsides. I bring you plants for hunger and illness, for weaving and dyeing. Hidden beneath My surface you will find minerals, ore, and clay of endless form. She took from the jar two flat stones. Attend with care My plainest gift: I bring you flint.

Then Pandora turned the jar on its side, inundating the hillside with Her flowing grace. The mortals were bathed in the changing colors of Her aura. I bring you wonder, curiosity, memory. I bring you wisdom. I bring you justice with mercy. I bring you caring and communal bonds. I bring you courage, strength, endurance. I bring you loving kindness for all beings. I bring you the seeds of peace.

From Charlene Spretnak, *Lost Goddesses of Early Greece*, Beacon Press, 1981.

MAID OF THE NORTH: FEMINIST FOLK TALES FROM AROUND THE WORLD

ETHEL JOHNSTON PHELPS

Twenty folk and fairy tales of spirited and independent heroines from a variety of ethnic and cultural backgrounds including African, Breton, Scandinavian, Zuni, Persian, Japanese, Pakistani. These "maids" have self-confidence, spunk, and a clear sense of their own direction, possess moral and physical courage, use magic and common sense to solve the challenges they face, An excellent source of female-affirming stories for young and old children. PW

Holt, Rinehart & Winston, 1981, 176 pgs. Available from A Child's Garden, 920 St. Helena Ave., Santa Rosa, CA 95404 ($8.25 ppd.).

MAKING THE CONNECTIONS: ESSAYS IN FEMINIST SOCIAL ETHICS

BEVERLY WILDUNG HARRISON

Noted feminist ethicist Beverly Wildung Harrison, in this collection of thirteen essays, argues for an ethical theory rooted in the embodiment of reason, the activity of love, and relationship. She then applies this theoretical framework to misogyny, homophobia, ageism, abortion, and energy policy. Finally, Harrison confronts the Christian tradition of which she is part, aiming to rid Christianity of its sexist propensities by recalling its profoundly human teachings. PB

Beacon Press, 1985, 312 pgs. Available from Beacon Press ($12.45 ppd.).

MARIA SABINA: HER LIFE AND CHANTS

ALVARO ESTRADA

"Sometime later I knew that the mushrooms were like God. That they gave wisdom, that they cured illnesses, and that our people, since a long time ago, had eaten them. That they had power, that they were the blood of Christ. . . . Years later, I gave myself up for always to wisdom, in order to cure the sicknesses of people and to be myself always close to God. . . . In truth I was born with a destiny to be a Wise Woman. To be a daughter of the 'saint children.' "

Maria Sabina was a shamanic healer and visionary who practiced a synthesis of pre-Columbian religious belief and Christian mysticism. This book is significant in that there have been few women shamans alive in this century whose life stories have been recorded. Except for her shamanic calling, Maria Sabina lived a simple life that was indistinguishable from that of her neighbors. The book contains a rare translation of the chants by which she healed those who came to her. AR

Ross-Erickson, Publishers, 1981, 239 pgs. Available from Ross-Erickson, 815C Delavina, Santa Barbara, CA 93101, (805) 966-2060 ($9.95 ppd.).

MEDICINE WHEEL EARTH ASTROLOGY

SUN BEAR AND WABUN

This book is an invitation to open to the magical world where all things are connected and where the cycles and rhythms of life are waiting to support you. The Medicine Wheel Earth Astrology system takes the moon, or month, in which you were born as your starting place, relates this to your totems in the mineral, plant, and animal kingdoms, and attunes you to spirit guides for healing and spiritual unfoldment. The gift in this system is its perception of the human life journey as movement on a circular wheel; the book provides a symbol system for understanding each position on the wheel. The result is living with greater integration, balance, and harmony with oneself and the Earth. RF

Prentice-Hall, 1980, 202 pgs. Available from The Gaia Catalogue Company ($8.45 ppd.).

MEDICINE WOMAN, FLIGHT OF THE SEVENTH MOON, JAGUAR WOMAN, STAR WOMAN

LYNN V. ANDREWS

As with Carlos Castaneda's Don Juan stories, the literal truth of Lynn Andrews's books has been questioned. Her narratives, especially her encounters with evil shaman Red Dog, seem too pat and too, well, exciting to be entirely believable. But even if

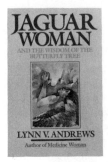

Andrews proves to be "only" a novelist, she's a good one! Her skill lies in illuminating the wounding and the healing of women's sacred powers within tales of extraordinary mind-body-spirit adventures.

In *Medicine Woman*, the first book of the series, a search for an Indian marriage basket leads Lynn to northern Canada where terrifying encounters with Red Dog serve as a testing ground for her personal power. Medicine women Agnes Whistling Elk and Ruby Plenty Chiefs, two feisty but often very wise crones, are her Cree Indian mentors. Lynn's often comic struggle to gain knowledge from these memorable characters may amuse some and annoy others. Yet, the medicine women's teachings offer much to ponder for the non-Indian mind—Agnes's lecture on the senses of stones and the vision of Crystal Woman are not to be missed!

In *Flight of the Seventh Moon*, which has less thriller narrative and more teaching than *Medicine Woman*, Lynn undergoes initiation into the Sisterhood of the Shields, a highly secretive shamanistic society of women who guard and cherish the lost sacred powers of womanhood. To earn her place in this inner circle of shaman women, Lynn constructs her personal medicine shields. "Learning to make a shield is the process of fitting together the shattered pieces of oneself into a whole. This puzzle becomes a working mandala, a shield we carry in our everyday life."

The adventures begun in the frozen wastes of northern Canada continue in the jungles of the Yucatán. In *Jaguar Woman* Lynn receives the next teaching of the Sisterhood: if we are to know ourselves as women we must reclaim the four hoops of female energy: Rainbow Woman's inspiration, Crazy Woman's wildness, the nurturance of the Great Mother, and Death Mother's transformative powers.

Lynn's fourth book, *Star Woman*, is a virtual phantasmagorian tale of supernatural visions and sensational ramblings, accompanied by the usual host of characters and a few new allies—Arion, the stallion, and Twin Dreamers, another Indian shamaness with ancient teachings to impart to the initiate. The writing style has deteriorated to the point where it takes allegiance to the saga to get beyond the first chapter . . . but if you are a Lynn Andrews fan there are a few glimmers of insight. Her struggle to understand the "fear addiction" that keeps her from owning her female power and the exploration of the difference between her female and male energies may prove insightful to women seeking answers in native traditions to questions of female identity and self-awareness.

In her fifth book, "Crystal Woman," Andrews describes a journey to Australia where she masters the Realing and psychic powers of crystals. Truth or fiction? Read and decide for yourself. PW/LY

Medicine Woman. *Harper & Row, 1981, 204 pgs.*
Flight of the Seventh Moon: The Teaching of the Shields. *Harper & Row, 1984, 203 pgs.*
Jaguar Woman and the Wisdom of the Butterfly Tree. *Harper & Row, 1985, 194 pgs.*
Star Woman: We Are Made from the Stars and to the Stars We Must Return. *Warner Books, 1986, 246 pgs.*
Lynn Andrews's books are available at many bookstores or by mail from The Gaia Catalogue Company.

STEALING BACK THE POWER OF WOMAN

LYNN ANDREWS

"I am sure a lot of people wonder what a white woman is doing talking about Native American medicine," says Lynn Andrews at the beginning of her audio tape series Practical Wisdom. *I was wondering that very thing as I sat across from Lynn at a Beverly Hills deli one winter day. Lynn Andrews is the author of five best-selling books that chronicle her adventures with shaman women Agnes Whistling Elk and Ruby Plenty Chiefs and an evil sorcerer, Red Dog. She is a woman who, in her own words, "can't stop writing."*

There are many who have serious doubts about the authenticity of her story as she tells it. I read these stories as metaphors of the soul's journey, offering insights particular to women's psychology and spiritual quests. Yet in spite of the controversy over her autobiographical claims, this much is true: Lynn's writings have inspired many women to pursue their spiritual vision and to risk sharing these visions in the world.

When the interview was over Lynn looked at me quietly and said, "Patrice, the Sisterhood is all of us. It is every woman who is keeping the dream alive. And the oldest dreamkeepers, the Grandmothers, are in danger at this very moment. We must write and we must act to keep the knowledge and the powers of woman alive."

—Patrice Wynne

The Native American is the conquered nation within the nation that we live in. So, naturally, their traditions have been very jealously guarded. The Sisterhood has made it clear to me that the balance between the male and the female is absolutely essential if we are to survive. If we do not act now to bring balance back to the Earth, there will be no tradition to jealously guard.

When I began my apprenticeship with Agnes I studied with her in a very secret way. Nobody even knew that I was going to Canada to learn the medicine ways from her. One of the most important things she taught me as a woman is the importance of making an act of power in the world. I write about this at the end of *Medicine Woman*. Agnes tricked me into making my act of power. After I had studied for some time with her, she said, "Oh Lynn, why don't you come up and live on the reservation with us." So I rented out my house for two years while my daughter was away in school. I had just gone through a divorce and I left, with no money, arriving in Canada with my suitcases in the middle of the night. Agnes was sitting out in front of her cabin by the fire. I was excited and thrilled to see her. She looked at me fiercely and said, "What are you doing here?" I said, "You asked me to come live on the reserve with you." She replied, "You are not Indian. You are a white woman. You do not belong here." She held out her hands and pointed her fingers upward. "It is time for you to let the eagle fly. Take what you have learned from the Sisterhood, the teaching of the old ways and the power of woman, and take them back to your people."

I said, "But I thought it was a secret. I thought I wasn't supposed to tell anyone!" She said, "No. We live in a time of vision, when the Earth is in need of healing and in danger of wobbling off and dying. Take your notes and write the first of many books on this knowledge. Do not return here until the first of those manuscripts is written." That was the end of the conversation. She did not dream me nor did she talk to me until that book was done. She tricked me by placing me in a position where I had cut off all the props in my ordinary life to go study with her. I realized I would never see her again until I wrote my first book.

I am telling you this because I find that the women who are coming to me, and the men too, tend to be people who, in one way or another, need to make their act of power in the world. In other words, we have come through the sixties, the dark time of the seventies, knowing what it is we do *not* want, but not being able to define what it is that we do want in the eighties. And it is what we *do* want that is especially important at this time of great danger on the planet.

A woman is in a very interesting position in this lifetime. She is born onto a female planet. Most places on the Earth you are told, "You are second class. This is not your planet, it's a man's world." And yet women know instinctively that they understand certain things, even though they may not be able to define it. So they hide their truth out of fear that they won't be loved by the men in their lives. And many women take their power and become middle-class men, taking on the very attributes of a sex they don't particularly admire. It's strange to me because women are so very beautiful and powerful as females.

Men, on the other hand, are born into this earthwalk not understanding the energy of the Earth at all. It's very foreign to them. They come here to heal their female side. Women have to take their power to be able to heal men, to be able to teach them how to live. If we don't do that, we're never going to be balanced. Women can balance themselves as individuals, but they have to teach men how to live in balance. However, women can't just say, "I'm your teacher." Women have to *live* their teachings as an example.

Power is never given to a woman. I told the story of the marriage basket in *Medicine Woman* because if you look at it in symbolic terms, the marriage basket essentially is the power of woman stolen away by the sorcerers of the world. Women need to know how to enter the world to steal back that power. It's stealing back what is rightfully theirs, making a place receptive within themselves for their prey, which actually is their power. I don't mean this in a manipulative way. I mean that they have to see what opportunities are there and go for them. And women are afraid to do that for the most part.

The most human thing in the world, really, is work, because it brings everything into focus. Everything springs off of that, which sounds odd for a spiritual woman to be saying. But this is true. You have to begin with work, with a functional process, and then off of that, your spirituality can grow. You can't do it the other way around. Now there is a great difference between your voice and your work. Your work is how you live with dignity in the world and how you support your family. Your voice is how you express your spirit. They do not necessarily have to be from the same endeavor. William Carlos Williams was a great poet. But he earned his living as a doctor in order to live with dignity in the world. He realized he couldn't support his family on poetry though certainly poetry was the expression of his spirit.

I look at human beings as icebergs floating on the sea of enlightenment. As an iceberg, you look down at the sea of enlighten-

Lynn V. Andrews.
Photo by Cynthia
MacAdams, 1984.

ment. You realize you're made of the same material. The only difference is in temperature. When you come to work with a shaman, you are coming for a mirror that's going to heat you up because you begin to notice where you were losing your energy. As you lose energy in addiction, that iceberg gets colder, bigger. As you begin to heal those places where you're hurting, you begin to heat up and the iceberg melts. That is the process of shamanism. It's very simple to understand. It's just very difficult to do it.

A lot of women today are dealing with loving too much. We'd rather fix someone else than fix ourselves. We're addiction-prone because we've come from very chaotic backgrounds. What comes out of that is that we are attracted to chaotic situations. We addict into great agony and pain and despair about our childhoods, and it disables us, which is exactly what we want from an addiction. That's its function, whether it's hitting up with smack or smoking a cigarette or addicting into an emotion. Shamanism deals with all that lost energy. When you addict into anything, you are literally throwing away energy, which is, in essence, a little bit of death.

You are already enlightened. You are the Goddess. All of this teaching is a process of remembering your origins in the center of the spiral. I think that to work with a teacher is enormously helpful, and sometimes that's an addiction, too. We're always looking for another workshop, another teacher, instead of dealing with ourselves. Yet we all have Agneses and Rubies and a Sisterhood in our lives. And Red Dogs, too, God knows. We just have to choose to see it. You don't need to go to the Yucatán to find medicine people. That medicine woman is within you. And certainly within your environment. Women desperately need to learn from women but, basically, we all need to work on our own. We don't need someone to hang on to.

You need to create a foundation for being in the world. You need to define who you are and what you want for yourself. If you don't define life, life defines you. As Agnes says, you can either live your life as an arrow or as a target.

MEDITATIONS WITH... SERIES
BEAR & COMPANY

Within Catholicism there is a life-affirming alternative to the mainstream fall-redemption theology of Augustine and Aquinas. Bear & Co. is publishing a series of small books that return the wisdom of the creation-centered prophets to the "hearts, minds and bodies of our people." Many of the most influential mystics of this holistic tradition were medieval women. From the corpus of the recorded visions of Hildegard,

Julian, Mechtild, and Teresa, the translators have chosen and interpreted brief passages that can be used in meditation and prayer for Catholics and non-Catholics alike. JIS

Meditations with Hildegard of Bingen by Gabriele Uhlein. Bear & Co., 1982. 128 pgs.
Meditations with Julian of Norwich by Brendan Doyle. Bear & Co., 1983. 135 pgs.
Meditations with Mechtild of Magdeburg by Sue Woodruff. Bear & Co., 1982. 132 pgs.
Meditations with Teresa of Avila by Camille Campbell. Bear & Co., 1985. 142 pgs.
Available from Bear & Company, P.O. Drawer 2860, Santa Fe, NM 87504-2860, (800) WE-BEARS ($8.95 ppd. each).

MEDIEVAL ECO-FEMINISM: POETRY OF THE WOMEN MYSTICS

———

HILDEGARD OF BINGEN (1098–1179), the Grandmother of the Rhineland mystics, was an extraordinary Renaissance woman: a doctor, a pharmacist, a playwright, a poet, a painter, a musician, a mystic, a prophetess who attacked church corruption, and an abbess of a dual (male/female) monastery. We possess much of her poetry, music, painting, and writing. She is amazingly ecological in her worldview, which is based on a micro-macrocosmic psychology.

"Glance at the sun. See the moon and the stars.

Gaze at the beauty of earth's greeting.

Now, think.

What delight God gives to humankind

with all these things . . ."

"Humankind is called to co-create.
With nature's help,
humankind can set into creation
all that is necessary and life-sustaining."

"Like billowing clouds, like the incessant gurgle of the brook the longing of
   the soul can never be stilled."

JULIAN OF NORWICH (1342–1415) is rightly famous for articulating in considerable detail the motherhood of God and even the motherhood of Christ. In spite of her living immediately following the Black Death and during very troubled times, she maintains a hope and joy that are remarkable for their sanity and groundedness. She truly develops a metaphysics of goodness, declaring that "goodness is God."

"When God was knitted to our body

in the Virgin's womb,

God took our Sensuality

and oned it to our Substance.

Thus our Lady is our Mother

in whom we are all enclosed

and in Christ we are born of her."

"Just as

    god is

        truly

            our Father,

So also

    is god

        truly

            our

                Mother."

MECHTILD OF MAGDEBURG (1210–1280) was an unmarried lay-woman who consistently attacked church corruption and was just as consistently driven from town to town for her efforts. She kept a journal/book through her adult life, which she published with the encouragement of her Dominican spiritual directors, entitled *The Flowing Light of the Godhead*. Her images in this book are amazing, and they influenced Meister Eckhart deeply, and most likely Dante as well. She ended her years as a nun at Helfta.

"What is the greatest kind of love?

Great Love

    does not flow with tears.

Rather,

    it burns in the great Fire of Heaven.

In this Fire

    it flows and flows swiftly

"The sea is the symbol for emersion into life, the subconscious and the reservoir of treasures within one's inner self. Fish and womb were synonymous in Greek; delphos meant both. The original Delphic oracle first belonged to the fish-goddess, Themis, who often incarnated as a dolphin. The Celts though fish-eating could place new life in a mother's womb. The center shell represents the

Sea Mandala
© Susan St. Thomas, 1982. Watercolor, 30" in diameter.

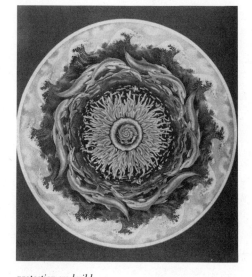

protection we build in our lives to allow inner growth and change" (Susan St. Thomas). For information on mandalas available for sale from the artist write: Susan St. Thomas, 19 Winfield St., San Francisco, CA 94110.

yet all the while

it remains in itself

in a very great stillness."

TERESA OF AVILA (1515–1591) was an indefatigable reformer of religious life in the Carmelite Order. She combined deep prayer with busy administrative duties and boldly faced constant political opposition. She was a fine psychologist of the interior life and she counseled the need for joy, moderation, humanity, and self-knowledge as well as compassion as the test of one's mystical life.

"All things must come to the soul

from its roots,

from where it is planted.

The tree that is beside the running water

is fresher and gives more fruit."

"God Herself

    becomes

the dwelling place we build for ourselves.

It seems I am saying

    that we can build up God

        and take God away

since I say

    that God is the dwelling place

    and we ourselves can build it

        so as to place ourselves in it.

        And indeed we can!"

Biographies from Matthew Fox, *Original Blessing* (see listing on page 67), Bear & Co, 1983. Poem meditations from the *Meditations with . . .* ™ Series (Bear & Co.): *Meditations with Hildegard of Bingen*, 1982; *Meditations with Julian of Norwich*, 1983; *Meditations with Mechtild of Magdeburg*, 1982; *Meditations with Teresa of Avila*, 1985.

Meetings with Remarkable Women celebrates the flowering of contemporary women teachers of Buddhism—a flowering wholly unprecedented and particular to this time, this place. Women teachers of Vipassana, Zen, and Tibetan Buddhism are represented in this work. Some have maintained close ties to inherited traditions while infusing them with a warmth and softness closer to their natures, while others have sloughed off traditional forms and are exploring new ways of practicing and transmitting the dharma. Their teachings represent the growing edge of American Buddhism today. Includes twenty-five photographs. PW

Shambhala Publications, 1987, 250 pgs. Available from The Gaia Catalogue Company ($11.45 ppd.).

MIDDLE EASTERN MUSLIM WOMEN SPEAK

ELIZABETH WARNOCK FERNEA AND BASIMA QATTAN BEZIRGAN, EDS.

A collection of biographical and autobiographical writings on and about Middle Eastern women. Poetry, interviews, excerpts from other works (including the Koran), many translations, and photographs cover a wide range of women from the early Islamic to contemporary times. The female personalities that emerge from the pages of this anthology are highly diverse—from the submissive and traditional lamenting the restrictions of femininity imposed upon them to the socially and politically active whose lives exemplify a dedication to freedom and justice. AB

University of Texas Press, 1977, 402 pgs. Available from University of Texas Press, P.O. Box 7819, Austin, TX 78712 ($14 ppd.).

MIDWIVES OF THE FUTURE: AMERICAN SISTERS TELL THEIR STORY

ANN PATRICK WARE, ED.

The nineteen authors in this collection of autobiographies began their religious lives in medieval habits, in awe-filled obedience to church authority and strictly regulated in the smallest details of their lives. In *Midwives of the Future* they describe the process of finding their own paths to spiritual empowerment and of developing sisterhood and inner authority—which, though different in form, echoes the experience of many women over the last twenty years. Each of these sisters, active agents of social change, remain within the Church but challenge it to a renewed future in which patterns of relationship, community, and mutual empowerment exist for all people. PW

Leaven Press, 1985, 237 pgs. Available from Leaven Press, P.O. Box 281, Kansas City, MO 64141-0281 ($10.45 ppd.).

Young women of Pushkar, India. UN Photo 153,017 by Oddbjorn Monsen.

MENOPAUSE NATURALLY: PREPARING FOR THE SECOND HALF OF LIFE

SADJA GREENWOOD, M.D.

Anthropologist Margaret Mead once said that the most creative force in the universe is the menopausal woman with zest. In this work, holistic practitioner Sadja Greenwood offers a practical and spirited approach to attaining the zestful life. She balances information on the medicinal with the natural, the cultural with the physical, and suggests ways of incorporating appropriate nutrition, emotional support systems, relaxation techniques, enjoyable exercises, and humor into our daily lives. Includes cartoon illustrations by Marcia Quakenbush. PW

Volcano Press, 1984, 202 pgs. Available from The Gaia Catalogue Company ($11.50 ppd.).

MIRIAM'S WELL: RITUALS FOR JEWISH WOMEN AROUND THE YEAR

PENINA V. ADELMAN

Rosh Hodesh, Jewish women's traditional celebration of the new month at the time of the new moon, is the

starting point for this book of symbols, stories, songs, rituals, history, and new insights. It is based on the author's pioneering experience in reviving the observance of Rosh Hodesh as well as the work of other contemporary Jewish feminists. In addition to information on topics such as the Jewish calendar and the origins of Rosh Hodesh, there is a section for each month that includes a discussion of themes, correspondences (astrological signs, mystical traditions, biblical figures, and so on), stories, guided imagery, special readings (blessings, poems), songs, foods, and rituals for the season. Rituals also relate to personal life cycle events such as fertility, childbirth, menstruation, mourning, and healing. A companion music cassette tape, "A Song a Month," is also available. PW

Biblio Press, 1986, 143 pgs. Available from Biblio Press, P.O. Box 4271, Sunnyside, NY 11104 (book and tape, $16.89 ppd.; book only, $10.64 ppd.; tape only, $9).

THE MISTS OF AVALON
MARION ZIMMER BRADLEY

"For this is the thing the priests do not know, with their One God and One Truth: that there is no such thing as a true tale. Truth has many faces and the truth is like to an old road to Avalon; it depends on your own will, and your own thoughts, whither the road will take you."

A powerful retelling of the Old Religion of the Goddess by the women of Arthur's court in pre-Christian Britain. Reading this book, you will leave the present for a time when Morgaine le Fey was a priestess of the Goddess and her brother Arthur was king of all Britain, when women controlled their own bodies and their own power, when men ruled by virtue of their relationship to a woman. For 876 pages you will live in an enchanted world and grieve as that world slips further into the mists. (Contributed by Rev. Jeanette Stokes, Resource Center for Women and Ministry in the South—see listing page 202.)

Alfred A. Knopf, 1983, 876 pgs. Available from The Gaia Catalogue Company, ($11.95 ppd.).

THE MOON AND THE VIRGIN: REFLECTIONS ON THE ARCHETYPAL FEMININE
NOR HALL

Nor Hall takes us into the land of myth, fairy tale, poems, and dreams. The book is intelligent, sensitive, and stimulating. Hall guides us through familiar landscapes peopled by Aphrodite, Artemis, Psyche, Hecate, the Wise Woman, and the Hetaira. The book provides women a refreshing look into the realm of archetypal psychology and the dark moist matter of the feminine unconscious. AG

Harper & Row, 1980, 284 pgs. Available from Harper & Row ($9.45 ppd.).

MOTHER WIT: A FEMINIST GUIDE TO PSYCHIC DEVELOPMENT
DIANE MARIECHILD

Diane Mariechild brings together a wealth of information on healing and female spirituality in *Mother Wit*, one of the most nurturing, feminine-wise books available today for developing our inherent psychic abilities. Includes chapters on deep relaxation,

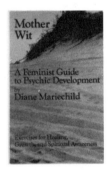

energy and vibration, psychic communication, creating your own reality, reincarnation, and using ritual for protection. Drawing on her life experiences as a woman and mother, the author honors both the child within and our own children as spir-

itual teachers. RF

Crossing Press, 1981, 155 pgs. Available from The Gaia Catalogue Company ($10.45 ppd.).

MOTHER WORSHIP: THEME AND VARIATIONS
JAMES J. PRESTON, ED.

Since women have started to reclaim the Goddess as their role model, many books have emerged to delve into Goddess legends and rediscover the significance of the Goddess in every world culture. The essays collected in *Mother Worship* are especially valuable for the women of color seeking awareness of the Goddess's presence in her ancestors' past. The book covers the less-recognized representations of the Goddess by organizing the contents cross-culturally: "Mother Worship in the New World," "The European Madonna Complex," "The Great Goddess in South Asia," and "The Divine Feminine in Southeast Asia and Africa." Written mainly by anthropologists and university professors, these essays are comprehensive, well-documented, and, though written from an academic viewpoint, reverently spiritual. In his conclusion, Preston addresses those of us who are seeking to recapture the feminine deity and empower ourselves to "correct the errors of those that came before," referring to the patriarchal move in history to negate the Mother, the Earth, the Goddess, Motherhood. Includes the Christian black madonnas, saints, and Witches. PCC

University of North Carolina Press, 1982, 360 pgs. Available from University of North Carolina Press, P.O. Box 2288, Chapel Hill, NC 27514 ($11.45 ppd.).

THE MOTHER'S SONGS: IMAGES OF GOD THE MOTHER

MEINRAD CRAIGHEAD

Mystic and artist Meinrad Craighead spent most of her life within institutional Catholicism, including fourteen years in a monastic order. Always, it was the image of God the Mother, rooted firmly in her motherline, that lived in her heart. This beautifully produced book is a collection of Craighead's paintings, each image juxtaposed with a description of a dream, or contemplative experience, a poem, or a childhood memory. The images are archetypal, earthy, and sensual—a deeply loving representation of female spirit. *The Mother's Songs* is an exquisite portrayal of the magic of the natural world and the presence of God the Mother in all her manifestations. JIS

Paulist Press, 1986, 88 pgs. Available from The Gaia Catalogue Company ($11.45 ppd.).

Garden
© Meinrad Craighead, 1984. (From *The Mother's Songs: Images of God the Mother,* Paulist Press, 1986.)

MY ROOTS IN GOD THE MOTHER

MEINRAD CRAIGHEAD

God the Mother came to me when I was a child and, as children will do, I kept her a secret. We hid together inside the structures of institutional Catholicism. Through half a lifetime of Catholic liturgies, during years of Catholic education, from first grade through college, in my professional work in Catholic education, for fourteen years in a Catholic monastery, we lived at my inmost center.

This natural religious instinct for my Mothergod gave me a profound sense of security and stability. She was the sure ground I grew in, in the groundsill of my spirituality. Yet we remained comfortably at home in the bosom of Holy Mother Church. My Catholic heritage and environment have been like a beautiful river flowing over my subterranean foundation in God the Mother. The two movements are not in conflict, they simply water different layers in my soul.

This personal vision of God the Mother, incarnated in my mother and her mother, gave me, from childhood, the clearest certainty of woman as the truer image of Divine Spirit. Because she was a force living within me, she was more real, more powerful than the remote Fathergod I was educated to have faith in. I believed in her because I experienced her.

Instinctively I knew that this private vision needed protecting: my identity, my very life depended upon its integrity. But as she guided me as an artist, illuminating my imagination, her presence in my life could not really be veiled. She erupted in my imagery. And it is as an artist that I am compelled to reveal this secret life we have shared for nearly fifty years. . . .

I draw and paint from my own myth of personal origin. Each painting I make begins from some deep source where my mother and grandmother, and all my fore-mothers, still live; it is as if the line moving from pen or brush coils back to the original Matrix. Sometimes I feel like a cauldron of ripening images where memories turn into faces and emerge from my vessel. So my creative life, making out of myself, is itself an image of God the Mother and her unbroken story of emergence in our lives.

From Meinrad Craighead, *The Mother's Songs: Images of God the Mother*, Paulist Press, 1986.

MOTHERPEACE: A WAY TO THE GODDESS THROUGH MYTH, ART, AND TAROT
VICKI NOBLE

Motherpeace: A Way to the Goddess through Myth, Art, and Tarot is an informative journey into the labyrinth of matriarchal cultures. Vicki Noble combines art, prehistory, mythology, ancient religions, and astrology to guide us in rediscovering the rich heritage of Goddess-worshiping cultures around the world. Vicki is one of the creators of the Motherpeace Round Tarot; this book can be used alone or in conjunction with the cards. Similar to the Motherpeace cards, the teachings contained in the book serve as a bridge to reclaiming a holistic sense of self, a prerequisite to creating a healthy, peaceful connection to Mother Earth. Contains sixteen full-color plates and sixty-two black-and-white line drawings of the Motherpeace Round Tarot. EF

Harper & Row, 1985, 276 pgs. Available from The Gaia Catalogue Company ($14.45 ppd.).

THE MOTHERPEACE TAROT PLAYBOOK: ASTROLOGY AND THE MOTHERPEACE CARDS
VICKI NOBLE AND JONATHAN TENNEY

In *The Motherpeace Tarot Playbook*, a series of clear and practical exercises guide the reader in using tarot

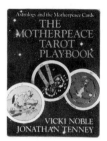

and astrological systems for personal awareness. The first half of the book teaches various ways of learning and applying the tarot; the second half contains insightful methods of relating the tarot to one's astrological chart. Throughout, the reader is encouraged to enter into "sacred play," a process that emphasizes joy and spontaneity rather than fear and judgment in readings. *The Motherpeace Tarot Playbook* provides guidelines for interpreting reversed or tilted cards, information not included in Vicki's first book, *Motherpeace: A Way to the Goddess through Myth, Art, and Tarot.* Though based on the Motherpeace Tarot (see listing on page 259), the information contained in this book can be used for any tarot system. EF

Wingbow Press, 1986, 206 pgs. Available from The Gaia Catalogue Company ($13.45 ppd.).

THE MYSTERIES OF THE GODDESS: A STUDY IN THE LORE AND CRAFT OF WOMEN
SHEKHINAH MOUNTAINWATER

In olden times, the mysteries of women were handed down by the crone mothers to the maiden daughters when their first bloods came. Learning and teaching was a personal exchange between women who loved and respected one another. *The Mysteries of the Goddess* offer a way to learn magic in the Old Way. It is a homespun study course for budding female witches in thirteen lessons, one for each lunar cycle of the sacred

year. The course includes discussion, reading list, and assignments, all infused with Shekhinah's exuberant personal style. Subjects studied: creating altars, raising power, casting spells, performing rituals, celebrating holy days, herbs, and divination. PW

Send $1 for course information and catalogue to Shekhinah Mountainwater, Box 2991, Santa Cruz, CA 95063.

NATURAL MAGIC
DOREEN VALIENTE

After a ten-year absence, *Natural Magic* is back in print. It covers the magic of herbs and flowers, the four elements, numbers and colors, amulets and talismans, traditional spells, planting a magical garden, the magic of birds and animals, and an unusual chapter on weather predicting and weather magic. PW

Phoenix, 1985, 184 pgs. Available from Phoenix Publishing, P.O. Box 10, Custer, WA 98240 ($8.95 ppd.).

NIGHT FLYING WOMAN: AN OJIBWAY NARRATIVE
IGNATIA BROKER

By telling the life story of one woman, fictional but realistic, Broker hoped to teach the children the old ways. We hear the people being guided by dreams, holding council with each other, choosing which ways to use and which not to use in dealing with the strange intruders on their land. As we watch the traditional ways changing bit by bit, there are lessons for all of us in reinhabiting the Earth in a new/old way. CS

Minnesota Historical Society Press, 1983, 135 pgs. Available from the Minnesota Historical Society, 1500 Mississippi St., St. Paul, MN 55101, (612) 297-3243 ($9 ppd.).

OF WOMAN BORN
ADRIENNE RICH

Many women experience a conflict between self-preservation and maternal feeling. In this classic work, Adrienne Rich unravels the institution of motherhood, which demands instinct rather than intelligence, selflessness rather than self-realization, and relationship with others rather than the creation of self. In tracing the history of motherhood, Rich describes the prepatriarchal societies where a woman's spirituality was validated in the images of the Goddess. The core of her book is the chapter "Motherhood and Daughterhood" in which she advises us to be courageous mothers and to nurture ourselves as well as our daughters. Rich closes with a plea to women to "think through our body" and thus come into a new relationship with the universe. MS

Bantam Books, 1976, 328 pgs.

ON BEING A JEWISH FEMINIST
SUSANNAH HESCHEL, ED.

Excluded so long from the domain of the written word, Jewish women are only now beginning to explore the past and present with feminist insights and to record our findings. This book offers responses from a variety of Jewish religious and secular perspectives, in twenty-five brief essays by women. These writers consider the difficulties of the past and attempt to break apart old myths and images that are negative and detrimental to Jewish women's spiritual growth and position in society. This work reveals how Jewish women are uncovering the powerful voices of women long buried within mounds of inaccessible material and provides a useful history of the Jewish feminist movement since the early seventies. LG

Schocken Books, 1983, 288 pgs.

ORIGINAL BLESSING: A PRIMER IN CREATION SPIRITUALITY
MATTHEW FOX

In *Original Blessing*, Matthew Fox, a Dominican priest and educator, turns Christian spirituality as we've known it upside down. He counters the past centuries' exaggerated emphasis on sin and redemption with a focus on celebration, creativity, and the blessedness of all created things. Fox describes a spiritual path, creation-centered spirituality, that is at once aesthetic, earthy, ecstatic, feminist, and justice-oriented. For women and men trying to reconcile their Christian roots with feminist values and an earth-based spirituality, this book can be a healing and a revelation. Scattered among lines from the Old and New Testaments, female mystics of the Middle Ages, and church teachers from Irenaeus to Aquinas are quotes from Susan Griffin, Chief Seattle, Mahatma Gandhi, Audre Lord, Rabbi Heschel, C. G. Jung, Starhawk, and other prophets of ecologically-wise spiritual traditions. CRS

Bear & Company, 1983, 348 pgs. Available from Bear & Company, P.O. Drawer 2860, Santa Fe, NM 87504-2860, (800) WE-BEARS ($12.95 ppd.).

OUR PASSION FOR JUSTICE: IMAGES OF POWER, SEXUALITY, AND LIBERATION
CARTER HEYWARD

Our Passion for Justice is a collection of essays, sermons, lectures, and liturgical poetry spanning a seven-year period in the life of Episcopal priest and radical feminist theologian Carter Heyward. Heyward treats complex topics such as male gender superiority, homophobia, and capitalist exploitation in tones that are both pastoral and prophetic, imaginative and analytical. In moments of waning energy and faltering vision, one can turn to this work to rediscover a vibrant and renewed faith. RK

Pilgrim Press, 1984, 264 pgs. Available from Pilgrim Press, 132 W. 31st St., New York, NY 10001 ($12.45 ppd.).

OVERLAY: CONTEMPORARY ART AND THE ART OF PREHISTORY
LUCY LIPPARD

In *Overlay*, feminist art historian Lucy Lippard draws parallels between the megaliths, hill drawings, labyrinths, and burial places of prehistory and the sculpture, earthworks, ritual, and body art of recent decades. Her thesis is that the matrifocal images of prehistory that are reemerging in modern feminist art hold powerful symbolic messages for re-entering into reverent relationship with the Earth. PW

Pantheon, 1983, 266 pgs. Available from Random House ($17.95 ppd.).

THE OWL WAS A BAKER'S DAUGHTER: OBESITY, ANOREXIA NERVOSA AND THE REPRESSED FEMININE
MARION WOODMAN

Jungian analyst Marion Woodman is on the leading edge of developing a genuine women's psychology. Her three books to date are profound in their pioneering research into women with eating disorders. In *The Owl Was a Baker's Daughter*, her first work, Woodman sets out her thesis: the feminine in Western countries has been devalued for centuries and is now profoundly distorted. As women we are alienated from our bodies and the feminine. "The way

back to the feminine for the obese and anorexic woman," she writes, "is no different than the way back for the rest of us." We must find and reclaim the lost Goddess within ourselves. MS

Inner City, 1980, 144 pgs. Available from The Gaia Catalogue Company ($11.50 ppd.).

PAGAN MEDITATIONS: THE WORLDS OF APHRODITE, HESTIA, ARTEMIS
GINETTE PARIS

Ginette Paris, a French Canadian therapist and scholar, writes in her introduction: "In contrast to a meditation which, like Buddhist meditation, seeks to find a void, a 'pagan' meditation allows all images, all possibilities to arise, all the fabulous personages who inhabit us, until, little by little, we perceive the web of their relations. Then a myth becomes a coherent scenario, and the part we play in the collective drama becomes clearer." Her book, an emotional and intellectual appreciation of three Greek goddesses, presents these archetypes as values of extreme importance to twentieth-century collective life—for men as well as women. Aphrodite, goddess of love, appears as civilized sexuality and beauty; Artemis, goddess of the hunt, is brought to presence as solitude, ecological significance, and a clarifying perspective on abortion; Hestia, goddess of home and hearth, comes before us in images of security, warmth, and stability. This book addresses the need felt by many women today for an imaginative, feminine feminism, one that validates our meditative interior as well as our role in the unfolding of culture. PW

Spring Publications, 1986, 204 pgs. Available from Spring Publications, P.O. Box 22069, Dallas, TX 75222 ($15 ppd.).

THE POLITICS OF WOMEN'S SPIRITUALITY: ESSAYS ON THE RISE OF SPIRITUAL POWER WITHIN THE FEMINIST MOVEMENT
CHARLENE SPRETNAK, ED.

"The title The Politics of Women's Spirituality *refers to our attitude toward life on Earth (i.e., spirituality) and the perception, manifestation, and use of power (i.e., politics) that stem from that attitude. The worldview inherent in feminist spirituality is, like the female mind, holistic and integrative. We see connectedness where the patriarchal mentality insists on seeing only separations. . . . The gains that we make in legal, economic, medical, and educational areas will be shortlived unless they are grounded in collective action that is continually fueled by a strong sense of our personal power and its elemental source. In fact, without that sense of inner power, without the sense that we are the source of change, our vision will not prevail."*

This anthology is one of the best sources on contemporary women's spirituality, and an essential record of our first decade. In the introduction, Spretnak presents her concept of "body parables" (birth, pregnancy, menstruation, orgasm) as spiritual teachings. Part One, Discovering a History of Power, is a cross-cultural look at our traditions and foremothers. Part Two, Manifesting Personal Power, brings together consciousness, ritual, art,

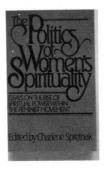

healing, and action. Part Three is Transforming the Political, where feminist spirituality manifests in new forms of political action. The appendix includes two debates, on hierarchy in women's spirituality and the historicity of matriarchies. It has been said that patriarchy is the current world religion; this book offers an alternative, and not a moment too soon. JIS

Anchor Press Doubleday, 1982, 590 pgs. Available from The Gaia Catalogue Company ($16.45 ppd.).

POSITIVE MAGIC: OCCULT SELF-HELP
MARION WEINSTEIN

Considered by many to be one of the best books on the principles and philosophy of Wicca, *Positive Magic* includes a brief history of the Craft, teachings on astrology, tarot, the I Ching, and an invaluable chapter on composing words of power. Ethical considerations and karmic effects of various forms of magic are presented. An excellent sourcebook of magical skills, written in Weinstein's characteristically witty and intelligent style. PW

Phoenix, 1984, 283 pgs. Available from The Gaia Catalogue Company ($10.45 ppd.).

PRAISE SONG FOR THE WIDOW
PAULA MARSHALL

Praise Song for the Widow describes the spiritual odyssey of an older black widow. When the story begins she is living a life without meaning, estranged from her children. Journeying to a festival on an island she has never heard of before, she awakens an ancestral memory: the Ibo slaves, upon landing on the Georgian Sea Islands, looked into the future, rejected what they saw, and walked, singing, across the water back home to Africa. In making peace with her ancestors, the widow makes a place not only for herself but for her children and the generations to come. This book is significant in that it portrays the living cultural legacy of black people that has persisted through the period of slavery and remains to this day as a source of spiritual and political sustenance. AR

E. P. Dutton, 1984, 256 pgs. Available from New American Library, 120 Woodbine St., Bergenfield, NJ 07621, (201) 387-0600 ($9.25 ppd.).

THE PREGNANT VIRGIN: A PROCESS OF PSYCHOLOGICAL TRANSFORMATION
MARION WOODMAN

The virgin archetype is "that aspect of the feminine, in man or woman, that has the courage to Be and the flexibility to be always Becoming." This is the essence of feminine consciousness (not to be confused with mothering), which Jungian analyst Marion Woodman defines in her most comprehensive book to date. Once again she focuses on eating disorders, but this time she is more concerned with how to transform them. Specifically, she suggests ways to free ourselves from the father and mother complexes that have left so many of us helpless and addicted. Our transformation involves becoming pregnant with ourselves and learning to love the abandoned child inside of us (the one our mothers didn't nourish). Woodman's final chapter is a moving account of her journey to India and her own initiation into womanhood. Her story began where many of us begin: "First I had to face my own hatred." MS

Inner City Books, 1985, 204 pgs. Available from The Gaia Catalogue Company ($16.50 ppd.).

ANOREXIA, BULIMIA, ADDICTION, AND THE LOST FEMININE: AN INTERVIEW WITH MARION WOODMAN

BY SALLY VAN WAGENEN KEIL

For the last six years, Toronto analyst Marion Woodman has been persistently exploring some of the most intractable of our modern illnesses, from alcoholism to anorexia. She has shared her powerful approach and insights in The Owl Was a Baker's Daughter: Obesity, Anorexia Nervosa and the Repressed Feminine; Addiction to Perfection; *and* The Pregnant Virgin. *Now that we have the capacity to annihilate ourselves through nuclear physics and to dehumanize our psyches through laser-speed technology, Woodman believes we are witnessing a groundswell of protest from our bodies and the Earth itself.*

Our insatiable pursuit of rationality, recognition, and material achievement has left us starving for the life force within. Our heady existence—even our ethereal spirituality—must now be grounded in the body. We have to listen to its wisdom if we want to save the planet and redeem the sacred in ourselves.

SK *Why are we seeing such an astonishing increase in eating disorders today?*

MW Anorexia and bulimia are more common because women are further away from their bodies than ever. This breeds a profound inner rage, one that compounds itself from generation to generation. Yet I believe illnesses like anorexia, far from being evil, are the means of healing on a larger scale if we can only understand their message.

Food represents nurturing by the mother, and when we reject it like the anorexic, we are rejecting life itself. Women today are being forced to deal with their own death wish—which is precisely what we must do on a global scale. The truth is we are moving toward annihilation because our culture does not respect the earth or feminine creativity.

SK   How is our rejection of the body related to our rejection of the feminine?

MW   All matter is feminine. On this level, men's bodies are embodiments of the feminine just as much as women's. The extraordinary thing is that matter is becoming conscious. For women, there is an anguished realization: "I hate this body!" For men, it comes out in the cry, "This hurts!" Matter is forcing many people to become aware of its sacredness. So we have these scourges of illness like messages from the gods.

SK   What generally is blocking life?

MW   A profound unconscious fear and rage that goes back to infancy. Because our mothers could not love themselves as complete feminine beings, they could not love us. So our fear is archetypal, monstrous. We have a tremendous sense of something within being shut off, abandoned. This is our own self, our soul.

SK   How do we proceed from here?

MW   You have to get at the meaning of the starving—what the soul is hungry for—in order to feed it. An addict attempts to fill a terrible emptiness inside. But it's a spiritual emptiness, not physical emptiness.

Dreams give us the images that can feed the soul. The dream can tell you exactly what the problem is and even where it is in the body, months before a doctor could have diagnosed it. The image doesn't usually come as a picture of the body, but as a symbol—a car, a house, a tree. Often the soul manifests as a plant or a tree which is broken or endangered somehow.

The Eastern sages knew about the relationship of symbols to the body. You can see it in their description of the chakras. But in our culture, there is a failure of imagination. We confuse spiritual or soul food with actual material food. As a result, the soul is left starving and the body is abandoned.

We also don't feed ourselves images that are healthy. The images of war and violence we see on television are actually soul-destroying. But more fundamentally, the soul is not being fed because people can't receive.

SK   So we've lost a sense of communion between the body and the soul?

MW   Yes. For me body work is soul work and the imagination is the key to connecting both. To have healing power an image must be taken into the body on the breath. Then it can connect with the life force, and things can change—physically and psychologically. We have no real contact with the feminine.

SK   What signs do you see of this deprivation?

MW   The need for feminine recognition of the body comes up in

The Nubian
© Thomas
McKnight, 1983.
Casein on canvas,
36" × 40".

dreams of lesbianism. When the female body has not been loved by a woman—the mother—the psyche tries to fill that gap. Often these dreams involve the analyst who is serving as a mother figure.

Once the body has experienced feminine love—in dreams or life experience—it will move on to a new plateau of sexuality. A symbolic union of woman and woman must take place before a real meeting with a male is possible.

SK Are our bodies trying to teach us how to live as women?

MW They certainly are. Take premenstrual syndrome, for instance. A lot of women find their bodies swelling up with water. If you look at that symbolically, you see the body filling up with the unconscious. In the olden days, women would have gone to the menstrual hut and looked inward, stayed with the unconscious, listened to the body, and brought this wisdom back to the tribe. But in our culture, there is no time given, no respect paid to that period.

It's like the dark of the moon. When we menstruate there has been a death. A child will not be born. But there is the possibility of new spiritual life, and evidence of our capacity to nourish it. If we don't take time to respect these mysteries, we feel a terrific tension. The body swells up and says, "Come down into my healing waters and I'll give you the symbols which will make it possible for you to go out into new life, into a new cycle."

SK Why haven't we been more sensitive to the female body and to these warnings?

MW   One of the problems is the taboo against death in our Western culture. People just don't want things to die. They are afraid to let go of the old and go on with the new. The true feminine knows life is cyclical, that the caterpillar must die for the butterfly to emerge. We all must experience this chrysalis stage periodically.

Women have such potential to bring into the world a totally new insight into the cyclical pattern of life. But if they keep trying to run that straight line of perfection and performance, the body catches up with them. And the body will only be outraged for so long before it takes revenge.

SK   What happens when we don't use the body fully?

MW   We are disconnected from soul, from the purpose of our lives. Life is a matter of incarnation—the soul is an entity we have to live with in our human body. The problem is too many people in our culture try to skip over this step and go straight up into spirit.

Overspiritualization is a real danger, but usually the body starts to scream. People will get symptoms or an addiction. Then they can start coming down to earth again.

We have got to face the agony and the ecstasy of being human— something we are not too good at in this culture. Many people don't want to be human, they'd rather live on idealization and perfection. They don't want to take responsibility for their lives because it's much easier to fly off into spirit and try to live out an archetypal dream.

SK   Has our overly masculine culture been seduced by ideas and left the body far behind?

MW   I see patriarchy as the power principle, not as genuine masculinity. It's the Father on the archetypal level. It is Jehovah, Father Law. Father Law upholds Mother Society, Mother Convention, Mother Church, Mother Social Insurance. Yet these archetypes leave us with a view of our own humanity that is very incomplete.

SK   What is the positive feminine that we're moving toward?

MW   Love is the essence of feminine consciousness—in men and women. It is the recognition and acceptance of the total individual, and loving the individual for who he or she is. The feminine is the loving container of all conflict, all physical and psychological processes. They must not be rejected, but safely, lovingly contained. Suffering and conflict are the only way to grow. As life moves from phase to phase, you have to suffer the death of one and the birth of the next.

SK   Tell us more about this rite of passage.

MW   The feminine soul is what grounds us, it loves and accepts us in our totality. Our challenge today is to embody this. For some time now I have been seeing dreams—hundreds of dreams from both sexes— about big, dark women: they appear as dancers, magnificent gypsies, a Portuguese cook or people they met in the Bahamas. These great wonderful black women are reminiscent of the Black Madonna,

Photo courtesy of
Marion
Woodman, 1988.

the dark earthy virgin who was worshiped in the Middle Ages and is still worshiped in many European countries today.

SK What happens when the body is finally listened to?

MW It becomes eloquent. It's like changing a fiddle into a Stradivarius. It gets much more highly attuned. As it becomes more sensitive, it protests against all manner of psychological and physical poisons coming in.

When people listen to the body, they also develop an acute sensitivity to nature. I have seen so many men and women come into my office crying over a tree that has been cut down, a bird that has been hurt. Once you come into contact with the pain of your own body and its devastation, you become more aware of the ravages of nature.

SK When you begin this dialogue with the body, are there different levels of communication?

MW Yes. Let me give you an example. At menopause women may be given pills to keep their rite of passage at bay. If, however, they listen to their own body, it finds a way of bringing about genuine transformation—psychically and physically. The pills work for awhile but then the body finds a way of getting its message through.

Warning signs are to be heard and obeyed. Rather than being ignored, starved, gorged, or made drunk, the body must be attended to. When the body is fully open, we can trust our own feelings and actions; they anchor us in an inner home. The body protects and guides us—its symptoms are the signposts that reconnect us to our own lost soul.

This interview is reprinted from *The Tarrytown Letter*, December 1985, edited by Valerie Andrews.

PROLEGOMENA TO THE STUDY OF GREEK RELIGION
JANE ELLEN HARRISON

Jane Ellen Harrison's *Prolegomena to the Study of Greek Religion* is an essential reference text for anyone engaged in study of the ancient Goddess or of prepatriarchal religion. *Prolegomena*, Harrison's first major work, is crammed full of ideas that were considered revolutionary by her colleagues. In many classics departments today, her work is ignored or simply forgotten. We must attribute this to the fact that Harrison seeks to elucidate, rather than obscure, the prepatriarchal foundations, including a "matriarchal substratum," of Greek religion. Throughout her writings, one finds perceptive statements about the Goddess, the evolution of ritual, and the Goddess religion rarely found in classical male scholarship. Harrison is very much a product of her times (1850–1928), and as such, is rather difficult to read. Nevertheless, any effort is amply rewarded. I recommend reading some of Harrison's other works before diving too deeply into *Prolegomena*, particularly the introductions to *Epilegomena* and *Themis*. In these two works, written later in her life, she further developed her ideas about magic, ritual, and the mysteries. AM

Merlin Press, London, 1962, 682 pgs. Although Harrison's work is out of print, most libraries have copies of her more popular titles.

PURE LUST: ELEMENTAL FEMINIST PHILOSOPHY

MARY DALY

"Primarily, then, Pure Lust names the high humor, hope, and cosmic accord/harmony of those women who choose to escape, to follow our hearts' deepest desire and bound out of the State of Bondage, Wonderlusting and Wonderlusting with the elements, connecting with auras of animals and plants, moving in planetary communion with the farthest stars. This Lust is in its essence astral. It is pure Passion: unadulterated, absolute, simple sheer striving for abundance of be-ing. It is unlimited, unlimiting desire/fire. . . . Choosing to leave the dismembered state, she casts her lot, life, with the trees and the winds, the sands and the tides, the mountains and moors. She is Outcast, casting her Self outward, inward, breaking out of the casts/castes of phallocracy's fabrications/fictions, moving out of the maze of mediated experience. As she lurches/leaps into starlight her tears become tidal, her cackles cosmic, her laughter Lusty." JIS

Beacon Press, 1984, 488 pgs. Available from Beacon Press ($13.95 ppd.).

THE QUEEN OF WANDS

JUDY GRAHN

Judy Grahn celebrates the many forms of the Goddess and sources of the mystical tradition in women's culture: the tarot's Queen of Wands, the ancient Sumerian goddess El-Ana, Helen of Troy, the Indian Spider Grandmother (here called Spider Webster), the Yoruba goddess Oshun, Hel, Frigga, Woman the Weaver, the Keeper of the Flame, the Stolen Queen whose beauty and power are taken captive. Grahn consistently presents us with the poetic vision of the ancient/new myths being woven in women's spirituality literature. LY

Crossing Press, 1982, 112 pgs. Available from Crossing Press, P.O. Box 1048, Freedom, CA 95019, (408) 772-0711 ($7.95 ppd.).

RADICAL LOVE: AN APPROACH TO SEXUAL SPIRITUALITY

DODY H. DONNELLY

Donnelly, a Roman Catholic, sees spirituality "not as some airy laxative that purges the bodily-sexual away, but as the oneness of our human existence lived in the light of faith—a faith that means we know we're loved, and by such a Lover, our God! I see sexuality as the greater intercourse we have with the world, the sensuous embracing of life." Donnelly names the dualism of sexuality and spirituality within the Christian church and tradition, and traces a

path toward healing and union. PB

Harper & Row, 1984, 135 pgs. Available from Harper & Row ($8.95 ppd.).

RITES OF ANCIENT RIPENING

MERIDEL LE SUEUR

Meridel Le Sueur is a cultural treasure, a wisewoman from whom seventeen books, twenty-three stories, articles, poems (many of them award-winning), and twenty-one great-grandchildren have grown. She lives in her beloved Midwest, where she has celebrated, defended, and protected working people through the decades. Less well known is that part of her work that proclaims a powerful Earth-based spirituality, full of erotic wisdom and the deeply rooted authority of a matriarchal voice. The first group of poems in this collection, "Winters of the Slain," are fiercely tender memorials to her Native American great-grandmother and prayers to the larger spiritual sense of "grandmother." In the second group, "Changing Woman," Le Sueur is one with the elements and the forces of procreation, "luminous with age." The third group, "Surround of Rainbows," are songs of harvest and thanksgiving to "grandmother of the center of the earth." In the final group, "Doan Ket" (Vietnamese for solidarity), Le Sueur mourns the plundered villages worldwide that have lain in the path of the conqueror and calls for "Roaring womb singing. Our sisters singing. Choruses of millions singing." (Contributed by Charlene Spretnak.)

West End Press, 1977, 57 pgs. Available from West End Press, P.O. Box 291477, Los Angeles, CA 90029 ($6 ppd.).

THE SACRED HOOP: RECOVERING THE FEMININE IN AMERICAN INDIAN TRADITIONS
PAULA GUNN ALLEN

"In the beginning was thought, and her name was woman. . . . She is the Old Woman who tends the fires of life. She is the Old Woman Spider who weaves us together in a fabric of interconnectedness. She is the Eldest God, the one who Remembers and Re-members; and though the history of the past five hundred years has taught us bitterness and helpless rage, we endure into the present, alive, certain of our significance, certain of her centrality, her identity as the Sacred Hoop of Be-ing."

The inherent wisdom of native traditions teaches us that each part is necessary for the well-being of the whole. In Native American spirituality, the sacred hoop represents the continuous circle of life within which everything in existence has its place. Yet while this worldview may be slowly permeating the Western white mind, patriarchal attitudes toward women remain firmly entrenched without knowledge of the contribution, traditions, and values of Native American women. *The Sacred Hoop*, a collection of essays by noted American Indian poet, novelist and scholar Paula Gunn Allen, provides the missing link in our understanding of the significance of female tradition within Indian spirituality. Allen argues that colonization altered and obscured what were once woman-centered cultures. Drawn from over a decade of writing, her essays demonstrate the crucial significance of mothers and grandmothers to Indian identity, unveil the honored place of lesbians in Indian culture, relate the history of gynocracies within several tribes, and explore a range of female deities.

The Sacred Hoop is a major contribution to feminist and American Indian scholarship. It provides modern people—and especially American Indian women—with a history though which to remember, validate, and resacralize ourselves and the planet. PW

Beacon Press, 1986, 309 pgs. Available from The Gaia Catalogue Company ($12.45 ppd.).

RECOVERING SPIRITUAL REALITY IN INDIAN TRADITIONS: AN INTERVIEW WITH PAULA GUNN ALLEN

BY PATRICE WYNNE

Paula Gunn Allen is a poet, novelist, and scholar of Laguna Pueblo/ Sioux/Lebanese-American ancestry. She is the author of Shadow Country *and four other books of poetry. Her novel* The Woman Who Owned the Shadows *is the first novel written by an American Indian woman about an Indian woman in fifty years. Her most recent book,* The Sacred Hoop: Recovering the Feminine in American Indian Traditions, *is a ground-breaking work that describes the varied lost female traditions within Indian culture and identifies their significance for all peoples—Indian and non-Indian, women and men. She is a professor of Native American studies at the University of California at Berkeley and a respected teacher of many women and men seeking a deeper understanding of the American Indian way.*

PW What spiritual teachers have been influential in your life?
PGA When I was in my very early twenties, my sister gave me a copy of *In Search of the Miraculous* by P. D. Ouspensky. I enjoyed it very much and then I forgot about it. But I had begun to practice the teachings of Gurdjieff, which Ouspensky writes about, and they had transformed my life.

Women come to me because I'm Native American and they want to learn how to be an Indian. The more I work with Gurdjieff, the more I know that he's how urban Western women can do Native American spirituality in the real Indian way. An Indian is somebody who connects with and takes responsibility for the spiritual life of this continent, who recognizes the spirit entities of the land and lives in congruence with them, who understands that every aspect of life is sacred; that is, it matters in the balance of the planet. This is what makes an Indian, not skin color.

What I do in teaching Gurdjieff's ideas or systems is to get women connected to reality. That's very difficult to do with white women. They have been so desperately turned against reality at every level. But that's where spirituality is.

PW What do you mean by reality?

PGA It's washing the dishes and doing the laundry and paying the bills and talking to your girlfriend and walking down the street and going to a movie and eating and combing your hair. It's being in your life. You can't *do* spirituality if you're trying to be someplace else. What I know about the tribal system is that it's based in your present reality. The way you do Indian spirituality is you belong to a tribe. You can't separate the religion from the people base. And if you're an Indian, one of the things about your reality is grief and pain and anguish and rage. You can't be an Indian and not know that's how it is. You struggle with those feelings. You don't kill people as a consequence of your feelings. It violates your spiritual integrity and basic commitment to life. The tribes that fought back on white terms lost so much of themselves. A lot of women who are feminists or lesbians are now learning that.

PW It seems to me that during the seventies, in our attempt to change the prescribed roles for women we lost the power of the feminine.

PGA If you are a woman, it isn't going to be real good for you to deny the centrality of the feminine in your life. How are you going to heal when you hate yourself? And that's the kind of thing that an Indian has to go through all the time. Self-loathing destroys not only the person caught in it but others and eventually the biosphere. You can't do feminine without masculine. You can't do stars without the void. You can't do light without darkness.

PW How would Gurdjieff teach us to experience our feelings, say, for example, of grief or anger, and then to transmute them?

PGA Transmutation is the key here. He would actually give people experiences that they hadn't had. So if they didn't know how to be bitter, he would do something that made them bitter toward him. OK, now, how does being bitter affect who I think I am? Could I come to terms with my own bitterness? Gurdjieff's teachings are about self-concept and learning to be an observer. The physicists say that what the universe appears to want is for us to observe Her. Absolutely.

Every Indian knows that. That's why they developed many ways to observe things carefully. She just likes to be looked at. Noted. Attended to. The most important thing my mother taught me was how to see, how to get all my social stuff, all my emotional stuff, all my personal stuff, out of the way, and just see what was there. It's a great gift she gave me. It's also a great pain. Because you can never do something disastrous to someone and feel justified about it. When you've learned to observe, you see the consequences of your action. Grief and pain are expressions of connectedness. Gurdjieff's system teaches practical compassion through right self-observation, which means *observe*: don't criticize, don't analyze, don't be judgmental, just observe *how* you function, honestly, sincerely, and in a balanced way.

PW What would Gurdjieff teach us about living life with reality in these times of massive cultural and personal change?

PGA If you stay alive, aware, intelligent, sensible, and in balance when everything in the situation is dragging you into your garbage, then you have healed. When you heal under great difficulty, you heal a lot of beings around you just because of the effort it takes to do it. That's why Indians would do things like go up on a vision quest and cut off a finger. Now, be in balance. Don't eat for seven days. Now, be in balance. Spend your life with a whole bunch of folks who're always making fun of you because Indians are good at that. Now be in balance. Be the leader and have everybody chewing on you because that's how Indians are. Now, be in balance.

PW Why do you think Gurdjieff's teachings are so translatable to women today?

PGA The core of his teachings are the ancient woman systems. Frankly, he stole them. He brought them to the West, where they were desperately needed. The people he got it across to were women. It was the wives, the dykes, the single women, who became his most important and later influential students. He knew the Westerners were suckers for foreground, for the hero. They never pay attention to background, matrix. But where the truth is is in the matrix. It's in the background, in the shadows, in the women. By the time he died, he had a group of women who were very capable teachers. They could teach by living the work, by their very presence in the room. They were that beautifully attuned.

PW What can women do to heal the masculine internally?

PGA For a long time, the idea was to heal the feminine in ourselves. I'm certain that doesn't mean destroying the masculine because that could not be healing. If I'm going to be a whole person, I can't possibly be whole at the expense of psychic, psychological, emotional, or physical destruction of another being because that's not wholeness, that's disease. At times the feminist movement has tried to buy the health of women at the expense of men. I know that the most brutal existence you could have in America today is to be a

Paula Gunn Allen.
Photo by
Catherine Busch,
1986.

male of color. This says something about feminist theory. I'm saying this not to deny the terrors and dangers and risks and horrors of being female, but rather to say that there's lots of people at risk in this situation. Actually, most of them are children.

I not only acknowledge but respect the masculine in myself. That creates an empowerment for me, a gentleness, a mellowness, an ability to nurture that I didn't have before. When I came out as a lesbian it was a process that healed me. I learned to see men as beings with their own problems, limitations, bad habits, wonderful-nesses, strengths, beauties, and joys. I don't mean to suggest that I'm now giving up my obligation, not to mention my right, to criticize men. But I also have the responsibility to nurture and respect what is male because I can't criticize what I can't love. A human being is like a bird. One wing is masculine and the other wing is feminine, but both wings are needed to fly.

PW What does the Indian tradition have to teach us about positive images of male power?

PGA Where I come from, which is Laguna Pueblo, the ideal of manhood is motherness. My book *The Sacred Hoop* talks about this at length. America has created an image of a brutal, bloodthirsty, macho man, who by and large never existed in the tribes. A man, if he's a mature adult, nurtures life. He does rituals that will help things grow, he helps raise the kids, and he protects the people. His entire life is toward balance and cooperativeness. The ideal of man-hood is the same as the ideal of womanhood. You are autonomous, self-directing, and responsible for your own spiritual, social, and material life within a matrix that includes the animal people, the spirit people, and the entire planet herself. As a definition of self it is enormous.

PW It seems a key to being our healthiest selves is nurturance, that is to nurture life in all that we do.

PGA I think so. And we have to quit saying only women nurture. For this is not true. Modern peoples have a very peculiar system where fathers are deprived of the babies and either can't or won't support them because they've been told for generations that they can't nur-ture. What does it do to a human being to be told, "You're not supposed to be connected to the sources of life. You're not supposed to hold the baby. You're not responsible for what the child thinks or how it grows"?

PW These are no longer simply women's issues or male/female issues but rather species issues. Mother Earth's.

PGA Absolutely, and we need to know that we're learning to nurture again. Since we used to know how, we can remember again. Nurturing women and nurturing men and strong men and strong women. Remember, none of this means not strong!

PW How is strength understood in Indian cultures?

PGA The ability to endure, the ability to remain centered within the self and within the biosphere no matter what's going on, the ability to insure all things are taken care of, nurtured, helped to prosper, and enjoyed. None of this includes the Puritan notion that you're not supposed to have a good time! If you're not having a good time, it's either temporary or there's something wrong. Not that everyone is expected to always feel wonderful. But if you don't feel centered for an extended period, attention is paid to that. It's important that everybody remain in a psychically healthy condition because otherwise the balance will be thrown off.

PW How is health maintained in Indian cultures?

PGA Health is not an individual affair. It's a systemic affair of keeping the whole healthy: the whole within the human community and the layers of nonhuman communities. Mothering for both men and women means not just bearing children but keeping this healthy balance.

Under the process of colonization you can see that definition of health tends to break down. In a perfect situation, there's water and it's clean. There's land that you can either grow things in or hunt and gather food. There's game. There's balanced rainfall and snow, plenty of food supplies. In a situation where the water has been taken away upstream, where what remains is dirty, where the water tables have been decreased because of agriculture and mining and dams and cities, where the air is filthy, and you have an invasion of disease systems that are not indigenous to you, what do you do? The entire system on which you depend for health is diseased.

What are the healing arts in these circumstances? Well, appropriate political consciousness becomes a healing art. Aesthetic consciousness, like painting, sculpture, dancing, and singing becomes a healing art. Community work becomes a healing art. Business enterprise and agriculture become healing arts. When the entire organism is diseased, every individual within it is suffering to one degree or another from that systemic disorder. And so healing becomes philosophy. It becomes religion, writing, storytelling. It becomes everything that you do and are.

PW There is an old proverb that says that when spiderwebs unite, they can halt a lion. What role does Grandmother Spider play in your culture?

PGA Grandmother Spider is Creation Thinker Woman. As she thinks, so we are. We call her Thought Woman. She's the galaxy herself. It is said that the universe has every characteristic that's possible in existence. There are more elements that are feminine in vibration than are masculine in vibration. Therefore the Keres Pueblo people refer to Creator as "She" because She's preponderantly feminine, though she includes the masculine. When an embryo is formed it is first female, then it might become male. What that says, at least organically, is first female, then male.

Grandmother Spider is a little bitty spider, but she's extraordinarily

Dancing the Solstice Fire © Bonnie Mc Rae Hernández, 1986. Acrylic on masonite, 18" × 24". Full color copies of this work and others by the artist may be obtained by writing: Bonnie Mc Rae Hernández, 4174 Third Ave. #27, San Diego, CA 92103.

powerful. Her strength is in competence, not in size. I think of it like baskets. There's a big basket and it's female, then there's a smaller basket that fits in it and it's male. I won't refer to traditional American Indian systems as matriarchal because the term implies female supremacy. But many are gynocentric systems. Some are not, I guess— but *none* are patriarchal as far as I know.

PW Who are the other Grandmothers in American Indian traditions?

PGA One of the group of Grandmothers are the Grandmothers of Fire. They are the spirits or the intelligence or the consciousnesses of the volcanoes, the spirits of the core of the Earth and the spirits of the sun. They're just as much the spirits of any kind of fire, my microwave or Chernobyl's radiation. These Grandmothers are very big and very scary! Walt Disney definitely did not create them. I have no idea what Grandmother Fire has in mind but I know she's come back.

PW For millennia, women's spirituality has been in the background. Now more and more of it is coming to the foreground. How do you interpret the emergence of women's spirituality at this time?

PGA In the West that's true. For Native Americans it's not. Feminine spiritual systems have been suppressed only for a few decades in some tribes or a century or two in others. But the situation is changing.

The feminine is waking up, I say. She's been asleep for a while and now She's waking up. You know how a Turkish carpet looks? It's all pattern. An American Indian rug looks the same way. There's a dynamic interconnectedness of everything. Women's quilts do the same thing. That's the matrix of the universe. And that's what's coming into focus. People of feminine consciousness—some of whom are female—are going to carry it in because we've spent centuries thinking about it. We'll be able to bring this pattern in because we have the capacity to do it.

Paula Gunn Allen can be reached % The Rainbow Path, a center for instruction, psychic readings, and spiritual counseling in Oakland, California. Paula's teachings, based on the ancient ways of Sophia, the goddess of wisdom, offer a female alternative to philosophy. For more information, call (415) 223-4353.

SANTERIA: AFRICAN MAGIC IN LATIN AMERICA
MIGENE GONZALEZ-WIPPLER

An important work for women who wish to better understand the spiritual paths of their ethnic sisters, this book provides an in-depth look at Santeria, a syncretic religion of magic rites of the Yorubas (Africa) and the traditions of the Catholic church. Like voodoo, Santeria is often misperceived as being entirely based on black magical practices. Wippler's scholarship challenges this misconception. She describes the relationship of the Santero deities and holidays to the Catholic holy days and saints (Virgin Mary and Christ/God included). Covers rituals, ceremonies, traditions, spells, herbs, and the Seven African Powers. Illustrated. PCC

Original Products, 1984, 192 pgs. Available from Original Products, 2486 Webster Ave., Bronx, NY 10458, (212) 367-9589 ($9 ppd.).

SAPPHO: A NEW TRANSLATION
MARY BARNARD

Sappho was the most renowned female poet of ancient times, leader of a tradition of women's poetry that flourished until later male scholars suppressed and destroyed much of her work. Few complete poems of Sappho survived, but those that have are very beautifully translated here. The book includes lovely prayers to Aphrodite that may have been used at rituals performed by Sappho and her students. DLP

University of California Press, 1958, 114 pgs. Available from The Gaia Catalogue Company ($6.95 ppd.).

SARAH THE PRIESTESS: THE FIRST MATRIARCH OF GENESIS

SAVINA J. TEUBAL

Teubal's insightful reading of the literary texts of Genesis has produced a significant and controversial interpretation of the life of Sarah. Arguing that the matriarchs were the heirs of nonpatriarchal traditions, the book outlines Sarah's position as one comparable to the high priestesses of Mesopotamia. Teubal reinterprets both biblical and cross-cultural material in original ways that respect both polytheistic and Jewish traditions of the ancient Near East. Her ideas provide new paths of envisioning women's spiritual history and leadership in biblical times. TDS

Swallow Press, 1984, 199 pgs. Available from The Gaia Catalogue Company ($10.45 ppd.).

SARAH: PRIESTESS, MOTHER, WOMAN OF STRENGTH

SAVINA J. TEUBAL

The narratives of the Sarah tradition represent a nonpatriarchal system struggling for survival in isolation in a foreign land. Nevertheless, women of strength emerge from the pages of Genesis, women who are respected by men. Their function in life, though different from that of men, is regarded as equally important to society.

Women's participation in society as described in the narratives presupposes a system in which women were able to maintain an elevated professional position into which were incorporated the roles of mother and educator. Just as significantly, these women were in control of their own bodies and their own spiritual heritage.

Sarah, Rebekah, and Rachel, in identification with a goddess, chose to remain childless for decades. They chose to conceive, late in life, because of the circumstances they encountered in exile. They were venerated during their lifetimes as pristesses and as women. It is not clear whether a priestess who became a mother was forced to relinquish her profession. If her progeny was the result of the sexual component in the *hieros gamos* [sacred marriage], was her child regarded as the offspring of a goddess, of a mortal woman, or of someone in between represented by a priestess? In other words, did the fact of conception during the ritual of the Sacred Marriage or the fact of birth at a later date establish the status of the mother or the child? In early versions of the ritual the priestess who participated in the *hieros gamos* was thought to be the goddess incarnate; if conception took place the offspring were regarded as part divine. In much later times, a child born of the sacred union was to be exposed to the elements and left to its fate. Sarah's son Isaac, however, was celebrated at a feast given by Abraham. Does this mean that Sarah lived at a time when the priestess was regarded as goddess incarnate and her son as semi-divine, as was the case with Gilgamesh? Or was the son's life spared because the priestess was living in safety in exile? What had become of Sarah's status in exile, in the society in which she was living?

From Savina Teubal, *Sarah the Priestess: The First Matriarch of Genesis*, Swallow Press, 1984.

THE SEA PRIESTESS
DION FORTUNE

Dion Fortune was one of the best known and most reputable occultists of the early twentieth century. In this novel and the companion *Moon Magic*, Fortune creates the character of Vivien LeFay Morgan, a reincarnated priestess of Atlantis and Egypt who recovers her knowledge and uses it to perform rituals that will affect modern culture. Fortune's novels are easier to read than her numerous occult treatises. They portray a great deal of ritual and also provide a rare insight into what a priestess and priest of the Goddess actually do. DLP

Samuel Weiser, 1979, 316 pgs. Available from Samuel Weiser, Inc., Box 612, York Beach, ME 03910 ($9.45 ppd.).

SHAMANIC VOICES: A SURVEY OF VISIONARY NARRATIVES
JOAN HALIFAX

A collection of narratives from shamans, both women and men, from cultures around the world, speaking in their own voices. Simply by remaining faithful to the stories told her, Halifax reveals truths of shamanic practices often ignored by male anthropologists: that women are shamans and healers; that male shamans frequently receive their power from female spirits; that gays, androgynes, transsexuals, bisexuals may be shamans—that sexual difference may even be required in order to be a shaman. CS

E. P. Dutton, 1979, 268 pgs. Available from The Gaia Catalogue Company ($13.45 ppd.).

THE SILBURY TREASURE: THE GREAT GODDESS REDISCOVERED
MICHAEL DAMES

"What followed from the conviction that everything, including the land, was alive, was the certainty, based on observation, that everything was subject to change. The monuments were not fixed objects but living events, volatile descriptions of the divine body in different conditions—puberty, sexual maturity, maternity, senescence—reinforced at the right season by appropriate human behavior, with the last act leading on to the first."

In this book and the later book *The Avebury Cycle*, Dames has exhaustively studied some of Britain's most famous megalithic monuments, showing that prehistoric peoples constructed them as sites for seasonal rituals, celebrating the Goddess's cycles of transformation. Silbury Hill is the pregnant Goddess squatting in birth; it is constructed in such a way that the rising full moon nearest Lammas (the August harvest festival) becomes the child to which she is giving birth. Each of the remaining Avebury monuments, including a maze sanctuary, a barrow grave, a henge, and a serpentine avenue, likewise embodies another turning point in this annual cycle. Dames draws parallels with other prehistoric sites in Britain and elsewhere, and he shows how these ancient traditions have survived for millennia in folk culture. JIS

Thames & Hudson, London, 1976, 192 pgs.

SISTER OUTSIDER: ESSAYS AND SPEECHES
AUDRE LORDE

A stunning collection of writings (1976–1983) by black lesbian poet and feminist Audre Lorde on a wide range of themes: language and poetry ("When I speak of knowledge . . . I am speaking of that dark and true depth which understanding serves, waits upon, and makes accessible through language . . . this depth within each of us which nurtures vision"), anger ("I have suckled the wolf's lip of anger and have used it for illumination, laughter, protection, fire in places where there was no food, no sisters, no quarter"), feminist motherhood. Includes her timeless work "The Use of the Erotic as Power." PW

Crossing Press, 1984, 192 pgs. Available from Crossing Press, P.O. Box 1048, Freedom, CA 95019, (408) 722-0711 ($9.95 ppd.).

SISTERS OF THE SPIRIT: THREE BLACK WOMEN'S AUTOBIOGRAPHIES OF THE NINETEENTH CENTURY
WILLIAM L. ANDREWS, ED.

As preachers of the Christian gospel, Jarena Lee, Silpha Elaw, and Julia Foote underwent a revolution in their own sense of self that helped to launch a feminist revolution in American religious life and in American society as a whole. In 1836, *The Life and Religious Experience of Jarena Lee* challenged traditional female roles with an argument for women's spiritual authority. Silpha Elaw's *Memoirs* (1846) recounts not only its author's struggle for legitimacy as a preacher but also her dangerous preaching missions to the slave states. After the Civil War, Julia Foote's *A Brand Plucked from the Fire* (1879) testifies to the growth of a more explicitly feminist message in black women's spiritual autobiography. These three autobiographies are important literary and historical documents in their own light, and are additionally valuable as self-portraits of major forebears of the black feminist literary tradition in America. PW

Indiana University Press, 1986, 256 pgs. Available from Indiana University Press, 10th and Morton Sts., Bloomington, IN 47405, (812) 335-6804 ($10.20 ppd.).

THE SKEPTICAL FEMINIST: DISCOVERING THE VIRGIN, MOTHER, AND CRONE

BARBARA G. WALKER

The Skeptical Feminist is Barbara G. Walker's personal story of her Christian upbringing and her quest for a more nourishing, nonviolent spiritual morality. She reveals her religious quandaries as a young girl: prayers unanswered, questions ignored, the search for a reasonable God. Writing in the concise, rational, and often satirical style that is her hallmark, she argues for a need to move past a belief in a deity to an appreciation of the Goddess as a way to structure just social systems and open up to the beauty in Nature. *The Skeptical Feminist* concludes with a universal plea for a saner world: "Women's

perceptions and women's morality must take charge of the future, if there is to be any future left to us." PW

Harper & Row, 1987, 224 pgs. Available from Harper & Row ($18.45 ppd.).

THE SKEPTICAL FEMINIST: AN INTERVIEW WITH BARBARA G. WALKER

BY GLORIA BERTONIS

With a certain amount of trepidation I approached the house of the enigmatic Barbara G. Walker. I had read her books, The Crone: Woman of Age, Wisdom, and Power *and* The Woman's Encyclopedia of Myths and Secrets, *which were merciless in their condemnation of patriarchal politics and religions. I was not prepared for the small, gentle, unassuming woman who greeted me in her knit sweater and slippers and who posed obligingly for pictures in her study. Instead of books, her study is filled with hundreds of miniature dolls lined up in neat rows, and dressed in original creations knit by Barbara. She is a study in contrasts: the angry, vocal critic of male power structures and the best-selling author of ten knitting books. "Isn't it odd," I asked, "that you would choose knitting as a hobby? Knitting is such a traditional way to keep women's hands and minds busy." "Oh no," she replied, "not at all. My mind is very active while I'm knitting." Obviously, for in the five books she has written, she scrupulously strips away layers of distortions in the patriarchal mind. She lives with her husband, a scientist, in a modest lakeshore home in a secluded community in New Jersey. Her home, sparkling with crystals and decorated with tablecloths and lampshades knitted in neat geometric patterns, reflects the neatly ordered processes of Barbara G. Walker's crystal-clear mind.*

GB *What major life events have shaped your feminist consciousness?*

BGW Growing up in a patriarchal society, which all of us go through, rubbed me the wrong way more than most people. The patriarchal religion I was exposed to struck me as a very cruel religion. The first time I walked into my Sunday school room I saw an enormous crucifix, life size, full of gore, with tortured, twisted limbs. Since I was a kindhearted child, it turned me off at that very moment that I was expected to worship a God who did this to his dearly beloved son.

GB   What was the religion of your birth?

BGW   I was confirmed into the Episcopal church, reluctantly. I had a dog that I loved very much, and the dog died. Shortly after, I went to the minister and asked him, if I went to heaven, would my dog be waiting there for me? The minister told me that under no circumstances were there any animals in heaven. I threw a tantrum and said I didn't want any part of this heaven. I didn't care if I met my aunts and uncles in heaven. They didn't mean as much to me as my dog. I embarrassed my mother horribly. I was a very willful child and very sensitive. Most of the things I was supposed to accept offended my sensibilities.

GB   What did you replace that religion with?

BGW   Nothing. I was an atheist and I still am. Psychologically, however, I feel the vital importance for women of the archetypal Goddess image.

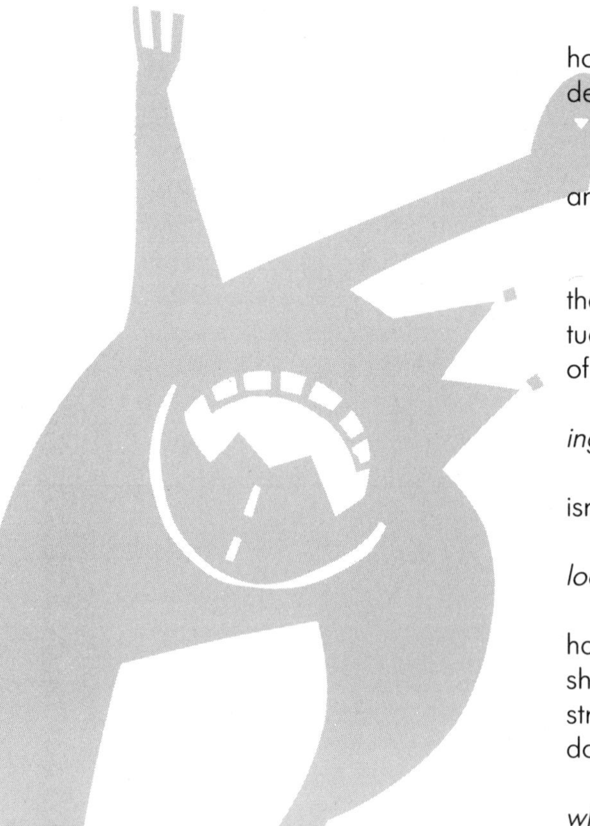

GB   Was lack of support for your atheism a problem?

BGW   No. I didn't feel I needed any support. It was what I thought and what I felt.

GB   Then that gave you tremendous intellectual freedom.

BGW   Absolutely! To be locked into a religious mold is slavery to the mind. Many people are afraid to express disbelief that they actually have. Many people profess a religion without the faintest idea of what their theology teaches.

GB   Do you see any hope of this kind of intellectual captivity changing in the near future?

BGW   Yes, I think it's bound to come. In a scientific age it just isn't possible to hold onto this kind of religious naiveté.

GB   In your book The Crone, *you take a very harsh and angry look at Western culture.*

BGW   I don't feel as much anger as I do disgust that men should have such unrealistic views about the female life cycle. That women should be seen as symbols, instead of being seen as real people, strikes me as just foolish. It's not that I'm furious at it; it's just that I do not suffer fools gladly.

GB   Where do you see the women's movement heading today and what do you think we have to concentrate on?

BGW   I definitely think we have to concentrate on reducing the amount of violence in our culture. I am horrified at the amount of violence on television, for example. Children are trained to think in violent terms from toddlerhood when they watch cartoons in which the animals blow each other up. Recently at a shopping mall in this area, Rambo dolls went on sale and the little boys were there to get them. Mothers' groups have objected, writing letters saying they hate the violence on TV, but it goes right on.

GB Do you see any form of female leadership emerging from the women's movement, as for instance, a female president in the near future?

BGW When you say leadership, and you mean political leadership, you are talking in masculine terms. It's been my experience in women's groups that one of the nicest aspects of women bonding is that there isn't a "leader." There isn't a pyramid. There isn't one person who makes the decisions and the others follow. Rather, decisions tend to be collective. So the very concept of leadership is, in some sense, unfeminine.

GB Can women have any real power in the world, without a leader? I don't mean symbolic power, but real power, economically and politically?

BGW Sure, but it's a different kind of power. Does a mother *lead* a child? Not really; the mother gets behind and pushes. She has the child's best interests at heart. She is not dragging the child, kicking and screaming, into doing things the child may not want to do. She shows the child things that he or she will like and enjoy. That's a different kind of leadership. It's not coercive.

GB Sidney Harris has said that "leadership lies in the genes, attacking, invading, subjugating others. The wrong types are almost always in charge. Every group tends to let power pass to the strong man, the one who wants it the most. The dream of sisterhood and brotherhood seems further away than ever, because the ones who want friendship and cooperation do not seek power over others or personal aggrandizement."

BGW I disagree. I don't think leadership necessarily involves force. If you look at primitive societies, where people are presumably more natural, it is *not* the strongest who leads. It is those who are thought to have the most *mana*, the most spiritual power. We had better start thinking along those lines in this country, or we will have a holocaust. Our choices are narrowing all the time. The fundamentalist Christian minister who is talking of running for president is not my idea of spiritual leadership. That's still patriarchy. He is totally commercial. He is exploiting for money a great many people. The person who leads in a primitive society leads by the consent of the led—because they are in awe of his or her spiritual force, which they call *mana* (which is, of course, a matriarchal term meaning moonness, mother power). Women naturally have more of this than men, because women naturally have power over the growing child. So a woman is a *natural* authority figure, as she is in all the early matriarchal societies. She knows moral leadership because she is a mother. A mother knows what's best. Mother teaches her child the rights and wrongs of her culture; because most children, even in our society,

are raised by women. I think this gives women a natural advantage when it comes to moral leadership. Men try to assume moral leadership, but they don't do quite as good a job.

GB Feminists talk of a "matriarchal morality," a morality based on considering the needs of others, situational relativism, morality in the context of a web of relationships. I wonder how far we are from that kind of morality?

BGW I think Christianity has *tried* to adapt that kind of morality to its own ends; but once you commercialize it, which is what Christianity does, it is no longer moral. I think you can sum it up by saying that what is moral is simply what does not hurt others. Kindness is probably the word that sums up everything, as far as morality is concerned. If you apply that standard to the things we do in this culture, it breaks down, all the time. It's simply an immoral culture, because there is so much *unkindness* in it. This is not a complicated idea. It's about as simple as you can get, and I think most women instinctively understand it.

GB "Do the least harm," as the Buddhists would say. Do you have any messages for posterity?

BGW Yes, many—I will continue to write those messages in my books.

SKY DANCER: THE SECRET LIFE AND SONGS OF THE LADY YESHE TSOGYEL

KEITH DOWMAN

The sacred biography of this Tibetan female Buddha has three levels: it is Yeshe Tsogyel's esoteric teachings on the Tantric path, particularly for women practitioners; it tells the story of her public life, which was integral to the historical events of the period; and it provides the means for worshiping her as a goddess. The second half of the book comprises Dowman's lively essays on the *dakini* (sky dancer) and the feminine as the perfection of wisdom in Tantric tradition. The *dakini* presented here is part of an overwhelmingly male tradition, but this book provides some useful understanding as we reclaim her for ourselves. Illustrated. JIS

Routledge & Kegan Paul, 1984, 379 pgs. Available from Routledge & Kegan Paul, 29 W. 35th St., New York, NY 10001, (212) 244-3336 ($19.45 ppd.).

SOPHIA: THE FUTURE OF FEMINIST SPIRITUALITY

SUSAN CADY, MARIAN RONAN, AND HAL TAUSSIG

This book finds in the biblical figure of Sophia, or Wisdom, an enigmatic link between Western religion and feminist consciousness. Drawing on a wide spectrum of biblical texts, the authors discuss Sophia as a powerful creator in the Hebrew Bible and examine the provocative way the Christian Bible associates her with Jesus. Sophia emerges as an evocative figure with broad potential for uniting herself with both feminism and the social, political, and ecological movements of our day. PW

Harper & Row, 1986, 128 pgs. Available from Harper & Row ($16.45 ppd.).

SPEAKING OF FAITH: GLOBAL PERSPECTIVES ON WOMEN, RELIGION AND SOCIAL CHANGE
DIANA L. ECK AND DEVAKI JAIN, EDS. (WITH FOREWORD BY ROSEMARY RADFORD RUETHER)

In *Speaking of Faith*, twenty-six women author/activists—including Carol Gilligan, Sisela Bok, Julia Esquivel, Nawal el Saadawi, Radha Bhatt, Judith Plaskow, Beverly Harrison, and Jean Zaru—from five continents and representing all world religions speak from personal experience, challenge religious institutions and leadership roles, and strive to build a common foundation for social change. These articulate and passionate voices of religious women reveal the connections between women's oppression and religious symbols and practices, the means by which religion can serve as a structure of oppression while simultaneously offering a vision of equality that has historically generated powerful liberation movements. PW

New Society Publishers, 1987, 308 pgs. Available from New Society Publishers, P.O. Box 582, Santa Cruz, CA 95061, (408) 458-1191 ($11.45 ppd.).

SPIDERS AND SPINSTERS: WOMEN AND MYTHOLOGY
MARTA WEIGLE

Starting from the archetype of the Goddess as spinster—Spider Woman, Athena—Weigle spins a fascinating web of myth and symbol, focusing strongly on Native American and Third World mythologies and relating them to European counterparts. Useful as a sourcebook of material for ritual as well as insight and inspiration, especially regarding the Crone aspect of the Goddess, so often shortchanged in works on mythology. DLP

University of New Mexico Press, 1982, 320 pgs. Available from University of New Mexico Press, Albuquerque, NM 87131, (505) 277-2346 ($15.95 ppd.).

SPINNING A SACRED YARN: WOMEN SPEAK FROM THE PULPIT

Women speak from the pulpit in this collection of thirty-six sermons from Protestant, Catholic, and Jewish women. The sermons—scriptural, personal, moving, inspiring—serve as testimony to the power unleashed when women give voice and interpretation to religious symbols and traditions. The speakers address suffering, resurrection, reconciliation, mercy, creation, and more from the unique perspective of women. Contributors include Sister Margaret Ellen Traxler writing on women in prison; Carter Heyward on the enigmatic God; Laura Geller on Rosh Hashanah; Rosemary Radford Ruether on the ambiguity of the role of women in biblical times. PB

Pilgrim Press/United Church Press, 1982, 256 pgs. Available from Pilgrim Press, 132 W. 31st St., New York, NY 10001 ($10.45 ppd.).

THE SPIRAL DANCE: A REBIRTH OF THE ANCIENT RELIGION OF THE GREAT GODDESS
STARHAWK

"It dawned on me as I was participating in a Summer Solstice ritual: at that moment, I and many other women across the land were joined in common practice of worshiping the Goddess largely as a result of Starhawk and *The Spiral Dance*" (Pat Camarena). Perhaps more than any other body of work in the field of women's spirituality, Starhawk's writings have empowered women to discover within the Goddess religion a life-affirming, female-centered basis for the unfolding of our spirituality. *The Spiral Dance* is a collection of rituals, invocations, and magical exercises to invoke the Goddesses and Gods of the Old Religion. For those interested in Witchcraft, it offers information on how to start your own coven and do rituals based on Goddess worship, and practices; explains the significance of the holidays and celebrations (Wheel of the Year); and offers exercises in doing trance and psychic work. Starhawk's focus on the positive use of power to transform our personal and political lives and her emphasis on the ecological application of Witchcraft have led many women and men to reclaim the Old Religion of the Goddess as a spirituality relevant to our times and a spiritual pathway to a healthy future. PCC/PW

Harper & Row, 1979, 218 pgs. Available from The Gaia Catalogue Company ($12.45 ppd.).

THE SPIRITUAL DIMENSION OF GREEN POLITICS
CHARLENE SPRETNAK

"I don't know whether 'everyone' will ever come to Green politics, but I do believe that a 'spiritual infrastructure' is essential for a successful

transformation of our society in post-modern and Green directions. A spiritual grounding would not only answer a deep hunger in the modern experience, it would also be harmonious with various Green tendrils that have already begun to sprout: the bioregional movement, which teaches us to 'live in place,' to know and appreciate the heritage and ecological character of our area; the evolving philosophy of deep ecology; the emergence of community-based ecological populism; the Green-oriented activism in mainline religion; the work of cultural/holistic feminists; the spiritual dimension appearing in the discussions of global responsibility—and the worldwide network of Green parties and organizations. . . . There is just cause to celebrate the frail but stubborn budding of a new vision—based on the oldest wisdom we contain. If we nurture that vision with the lifeblood of our ideas and our efforts, we—and our children—may be rewarded with a future worth living."

Charlene Spretnak, a pioneering author in the feminist spirituality movement (*The Politics of Women's Spirituality*—see listing on page 68; and *Lost Goddesses of Early Greece*—see listing on page 53), has in the last few years become a spokeswoman for the Green political movement (see listing for *Green Politics: The Global Promise* on page 33). Her most recent book, *The Spiritual Dimension of Green Politics*, was originally presented as the 1984 lecture of the E. F. Schumacher Society of America. Here she integrates her incisive, Green political analysis and compassionate pragmatic spirituality in answering three questions: Who are we? or What is our nature? How shall we relate to our context, the environment? and How shall we relate to other people? This body of work fills a gap in the Green vision. For if the Green movement is to be truly holistic, its politics must offer a vision

of a sustainable spiritual ethic as well as envisioning a sustainable economics, health, education, and world order. What many feminists know is that, in fact, there is no other way for our political vision to be realized. PW

Bear & Co., 1986, 95 pgs. Available from The Gaia Catalogue Company ($6.45 ppd.).

GAIA, GREEN POLITICS, AND THE GREAT TRANSFORMATION

CHARLENE SPRETNAK

"It is essential that people realize at a rational and an intimate, spiritual level that we come out of the Earth, that we don't exist separately from Her, that our health depends on Her health, so deeply are we linked."

—Charlene Spretnak
Gaia Conference, Amherst, Mass.
August 1985

Charlene Spretnak has worked, with her four books and her political activism, to help move our society in the direction of an Earth-based spirituality of wisdom and compassion. In her first book, Lost Goddesses of Early Greece, *she reconstructed the sacred myths of the pre-Hellenic cultures, revealing that our oldest heritage in Western religion honors women and Nature. In* The Politics of Women's Spirituality, *Spretnak demonstrated the depth and breadth of postpatriarchal spirituality in some fifty essays she gathered and edited by leading spokeswomen of the women's spirituality movement. In recent years she has focused attention on the growing worldwide movement called Green politics. In addition to writing* Green Politics: The Global Promise *with Fritjof Capra and* The Spiritual Dimension of Green Politics, *Spretnak co-founded, in 1984, the major Green political organization in the United States today, the Committees of Correspondence. She is currently at work on a book about spiritual values and contemporary issues. She maintains a practice of Vipassana (Insight) meditation and hatha yoga. This article is excerpted from an interview conducted by Lish Hanhart at Charlene's home in Berkeley, California.*

During the pre-Olympian era of the history of Western religion, Gaia, the Earth Goddess, was revered as all forces: active and receptive, creative and destructive, fierce and gentle. Her presence was immanent in people's daily lives and honored through art and ritual. Early Goddess statues seem to be expressions of the female body as a living microcosm of the larger experiences of cyclic change, birth, renewal, and nurturance. While no one claims that the pre–Indo-European Neolithic era was perfect nor that we should attempt to return to it, I do feel that the art and artifacts—for instance, a statue that is half bird and half woman—carry lessons for us in our interrelatedness with Nature and her cycles.

Ecologically wise spirituality went into eclipse when Gaia, and all manifestations of the bountiful Mother, were diminished and eventually suppressed almost to extinction by the introduction of the sky-God concept. That notion was brought into Europe by the Indo-European invaders, nomadic cattlemen who first migrated from the Eurasian steppes into southeastern Europe in about 4500 B.C. Eventually they spread all across Europe, establishing a patriarchal chieftain system, adoration of the warrior, and their Thunderbolt God. The sky-God, in addition to being a judgmental, vindictive patriarch, was alienated and spatially distant from experiential Earth wisdom. So were most of his followers—until recently.

The current development in both Judaism and Christianity that I find encouraging is *creation spirituality*, which honors and holds sacred the natural world as the most profound expression of the divine. Rabbi Abraham Heschel emphasized that the appropriate response to the intricate wonders of the natural world, of which we are a part, is awe. From that comes gratitude and celebration, the roots of worship. The awakening of Earth-based spirituality today is also reflected in the growing interest in the creation-centered Western mystics, many of whom were women: Mechtild of Magdeburg, Hildegard of Bingen, Julian of Norwich, and, of course, St. Francis of Assisi and his colleague, Claire. Their meditations and their art find resonance with just about anyone seriously following a practice within any of the other Earth-based traditions: Goddess, Native American, Taoist, and so forth.

It's a sad situation we have today with most congregations afraid to honor the natural world in their liturgies for fear of being called pagan. Creation spirituality (not to be confused with fundamentalist creationism!) could change all that, moving organized religion beyond our ultimately suicidal alienation from Nature—and not a moment too soon for the survival of this unique and glorious planet.

One of the core teachings of creation-centered spirituality—that we need to find our place *within* the web of life, rather than operating as if we were somehow on top of Nature—is also an informing principle

Charlene Spretnak. Photo by Nikki Ann Spretnak, 1986.

"There are certain beings who love the planet very much but who cannot act directly to express this love. The Christian tradition would call them angels. They are known as Devas to the Hindus and Sidhs to the Celtic people. They are acknowledged in traditions all over the world. I believe these beings are here to be of service and

The Great Goddess © Colleen Kelley, 1984. Pencil on paper, 16" × 10". For information on recent showings, commissioned work, and a forthcoming book on ceremonial art write: Colleen Kelley, #6 Frasco Place, El Dorado, Santa Fe, NM 87505.

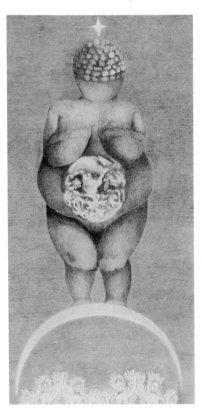

to inspire. They may communicate with us when we are in nature. We are a part of nature. Once we see the Sacred in nature, we may see it in ourselves" (Colleen Kelley).

of Green politics. Far more than mere environmentalism, Green politics is a comprehensive politics that incorporates many of the values found in women's spirituality and ecofeminism: ecological wisdom, social responsibility, nonviolence, postpatriarchal consciousness, spiritual values, grassroots democracy, respect for diversity, real security in the global community, and sustainable future focus. Our goal is for human society to operate in a learning mode and to cultivate biocentric wisdom and engaged compassion. Green politics is a beyond-left-and-right approach to our problems that emphasizes sustainability and interrelatedness. We simply must move from rapacious growth-mania economies, both socialist and corporate-capitalist, to more rational modes.

A Greening of all human culture is the transformation beyond the cult of industrialism necessary to alter the death-oriented course of patriarchal-military-industrial society. Hence, Green politics counters patriarchal values. In a narrow sense these entail male dominance and exploitation of women. In a broader sense the term *patriarchal culture* connotes not only injustice toward women but also the accompanying cultural traits: love of hierarchical structure and competition, love of dominance-or-submission modes of relating, alienation from Nature, suppression of empathy and other emotions, and haunting insecurity about all of those matters.

The spiritually grounded transformative power of Earth-based wisdom and compassion is our best hope for creating a future worth living. Women have been associated with transformative power from the beginning: we can grow people out of our very flesh, take in food and transform it into milk for the young. Women's transformative wisdom and energy are absolutely necessary in the contemporary struggle for ecological sanity, secure peace, and social justice. We are passing on to our children a critically degraded planet, and with each day the damage worsens. Where can we, as a species caught up in rootless modernity, seek guidance? From spiritual teachings that do not separate themselves from Nature, from our bodies, and from the female.

Correspondence regarding lectures by Charlene Spretnak at conferences and colleges should be sent to P.O. Box 9997, Berkeley, CA 94709.

For information on Green politics groups in your geographical area write: Committees of Correspondence Clearinghouse, P.O. Box 30208, Kansas City, MO 64112. (See listing on page *184* for organizational description.)

Information about Vipassana (Insight) meditation retreats, most of which are co-led by women, can be obtained by writing Vipassana Meditation Center, P.O. Box 51, Shelburne Falls, MA 01370, or calling (413) 625-2160.

STAR WARS AND THE STATE OF OUR SOULS: DECIDING THE FUTURE OF PLANET EARTH

PATRICIA M. MISCHE

An innovative exploration of the current armament/disarmament debate. For Mische, the Star Wars debate is not a debate about weapons systems but a "battle being waged within our souls" between the mechanistic/divisive and the organic/holistic worldview. She proposes a system of world ordering featuring a permanent international peacekeeping force trained in nonviolence. This book adds a depth dimension too often missing from arms discussions. PW

Harper & Row, 1985, 136 pgs. Available from Harper & Row ($6.95 ppd.).

STAR WOMAN: WE ARE MADE FROM THE STARS AND TO THE STARS WE MUST RETURN

LYNN Y. ANDREWS

See listing on page 55.

Warner Books, 1986, 246 pgs.

TAKING THE FRUIT: MODERN WOMEN'S TALES OF THE BIBLE

JANE SPRAGUE ZONES, ED.

"Making midrash," telling stories to flesh out the bare bones of the text, is an ancient Jewish spiritual practice. As the prologue to this collection comments, "In the beginning women told their stories . . . and shared the glorious deeds that had been their spiritual inheritance." Sadly, most of these tales have been lost, but a new tradition of women's midrash is in the process of creation. This anthology represents an early milestone in that process. The cooperative effort of eight women, the book contains fifteen stories commenting on texts from Genesis to Judith. It is an important resource, not only for the tales themselves, but also for the prologue and source list,

which enable and encourage the reader to become part of this new and old tradition by making her own midrash. LG

Women's Institute for Continuing Jewish Education, 1981, 60 pgs. Note: Taking the Fruit, plus San Diego Women's Haggadah, Midlife and a Rite of Passage Ceremony, On Our Spiritual Journey: A Creative Shabbat Service, and Educating the New Jewish Woman: A Dynamic Approach (see listing on page 24) are the materials published by the Women's Institute for Continuing Jewish Education, under the guidance of educator and writer Dr. Irene Fine. These books can be ordered from the Institute, 4079 54th St., San Diego, CA 92105 (619-442-2666). (See listing on page 209.)

TAROT FOR YOURSELF: A WORKBOOK FOR PERSONAL TRANSFORMATION
TAROT MIRRORS: REFLECTIONS OF PERSONAL MEANING

MARY K. GREER

These books, written in a skillfully designed workbook format, are one of the best tools on the market for entering the world of the tarot. Mary Greer combines warm feminine intuition with a comprehensive scholarly approach to the tarot. Mary's obvious ease in working and playing with the tarot becomes an inspiration for developing one's own personal relationship with the cards. These books are rich in correspondences, meditations, charts, spreads, interpretations, and, best of all, insightful questions and healing affirmations for each of the seventy-eight cards. To contact the author for workshops and private consultations on the tarot, intuitive writing and women's mysteries send a SASE to T.A.R.O.T., P.O. Box 31123, San Francisco, CA 94131 (415) 824-8938. EF/PW

Newcastle, 1987/1984/1988. Available from The Gaia Catalogue Company ($14.95 ea. ppd.).

THAT'S WHAT SHE SAID: CONTEMPORARY POETRY AND FICTION BY NATIVE AMERICAN WOMEN

RAYNA GREEN, ED.

This book exemplifies the closeness to the Earth, to ancestors, to the mythic spirits that modern Native American writers such as Joy Harjo and Paula Gunn Allen seem to possess to such an amazing degree. Some of these poems and stories address contemporary concerns of alcoholism, race prejudice, and cultural breakdown, but their real strengths are timeless. These poets seem to be able to enter "the Dreamtime" at will yet remain lovingly grounded in the elemental particulars of the physical world. LY

Indiana University Press, 1984, 329 pgs. Available from Indiana University Press, 10th and Morton Sts., Bloomington, IN 47405, (812) 335-6804 ($13.75 ppd.).

THIS WAY DAYBREAK COMES: WOMEN'S VALUES AND THE FUTURE

ANNIE CHEATHAM AND MARY CLARE POWELL

This book chronicles a feminist vision quest. Rather than seeking vision on a mountaintop, the authors set out across America, traveling more than thirty thousand miles to

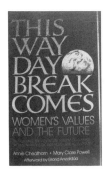

interview women engaged in creating a new culture, one largely ignored by mainstream media. Includes sections on family, art, peace, technology, and the Wise Woman within. PW

New Society Publishers, 1986, 288 pgs. Available from New Society Publishers, P.O. Box 582, Santa Cruz, CA 95061, (408) 458-1191 ($14.45 ppd.).

THROUGH THE FLOWER
THE DINNER PARTY: A SYMBOL OF OUR HERITAGE
EMBROIDERING OUR HERITAGE: THE DINNER PARTY NEEDLEWORK
THE BIRTH PROJECT

JUDY CHICAGO

Perhaps more than any other contemporary artist, Judy Chicago has enabled women to reclaim their talents, pride, and heritage as artists of the world. The techniques that Judy Chicago honors—weaving, embroidery, applique, crochet, knitting—are art forms that women have always done as art but that, until the recent wave of feminism, have rarely been honored.

In her autobiography *Through the Flower*, Judy Chicago describes her struggle to put female images into her art and still be acknowledged as an artist in the Establishment. Her butterfly vagina paintings on porcelain shown in art galleries in 1975 were the beginning of the modern artistic celebration of the sacredness of the female body.

The Dinner Party chronicles the making of the extraordinary artwork

of the same title: three large tables placed in a triangle (symbol of female genitals) with place settings honoring 39 female heroines and goddesses. Each setting contains a porcelain plate and runner designed by Judy Chicago to symbolize the woman's contribution to culture. The table sits on a platform covered with smaller triangles with the names of 999 women written in gold. *The Dinner Party* includes color and black-and-white photographs of the plates, biographies of the 39 women honored, and shorter biographies of the 999 historical women whose names are on the tile base.

Embroidering Our Heritage describes the making of the Dinner Party needlework. It includes black-and-white photos of the needlework, firsthand accounts of the women doing the work, and color photos of the runners with many fine details of the needlepoint.

In response to the difficulty of housing the immense Dinner Party, Judy Chicago created *The Birth Project*, art done on cloth that could be rolled up and easily transported. Like *The Dinner Party* and *Embroidering Our Heritage*, *The Birth Project* book tells the story of how the art was created, invites us into the lives of the women artists, and is rich in photography of the artworks themselves. Most important, *The Birth Project* reclaims the sacredness of the birth process in human culture as a primal act of creation. (See also listing for Through the Flower on page 204.)

Through the Flower. *Doubleday,*

1975. 226 pgs.
The Dinner Party: A Symbol of Our Heritage. *Anchor Press/Doubleday, 1979. 225 pgs.*
Embroidering Our Heritage: The Dinner Party Needlework. *With Susan Hill. Anchor Books, 1980. 287 pgs.*
The Birth Project. *Doubleday, 1985. 231 pgs.*

TO HEAR THE ANGELS SING: AN ODYSSEY OF CO-CREATION WITH THE DEVIC KINGDOM

DOROTHY MACLEAN

Dorothy Maclean tells, in a quiet, clear way, the story of her spiritual journey and, within it, the tale of how she communicated with great beings of light—known in scripture as angels or devas and in myth as gods and goddesses. A co-founder of Findhorn, a New Age community in northern Scotland, Dorothy relates how at first she learned from the devas practical ways she and her partners, Peter and Eileen Caddy, could cooperate with the devas in growing Findhorn's now-famous garden. Later, she speaks of the deeper realities she came to understand about the relationship between humans and devas, the nature of God, the sacredness of Earth and body, and the work/play synthesis needed to restore balance to our planet. This is an inspiring story about a woman whose trust in her inner knowing guided her along uncharted paths to a world of wholeness, beauty, and joy. CRS

Lorian Press, 1980, 217 pgs. Available from The Gaia Catalogue Company (9.50 ppd.).

TO WORK AND TO LOVE

DOROTHEE SOELLE WITH SHIRLEY A. CLOYES

In this book, Soelle weaves liberation theology with a creation-centered spirituality. She maintains that God created the world out of a desire for relatedness and relationship. As a result, we are called to be co-creators with God, shaping the world and the human community through work and love. She offers a vision of economics and work, love and solidarity, that is rooted in Christian theology. RK

Fortress Press, 1984, 165 pgs. Available from Fortress Press, 2900 Queen St., Philadelphia, PA 19129, (800) 367-8737 ($9.39 ppd.).

TRUTH OR DARE: POWER, AUTHORITY AND MAGIC
STARHAWK

Truth or Dare, Starhawk's third work, is a blend of theory, history, personal experience, and ritual. Deepening her examination of the nature of power and authority in women's experience, she contrasts the culturally dominant power-over model, which depends on controlling resources, with the power-within model, based on human connection and bonding with the life of the environment. She explores power-with, originating not in a role, a principle, or a law, but in the internal power of the person, the idea, and the action to focus the group will and process. An empowering book that reflects the new structures, new societies, new cultures, and new values that women are bringing into being. PW

Harper & Row, 1987, 320 pgs. Available from Harper & Row ($21.95 ppd.).

POWER FROM WITHIN, THE ABILITY TO DO: MAGIC, RITUALS, AND DIRECT ACTION

STARHAWK

Perhaps more than any other written works, Starhawk's books The Spiral Dance, Dreaming the Dark, *and* Truth or Dare *have educated the public about the ecological wisdom and political implications of the Old Religion of the Goddess. Witchcraft or Wicca is a pre-Christian tribal religion of Europe that sees the Goddess as immanent in life. Within this Earth religion, seasonal celebrations establish the bond between individuals, the community as a whole, and the land and its resources. From the power within this relationship comes the ability to heal, to create communities, and to build culture—always with the primary consideration of humankind's interconnectedness with Nature. As a writer, a teacher, a counselor, a ritualist, a peace activist, and a Witch, Starhawk has distinguished herself as a woman of courage, dedication, and truth. I recorded Starhawk's words as we sat in the garden of her communal household in San Francisco.*

—Lish Hanhart

Last May when I was in England, I celebrated Beltane or May Eve on Silbury Hill, an ancient Goddess site in England, with women from Greenham Common (the women's peace encampment at the gates of the U.S. air base where missiles are deployed). Our ritual on Silbury was the beginning of a five-day walk to Stonehenge, which took us across Salisbury Plain, the ancient sacred land of the British Isles. For days we sang, danced, and walked our pilgrim way across the green wind-scoured fields, escorted by our footsore guard. We marched, accompanied by dogs and babies, drums and bright banners, smelling the cropped grass and hearing the wind singing as it has since before Stonehenge was new.

Salisbury Plain today is one large artillery field, and in order to complete our pilgrimage we had to confront the military police and risk getting arrested. We did a ritual at Stonehenge on the full lunar eclipse, an amazing experience. The point and heart of our walk was

Temple of Artemis/ Harmonizing our Intuitive Self © Ursula Kavanagh, 1981. From the Estrella Postcards.

to reclaim the Plain, if only for a few short hours, to symbolically establish our right to walk freely in peace over sacred land, and for that time to disrupt the work of war!

When I was sixteen years old I discovered the Goddess in deeply connecting with everything alive in Nature. I knew even then that goddess religion had political implications for women, especially for the feminist movement. The Goddess brings a sense of connection with a woman's own creativity, her power, and her ability to value herself and her connections with other women in a very deep way. The Goddess entails the recognition that spirit, whatever we want to call spirit, is immanent in Nature and in the world. With that realization you start to see the world as something alive, not just a trash pile of minerals. I always felt the split between the spiritual and the political was a false division that came out of a consciousness of disconnection. If you believe that the Earth is sacred and that human beings have value, then you are necessarily propelled into taking political action and resisting the power structure that we live in right now.

The way we usually think about power in this society is power-over: the ability to control other people, to make decisions that affect others and in which they have no say. Power-over is based on a model in which the universe is something mechanical and is controlled by a God located outside the world. There is another kind of power that I call power-from-within, which is closer to the root of the word itself, which means to do, to be able. Power-from-within is based on a different model of the universe. The world is seen as God, alive and with a consciousness of its own. Each living being—a tree, a flower, a bird—has inherent value. We don't have the right to destroy those things!

To reshape the very principle of power upon which our culture is based, we must shake up all the old divisions. The comfortable separations no longer work. The questions are broader than the terms *religious* or *political* imply. They are questions of complex connections. For though we are told that such issues are separate—that rape is an issue separate from nuclear war, that a woman's struggle for equal pay is not related to a black teenager's struggle to find a job or to the struggle to prevent the export of a nuclear reactor to a site on the edge of an earthquake fault in the Philippines—all these realities are shaped by our power relationships. Those relationships in turn shape our economic and social systems—our technology, our science, our religions, our views of women and men, our views of races and cultures that differ from our own, our sexuality, our gods and our wars. They are presently shaping the destruction of the world.

We have a lot of realistic fears, especially about radiation, technology, and war. We feel so tremendously disempowered. When we feel fear, or rage, it disappears into a void. It is very hard to get people to move into action because we feel we can't have any impact or effect. Ritual is important in that it empowers us and gives us a feeling of support, in the sense that, yes, there is a value in action whether it is effective or not. A ritual is a movement of energy that is directed toward transformation or change. When I do a ritual I usually think about what is going on in the world, the energies around, the seasons, the timing, and what kind of personal transformation I need from the ritual. There are certain structures that are traditional, such as grounding, doing a meditation to connect with the Earth, casting a circle, calling in the directions, calling in the Goddess or a certain aspect of the Goddess. When you do rituals nonhierarchically you create a space in which people can share directly out of their own freedom and spontaneity. This creates a very strong sense of connection.

When we practice magic we are always making connections, moving energy, identifying with other forms of being. Magic is an applied science that is based on an understanding of how energy makes patterns and patterns direct energy. To put it another way, at its heart is a paradox: consciousness shapes reality, reality shapes consciousness. Magic comes out of the consciousness that sees everything as being alive and interconnected, and sees the Earth as being literally the body of the Goddess.

Magic can be very prosaic. A leaflet, a lawsuit, a demonstration, or a strike can change consciousness. Magic can also be very esoteric, encompassing all the ancient techniques of deepening awareness, of psychic development, and of heightened intuition. Learning to work magic is mostly a process of learning to think-in-things, to experience concretely as well as to think abstractly. Though abstractions have their uses, they separate us from the deeper levels of our feelings. Relearning the language of things requires that we reconnect with our emotions.

One of the principles of magic is that you don't run away from something because it feels negative. Anything that is negative has a potential for something positive. The word *Witch* is important for me because it is so connected with how we view women and women's power and how we view any kind of power that is not approved of by the authorities. I use it very deliberately—it is not that I have not noticed the reaction against it—but I feel the only way to counter unconscious assumptions is to bring them out into the open and examine how we react to words.

Witchcraft, the Old Religion of the Goddess, was deliberately stamped out and persecuted in Europe as part of the political shift in the sixteenth and seventeenth centuries. During that time both the Catholic and Protestant churches and the secular powers were instituting a new type of control in society. Feudal society was still very much rooted in the land. In order to exploit the land and the resources of the Earth in levels that had not been done yet, there was a need to sever the connection of spirit with the land. This was a way to institute a new attitude in relation to work. Work on the land was determined by real things like does the hay need to be harvested today, whereas work in a factory was a way of turning people into

Solstice at Stonehenge/ Remembering our Connections to the Great Mother © Ursula Kavanagh, 1981. From the Estrella Postcards. To order write: Ursula Kavanagh, 196 Court St., Brooklyn, NY 11201.

machines with no relationship to Nature. So there were four hundred years of persecution and propaganda directed against women and men who held the older worldview and continued to believe that the world was alive.

I use the word Witch because it is the correct word. Witch in English comes from the Anglo-Saxon root *Wic*, which means to bend or shape. If you call yourself a Witch, it becomes a powerful statement about who you are, whom you identify with, and who you are allied with. It becomes a way to reconnect with the Earth wisdom once practiced by the women and men who held on to their belief that the Earth is sacred. There is power in such a statement!

Power is the thing we fear most, ultimately, because what it means is responsibility. What happens is we mistake power-from-within for power-over. People who have been oppressed don't want power because they see how destructive it is. We become afraid of what we will turn into when we have it. But I think it is crucial to say, "Wait a minute, there is a difference between power-over, which is the power to control, and power-from-within, the ability to act . . . !"

The groups that I have seen stay together consistently over a long period of time, especially now in this period, a very discouraging one politically in America, are groups that have a spiritual connection. I think part of what we need to do politically is build community, and that means long-term connections. We have to have a strong base where we can be creating the culture that we want to live in and, as much as possible, living in that. Community involves being there for people emotionally and in practical ways as well as working together on political action. I live collectively and it is always challenging.

What is becoming more and more important is just staying centered and knowing that the means are the ends, the struggle is the victory. We can't drive ourselves crazy now to create a better world in twenty years. We have to act as if we are living in a world that is going to last, that can be sustained, and work steadily toward that! Because the thing about changing consciousness and developing power organically is that it is not a fast process; it takes time.

The most important tool is to get together with other people and develop support systems. An effective way to do that is in small groups, such as affinity groups, covens, consciousness-raising groups. Meet with other people, do many kinds of ritual, pick different topics and talk about them from your own experience without being interrupted, challenged, or argued with. This is how the women's movement developed its theory in the seventies. One of the things about valuing spirit inherent in the world is that you value Nature's diversity. Where our strength comes from is having many, many, many different ways of taking action to protect the Earth.

Starhawk requests that booking inquiries be directed to: Jodi Sager, P.O. Box 9725, Berkeley, CA 94709. All other correspondence send to: Harper & Row, Icehouse One—401, 151 Union St., San Francisco, CA 94111-1299.

SALISBURY PLAIN, MAY '85

Starhawk

here we are free

    and the light grows

a crescent   between stone thighs

it has been a long long time   since we were free

since we sang the moon here

    and the light grows

and we will not be free for   long

    a moment   eclipsed out of time

    a hole   clipped in barbed wire

tomorrow   they will jail us

tomorrow   they will repair the fence that surrounds us

    but never completely

for tonight   we touch   freedom

    and the light grows

a crescent wedded to our own shadow

pulling a rising   invincible river

the moon is full   and the dark is holy

and we are women who live in the open

Starhawk. Photo by Catherine Busch, 1985.

TURNING THE WHEEL: AMERICAN WOMEN CREATING THE NEW BUDDHISM
SANDY BOUCHER

Turning the Wheel profiles contemporary American Buddhist women, revealing their profound effect on an ancient spiritual practice that has been dominated by male traditions. Sandy Boucher, author of *Heartwomen* and three other books, is a practicing Buddhist. Her book deals with controversial issues within Buddhist communities and discusses the relationship between political movements, Buddhism, and family life.

Harper & Row, 1988, 256 pgs. Available from Harper & Row ($19.45 ppd.).

VETAHER LIBENU (SHABBAT PRAYERBOOK)
CONGREGATION BETH EL OF THE SUDBURY RIVER VALLEY

This unique prayerbook was written, translated, and edited by members of a Reform synagogue near Boston. Wishing to integrate their desire for more traditional prayer with their concern for personal and inclusive spiritual language, they produced a remarkable text. While the Hebrew prayers retain their standard masculine gender (with the exception of the addition of the mothers, Sarah, Rebecca, Leah, and Rachel), the English incorporates both feminine pronouns and gender-nonspecific phrasings. These new translations also provide a powerful and beautiful theological reinterpretation. For example, the blessing formula usually rendered as "Praised art Thou, Lord our God, King of the Universe," is transformed into "Holy One of Blessing, Your Presence fills creation." TDS

Congregation Beth El, 1982, 168 pgs. Available from Congregation Beth El, Hudson Road, Sudbury, MA 01776 ($10 ppd.).

WAKING UP IN THE NUCLEAR AGE: THE BOOK OF NUCLEAR THERAPY
CHELLIS GLENDINNING

Chellis Glendinning is one of the early feminist writers and activists whose work launched the women's spirituality movement. In the early 1980s she began to apply her insights as a psychologist and experiences in feminist ritual to the danger of human extinction through nuclear war. She founded Waking Up in the Nuclear Age, the first organization of mental-health professionals offering help to the public with nuclear-related distress, and was a co-founder of Interhelp (see listing on page 186). In *Waking Up in the Nuclear Age*, Chellis helps the reader confront the "psychic numbing" and hidden anxieties of living in the nuclear world and guides us in a modern-day rite of passage that will enable us to respond constructively to the nuclear threat. Her cogent vision of new myths and heroes, those willing to cross the line of business-as-usual to express a passionate commitment to planetary survival, is particularly important today. *Waking Up in the Nuclear Age* integrates personal story with astute political analysis, despair and empowerment work with concrete ways we can eliminate nuclear arsenals in the world. PW

Beech Tree Books/William Morrow & Co., 1987, 237 pgs. Available from Beech Tree Books, 105 Madison Ave., New York, NY 10016 ($12.45 ppd.). The author is available for public speaking, workshops, events, and po-litical actions. Write to her c⁄o Waking Up in the Nuclear Age, P.O. Box 381, Tesuque, NM 87574.

WALKING ON THE WATER: WOMEN TALK ABOUT SPIRITUALITY
JO GARCIA AND SARA MAITLAND

The first of its kind to be published in Britain, this book is a collection of essays, autobiographies, poems, artwork, cartoons, and fiction pieces by women from orthodox and unorthodox spiritual traditions as well as women who question and even oppose spiritual/religious convictions. Writings cover a diverse range of topics including myth and religion, feminism and Christianity, love and sexuality, grief and childbirth, women priests and Jewish feminism. PW

Virago Press, 1983, 214 pgs. Available from Merrimack Publishing Circle, 462 Boston St., Topsfield, MA 01983, (617) 887-2440 ($5.95 ppd.).

THE WANDERGROUND: STORIES OF THE HILL WOMEN
SALLY MILLER GEARHART

This classic of feminist visionary writing, long out of print, has made a welcome return. First published in 1979, Gearhart's tales are set in a future time when women have fled the increasingly violent cities to create a new culture. From their encampments in the hills, they explore and celebrate their newly developed psychic powers, develop an organic relationship with animal and plant life, and establish a plan for the future of mankind. Full of discovery, suspense, and intrigue, this collection reveals a world where women live happily without men and deal compassionately with the consequences. PW

Alyson Publications, 1984, 196 pgs. Available from Alyson Publications, P.O. Box 2783, Boston, MA 02208 ($8.45 ppd.).

WE ARE ALL PART OF ONE ANOTHER: A BARBARA DEMING READER

JANE MEYERDING, ED.

"I feel a queer stirring in me, and it is as though my heart first bursts the bars that are my ribs, then bursts the bars of this cell, and then travels with great lightness and freedom down the corridor and into each stinking cell, acknowledging: Yes, we are all of us one flesh" ("Prison Notes").

Barbara Deming was one of the most beloved and compassionate voices in the peace and feminist movements. "Prison Notes," written during her month-long imprisonment for nonviolent resistance during a 1966 peace march, is one of the classics of contemporary pacifism. This volume is a collection of her essays, poems, speeches, stories, and letters spanning four decades of social justice and peace activism. A deeply spiritual woman who died of cancer in 1984, her words serve as an inspiration to those carrying forth her commitment to a nonviolent world. PW

New Society Publishers, 1984, 320

pgs. Available from New Society Publishers, P.O. Box 582, Santa Cruz, CA 95061 ($12.45 ppd.).

WHEN GOD WAS A WOMAN

MERLIN STONE

The first part of this extensively researched book is one of the best single sources on various aspects of early gynocentric religion: The Great Goddess of prepatriarchal times, the status of women in Goddess-worshiping cultures, the patriarchal Indo-European destroyers of these cultures, the *hieros gamos* (Sacred Marriage) and rite of the dying god, and sacred (hetero) sexuality. The second part deals with the origins of Judeo-Christian religion: Goddess worship in Canaan and its suppression, the Garden of Eden myth, and the role of women in Christianity. This later section has proved controversial; some of Stone's assertions have been assailed as inaccurate and even anti-Semitic. Nonetheless, this is an essential volume in any library on women's spirituality. JIS

Harcourt Brace Jovanovich, 1978, 265 pgs. Available from The Gaia Catalogue Company ($8.45 ppd.).

WHEN SOCIETY BECOMES AN ADDICT

ANNE WILSON SCHAEF

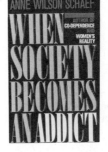

While many writers have acknowledged the pervasiveness of addiction in our society, Anne Wilson Schaef is the first to identify the addictive process as the underlying malaise of our culture. We operate in addictive ways, she says, because the foundations of our social structures are fundamentally addictive. Schaef identifies the multitude of addictions that affect our individual and collective emotional, physical, and spiritual health. She discusses substance addictions (alcohol, drugs, nicotine, caffeine), process addictions (accumulating wealth, sex, work, religion, worry) and relationship addictions (characterized by dominator and victim roles). Schaef, author of *Women's Reality* and *Co-Dependence*, brilliantly integrates feminist, chemical dependency, and psychological theories, explores the norms of the addictive process (self-centeredness, dishonesty, and constant crises) and points the way to functioning as whole and healthy people in life-affirming ways. PW

Harper & Row, 1987, 192 pgs. Available from The Gaia Catalogue Company ($17.45 ppd.).

THE WISE WOMAN HERBAL FOR THE CHILDBEARING YEARS

SUSUN S. WEED

It is particularly essential for women in the childbearing years to live in concert with their bodies' natural wisdom. In this book, practicing herbalist Susun Weed presents basic herbal information to show how herbs can support the natural functions of pregnancy and childbirth. There is material on everything from morning sickness to fatigue, from labor pain to nursing, as well as information on general health concerns of women—

menstruation, nutrition, birth control, and recipes for herbal remedies. A valuable resource/reference book for anyone interested in women's health and natural healing power. (See also listing for Wise Woman Center on page 205.). RF

Ash Tree Publishing, 1985, 192 pgs. Available from Ash Tree Publishing, P.O. Box 64, Woodstock, NY 12498 ($8.95 ppd.).

WITCHCRAFT FOR TOMORROW
DOREEN VALIENTE

A review of Witchcraft practices by an English Witch who suggests ways to practice the Old Religion in the modern world. Includes chapters on Witch ethics, festivals, signs, tools, and symbols. The final chapter is the author's version of the Book of Shadows, the Witch's handbook of rituals and instructions. It contains directions on casting the circle, rites, invocations, chants, and dances. PW

Phoenix, 1978, 205 pgs. Available from Phoenix Publishing, P.O. Box 10, Custer, WA 98240 ($15.95 ppd.).

WITCHES, MIDWIVES, AND NURSES: A HISTORY OF WOMEN HEALERS
BARBARA EHRENREICH AND DEIRDRE ENGLISH

A women's movement classic, this slim volume has awakened thousands of women to our heritage as healers and to the way the modern medical profession has kept us from claiming this birthright. The booklet traces the roots of today's medical profession back to the Witch burnings of the late Middle Ages and follows its rise, first in Europe and later in the United States. The authors show how, at every stage, this new male-dominated profession, often unscientific and dangerous in its practices, suppressed and discredited the widespread and effective practice of medicine and healing by women, most serving as herbalists, nutritionists,

and midwives to the common people. The medical profession split head from heart and curing from caring, creating a rigid pyramid of an institution in which men are concentrated at the top as the all-powerful, highly respected diagnosticians and decision makers and women are at the bottom as the obedient, low-status caretakers. CRS

Feminist Press, 1973, 44 pgs. Available from The Feminist Press at CUNY, 311 E. 94th St., New York, NY 10128, (212) 360-5790 ($5.70 ppd.).

THE WITCHES' QUABALA: THE GODDESS AND THE TREE
ELLEN CANNON REED

The Witches' Quabala is a practical guide for channeling kabalistic energies for rituals and other magical works. Pagans and Witches, who have steered clear of kabalism, defining it as too solemn and monotheistic, will find in Reed's book an unpretentious and basic understanding of the Kabala in relation to Witchcraft, paganism, and spirituality. Reed's interpretations follow the traditional charge of the Goddess, from "Listen to the Words of the Great Mother" for Binah, to "I have been with you from the beginning" for Chokmah. PCC

Llewellyn Publications, 1986, 192 pgs. Available from Llewellyn Publications, P.O. Box 64383, St. Paul, MN 55164, (800) THE-MOON ($9.45 ppd.).

WOMAN, EARTH AND SPIRIT: THE FEMININE IN SYMBOL AND MYTH
HELEN M. LUKE

Drawing upon ancient mythology and informed by a Christian and Jungian perspective, Luke explores the mysteries and meaning of the feminine principle as spirit, fire, and symbol. She emphasizes the importance of the feminine for women and men and

entreats us to restore the values of nurturance, relatedness, and contemplation in the home. Contains an unusual chapter on the relationship of the feminine principle to money. PW

Crossroad Publishing, 1985, 102 pgs. Available from The Gaia Catalogue Company ($8.45 ppd.).

WOMAN AND NATURE: THE ROARING INSIDE HER
SUSAN GRIFFIN

Poet Susan Griffin takes on the awesome task of allowing Nature to speak through her in this hauntingly lyrical prose-poem. If one were asked what it is we as conscious women know at the deepest levels of our being, there could be no better answer than this book. And she articulates what forest and cow and wind know as well. Books One and Two, "Matter" and "Separation," explore the patriarchal experience of woman and Nature, and its inevitable cataclysmic results. Books Three and Four, "Passage" and "Her Vision," speak of what happens when the separate is rejoined and the "power he could not tame" is free to dream and dance, rage and name. JIS

Harper & Row, 1978, 263 pgs. Available from The Gaia Catalogue Company ($8.45 ppd.).

THIS EARTH:
WHAT SHE IS TO ME

SUSAN GRIFFIN

As I go into her, she pierces my heart. As I penetrate further, she unveils me. When I have reached her center, I am weeping openly. I have known her all my life, yet she reveals stories to me, and these stories are revelations and I am transformed. Each time I go to her I am born like this. Her renewal washes over me endlessly, her wounds caress me; I become aware of all that has come between us, of the noise between us, the blindness, of something sleeping between us. Now my body reaches out to her. They speak effortlessly, and I learn at no instant does she fail me in her presence. She is as delicate as I am; I know her sentience; I feel her pain and my pain comes into me, and my own pain grows large and I grasp this pain with my hands, and I open my mouth to this pain, I taste, I know, and I know why she goes on, under great weight, with this great thirst, in drought, in starvation, with intelligence in every act does she survive disaster. This earth is my sister; I love her daily grace, her silent daring, and how loved I am *how we admire this strength in each other, all that we have lost, all that we have suffered, all that we know: we are stunned by this beauty*, and I do not forget: what she is to me, what I am to her.

From Susan Griffin, *Woman and Nature*, Harper & Row, 1978.

Passage, © Aline Lapierre, 1983. Four-color lithograph from original watercolor, 27″ × 30″. Reproduced as four-color lithograph available for purchase. Write: The Salamander Press, 1341 Ocean Ave. #349, Santa Monica, CA 90401.

WOMAN AS DIVINE: TALES OF THE GODDESS
MARIAM BAKER

A global treasury of women's spirituality myths and rituals, *Woman as Divine* is a spiritually evocative and beautifully illustrated book. Drawn from Buddhist, Jewish, Native American, Hindu, Moslem, Sufi, Christian, Taoist, Druidic, and Pagan traditions, these rare tales bring to life the forgotten aspect of the divine female principle as she exists within all religions and within all living things—rocks, trees, music, art, human love. Includes stories of Ma Kali, Shekinah, Isis, Kuan Yin, Changing Woman, Joan of Arc, Aphrodite, The Shabbos Queen, Noor-un-nisa, Mother Teresa, Mother Krishnabai, meditations and blessings. Recommended for women's ritual groups and children's nonsexist educational curriculum. PW

Crescent Heart Publishing, 1982, 68 pgs. Available from The Gaia Catalogue Company ($10.45 ppd.). A tape of songs to accompany the book is available for $10 from Crescent Heart Publishing, 150 Cerro Crest Drive, Novato, CA 94947.

WOMAN TO BE FREE: FREE TO BE GOD'S WOMAN
PATRICIA GUNDRY

The best short book to give to individuals who are traditional in outlook and concerned about being "true to the Bible." Gundry discusses such topics as women as second-class Christians, common threats to hold women down, misuse of Scripture in the past as ammunition for repression, and problem passages. Her treatment throughout is gentle, winsome, logical, thorough, and convincing. VH

Zondervan, 1977, 112 pgs. Available from Daughters of Sarah, 3801 N. Keeler, Dept. 1114, Chicago, IL 60641, (312) 736-3399 ($6 ppd.).

THE WOMAN WHO SLEPT WITH MEN TO TAKE THE WAR OUT OF THEM/TREE
DEENA METZGER

These two works in one volume by poet, novelist, and playwright Deena Metzger explore the fundamental processes of war—in gender roles and in the body. Deena writes in a powerful, rhythmic, and ancient voice, blending dreamlike material of the unconscious with the topical dialogue of our daily lives. In *The Woman Who . . .* Ada "walks down the street of an occupied village from the cemetery, passing her own house to the General's house which she enters without a word, to lie down unashamed on his bed. She does this—with the full cognizance that she is committing a political act." Voices narrate versions of Ada's actions and ask why she would choose to lie down with the enemy. Can the act of loving banish the impulse to war? Is it possible to be free of domination by the General without resorting to the weapons of the General? *Tree*, the journal Deena kept from the time she discovered she had breast cancer through her post-surgery period, in-

vestigates the inner and outer, personal and political causes of cancer. This book similarly asks, Can we heal cancer without making war on the body? Virtually a map of the healing journey, *Tree* details precisely the inner voyage. Deena implores us to create healing communities, to live on the side of the life force, and not to be silent in the face of death. PW

Wingbow Press, 1981, 220 pgs. Available from The Gaia Catalogue Company ($9.45 ppd.).

WOMANGUIDES: READINGS TOWARD A FEMINIST THEOLOGY
ROSEMARY RADFORD RUETHER

Womanguides is a remarkable collection of religious reading from ancient and contemporary sources that provides an affirmation of female divinity as an alternative to the exclusive male-gender imagery found in patriarchal religions. A renowned scholar in ancient history and Christian origins, theologian Ruether has provided a wealth of historical background information about the evolution of theological symbolism and themes. Included in this anthology are psalms affirming the sacredness of life, from Sumerian odes to Isis up to the present-day Mother/Father God of Mary Baker Eddy, founder of Christian Science. The ode to Ishtar, shepherdess of the Sumerians, is especially poignant. Ruether's essays and exercises at the beginning and end of each chapter are designed to foster the growth of Women-Church, a grassroots movement among feminists interested in transforming Christianity through feminist liturgies. GB

Beacon Press, 1985, 274 pgs. Available from Beacon Press ($12.95 ppd.). (See also listing for Women-Church on page 208.)

THE WOMAN'S BIBLE
ELIZABETH CADY STANTON

In the 1880s, Elizabeth Cady Stanton and her friends published this series of commentaries and essays on those parts of the Bible that deal with women and those sections in which women are glaringly excluded. Although the writing is uneven and the biblical scholarship often riddled with inaccuracies (and overlaid with Victorian viewpoints), *The Woman's Bible* offers a fascinating biblical analysis for contemporary women of faith and reveals insights into the minds of our feminist foremothers. RK

Coalition Task Force on Women and Religion, 1978, 217 pgs. Available from Coalition Task Force on Women and Religion, 4759-15th Ave. NE, Seattle, WA 98105 ($12.95 ppd.). A Study Guide to The Woman's Bible is also available ($5.95 ppd.).

THE WOMAN'S ENCYCLOPEDIA OF MYTHS AND SECRETS
BARBARA G. WALKER

A veritable gold mine gleaned from twenty-five years of cross-cultural research into word origins, mythology, religion, folklore, history, psychology, and philosophy. From A, the Babylonian Creatress who invented alphabets, to Zurzan, the dark divinity of Zoroastrian symbolism, Walker traces many words back to prepatriarchal origins and presents new information you will undoubtedly not find in the *Encyclopaedia Britan-*

nica. Walker's feminist interpretations are the most daring, entertaining, and provocative when she breaks through gender barriers and reexamines our outmoded views of love, romance, sex, and marriage. A major step in reclaiming herstory, this book is a treasured reference source in my personal library. GB

Harper & Row, 1983, 1100 pgs. Available from The Gaia Catalogue Company ($23.95 ppd.).

HOW I DISCOVERED KNITTING . . . AND WHY

BARBARA G. WALKER

Barbara G. Walker is a feminist writer who has spent the last twenty-five years researching religious symbolism and women's religion. She has authored the monumental Woman's Encyclopedia of Myths and Secrets, *as well as* The Secrets of the Tarot, The Crone, The I Ching of the Goddess, The Skeptical Feminist, *and* The Womens' Dictionary of Symbols *(forthcoming from Harper & Row, 1988). She's designed a feminist tarot deck, the Barbara G. Walker Tarot, and undoubtedly has at least several more book projects brewing at this very moment.*

Readers of this book may be less familiar with Barbara G. Walker's other talent and focus of prolific research: she is a leading world authority on knitting. Between 1968 and 1976 she authored ten books on knitting, now considered classics in the field. In this article Barbara reveals her "addiction" to knitting and gives the reader a glimpse into the patterns connecting the passions in her life: women's religion and knitting.

—Patrice Wynne

Back in the Old Stone Age when I was in college, the "in" thing for girls to do was knit argyle socks for their steady boyfriends. I didn't have one of those useful male attachments, a steady boyfriend. But I thought it might improve my image if I sat in class knitting socks like everyone else. I asked an expert argyle-knitter to teach me. She tried. Unfortunately, I was an abysmally slow learner and an uncoordinated klutz.

My first project was a small shapeless swatch demonstrating holes, knots, split yarn, and dropped stitches. It was good for nothing except maybe to wash a car, but it was thrown away before the car got dirty enough. With no regrets whatever, I said good-bye to knitting. I figured if I wanted to do something with my hands I could always doodle, play solitaire, hook a rug, or paint my room. Who needed knitting? My real interest at the time was riding horses. I hoped somehow to earn enough money to buy a ranch in Wyoming and breed mustangs.

Years later, as a wife and mother with no ranch, no mustangs, and only moderate funds, I got the urge to try knitting again. I loved sweaters with the handmade look—so expensive to buy. Even if the price should be right, a store-bought sweater might be an acceptable size and shape but a wrong color. Or it might be a pullover, when I wanted a cardigan. I yearned to create my own exactly-right sweaters with the aristocratic aura of the handmade. Next winter, I told myself, I will master knitting.

Since I was married I made it a habit to set a course of study for myself each fall, to fill in spare time during the cold months. I would collect all the books in the library on my chosen subject, read them, and take notes. In this way I studied architecture, astronomy, geology, ancient history, psychology, painting, sewing, folklore, anthropology, and many others year by year. This year I began by buying some yarn and needles and a paperback learn-to-knit booklet published by a yarn company.

My knitting was as clumsy as I remembered, but this time I persevered. In due course the learning passed from my head into my fingers. I got the rhythm. But halfway through my first plain stockinette sweater, I struck another snag—boredom. I thought: knitting is dull, dull, dull. How can a person make the same motions over and over? Knit another row, purl another row. Is that all there is to it?

Of course, like any beginner, I was naive. When I studied the pictures in knitting magazines, it began to dawn on me that this was *not* all there was to it. There were different-looking textures, fancy lacy patterns, embossed patterns, twists, cables. I wanted to know how all these were made. I read and practiced. I looked for a nice big book that would give directions for many patterns. There was no such book published in the U.S. at the time, so I began my own collection. I copied patterns from magazines, foreign books, old pamphlets, yarn-company publications. I began to invent my own patterns by trying out variations.

This initial collection formed the basis of my first published book, *A Treasury of Knitting Patterns*, which I thought must be quite complete, with its directions for about 550 patterns. Wrong again. Two years later I had over 700 additional patterns, gathered from back issues of knitting magazines, from correspondents' contributions, from a private library of old pamphlets, from the Library of Congress collection, even from an archeological text that yielded a pattern more than 2,000 years old, taken from a dig in Mesopotamia. These went into *A Second Treasury of Knitting Patterns.*

Then I stopped collecting and concentrated on inventing. From my own designs evolved the subsequent ten years' production of the following swatches and knitted projects for photographs in my next five published books; 79 blouses and pullover sweaters; 33 suits and two-piece dresses; 28 knitted handbags; 27 cardigan sweaters; 25 table mats and doilies; 18 skirts; 17 bed-size afghans; 16 hats; 15 scarves or shawls; 12 pillows; 12 capes or ponchos; 11 one-piece dresses; 7 coats; 6 pants; 6 wall hangings; 5 knitted lampshades; 4 lace tablecloths; 3 neckties; 2 swimsuits; and one—no, not a partridge in a pear tree—bedspread. Plus commercial designs. On seeing my album of photographs, visitors often ask, "Who could find time to do all this?" I have a standard answer. I didn't watch television. Not at all. It's astonishing how much time one has for creative activities when the idiot box is eliminated from one's life.

Naturally, that's not the whole story. I was altogether addicted to working out the puzzles of patterning and garment shaping that I set for myself. I knitted day and night. I never wasted a minute in life's miscellaneous waiting spaces: offices of dentists, doctors, pediatricians, veterinarians, train stations, bus terminals, airports; as a passenger in any form of transportation; waiting for coffee to perk, for hair to dry, for guests to arrive, for a concert to begin, whatever. I knitted. I knitted so many acres of yarn that a friend said I should create a house-cozy to keep our house warm in winter.

In my own way I even solved the problem so many dedicated knitters complain of: idea explosion. This is what happens while you are working on one project and suddenly think of six more ideas you want to try right away. It's always an effort of will to hang in there and finish the job in hand, before rushing on to the next. My solution was to stop creating full-size garments and start creating miniature garments for dolls, which can be finished sooner, so many more ideas can find expression in any given time period. This is still my hobby.

Doubtless I'll keep on inventing puzzles for myself to solve until I am hauled away to the great yarn shop in the sky. Others who have become hooked on this endlessly fascinating craft will know exactly what I mean. There will never be Knitters Anonymous, because we addicts don't want to be cured.

This article is reprinted from *Vogue Knitting Magazine,* Spring/Summer 1984. Barbara G. Walker can be reached ℅ Harper & Row, Icehouse One—401, 151 Union St., San Francisco, CA 94111-1299.

WOMAN'S MYSTERIES, ANCIENT AND MODERN: A PSYCHOLOGICAL INTERPRETATION OF THE FEMININE PRINCIPLE AS PORTRAYED IN MYTH, STORY AND DREAMS

M. ESTHER HARDING

Harding's premise is that whether or not we believe in them, we are motivated by subconscious forces that are expressed in archetypal symbols. For women, the symbols associated with the lunar goddess are the most powerful, and understanding them is essential to emotional development. The book contains a lot of fascinating ethnographic and textual material, though Harding's interpretations are biased in the direction of Jungian psychology in general and her own premise in particular. Read it for the facts and interpret them yourself. DLP

Harper & Row, 1976, 256 pgs. Available from Harper & Row ($8.95 ppd.).

WOMANSPIRIT: A GUIDE TO WOMEN'S WISDOM

HALLIE AUSTEN IGLEHART

Womanspirit, as Hallie Austen Iglehart (now Hallie Iglehart Austen) writes of it, is not another religion or set of fixed spiritual practices passed down through formal teachers. Instead, it is a way of life that taps deep into the spiritual heritage of women yet is created anew daily by each woman as she goes about her ordinary life with a sense of connection to herself and the whole. Austen, a creator and teacher of Womanspirit since the early seventies, makes such often arcane subjects as meditation, ritual, and healing as accessible as breathing, brushing our teeth, and holding hands in a circle. Austen reminds women that we carry within us all we need to know. She weaves her own story of self-discovery and political and spiritual awakening with ancient roles and images of women as shamans, healers, and creators. Her book serves as a guide, offering exercises and suggestions for how women today can tap their inner wisdom—individually and in groups—through meditation, dreamwork, collective and personal mythology, healing, and ritual making. CRS

Harper & Row, 1983, 176 pgs. Available from The Gaia Catalogue Company ($9.45 ppd.).

WOMEN'S SPIRITUALITY FROM THE ROOTS TO THE HEART

HALLIE IGLEHART AUSTEN

A pioneer in the women's spirituality movement, Hallie Iglehart Austen (formerly Austen Iglehart) began teaching Womanspirit classes and rituals in 1974. Her teachings stress the importance of incorporating ritual and spirituality into our everyday lives as a way to bring about personal and political transformation. She is the author of Womanspirit: A Guide to Women's Wisdom, *co-creator with harpist Georgia Kelly of the* Womanspirit Meditation Tape, *and the founder of Women in Spiritual Education (WISE). One winter day while working on the Sourcebook I invited Hallie to my home for a discussion on the roots and the direction of the women's spirituality movement. Our conversation soon turned to the source of our power in love and compassion, the active love needed to bring about peace on Earth. The following article is an excerpt of our conversation.*

—Patrice Wynne

I believe that women's spirituality is extremely radical at its core. We are talking about reordering all aspects of ourselves and the culture in a fundamental way. The transformation from the absolute rule of the Father God to a spirituality that honors all forms of life as divine has been a major change in our understanding of reality. The circle, which is the form in which we gather, is an ancient model for sharing power. Everyone's experience and contribution to the whole is honored. There may be a leader, but the basic structure is more empowering and egalitarian than in most religious groups.

The movement has grown very quickly. It's a grassroots movement, and that is its power. It's not as if someone had a plan—"OK, we're going to go out and convert people to this idea." It is a seed that is bursting, a long-repressed seed, bursting inside people. The ideas spread because people are moved to find others who resonate with what they value.

Interviewers often ask me how large the women's spirituality movement is as they try to grasp the idea of a spiritual and/or political group that does not have a membership, a leader, or a creed. More important than the numbers, I reply, is the size and subtlety of the movement inside each of us. Women's spirituality is as large as the first flash of awakening when a woman realizes she can trust herself and be guided by her own wisdom. It is as large as the power that we feel when we affirm our birthright to be whole and the planet to survive. This movement is breathing and growing—inside of you right now, in all people who love the Earth and the feminine, and in the spirits of those who have gone before us and will come after us as caretakers of the Earth.

Women's spirituality is a process of demystifying spirituality. It is about making spiritual practice accessible to each of us in our everyday lives. We can write our own scriptures, create our own rituals, since each of us has access to the inner wisdom from which all great practices come. A daily practice of sitting in meditation can be as powerful a spiritual tool as the more public role of leading a ritual. We always need to come back to our own inner selves where the heart of our wisdom resides. When the spider is building her web, she moves out, then she returns to the center, and then she goes out again, and comes back to the center, and on and on. In our lives it is important to balance our outer-directed activities with our commitment to self-reflection and self-renewal.

It is also vitally important that we honor women's regenerative power. Whether we bear children or not, it is from our life-giving, life-sustaining capacities that we bring about a shift in global consciousness. Women know the value of life—we know what birth is like, that life is not easily come by. More men, by participating in the birth process, are learning this now, too.

The Zen teachers say that spiritual practice is as simple as following the breath. I would add: spirituality is as ordinary and as special as doing bodywork with a friend or doing a ritual to honor a transition in our life. These are very basic human practices. You can see them in all cultures. People touch one another. People follow their intuition. People love to do ritual, to play with the elements, to celebrate their lives and to activate changes.

Ultimately, I believe, women's spirituality is about love. Now, *love* is a loaded word in our culture. Women have been raised to live for others' love and, at the same time, to love all others before ourselves. We have a whole culture built on very tenuous and fragile emotional relationships. You can see this in its extreme form in international relationships. The power of the civil rights movement, the feminist movement, all social and political people's rights movements is that they are all processes of people learning to love themselves, to believe in themselves.

Female and feminine consciousness—and their practical applications—have been nurtured in the alchemical vessel of the women's

spirituality movement for the past fifteen years. We have begun to love ourselves—our heritage, our intuition, our bodies, our nurturing capacity, as well as our intelligence and strength. And now we turn to the possibility of learning to love the world in which we live—with a love that is at once compassionate and truthful. I am not talking about a self-sacrificing or self-denying or exclusively romantic love, which is what love usually means for women in this culture. Nor am I talking about a love that ignores harsh truths in order to keep peace at all costs. I am talking about a love that is freed from the cages that have deformed it—a dynamic, powerful, and self-loving love that is able to encompass our larger selves, the world.

The love I speak of is beautifully depicted in a painting by Mayumi Oda. She portrays a playful, sensuous yet dignified Kuan Yin, the Buddhist goddess of compassion. Mayumi's Kuan Yin looks out onto the world with serenity and love—and a sword in her hand. With this sword she is able to cut through fear. For women, these fears range from being afraid of not having a man, of the night, of being alone in the wilderness, of asserting ourselves, of losing approval. Often these fears are based on the realities of being attacked, of being poor, or of losing community and family. However, the basis of these fears is changing as women learn physical and psychic self-defense, gain more economic independence, and create families and communities that are based on equality and mutual respect. In short, we lose our fear as we learn to love ourselves and *take action based on that love*. This is an active love, a strong emotional and psychic force for planetary transformation.

At this point in time, feminine consciousness in women and men is the peacemaking impetus on the planet, the true custodian of human life. The women's spirituality movement has helped us tremendously to love ourselves and the feminine. It's as though we've turned on our inner lights and are waking up to ourselves, one another, and the planet. It is very important. The survival of the planet depends on us.

Hallie Iglehart Austen teaches Womanspirit workshops throughout the country and is currently developing her work through the mediums of slide shows, meditation tapes, and video tape. For information contact WISE (see listing on page 208).

WOMANSPIRIT RISING: A FEMINIST READER IN RELIGION
CAROL P. CHRIST AND JUDITH PLASKOW, EDS.

"The symbol of the goddess has much to offer women who are struggling to be rid of the 'powerful, pervasive, and long-lasting moods and motivations' of the devaluation of the female body, distrust of female will and denial of the mother-daughter bond and women's heritage that have been engendered by patriarchal religions. As women struggle to create a new culture in which women's power, bodies, will and bonds are celebrated, the symbol of the goddess naturally reemerges and speaks to the deep mind, expressing our new vision of the beauty, strength, and power of women" (Carol Christ, "Why Women Need the Goddess").

Womanspirit Rising offers a comprehensive overview of the most brilliant and creative feminist thought in religion, theology, and ritual. The myth of Adam and Eve is reexamined by Phyllis Trible; Merlin Stone writes about finding records of Goddess worship in widely diverse cultures; Mary Daly explores the Christian symbol system she repudiated in 1971; Zsuzsanna Budapest offers a self-blessing ritual for increasing self-esteem; and Carol P. Christ makes one of the strongest presentations on the relevance and necessity of the Goddess in women's lives. Other essays address the woman-centered post-technological religions

that reclaim the body, examine the way words shape our perceptions and reality, and discuss the power of myths to guide behavior. GB

Harper & Row, 1979, 287 pgs. Available from The Gaia Catalogue Company ($12 ppd.).

WOMEN, MEN AND THE BIBLE
VIRGINIA RAMEY MOLLENKOTT

A readable study that responds to the many "total woman" oriented books pouring off the presses by pointing to Jesus' way of relating to women. Mollenkott challenges Christians to depart from cultural mores past and present and live in a spirit of "mutual submission" toward one another. PB

Abingdon, 1977, 144 pgs. Available from Daughters of Sarah, 3801 N. Keeler, Dept. 1114, Chicago, IL 60641, (312) 736-3399 ($8 ppd.).

WOMEN AND JUDAISM: MYTH, HISTORY, AND STRUGGLE
ROSLYN LACKS

Roslyn Lacks offers us the effort of one woman to come to terms with the negative images of women's body and spirit that pervade traditional Jewish materials. She gets at the root of the problem by tracing myth and image to ancient times, and records Jewish women's connection to the suppressed goddesses, to the figures of Eve, Lilith, to biblical women, and to women's images in rabbinic law. It is for the memory of the suppressed goddesses and for future generations that she writes, attempting to free treasures of spirit buried within. LG

Doubleday, 1980, 280 pgs.

WOMEN AND SPIRITUALITY
CAROL OCHS

Ochs has written this book to provide us with a new spirituality based on the experiences of women as moth-

ers. She defines spirituality as coming into relationship with reality, and demonstrates how mothering is well-suited for the spiritual life. For example, the kind of knowing through love of which the mystics speak is an ordinary experience for many women in the daily care of their infants. Ochs urges women to discover new spiritual role models that conform to female rather than male concepts of heroism. She gives us the biblical women Hagar and Leah as two such models. Ochs devotes little space to the dark side of mothering that Adrienne Rich addresses in *Of Woman Born*. Read together, Ochs's book and Rich's cover the range of complexities of motherhood. MS

Rowman & Allanheld, 1983, 156 pgs. Available from Rowman & Allanheld, 81 Adams Dr., Totowa, NJ 07512, (201) 256-8600 ($12.45 ppd.).

WOMEN-CHURCH: THEOLOGY AND PRACTICE
ROSEMARY RADFORD RUETHER

"We do not form new communities lightly, but because the crisis has grown so acute and the efforts to effect change so unpromising that we often cannot even continue to communicate within these traditional church institutions unless we have an alternative community of reference that nurtures and supports our being."

In *Women-Church*, Ruether summarizes the Women-Church phenomenon, presents the historical and theological understanding of church as community of liberation, and provides a wealth of women's symbols, rituals, and liturgies as vehicles for healing the wounds of patriarchal religion. The liturgies, which form the heart of the book, can be adapted by women everywhere as nourishment for our souls. *Women-Church* is the best sourcebook currently available for women's rituals. Besides an extensive bibliography of Pagan, Jewish, Christian, and ecumenical feminist liturgies, the book includes over fifty rituals: rites of healing from violence, a rite of healing from an abortion, rededication of a house after a burglary or other violence, a coming-out rite for a lesbian, a puberty rite for a young woman, covenanting celebrations for creating new families, moon rituals, and yearly cycle remembrances. PW

Harper & Row, 1986, 306 pgs. Available from Harper & Row ($18.45 ppd.).

MENOPAUSE RITUAL

ROSEMARY RADFORD RUETHER

Women gather in a circle. Women who have not yet reached menopause are given purple candles. Those who no longer menstruate are given yellow candles. The candles are lit, and each woman meditates on her candle while the meditation is read:

In woman is the great birthing and creating energy. This creating energy takes many forms. It is the power of ovaries to create eggs and womb to nurture the seeded egg into another human being. It is the creative energy to bring forth poetry, song, image. It is the creative energy to reflect on all reality, to mirror the world in the mind and bring forth rational discourse, and to teach others of the secrets of the workings of the world around us. It is the creative energy to create homes, communities, gatherings of people to accomplish tasks and to live together as friends. It is the creative energy to work the clay of the earth, the fibers of plants, and the wool of animals into useful vessels to carry things and many-colored clothes to vest our bodies and the walls and floors of our homes. All of these are our many creative mother-energies. Today one among us lets go of one kind of birthing energy, the energy to create other human beings. As she relinquishes this one kind of birthing energy, she takes up all the more fully the other kinds of birthing energies, the energy to create poetry, art, song, vessels, textiles, knowledge, and communities of people who work and live together. As one kind of birthing energy ebbs away and is no more, she enters fully into her many other birthing energies. We pause for a moment of regret for the one birthing energy which is no more. (All turn their candles upside down and pour out a drop of wax, and then turn them right side up again.) We rejoice as she enters into her full powers in the many other birthing energies which are hers.

The menopausal woman extinguishes her purple candle and is handed a yellow candle which is lit by one of the other women with a yellow candle. The women with yellow candles say to her:

Welcome to the community of women who no longer ovulate and bleed and who create now with their minds and their spirits.

The Autumn Deva
© Azra Simonetti,
1986. Oil on
canvas,
16" × 24".

WOMEN IN BUDDHISM: IMAGES OF THE FEMININE IN THE MAHAYANA TRADITION
DIANA Y. PAUL

This is a scholarly feminist examination of the way women have been treated in the Buddhist literary canon. Paul's essays and translations of original texts cover traditional views of women (temptress and mother), paths to salvation for women (nun, teacher of the dharma, and bodhisattva), and images of the feminine (Kuan Yin and Queen Srimala). JIS

University of California Press, 1985, 333 pgs. Available from University of California Press, 2120 Berkeley Wy., Berkeley CA 94720, (800) 822-6657 ($12.45 ppd.).

WOMEN IN THE WILDERNESS
CHINA GALLAND

"Once you live with the issues of women and the landscape for awhile, you find that you cannot separate them from notions of peace, spirituality, and community. As women we must learn to become leaders in society, not just for our own sake, but for the sake of all people. We must support and protect our kinship with the environment for the generations to come." (China Galland)

This book is a rare synthesis of women's adventure stories, spiritual quotes, wilderness rituals, personal anecdotes, and resource/organizational listings. China documents the

The woman now has an opportunity to reflect on what this transition moment means in her life. She may speak of pleasures and regrets she had in her years as one who bled and could bear children, and what hopes she sees ahead of her as a creator of culture.

A cup of herbal tea (with hazel) is raised and is blessed with the words:

This is the healing tea which our mothers and their mothers before them drank to calm the distresses of the monthly cycle of egg and blood. This healing tea links all women—those who do not yet bleed, those who bleed, and those who no longer bleed—in one community of creators and caretakers of life in its many forms.

The cup of tea is passed and shared among all present.

From Rosemary Radford Ruether, *Women-Church*, Harper & Row, 1986.

vision of the woman we have become: competent, adventuresome, courageous, spirited, and willing to take risks, to venture beyond the boundaries of culture and personal fear in reclaiming the wilderness as a woman's place. Reading of women who have tested themselves in the wilderness releases the secret adventurer in us all. PW

1980, 162 pgs. Available from the author: China Galland, 25 Loring St., Mill Valley, CA 94941 ($9.95 ppd.).

WOMEN OF WISDOM
TSULTRIM ALLIONE

"I realize now that, for me, spirituality is connected to a delicate, playful spacious part of myself which closes up in militantly regimented situations. The more I try to limit my mind in outward forms, the more this subtle energy escapes like a shy young girl. . . . I think that this luminous, subtle spiritual energy is what is meant by the dakini principle. She is the key, the gate opener, and the guardian of the unconditional primordial state which is innate in everyone. If I am not willing to play with her, or if I try to force her, or if I do not invoke her, the gate remains closed and I remain in darkness and ignorance."

The author, an American who became a Buddhist nun and then returned to the householder's life, reclaims for us the compelling biographies of six Tibetan holy women from the eleventh to the twentieth centuries. They study and practice, confront violence, perform miracles, struggle with the demands of society and family, spend years in solitude, act as teachers and healers—all the while remaining true to their vision and so becoming women of wisdom. Tsultrim tells her own story as well: her commitment both to the inner call that led her on a profound spiritual journey, and to

life in the world with all its joys and sorrows. JIS

Routledge & Kegan Paul, 1984, 282 pgs. Available from The Gaia Catalogue Company ($12.45 ppd.).

WOMEN SAINTS: EAST AND WEST
SWAMI GHANANANDA AND SIR JOHN STEWART-WALLACE, C.B., EDS.

A collection of twenty-five biographies of women saints and mystics written by Eastern and Western scholars, both male and female. The women saints and mystics belong to Hindu, Buddhist, Jain, Christian, Judaic, and Sufi faiths. There is a unity to the lives of these remarkable women, a unity that comes from their total dedication to the spiritual path and selfless service to the divine and humanity. The biography of Sri Sarada Devi, the wife of the renowned Hindu saint Sri Ramakrishna, is the central article in this anthology. In fact, this volume was published in honor of Sarada Devi's birth centenary. Sarada Devi symbolized the essence of Hindu womanhood in her unswerving devotion to husband and family. Yet, as her biographer points out, her greatness rests in her spiritual motherhood: " . . . when we think of God as the Divine Mother, the Holy Mother and God are inseparable." AB

Auromere/Aurobindo, 1979, 275 pgs. Available from Auromere, 1291 Weber St., Pomona, CA 91768 ($10.45 ppd.).

WOMEN UNDER PRIMITIVE BUDDHISM
I. B. HORNER

A scholarly reconstruction of the lives of the first Buddhist nuns, who overcame great resistance to be accepted into monastic life. One of the book's treasures is its collection of verses by these women about the sufferings they were leaving behind, their spiritual awakening, and the

bonds they forged with their sisters. It is another testament to women's ability to find personal meaning and make community even within an unsupportive patriarchal environment. JIS

Motilal Banarsidass, 1975, 391 pgs. For ordering information for this and other titles pertaining to women in Eastern religions, write for a free catalogue: Orient Book Distributors, P.O. Box 100, Livingston, NJ 07039, (201) 992-6992.

WOMEN WHO LOVE TOO MUCH
ROBIN NORWOOD

Jung once wrote to the founders of Alcoholics Anonymous that the cure for addiction must include the spiritual. Therapist Norwood reaches the same conclusion in this landmark book, which describes the relationship addictions that often pass for love in our society. According to Norwood, loving too much is a pattern of both emotional and biological dysfunctioning, often stemming from the lack of bonding in addictive families. Though Norwood sees the problem as an epidemic, she is ultimately hopeful that through counseling, group support, bodywork, and commitment to spiritual growth we can transform the very cellular nature of the disease of relationship addiction. For many women, this book has changed addictive patterns of relating to those they love and, most important, has helped them to deepen their relationship with the divine within themselves. The last two chapters feature instructions for setting up a support group to break addictive patterns and to assist in the healing process. GB

Tarcher, 1985, 266 pgs. Available from The Gaia Catalogue Company ($5.95 ppd.).

WOMEN'S REALITY
ANNE WILSON SCHAEF

Women new to the feminist movement continue to find Schaef's 1981 book provocative, disturbing, and challenging, naming what women already know in unspoken parts of themselves. Schaef critiques the white male system, and explores the emerging female system. While nothing in the book is apart from spirituality (chapter 2 is entitled "The Original Sin of Being Born Female"), Schaef takes up "female system theology" specifically in her last chapter, describing God as process. Process, she writes, "is never constant or static. Our natural, human process is god—yet god is not just our process (paradox!). To live and follow our personal life process is to be with god." "Women's Reality" audio tape is also available. PB

Harper & Row, 1981, 169 pgs. Available from The Gaia Catalogue Company (Book $9.45 ppd., tape $11.45 ppd.).

THE WOMEN'S SPIRITUALITY BOOK
DIANE STEIN

This is a book of herstory and hands-on practice of Goddess religion. Beginning with creation and creation goddesses drawn from a variety of world sources, Stein illuminates the significance of women/goddess-centered Wicca. The first half of the book, which leads the reader through the yearly progression of moon and Sabbat rituals, is interspersed with Goddess myths and tales. The second half of the book centers on healing, chakras, networking, crystal and gemstone magic, transformational tarot, and the women's I Ching. Stein, the author of *The Kuan Yin Book of Changes*, has been active and instrumental in the growth of women's spirituality as a writer, healer, and priestess. Her book defines and traces the herstory of the movement and is filled with rituals

for groups and individuals seeking closer union with the Goddess as a source of personal and collective empowerment. PW

Llewellyn Publications, 1987, 250 pgs. Available from The Gaia Catalogue Company ($11.40 ppd.).

WRITTEN OUT OF HISTORY: OUR JEWISH FOREMOTHERS
SONDRA HENRY AND EMILY TAITZ

An introductory but essential resource on Jewish women's history, including our spiritual history. To date, this book contains the only published collection of *techinah* literature (women's devotional prayers) translated into English. It also relates the stories of female religious leaders from biblical times to the modern period. Autobiographical writings, letters, and poetry, as well as liturgy, illustrate the rich and diverse spiritual legacy of Jewish women. Originally published in 1978; revised edition published in 1986. TPS

Biblio Press, 1978, 300 pgs. Available from Biblio Press, P.O. Box 4271, Sunnyside, NY 11104 ($9.69 ppd., $12.94 ppd. hb).

YOU SAID, WHAT IS THIS FOR, THIS INTEREST IN GODDESS, PREHISTORIC RELIGIONS?
SUSAN LEE/SUSANAH LIBANA

Susan Lee/Susanah Libana is a jeweler based in the South best known for her cross-cultural primitive Goddess images. In this small press work, her poetry voices a passionate love of the Goddess. It is the voice of a woman crying out for memory of the Goddess ("With her flow / Exhaling stars / Inhaling butterflies"), remembering freedom in the Goddess ("Handling serpents / Running with beasts / Making music for feasts"), whole in union with the Goddess ("Integrating flesh and mind / Crop and quilt / Culture and

magic / Mountain and molecule"). Images of Yemonja, Freya, Nuit, Themis, Chicomecoatl dance across the pages and reach back into our collective memory: "Set us free to ecstasy / In love's meadows / Yemonja Oyo Tara Coyolxauhqui / Offer us a vision. . .." This interest in Goddess religion, we reply, is for healing, for protection, for nurture, for life. PW

Plain View Press, 1985, 12 pgs. Available by writing: Plain View Press, 1509 Dexter, Austin, TX 78704.

THE ZEN ENVIRONMENT: THE IMPACT OF ZEN MEDITATION
MARIAN MOUNTAIN

"Tassajara was my zen womb. During the two years that I lived in the monastery, the high rocky walls of the canyon formed the pelvic bones of my zen environment, the monks and priests its soft uterine lining, the monastic schedule the strong uterine muscle, the beast of the great drum in the meditation hall the rhythm of its heart-mind, and the cascading song of the canyon wren the hint of other awakenings."

Marian Mountain was an affluent suburbanite whose Zen practice led to a profound spiritual/personal transformation. She gave up her previous comfort for a radically simplified life in the Big Sur wilderness, from where she wrote these meditative essays—often deeply moving, sometimes infuriating, always with that rare thing, the unique and rich voice of a contemplative woman. JIS

William Morrow & Co., 1982, 233 pgs. No longer in print.

THE

WOMANSPIRIT

GATHERING

GROUND:

MAGAZINES, NEWSLETTERS,

JOURNALS

THE WOMANSPIRIT
SOURCEBOOK

P E R I O D I C A L

R E S O U R C E S

ANIMA—AN EXPERIENTIAL JOURNAL

Anima magazine is concerned with the quest for human wholeness through the spiritual development of the feminine—"the inner part of the person, the vital principle, the breath of life." Each issue combines intuitive wisdom and scholarship in a rich blend of articles, fiction, poetry, mythology, photography, and graphic arts. *Anima* contributors, leaders in the fields of feminism, religion, Jungian psychology, and the arts, explore some of the major questions of our times with intelligence, sensitivity, and depth. Published semiannually, subscription $9.95 per year.

To order write: Anima, 1053 Wilson Ave, Chambersburg, PA 17201, (717) 263-8303. Note: Back issues of An-ima, dating from 1974, are available for purchase.

BAY AREA WOMEN'S NEWS
SUSAN THOMPSON, PUBLISHER

Bay Area Women's News (BAWN) was created to celebrate the positive ways women are birthing a new culture on Mother Earth. The focus is on ways women support and heal themselves spiritually, politically, and culturally. Though many of the writers are Bay Area women, the articles address global concerns that affect us all. Reviews of women's music and books, feature articles on women's spirituality and feminist theory, calendar of events, and women's health concerns make this paper both informative and inspiring. Published bimonthly, subscription $9 per year bulk, $12 per year first class. Sample issue: $1.50. Call or write for advertising, bookstore rates, and article guideline information.

To order write: Bay Area Women's News, 5251 Broadway, Box 557, Oakland, CA 94618, (415) 652-2390.

THE BELTANE PAPERS: A NEWS-JOURNAL OF WOMEN'S SPIRITUALITY AND THEALOGY OCTAVA

HELEN G. FARIAS AND JUDITH G. MAXWELL, EDS.; NEW MOON COLLECTIVE, PRODUCERS

The Beltane Papers (*TBP*) is published four times a year; *Octava* supplements the larger journal. Both publications aim to provide a safe place in which to reveal, share, expand, trade, and nurture women's visions. Regular features include "The College of Hera" (resacralizing the female cycle), "Dreaming Numinous," "Moon/Feast Calendar," announcements, letters, poetry, festal music and food, women and the sky (constellation myths), gardening; book, music, and performance reviews; short stories and children's

fantasies; bibliographies, reading lists, graphics. Beautifully designed, filled with womanwisdom, full of practical and visionary tools, and a bargain at $12 a year (U.S.) for four issues of *TBP* and eight of *Octava* ($20 foreign or first class). Sample issue *TBP*—$2.50 and *Octava*—$1.25.

To order write: Beltane Papers, P.O. Box 8, Clear Lake, WA 98235, (206) 856-5469.

BROOMSTICK

MICKEY SPENCER AND POLLY TAYLOR, EDS.

Broomstick is a national magazine filled with wit and wisdom by, for, and about women over forty. The name of the magazine was deliberately chosen as a symbol of the strength and wisdom of older women:

skills—homemaking and paid jobs, *change*—the new broom sweeps clean, *power*—the witch flies on the broom, *healing*—witches were the ancient healers, *confrontation*—exposing what society considers not useful. Regular features include a health column, book reviews, resources of interest, letters and conversations between readers, networking, and witches' cauldron, women-brewed advice culled from reader's direct experience. Annual subscription: $15 U.S./$20 Canada. Sample issue: $3.50.

To order write: Broomstick, 3543 18th St. #3, San Francisco, CA 94110.

CIRCLE NETWORK NEWS: A MAGICKAL PAPER FOR MAGICKAL PEOPLE

Circle Network News is a 24-page international quarterly newspaper published by Circle, a Wiccan church serving people around the planet. Each issue is filled with a variety of articles, rituals, meditations, illustrations, invocations, contacts, herbal formulas, book and music reviews, chants, resources, and goddess spirituality news. *Circle Network News* is the best publication for keeping informed of activities, news, and resources in the Pagan community. One-year subscription, $9/bulk mail to U.S., $13/first class to U.S. and Canada, $17/airmail elsewhere.

To order write: Circle, Box 219, Mt. Horeb, WI 53572.

CREATION
FRIENDS OF CREATION SPIRITUALITY, PUBLISHERS

Within the pages of *Creation* magazine are the prophetic voices of creation-centered poets, artists, theologians, feminists, scientists, native peoples, mystics, ecologists, and political activists. *Creation* provides a forum for the renewal of Western mystical spirituality found in the Judeo-Christian heritage, "the kind of spirituality that can help sustain the earth; a spirituality of creativity, generativity, earthiness, wholeness that celebrates the beauty and goodness of the universe." Each issue features a rich stew of practical ritual, art-as-meditation, new cosmic stories, mysticism, photographic images, startling conversations, and thought-provoking articles by some of the leading thinkers of our day. Published bimonthly, subscription $17/individual, $29/institutional. Sample issue $3.

To order write: Creation, P.O. Box 19216, Oakland, CA 94619, (415) 253-1192.

POWER IN A NEW KEY

KATHLEEN HURTY

Dr. Kathleen Hurty is an author, lecturer, wife, mother of four, and assistant general secretary and executive director of the Commission on Regional and Local Ecumenism at the National Council of Churches in New York City.

Visible signs of brokenness are all around us. We long for visible signs of hope. Take a look at the broken dawn. Each morning the dawn breaks and a new day opens up to us. Or consider broken barriers that can tear down the fences of isolation between mother and daughter, husband and wife, nation and nation; between sexes and races, classes and ages. Or taste broken bread—life-giving, sustaining shared bread—"this is my body, broken for you," connecting us to each other and to God through the power of faith.

I turn here to the story of Martha as discovered by Elisabeth Moltmann-Wendel. It is a story about responsible active faith lived out passionately in ways hidden from view by the masculine tradition. Moltmann-Wendel tells about a feminist movement in the Middle Ages, until now barely recognized, which produced legends about Martha that reveal amazing insights into power and possibility. A number of paintings and carvings from this period show Martha as a dragon tamer—binding the dragon (which was the symbol of evil and the victimizer of women) with her girdle, or standing on it with her bare feet. This image was seen alongside, and later almost replaced by, images of George, the dragon slayer, sword in hand. The distinction between the two pictures is striking: In the masculine version, force counters force by killing, while in the feminine version evil is bound and transformed. Martha was victorious by conquering the dragon in a new way. Here we see the power of life transforming death, the power of nonviolent action against evil, the power of assertive love.

Brokenness and connectedness are not opposites, but exist in a creative tension. Connectedness encircles brokenness by mending the torn pieces, by healing the hurt, by binding the broken bones of our human accidents. Connectedness does not ignore or deny brokenness. Rather, the evil aspects of brokenness are transformed, resolved, made new. It is a both-and way of thinking. It is possible to acknowledge and counter evil, exploitation and conflict while, at the same time, acknowledging and working for the possibility of change, reconciliation and a new community. Perhaps it is women who have the ability to live with this paradox. Perhaps it is women who can lead the way in understanding power, not as force to kill but as energy to live and to make new.

Such a vision does not represent a pinnacle mentality or a hierarchical ordering of the world into dominant and subordinate. Rather, this vision that women have, this connected way of being in the world, is a nurturant, caring interdependent vision, a both-and approach that says, I can both love you and discipline you, I can both critique and care for you, I can be both an individual and a member of a community. It is a creative tension, a delicate balance.

Brokenness, the kind that separates people from each other and all of us from God—this kind of brokenness is the abuse of power. Connectedness, thinking interdependently and working in caring ways toward global problem-solving is power in a new key. It is the power of gutsy, grace-filled Holy Spirit, groaning with us in travail for the birth of the new community. It is this kind of power that women know something about. Together we can model, describe, use and expand our hidden resources of empowerment. It is not that all women are alike (any more than all men are alike); but there are some commonalities among women that make us sisters under the skin. For all its rich diversity, there is a world sisterhood whose power has, as yet, no name.

Consider the power of emotional energy: If you have ever cried with a friend in pain or distress; if you have recognized the hurt in another and acknowledged your own vulnerability; if you have anguished over injustice and turned your anguish into action; if you have thrilled to the music, dance and sculpture of artists and supported their endeavors; if you have shared agony and ecstasy with your children in their failures and their accomplishments, then you have used the power of emotional energy.

Consider the power of nurturance: Think of those you nurture and those who have nurtured you. Imagine the inner strength required to care deeply, to speak in love, to guide, to model fairness, to discipline, to challenge, to support, to share. You who nurture, empower others to grow—and that includes nurturing both children and adults. Nurturance is a hidden resource of power—valuable, yet untried in terms of global relation. Nurturing a global community can be done. The power of nurturance is a hidden resource, remarkably valuable for international relations.

Consider the power of reciprocal talk: Reciprocal talk is talking together, feeling with the other, both listening and speaking. Women talk about an idea, check it out with those who would be affected, listen, talk it over more, bring others into the conversation and eventually come to a consensus that is workable for everyone. The idea of reciprocity is important. It means shared conversations in which

DAUGHTERS OF SARAH: THE MAGAZINE FOR CHRISTIAN FEMINISTS

Daughters of Sarah began in 1974 as a six-woman study and support group seeking to discover what the Bible says about women. After a year, the group adopted the name Daughters of Sarah to parallel the biblical designation "sons of Abraham." Today, *Daughters of Sarah* is a 40-page magazine by Christian women who share their discoveries, struggles, and spiritual journeys. It addresses contemporary issues and their effect upon women—spirituality, work, peace, aging, singleness, marriage, family structures, addictions, racism, sexuality, poverty, crime, language. The tone is supportive, loving, hopeful, embracing, and nondogmatic. Subscription $14.75 annually (six issues).

To order write: Daughters of Sarah, 3801 N. Keeler, Dept. 1114, Chicago, IL 60641, (312) 736-3399.

Cover photo by Jan Phillips, 1987.

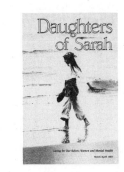

the ideas are collaboratively adjusted to find the best fit for all. Reciprocal talk is a diplomatic strategy—an imperative tool for problem-solving, a hidden resource of empowerment.

Consider the power of pondered mutuality: When you ponder, ruminate and reflect on your own needs and the needs of others, you are using the power of pondered mutuality to move beyond brokenness to the wholeness of an inner life in the context of community. Mary, the mother of Jesus, through that bloody groaning night of labor and the birthing joy of mothering her special child, took time to ponder all these things in her heart. Here we see the power of memory, the power of reflection, the mutuality of sharing God's work of world-loving.

Consider the power of collaborative change: Meet Julia Mora de Ussa from Colombia, a sixty-seven year old woman with a second-grade education who worked on a rural electrification project in her village, traveling mostly by horseback to secure the participation of all the people. Meet Jan Gallkager who works in Ecuador alongside the Inca Indians to create a sustaining community through farming, education and crafts. Meet Lynn Suter who lobbies for the city of Oakland, California, working as a persuader and mediator at the state level to improve the quality of life for the multicultural residents of that urban community. Meet women like Randall Forsberg, Helen Caldicott, Jihan Sadat, Mother Teresa, Alice Walker, Madeleine L'Engle and Zinzi Mandela who work against enormous odds and with their own special gifts to bring about change in collaboration with others.

These are the hidden resources of empowerment that connect us to ourselves in the integrity of our woman-ness, and connect us to each other, to the earth and to the human family. We are gifted by God, in unique and individual ways, to love and live together in community. These resources come straight out of our experience as women. It's just that we've never called them power. Oh, we do mess up a lot. Women have no edge on perfection. Yet, power in this new key is pregnant with possibility. The kind of power I am talking about is coactive empowerment—power with others. It is our heritage and our possibility, no matter how ordinary we may consider ourselves to be. It is available to men as well as women. Together we can create a new vocabulary of connectedness and a new grammar of power. Together, in God's name, we can begin to mend the brokenness, share in God's world-loving work and empower the human family to live in peace. All this brokenness, all this incredible brokenness. All this connectedness, all this audacious connectedness. All the possibility, all the glorious possibility.

This article, which was first published in *Concern*, Winter 1986, is excerpted from a presentation entitled "Beyond Brokenness: Women, Power, Possibility." Dr. Hurty's research on coactive empowerment ("Women in the Principal's Office: Perspectives on Leadership and Power" Ph.D. dissertation, University of California, Berkeley, 1985) is noted in *Dissertation Abstracts International*, vol. 47, no. 3, 1986, and is available from UMI, 300 N. Zeeb Rd., Ann Arbor, MI 48106, (800) 521-3042 or in Michigan (313) 761-4700.

A Rainbow Path: Green—The Heart Chakra Mandala © Gina Halpern, 1984. Acrylic painting, 10" × 10". From *A Rainbow Path*, a collection of eight mandalas for meditation and healing. Photo by Margaret E. Kauffman for Healing Through the Arts. For more information see page 184.

HEARTSONG REVIEW
WAHABA HEARTSUN, ED.

Filled with detailed reviews of vocal and instrumental New Age music and of music that integrates political, spiritual, and ecological concerns into the lyrics. Many spiritual traditions including Goddess/Earth religions, Sufi, Christian, and Hindu are represented, as well as special recordings for children, for ceremonies, and for spiritual practices. Reviews include suggestions for use of each recording, where and how to order. Semiannual subscriptions: $10 for four issues, $6 for two issues, $4 for a single issue.

To order write: Heartsong Review, P.O. Box 1084, Cottage Grove, OR 97424.

HERESIES: A FEMINIST PUBLICATION ON ART AND POLITICS

Since 1987, *Heresies* has provided a unique forum where women artists, anthropologists, political activists, tradeswomen, writers, therapists, former prostitutes, filmmakers, and musicians have worked in collaboration, creating a stimulating, self-probing, celebratory journal of our ever-evolving lives as women. Visually exciting and idea-oriented, each issue focuses on a different theme and is edited by women with expertise and dedication to the subject matter. One of its most popular back issues, *Heresies: The Great Goddess*, is one of the primary references on the Goddess. Prose, poetry, photography, symbols, dreams, art images, sacred places, jewelry, religious manuscripts, and masks combine to form a tapestry of homage to The Mother of Us All. Historical and cross-cultural, *Heresies: The Great Goddess* ($8 ppd.) presents a vision of the Goddess as she appears in her many manifestations. Other theme issues published by *Heresies* are: "Feminism and Ecol-

ogy" ($6 ppd.); "Racism Is the Issue" ($6 ppd.); "Film, Video, and Media" ($6 ppd.); "Women and Music" ($6 ppd.); "Acting Up! Women in the Theatre!" ($6 ppd.). The newest issue "Food as a Feminist Issue" ($5.50 ppd.), explores the cultural-political impact of food on women's lives from kitchen conversations to recipes to images of nurturance. A perfect antidote to the glut of diet books and pop-psychology treatises available to women in our culture.

To order write: Heresies, P.O. Box 1306, Canal Street Station, New York, NY 10013, (212) 227-2108.

IN CONTEXT: A QUARTERLY OF HUMANE SUSTAINABLE CULTURE
ROBERT AND DIANE GILMAN, EDS.

Through well-researched and experiential articles and art, *In Context* seeks to explore and clarify how we can develop socially ecological cultures and thus enable the world cultural shift to take place gracefully and positively. Each thematic issue offers practical steps and useful insights to getting there. The articles are intelligent without being inaccessible; emotional without being maudlin. Plenty of humor and hope! The backlist gives an idea of the breadth and nature of topics covered: #1 "Being a Planetary Villager," #10 "Friends and Lovers," #11 "Living Business or Turning Work into a Positive Experience," #13 "Play and Humor," #16 "Gender." Subscription $16/year or $28/two years. Back issues are available at $4 each.

To order write: In Context, P.O. Box 2107, Sequim, WA 98382.

INQUIRING MIND
BARBARA GATES AND WES NISKER, EDS.

Inquiring Mind, the journal of the Vipassana community, is a 22-page newspaper filled with news of interest

to practicing and would-be Vipassana meditators. The editorial content is diverse: recent issues have featured interviews with Vietnamese poet Thich Nhat Hanh, artist Mayumi Oda (*Goddesses*—see listing on page *28*), women's spirituality retreat facilitators Christina Feldman, Michele McDonald, and Ruth Denison (see page *171*). Regular features include poetry and "not poetry," book reviews, refreshing doses of comic relief, a international Vipassana retreat schedule and sitting groups, including women-only groups, around the country. Subscription by dana/donation.

To order write: Inquiring Mind, P.O. Box 9999, North Berkeley, CA 94709.

JOURNAL OF FEMINIST STUDIES IN RELIGION
JUDITH PLASKOW AND ELISABETH SCHÜSSLER FIORENZA, EDS.

The *Journal* disseminates information on feminist scholarship in religion and provides a forum for scholarly discussion and dialogue among women and men of differing feminist perspectives. Its editors are committed to the transformation of religious studies as a discipline and the feminist transformation of religious and cultural institutions. Published semiannually, subscription $15/individual, $25/institutional, $12/student.

To order write: Journal of Feminist Studies in Religion, P.O. Box 1608, Decatur, GA 30031.

Kannon, Bodhisattva of Compassion by Abby Terris. From *Kahawai, Journal of Women and Zen.*

KAHAWAI: JOURNAL OF WOMEN AND ZEN

Kahawai (KAH-hah-WAH-ee, Hawaiian for stream) chronicles one of the most important events in the transmission of Buddhism to the West: the meeting of Zen and feminism. The purpose of *Kahawai* is to encourage women's practice and full participation in Buddhist institutions as they establish themselves in the West. Theme issues have included "Nonviolence, Peace and Our Practice"; "Abortion"; "The Kahawai Koans"; "The Feminine in Zen Buddhism"; and "Practice and Relationships." No subscription fee but donations welcomed.

To order write: Kahawai, 2119 Kaloa Way, Honolulu, HI 96822, (808) 946-0666.

LADY-UNIQUE-INCLINATION-OF-THE-NIGHT

KAY F. TURNER, ED.

A matriarch of the feminist spirituality publications network, *Lady-Unique-Inclination-of-the-Night* was a leading voice in the emerging women's spirituality movement from 1976 until it ceased publication in 1983. *Lady-Unique* (the name is derived from the Mayan moon goddess) explored and expanded the positive meaning and political efficacy of a feminine aesthetic rooted in the image of the Goddess. To the women of *Lady-Unique*, love of the Goddess was/is first and foremost a love of the freedom of women to imagine ourselves powerful, to discover images rooted deep in the soil of our souls. The closing issue of *Lady-Unique* is a rare jewel devoted to an often-overlooked theme, women's altars. This issue presents photo documentation and essays on altars made by women in traditional cultures and contemporary feminists and artists. Issue price $7 ppd. Three back issues of *Lady-Unique* available at $4 each

ppd.

To order write: Lady-Unique-Inclination-of-the-Night, 704 Carolyn Ave., Austin, TX 78705.

NEW OPTIONS

MARK SATIN, ED.

New Options, though hardly a women's spirituality publication, deserves recognition. The board of advisers includes cultural and spiritual feminists Charlene Spretnak, Joanna Rogers Macy, Starhawk, Margot Adler, Robin Morgan, Hazel Henderson, Petra Kelly, Winona La Duke, and Elizabeth Dodson Gray. An 8-page newsletter published monthly, *New Options* explores the themes, issues, and values in postpatriarchal/globally responsible politics. It includes lively letters between readers, reinterprets topics ranging from sustainable agriculture to terrorism to ecological business principles, and looks constructively yet critically at social change groups and political books. In essence, it's a refreshing voice of future vision and current realities, a network of people seeking a spiritually-integrated new political agenda, and an excellent way to stay informed of the diverse threads of progressive movements for social change. Suggested subscription $25 annually. (From the publisher: "If you can't afford $25, send in what you can.")

To order write: New Options, P.O. Box 19324, Washington, DC 20036, (202) 822-0929.

OF A LIKE MIND (OALM)

LYNNIE LEVY, ED; JADE, COORDINATOR

An international newspaper and spiritual network founded to enable womyn to share their knowledge, feelings, dreams, visions, and resources. Focus is on Goddess religions, womyn's mysteries, Paganism, native and natural traditions from a feminist perspective. The *OALM Newspaper*, published quarterly, includes articles, dialogues between womyn, extensive resource listings, and announcements. The OALM Network is a computerized information resource bank that includes teachers, healers, groups, publications, community contacts, artists, centers, stores. OALM publishes this information annually in directory form. OALM is a project of the Re-formed Congregation of the Goddess, Inc., a legally recognized tax-exempt womyn's religion. Send SASE for subscription and membership information. Sample issue $3.

To order write: Of a Like Mind, P.O. Box 6021, Madison, WI 53716, (608) 838-8629.

Medusa's Song, © Ea Zü-En, 1980-9980 a.d.a. One of a series of feminist notecard designs available from Zü-en Graphics Studio, 8742 Luella Ave., Chicago, IL 60617.

SAGEWOMAN

LUNAEA WEATHERSTONE, ED./ PUBLISHER

Sagewoman is a feminist grassroots quarterly magazine dedicated to strengthening our inner visions and using those visions to transform our world. It focuses on women's spirituality in the tradition of *Womanspirit* and *Country Women* magazines—providing a way for women of all ethnic and cultural backgrounds to share and celebrate the Woman Shield: our sacred creativity, sacred intuition, introspection, Earth and our physical bodies, women's wisdom and women's mysteries. *Sagewoman* welcomes contributions of articles, drawings, poems, short fiction, black-and-white photographs, book reviews, rituals, music, and letters. Cover price is $4.50; yearly subscriptions are $13.

To order write: Sagewoman, P.O. Box 5130, Santa Cruz, CA 95063.

Logo for SageWoman magazine. Artwork © Abby Willowroot, 1984.

SNAKE POWER: A JOURNAL OF FEMALE SHAMANISM

VICKI NOBLE, PUBLISHER

"Goddesses like Kuan Yin (China) or Tara (Tibet) or Changing Woman (Navajo) or Ix Chel (Mayan) are . . . essentially shamanic, and they are also birthing mothers, the creators and sustainers of life. . . . They rule the cycles of life; they "hear the cries of the world" and respond; they oversee childbirth, help the dying, and heal all of us in between those two states. The Mother of All Life is the deity called upon by shamans all over the world and through all time. It is through her power and with her blessings that shamans work at all. And it is in her world that all shamanic activity takes place. The Siberian and Eskimo shamans inter-viewed by nineteenth and twentieth-century scholars confirm this view . . . The work can be done in no other way ." (Vicki Noble, "Female Blood Roots of Shamanism," Shaman's Drum, Spring 1986, Women in Shamanism Issue).

The word "shamanism" means to make heat and derives from the same root word as "shakti," the Indian word for female creative fire and the name of the primal Goddess. In available literature on shamanism women's unique experiences are frequently overlooked and their voices rarely heard. Yet the experience of the "medicine woman" or "woman of power" is often quite different from that of her male counterparts due to her unique psychic and biological capacities. *Snake Power: A Journal of Female Shamanism* will be a forum for the expressions of female shamanic points of view with an emphasis on the Goddess and feminist healing as a Western spiritual path.

For further information send a legal SASE to: Snake Power, P.O. Box 5544, Berkeley, CA 94705, (415) 658-7033.

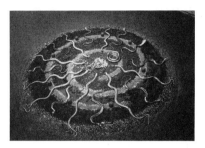

"The Magic Circle
Goddess Series
consists of both
indoor and outdoor
installations that
include drawings,
paintings, mixed
media, video,
environmental
sculptures, and
performances.
Initiated in 1978,
the series is my
lifelong project.
Inspiration for this
series derived from
my historical
heritage. Goddess
worship, the first
religion of
humankind, dates
beyond 35,000 B.C.
This omnipotent
Mother Goddess is
the underlying
symbol in my art.
Each Magic Circle
project celebrates

Woman God through
a visual and
multimedia art
installation. It
becomes complete
when a ritual video
performance occurs
on this site. The
Great Goddess has
been called by many
names and I have
included several in
my series. Coatlique
was an Omnipotent
Deity celebrated by
many American
Indian cultures. She
is still celebrated
today" (Kyra, P.O.
Box 6735,
Hollywood, Fl
33081).

PRESERVING WOMEN'S VISIONARY ART IN HUICHOL CULTURE

SUSANA EGER VALADEZ

In 1978 Susana Eger Valadez, an American, and her husband, Mariano Valadez, a Huichol Indian, founded The Huichol Center for Cultural Survival and Traditional Arts in the small coastal village of Santiago Ixcuintla. Some ten thousand Huichol Indians live in an impenetrable part of the Sierra Madre mountains in northern Mexico where they have preserved their existence much as it was in pre-Columbian times. The virtual isolation of the Huichols has enabled them to live in peace for thousands of years. The Huichol Center was founded to create a market in the United States for Huichol art so that Huichols can stay in their homeland and make a living as artisans rather than as poorly paid and badly treated migrant tobacco workers in settings where they are unable to maintain their vitally important religious and ceremonial life. Susana, one of only a few white people to be so closely associated with the Huichols, has dedicated her life to the preservation of traditional Huichol culture. With her husband and two daughters, Angelica and Rosie, she travels extensively raising funds for the Huichol Center and for legal aid and medical supplies. During a fund-raising tour of the West Coast, she spoke the following thoughts to me as we sat together in a children's playground in Oakland, California.

—Patrice Wynne

In 1975 I was a research director for the Foundation for the Indians of the Sierra, an organization dedicated to channeling medical supplies and other aid to indigenous populations. My work had both a scholarly and philanthropic focus. I first visited the Huichol people as an anthropologist, living in the culture for a month while doing field research. I saw a culture where one out of three babies dies, where four people sleep under the same blanket near the fire, and yet they were the happiest people I'd ever experienced. They joked often and they were very playful. I learned that for centuries the rugged and remote terrain of the Huichol homeland has provided a pocket of isolation where the Huichols have triumphed over the hardships of life. In this wilderness setting, their physical and spiritual needs have nurtured a value system and way of life that has carried itself through the generations. After awhile it became apparent that my reason for being there had more to do with my spiritual destiny than with my profession as an anthropologist. I put away my camera and academic's notebook and made a commitment to stay.

The Huichol believe themselves to be "mirror of the gods," which explains their beautiful dress and their artistic dedication. Being beautiful is an act of spiritual devotion. Before I became involved in the Huichol culture I was a lover of Renaissance and Impressionist art. The art that I knew was placed on walls in museums and had no relationship to daily life. To understand that the creation of art is an extension of our souls was a major turning point in my life. Traditional Huichol art, whether it be the striking costumes, the personal adornments, the meticulously executed beadwork, fulfills a prime purpose of their lives: encoding and channeling sacred knowledge, ensuring the continuity and survival of the legacy left to them by their pre-Columbian ancestors. Their highly ornate and colorful dress is said to give pleasure to the gods and goddesses, ensuring the benevolent protection of the divinities. In turn, the deities teach the Huichols a variety of esoteric techniques they may employ to influence the elements and maintain the delicate balance between life and death, sickness and health, abundance and misfortune. To the Huichols then, religion is not a *part* of life, it *is* life!

The Huichol Center for Cultural Survival and Traditional Arts began when I installed a small museum of traditional weaving patterns in my house in the Huichol homeland. The patterns were taken from embroidery on traditional costumes, which are direct statements of Huichol religious values and cultural identity. The Huichol Center makes available embroidery, beadwork, and weaving designs plus the necessary materials to make the designs. This is our approach to enabling the Huichol culture to remain self-sufficient. At a time when the Huichols are being forced to leave their homelands in search of jobs, this project is of vital importance for Huichol families who want to work at what they are skilled in, while at the same time keeping alive and thriving the precious knowledge that's been incubating in the culture and in their art.

The way that the Huichol women traditionally get their designs is by going through a process that is parallel to shamanic initiation. A good Huichol artisan, a woman, has the ability to see into her visionary mind from the use of sacred plants and to recreate these messages in a traditional form of art. A Huichol woman who undergoes this form of initiation has the ability to "dream" her designs and remember them. This is a path that women can take that equates to male shamanic powers. To keep these patterns going in her needlework is a way of recording the wisdom received in her visions and passing it on to future generations.

In the beginning I had a problem thinking, "If I graph out these patterns and make them available to the world, aren't I altering the natural system of how they acquire this secret language?" Yet, as Western influence is becoming more intrusive in their culture, traditional designs are disappearing and the integrity of the Huichols is

Susana Valadez with daughter, Angelica, and Huichol woman. Photo by Mariano Valadez, 1985.

diminishing. Designs of eagles, deer, peyote, and shamanic animals from their ancestral heritage are being replaced by cars, cowboys, cupids, and Disney characters. Their marvelous system of symbols and Huichol hieroglyphs, which have transmitted the spiritual values of the Huichols for centuries, is being replaced at a remarkably fast rate.

What I set out to do was to record the traditional designs from Huichol women throughout the Sierras wherever they could be found, very clearly showing how they can be copied onto embroidery or beaded into jewelry. Some women have found designs that their great-grandmothers once used but that had since become lost with the shift to a Western value system. Entire families come to the Center on the weekends for the sole purpose of copying beadwork or weaving designs. Seeing the hundreds of patterns all at once has renewed a sense of pride in their artistic skills and enthusiasm for their heritage.

In the Huichol culture, the ongoing dynamic is a struggle between the wet and the dry seasons. It's not enough to ask the god to make it rain so that the corn will grow. The rain has to stop so that the corn will dry on the stalks and be good to make tortillas. This is seen as a struggle between the male god, which is sun and fire and heat, and the female goddesses of rain and earth and fertility. If the people as intermediaries didn't intercede in the process then the earth would burn up or flood. Their mission on earth is to be the ambassadors of peace and keep the beings of the cosmic world in balance.

Today the Huichol culture survives as a window to the past revealing the legacy of indigenous ways that have become, for the most part, long extinct in many parts of the Americas. While many native peoples in the Western Hemisphere have become absorbed into the mainstream of the modern world, the Huichol people have maintained their traditional worldview. Yet, with the Huichols coming under increasing pressure to integrate into the modern world, the future of their culture has become uncertain. Unless something is done to help the Huichol people hold onto their religious and artistic traditions, the wisdom of this ancient peaceful culture will soon become another echo of a lost tribe.

Additional information on Huichol arts and culture and a newsletter of the Huichol Center can be obtained by sending a SASE to: Susana Valadez % Susan Page, 414-41st St., Oakland, CA 94609. Contributions of any size are deeply appreciated. See also the *Shaman's Drum* special color issue on the Huichols, Fall 1986. Huichol beadwork and native crafts are available through The Gaia Catalogue Company.

SOJOURNER: THE WOMEN'S FORUM
KAREN KAHN, ED.

Sojourner is a national women's monthly, offering reporting and analysis of national and global issues from a perspective that you will seldom find in your hometown tabloid. Named after Sojourner Truth, the black woman abolitionist and truthspeaker, *Sojourner* focuses on women's opinions and personal narratives with a special emphasis on spiritual growth. The letters to the editor column allows feminists of every persuasion—Pagans, Christians, ecofeminists, women of color, differently abled women, crones, and young sisters—to express their thoughts and feelings to one another on issues of mutual concern. Annual subscription: $15 U.S./$25 foreign. Sample: $2.

To order write: Sojourner, 143 Albany St., Cambridge, MA 02138, (617) 661-3567.

SPIRITUAL WOMEN'S TIMES: WOMEN LEARNING FROM WOMEN
KRYSTA GIBSON, PUBLISHER

Spiritual Women's Times is a quarterly newspaper devoted to the growth of women's spirituality. The paper provides a written forum where women can learn from and connect with women like themselves whose spirituality is an integral part of their lives. Published in the Pacific Northwest, much of the paper focuses on women and spiritual resources in that region, yet many of the themes and ideas are relevant to women and interested men everywhere. Articles, poetry, press releases, photographs, and artwork by women that define, strengthen, and nurture the feminine energies within all women are encouraged. Subscription $7.50 per year. Advertising information is available upon request.

To order write: Spiritual Women's Times, P.O. Box 51186, Seattle, WA 98115-1186, (206) 524-9071.

THESMOPHORIA
Z. BUDAPEST, ED.

In early Greece, the Thesmophoria were the rites practiced by women that later emerged as the Eleusinian Mysteries, the most revered and politically influential of all the Greek rituals. *Thesmophoria* means Law Bearer, Demeter's law of life. The newsletter of the Susan B. Anthony Coven, founded by Z. Budapest, is named *Thesmophoria* in honor of the connection between the rites of our ancient Greek sisters and the women of the new future who live in service to the Goddess. It features Goddess lore, feminist spirituality articles, a calendar of events, and letters between readers exploring areas of mutual concern related to the Goddess spirituality movement. Subscription $13 a year, issued eight times a year, close to the major Sabbaths.

To order write: Thesmophoria, P.O. Box 11363, Oakland, CA 94611.

VENUS RISING
DALE LEWIS, PUBLISHER AND ED.

Venus Rising is dedicated to the emerging feminine impulse and to the empowerment of women in all areas of our lives. Feature articles in each edition explore feminine ways of knowing our sexuality, the process of aging strong, death and dying, women and addiction, marriage, and the artistic impulse. Contributions from women and men who are engaged in healing and balancing the feminine and masculine powers are welcome. Subscription: $20.

To order write: Venus Rising, P.O. Box 21405, Santa Barbara, CA 93121, (805) 962-9345.

WISE WOMAN
ANN FORFREEDOM, ED.

Quarterly national newsletter focusing on feminist issues, feminist spirituality, Goddess lore, and feminist Witchcraft. Features articles, poetry, art, cartoons, exclusive interviews of "Inspirational Women of Our Time," photos, news analysis, and more. Annual subscription $6. Sample issue $2.

To order write: Wise Woman, 2441 Cordova Street, Oakland, CA 94602.

WOMAN OF POWER: A MAGAZINE OF FEMINISM, SPIRITUALITY, AND POLITICS
CHAR MCKEE, ED.

Woman of Power magazine, a 96-page international quarterly publication, honors the literary and artistic works of contemporary women activists and visionaries. Issues explore themes central to the emerging women's consciousness—"Womanpower," "Healing," "Women of Color," "ReVisioning the Dark," "Nature," "Envisioning a Feminist World,"—through interviews, articles, artwork, fiction, poetry, photography, and profiles of women of power. Material is selected with the goal of inspiring new visions of where women's power will lead us, nurturing women's spirituality as a planetary spiritual-political movement, and providing a multicultural and multiracial network for women of spirit, power, and vision involved in the many traditions of women's spirituality. Single issues available at women's bookstores or through The Gaia Catalogue Company. Back issues are also available, except for the premier issue, which has sold out ($6 each, plus $1 postage) Subscription $22.00

To order write: Woman of Power, P.O. Box 827, Cambridge, MA 02238-0827, (617) 625-7885.

FEMINISM— A VISION OF LOVE

CHAR MCKEE

The wisdom of women's experience is generating a reconceptualization of the meaning and power of love. More and more women are coming to recognize feminism as a powerful awakening force which opens the mind and heart, a moral force whose message is love of life, love of self and others, love of all forms of life and the earth. We are rethinking and revisioning love as a powerful force which knows the integrity and the interrelatedness of all life forms, and which seeks to manifest this knowing by creating those conditions which best promote the economic, social, political, and spiritual well-being of all womankind, and the abundant welfare of all creation.

Emerging from the wisdom of feminist spirituality is the mystical vision of love as the natural state of our true selves, the place which remains in the unconditional space, when the thought-forms of patriarchy have been excised. It is in this unconditioned space where we know our deepest love for ourselves and our deep love for other women, and find the courageous love we need to be powerful warriors in our work of healing a troubled world.

From *Woman of Power* magazine, Issue Two: "Envisioning a Feminist World," Summer 1985.

WOMANSPIRIT MAGAZINE
JEAN MOUNTAINGROVE, ED.

WomanSpirit gives voice to women worldwide discovering our own spirituality in the decade 1974–1984. In forty timeless quarterly issues the chorus of our diverse feminist sisterhood sings in art, music, stories, poems, plays, essays, photographs, affirming that our lives are grounded in our experiences and soar into every dimension. The multiple themes of the women's spirituality movement—Nature, intuition, our bodies, birthing and dying, healing, ritual, herstory, endurance, vision, our loving spirits—are explored in ongoing dialogue. All forty back issues and a comprehensive index are available from the publishers.

Send SASE to WomanSpirit, 2000 King Mountain Trail, Wolf Creek, OR 97497 for additional information.

THE WEB OF WOMANSPIRIT

JEAN MOUNTAINGROVE

"The Beginning Urge to create WomanSpirit was centered in our own spiritual awakenings. When we travelled we discovered that other women, too, were having intense inner experiences. We sensed that something global was happening. We suspected that our growing awareness of sacredness could be the basis of a new web of values and attitudes leading us in a new direction, unfolding a new culture."

—WomanSpirit Magazine, Summer 1975

The global vision and life-affirming content of WomanSpirit magazine had a profound effect on the emerging women's spirituality movement. During the ten-year period from Fall Equinox 1974 to Summer Solstice 1984, the magazine served as a lifeline to a web of woman-spirited seekers throughout the world. In prose, poetry, ritual, song, artwork, letters, essays, and analysis, women's words and images reflected a reality beginning to be gleaned in the lives of a multitude of women.

From its birth, WomanSpirit was a testimony to the power of women's love. "Our intention was to put so much love and care into the pages that reading the magazine would in itself be an experience of love, support, beauty and woman-affirmation, renewing hope and strength." Reviewers called WomanSpirit uneven. Yes, we are uneven, said the founders, and each issue celebrated the marvelous diversity and unevenness in women's lives. Intensely personal and more spherical than linear, material was arranged to reflect the relationships among themes and moods in a woman's inner life.

Knowing the risk they were taking in publishing a magazine of this sort, they were nervous about the response they would get. "Alive, full of hope, exuberance, and above all, of a profound honesty." The words of lesbian poet Elsa Gidlow, spoken for many, allayed their fears. "When I received Elsa's letter, I cried . . . with relief," wrote Jean. "She understood what we were trying to do. I knew we were on the right track."

When I began compiling material for this book, I wrote to Jean Mountaingrove asking for the herstory of WomanSpirit *magazine. I felt that the magazine's publication was a significant chapter in the unfolding life story of women's spirituality. Since I couldn't make the trip to her home in Oregon she agreed to send a tape in which she told her story of the magazine. The profound honesty that Elsa lauded in her letter to* WomanSpirit *continues in the words of Jean Mountaingrove. When I received the tape I, too, cried, for I was reminded by her words: We are the Weavers. We are the Web.*

When they met in Philadelphia in the early 1970s, WomanSpirit *founders Jean and Ruth Mountaingrove were suburban single parents with teenage children. Consciousness raising and sisterhood had revolutionized their lives and the magazine they later envisioned was grounded in these values.*

—Patrice Wynne

Jean Mountaingrove. Photo by Aggie Agapito, 1986.

In the fall and winter of 1973, Ruth and I traveled the West Coast looking for our home and our "work." In February of 1974 we visited Albion, in northern California, to work on the "Spirituality" issue of *Country Women* magazine. The volume of material submitted for that issue combined with the answer to an I Ching reading in which we asked: "What shall we do with our lives now?"

The hexagram *Pushing upward* changed to *Coming to meet*. I didn't understand the answer but it seemed positive. The next day upon awakening, the first thing I saw was a letter on the table next to the bed. As I read that letter I thought, "There is such a response to this special Spirituality issue. There needs to be a continuing journal of women's spiritual thought and experience." At a spirituality festival months later in Wolf Creek, Oregon, after the magazine went into production, I met the woman who wrote that letter. I learned she had been dreaming of starting a magazine devoted to women's spirituality when she wrote to us. So I believe there was a psychic connection that brought the vision of *WomanSpirit* to me that morning.

Doing the magazine was a spiritual discipline. It developed my trust and faith in miracles. I began to see that my life was guided by a power in the universe that would help me. The first time this came to me was after the WomanSpirit Tribal Gathering in the summer of 1975. The women stood around the final campfire and sang, "Ruth and Jean have strong faces." I could cry right now thinking about it. I

Photomythology
Series, *The
Archer's Aim*
© Marcelina
Martin, 1985.

became an elder of the tribe at that moment. Something in me that had been timid or lacked faith in myself was consolidated. There were many hard times after that, but I do go back and look at that as a turning point in my inner life.

The obstacles were tremendous. It was the kind of project that any intelligent, sane person would have said was ridiculous. We had no place to live. We had no money. We had no experience in publishing. We found indeed that money would come and facilities would be loaned and experience would be shared and the resources would be there. Being women, we had learned to improvise for years. And we just kept right on improvising.

Eventually we were able to buy a typewriter, but we lived without a telephone. We conducted an international business for ten years without business cards or telephone. Being away from the center of business orientation meant that we lacked the access to resources that women have in the city. I mean it was years before we learned about the little black strips that you can use around photographs in order to make them stand out on the page better. But what we did have was the privacy to be away in the country, which facilitated a spiritual focus. Our lack of resources became an asset. It was an obstacle on a physical plane but a resource on the emotional and spiritual plane.

A main theme in *WomanSpirit* was that our bodies are a source of wisdom. As such, there was an emphasis on menstruation, menopause, and childbirth as a spiritual experience. We stressed the full breadth of women's creative expression. Songs, photographs, and artwork were as important as the writing. And, of course, the writing, art, and music were always used as a contextual unit that I believe is basic to how women relate to the world. We're sensitive to our environment around us as well as what's going on inside of us. Even if we had something absolutely wonderful existing by itself, I would hold it for a later issue until we could find other material that would surround it and give other dimensions to it. The message is that women can trust their own inner experience, their own intuitions, and grow from inside themselves. Today that message is becoming widely available.

As a crone of sixty and that's a rather young crone, you understand, I have some observations that might help us through these times. As women move into more skilled, responsible, and powerful positions we need to focus on healing as well as work. During the early stages of the women's spirituality movement, healing was a major consideration of our work. We saw how we had been so wounded. And indeed we are going to be in need of healing for a long time. Healing the relationship breaks that the patriarchy encourages has been very important in my life. I believe it's because of the women's movement and the emphasis on respecting, loving, and valuing the lives of our mothers and grandmothers and foremothers that I was encouraged within myself to seek that union with my own mother and reconciliation with my sisters. And that has given me a great deal of pleasure at this period of my life.

I would advise women to pace themselves better than I did and to take time for renewal. I collapsed every once in awhile but that is not renewing, just simply getting back to maintenance. Another lesson, I would say, is that you can do anything even if it looks impossible. Don't be rational about your dream. If you feel an inner intuitive urge, if a dream captures you, do it. It doesn't matter if you don't have resources or experience or the things that logically support it, what is most important is inner conviction and desire. If the idea is a good one, if the time is right for it, the resources will come.

Tell other people what you need. This is not a selfish thing. A dream is not a personal possession. When we asked for typewriters or a loan, we were asking because of something that was larger than either of us and so things came. Birthing a dream into reality is 99 percent perspiration. But that other 1 percent of determination and inspiration is absolutely crucial.

What is my life like today? It is close to Nature by choice. It is close to my family, my grandchildren and my adult children. My granddaughter laughs so easily. We need to be in touch with that. I am close to my community of lesbian women. It's very helpful and stabilizing for me to feel that I have a group of women who've known me for ten or twelve years and accept me as an important part of their lives just as they are for me.

A large factor in keeping my sanity is my participation in a self-help group that uses a twelve-step program. Its spiritual emphasis is helping me make changes in my life I didn't think possible. I don't know that I am sane, but I am getting saner.

I'm working on the importance of the menstruation experience for women's spiritual lives, for their intuitive and psychic abilities. I believe menstruation is an extremely potent avenue for women's wisdom. My mind can fantasize doing conferences and workshops and art projects, but my emotional strength is not at the point where I could take on those kinds of projects. I know about the 99 percent perspiration! This past winter I have been more content than I have been in many years. And while my mind can race ahead, the slower pace is the one I will adjust myself to. I trust that the Goddess is preparing me for what she wants me to do.

Jean Mountaingrove lives at Rootworks and is part of a community of women who live in the southern Oregon mountains. Summer visitors are welcomed to Rootworks. For additional information send a SASE to: Rootworks, 200 King Mountain Trail, Wolf Creek, OR 97497. Back issues and a comprehensive index to *WomanSpirit* magazine can be ordered from the same address.

THE POWER

AND

THE SPIRIT:

WOMEN'S SPIRITUAL

MUSIC TODAY

**THE WOMANSPIRIT
SOURCEBOOK**

MUSIC

RESOURCES

A CIRCLE IS CAST
LIBANA

I can't imagine a better recording than *A Circle Is Cast* to recommend to anyone seeking devotional women's music from many cultures and spiritual traditions. From the day it arrived in our store, *A Circle Is Cast* has been the chosen favorite of staff and customers. The hauntingly beautiful chants, rounds, and melodies are drawn from Native American, African, early European, and Jewish sources. Libana derives such pleasure from sharing these songs that the listener is irresistibly drawn into an experience of the sacred. Libana is a performing ensemble dedicated to rediscovering women's ancient and often undocumented musical heritage. Artistic Director Susan Robbins founded Libana in 1979 to explore music that derives directly from women's experience. Named after a tenth-century Moorish woman poet, philosopher, and musician, Libana later learned that their name derives from an Arabic verb meaning "to nur-

ture from the breast." In the spirit of community and celebration, *A Circle Is Cast* is dedicated to the singer that lies in each of us. Twenty-two songs, including "The Earth Is Our Mother," "A River of Birds," "Kore Chant," "In May, That Lusty Season," and "Sister, Now Our Meeting Is Over." Also available is a companion songbook so that you can learn the songs to share them with others and thus enable the circle to grow. PW

Spinning Records, 1986, Ritual World Music. Available from The Gaia Catalogue Company (cassette only $11.50 ppd., book $8 ppd.).

A FEATHER ON THE BREATH OF GOD
HILDEGARD OF BINGEN

Hildegard of Bingen (1098–1179) was the original Rhineland mystic, abbess of her own convent, a prolific musician, scientist, poet, and the foremost sage of her time. Her creation-centered spirituality, rooted in

Kay Gardner.
Photo by Janet
Ryan, 1983.

her experience of the Motherness of God, was the source of a lifetime of creativity. She juxtaposed plain chants and sacred hymns of the twelfth century with a musical style reminiscent of the modern age. This exquisite recording of eight of Hildegard's sequences and hymns is by Emma Kirkby and other soloists from the Gothic Voices, directed by Christopher Page. With occasional drone accompaniment, *A Feather on the Breath of God* is a delight for the ear and a balm for the soul. NVS

Hyperion Records, 1982, Classical/liturgical. Available from The Gaia Catalogue Company (LP or cassette $13.95 ppd., CD $19.45 ppd.).

A RAINBOW PATH
KAY GARDNER

The culmination of Kay's studies concerning the healing properties of sound and color, *A Rainbow Path* is truly an awakening experience. The eight compositions are related to the eight chakras, which in turn correspond to different colors, distinct modes or scales, and separate syllables for intoning. But this is not boring, incantatory music. Although repetition is used (as always is the case in chanting) and a drone is maintained throughout each piece, the variety of instrumentation (bassoon, French horn, trombone, tim-

WORLD VIBRATION AND WOMEN'S MUSIC

KAY GARDNER

In order to make changes in the world, the vibrations of the world must change. How can they change if we're stuck in the same musical language? We are still using harmonies dictated to us by the Roman Church centuries ago, and by a harmony system invented 300 years ago. We are limited by the equal-tempered scale, which came to use when the piano was invented. It's a technocratic scale, not the one we hear in Nature. The natural scale is much more interesting. With the invention of the synthesizer and computer-generated sound, we may more accurately approach the natural scales.

In my research over the past 10 years, I have found several woman-identified scales from both Greek and Hindu cultures. The ones I tend to use are the Lydian and Lesbian (Mixolydian) modes (or scales), and the Saraswati Raga (a raga, too, is a scale). These scales were invented by women, and speak to women and to men who aren't afraid of their female sensibilities. This is probably why so many say that my music is evocative, haunting, etc. An ancient "memory" has been stirred just by listening to these women's scales.

I'm interested in exploring a new music theory, one based upon healing, unity of peoples, peace, and womanstrength. This requires synthesizing the commonalities of women's music and healing music from many different cultures, and redefining the musical language. New scales, new harmonies, new ways of performing.

Kay Gardner is an internationally recognized composer and teacher of the healing properties of music. She can be reached % Healing Through the Arts (see listing on page 184). This article is excerpted from an interview with Kay Gardner by Toni L. Armstrong that first appeared in the March 1986 issue of *Hot Wire: A Journal of Women's Music and Culture* (1417 W. Thome, Chicago, IL 60660).

pani, gong, harp, cello, double bass, recorder, English horn, viola, violin, oboe, clarinet, vibraphone, chimes, other percussion), harmonic invention, and sheer melodic beauty make this a recording worthy of Saraswati, the Indian goddess of music. The cover art to *A Rainbow Path* is an exquisite healing mandala, a celebratory, sensual, and empowering image of the feminine life force. A spectrum of brilliant colors illuminates the chakras or energy centers of the body. In an effort to make these images available to large numbers of people, the artist, Gina Halpern, has produced *A Rainbow Path* poster. Recommended for meditation, healing, visualization, harmonizing and balancing the mind. NVS/PW

Ladyslipper Records, 1984, Meditative/New Age. A Rainbow Path *recording and poster are available through The Gaia Catalogue Company (LP or cassette $11.50 ppd., CD $18.95 ppd., poster $15 ppd.).*

ACCORDION AND VOICE
PAULINE OLIVEROS

After many years of experimental electronic music, Pauline Oliveros is now recording meditative improvisation for accordion and voice. "Horse Sings from Cloud" (side 1 of this album) is a slow-changing meditation: chanting "om" on one tone is sustained until interest wanes and another tone is initiated; the accordion accompaniment is also breathlike, adding tones steadily to become more and more dissonant. "Rattlesnake Mountain," played on the accordion, sounds like an Indian harmonium playing a raga with a constant drone. Since Oliveros feels that it is "important for people to make their own music," I think she would be delighted if you chanted along with the record. NVS

Lovely Music, Ltd., 1982, Meditative/new music. Available from Pauline Oliveros Publications, P.O. Box 1456, Canal St. Station, NY, NY 10013,

(212) 219-0615 (LP only, $10 ppd.). Note: *Information on ordering other records, tapes, musical scores, and books by Pauline Oliveros is available upon request.*

AEOLUS
RUTH BARRETT AND CYNTIA SMITH

Barrett and Smith sing traditional melodies with updated, feminist lyrics and accompany themselves on dulcimer. Their exquisitely clear folk voices and clean accompaniments with flute, cello, and concertina make this a beautiful recording. "Every Woman Born," with a traditional tune and Ruth Barrett's new lyrics, is one of the most powerful songs to the Goddess I've ever heard. NVS

Kicking Mule Records, 1981, Folk/traditional. Available from Aeolus Music, 4111 Lincoln Blvd. #211, Marina del Rey, CA 90292, (213) 851-3201 (LP or cassette $10 ppd.).

ALIVE! ALIVE!
ALIVE!

The spirit of women's music is Alive! When these five women join forces they become one of the most dynamic ensembles in jazz, weaving instrumental and vocal improvisation with jazz and classical sounds, traditional African and Latin polyrhythms with female imagery and woman-affirming lyrics. This album is compelling, intelligent, and masterfully performed. The message: women's energy is pervasive and powerful. The words are delivered in sparkling songs like "Somebody's Talking to You," and "Spirit Healer," an anthem to women's spiritual power. AL

Urana Records, 1979, Jazz. Available from Ladyslipper (LP or cassette $9.95 ppd.).

ANCESTRAL DREAM: IMPROVISED RITUAL MUSIC
JANA RUNNALLS

This wonderful tape of improvised ritual music contains, among others, songs to Aeaea (a Celtic sky goddess), Tiamat ("all-embracing mother of the ocean"), Kore (a Greek earth goddess), and Kali (a Hindu goddess of fire), thereby invoking the four directions. It's hard to imagine someone more talented than Jana Runnalls, who composed, sang, and played all music on this cassette, including various flutes, clarinet, temple bells, African kalimba, dulcimer, African drums, Indian tabla, and many other percussion instruments. Sometimes her music is fairly far-out jazz with quite a bit of Indian influence, but it is always passionately and exquisitely performed. NVS

Stroppy Cow Records, 1986, Ritual/world music. Available from Ladyslipper (cassette $10.70 ppd.).

ANNIE OAKLEY RIDES AGAIN!
KAREN MACKAY

Annie Oakley Rides Again! may sound like an unlikely title for a spiritual record, but this bluegrass album has some of the most rejuvenating songs for women on a spiritual path today. Karen Mackay is a real West Virginian woman with a gutsy voice and the courage and joy to go with it. "Green Growin' Tree," which takes the listener on a healing guided meditation, and "If Every Woman," a women's anthem of peace, are my personal favorites. NVS

West Virginia Woman Records, 1984, Country/bluegrass. Available from West Virginia Woman Records, 526 Sherwood Lane, Hatboro, PA 19040 (LP or cassette $10.50 ppd.).

BIRDS OF PARADISE
GEORGIA KELLY

Birds of Paradise contains several

tone poems for solo harp or harp/flute duet by New Age composer Georgia Kelly, herself a consummate harpist. Each of these pieces of program music is meant for meditational purposes: "Rainbow Showers" begins with a clap of thunder and arpeggiated showers of harp chords; "Primavera" is concerned with cyclical growth; and "Birds of Paradise" is a relaxing duet for flute and harp. This album is soothing and refreshing. NVS

Heru Records, 1980, Meditative/New Age. Available from Heru Records, 845 Via de la Paz, Suite 454, Pacific Palisades, CA 90272 (LP or cassette $11.98 ppd.).

BLACK WOMAN
JUDY MOWATT

After years in mainstream reggae, Judy Mowatt, a Rastafarian woman who knows her own worth, has come out with her first solo album of six original songs. *Black Woman* is exciting reggae with a feminist slant, danceable, political, and, of course, spiritual. "Sisters' Chant" and "Strength to Go Through" offers women inspiration in shaping our personal and political futures. Judy advises the "Slave Queen" to "remove the shackles from your mind" and dedicates her recording to the remarkable strength and beauty of every Black woman. NVS

Shanachie Records, 1981, Reggae. Available from Shanachie Records, Dalebrook Park, Department R, Ho-Ho-Kus, NJ 07423 (LP or cassette $8.40 ppd.). Free catalogues of reggae, African, or folk music available upon request.

B'LIEVE I'LL RUN ON ... SEE WHAT THE END'S GONNA BE
SWEET HONEY IN THE ROCK

The spirit of Black women rings in the voices of Sweet Honey in the Rock. Their music is a stirring blend of a cappella vocal styles rooted in Black history. The voices of these five women are like the pipes of an organ; each has a unique tone color and spirit that is shaped and tuned to blend with the others, creating the sound of one instrument. The name Sweet Honey in the Rock is taken from the traditional spiritual that opens the album. It speaks of the range of colors worn by Black women: strength, consistency, warmth, and gentleness. As their voices weave through songs like the evocative "Dream Variations," set to a poem by Langston Hughes, and the classic "Are There Any Rights I'm Entitled To?" these colors are more readily perceived and understood. The quiet dignity and sincerity of Sweet Honey is always inspirational. AL

Redwood Records, 1978, Gospel. Available from Redwood Records (LP or cassette $9.98 ppd.).

CANTICLES OF LIGHT
CHARLIE MURPHY AND THE TOTAL EXPERIENCE GOSPEL CHOIR

Canticles of Light combines the ecstasy inherent in gospel music with rhythmic world fusion instrumentation. Listening to this tape will lift your spirits and your feet off the floor! It includes the rocking "We Remain Faithful," recorded live at the Prince of Peace Baptist Church, "Time to Love," a chant song written by poet Deena Metzger, and the Winter Solstice chant, "Light Is Returning." The message here is clearly hopeful, welcoming the dawning of a new worldview. PW

Out Front Music, 1984, Ritual/chant. Available from Meridian Distributors, P.O. Box 93458, Milwaukee, WI 53203, (800) 752-5437 (cassette $11.50 ppd.). Note: As the Sourcebook goes to press, this tape was not available from the distributor and may be going out of print.

Judy Mowatt. Courtesy of Shanachie Records.

CATCH THE FIRE
CHARLIE MURPHY

Recently re-released, *Catch the Fire* includes Charlie Murphy's classic "Burning Times," which has become an anthem in the Goddess movement. This song commemorates the resistance of Witches, women and men who chose to honor the Goddess and the Earth at a time when the wheels of patriarchal religion had set out to destroy the remnants of the Old Religion. The Goddess chant ("Isis, Astarte, Diana, Hecate . . ."), which serves as a refrain to the song, was written by poet-healer Deena Metzger and is well known in spirituality circles. "Mother Ocean," another beautiful and powerful song on the recording, celebrates our primal connection to the sea. A moving recording of progressive, gay, and neo-pagan themes. PW

Icebergg Records, 1986, Folk/ritual. Available from Meridian Distributors, P.O. Box 93458, Milwaukee, WI 53203, (800) 752-5437 (LP or cassette $11.50 ppd.).

CELEBRANT: HISTORICAL HARP VOLUME 1
THERESE SCHROEDER-SHEKER

Through her pioneering work with medieval music and historical harp, Therese Schroeder-Sheker has established a career as both a concert artist and a music scholar. On this magnificent recording, Therese performs medieval hymns, carols, dance-songs, antiphons, and ballads on seven harps and two psaltries built by Lynne Lewandowski. The wide diversity of timbres reflects the diversity of harp sounds typical of Romanesque, Gothic, Celtic, and early Renaissance music. Some compositions are accompanied by voice. This recording has a devotional quality to it, making it ideal for spiritual reflection and healing. PW

Lady Reason Records, 1984, Meditative/early music. Available from Lady Reason Records, P.O. Box 1911, Brattleboro, VT 05301 (LP or cassette $11.95 ppd.).

THE CHANGER AND THE CHANGED
CRIS WILLIAMSON

This is the best-selling record in the women's music business—with good reason. Cris Williamson has a great voice, sings with feeling, and writes music that speaks to all people. True to her reputation as the "spirit healer" of women's music, Cris will lighten your soul and warm your spirit. Her "Waterfall" ("Sometimes it takes a rainy day") fills up your heart until it's spilling over with smiles and laughter. This album also includes "Song of the Soul," "One of the Light," and "Sister." Olivia

Records has received thousands of letters over the years from people whose lives have been profoundly impacted by the deeply healing nature of these songs. NVS

Olivia Records, 1975, Folk/spiritual. Available from Olivia Records (LP or cassette $11.50 ppd., CD $15 ppd.).

CITY DOWN
CASSELBERRY-DUPREÉ

These two Black women form an artistic unit that is linked vocally, harmonically, and spiritually. Their music is a blend of reggae, gospel music, R&B, and African chants enriched by the group's unique interpretations. The anchor is J. Casselberry, whose crisp rhythm guitar chordings and almost basso vocal lines are the rock-steady strength under the flowering, spontaneous, punctuated, rastafied upper register of Jacque DuPreé. Add to this DuPreé's effective use of nontraditional vocal sounds ranging from wails and moans to clucks and warbles and it's easy to see why this group's sound is so appealing. Winner of the 1986 Best Reggae Album Award by the National Association of Independent Record Distributors and Manufacturers, *City Down* demonstrates the breadth of Casselberry-DuPreé's musical talents (omitting the customary "and" between their

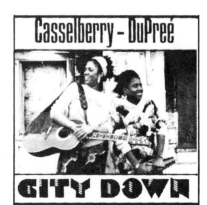

names is an expression of their unity). With an Opening and Closing Elegba, *City Down* is a ritual musical feast for the modern soul! AL/PW

Icebergg Records, 1986, Reggae/spiritual. Available from Meridian Distributors, P.O. Box 93458, Milwaukee, WI 53203, (800) 752-5437 (LP or cassette $10.50 ppd., CD $16.50 ppd.).

CRY OF RAMAH
COLLEEN FULMER AND MARTHA ANN KIRK

Cry of Ramah is a tape of songs and dances celebrating feminist biblical images of God. Colleen and Martha are affiliated with the Loretto Spirituality Network, a West Coast center for the Women-Church movement (see listing on page 208). Songs from *Cry of Ramah* have been sung at Women-Church gatherings around the country. Titles include: "Washerwoman God," "God Mother of Exiles," "La Mujer Biblica," "Ruah," "Blessed Is She." *Cry of Ramah*, a book of lyrics and dances choreographed by Sister Martha Ann Kirk, can also be ordered. PW

Loretto Spirituality Network, 1985. Christian feminist. Available from Loretto Spirituality Network, 529 Pomona Ave., Albany, CA 94706 (cassette $9.50 ppd., book $5 ppd.).

DANCING TOWARD THE ONE/ SACRED ROCK
GABRIELLE ROTH AND THE MIRRORS

Spirits fly to a new-wave beat with conscious lyrics! Gabrielle Roth is a dancer, composer, healer, choreographer, ritualist, and founder of The Moving Center in New York City. Each side of this recording is one long, extended sound piece to be danced, rocked, howled, and silently moved to alone or with others. Side 1, "Sing the Body," is a power chant, a rhythm ride taken by "devotees to a dancing god" drumming and dancing their way toward an unnamed shrine. The lead vocals invite you to "Get your mind in your feet/Get your body in the beat!" Side 2, "Can You See Me?" was created in a healing circle at The Moving Center as a dance meditation to be done in pairs. Find a partner and dance! PW

The Moving Center, 1982, Ritual/ dance. Available from The Gaia Catalogue Company (cassette $11.50 ppd.).

Dancing Toward The One
Gabrielle Roth and The Mirrors

DEEPENING

RUTH BARRETT AND CYNTIA SMITH

A beautiful record by priestesses Barrett and Smith, *Deepening* contains perhaps their most moving piece to date. "Allu Mari Mi Portati," written by Catherine Madsen, was the hymn sung by Italian women as they marched to their death in the sea in order to escape the Inquisi-

tion. Barrett and Smith's rendition is exquisite. "Song of the Wandering Aengus," a poem by W. B. Yeats and set to music by Ruth Barrett, is another gem, especially with the intertwining string trio that accompanies it. NVS

Icebergg Records, 1984, Folk. Available from Aeolus Music, 4111 Lincoln Blvd. #211, Marina del Rey, CA 90292 (LP or cassette $10 ppd.).

DON'T HOLD BACK

HOLLY NEAR

Holly Near is a versatile, dynamic performance artist who never allows her music to be categorized. *Don't Hold Back*, her latest release, is by far her most commercially accessible recording, but as always, her integrity and commitment to human rights and world peace remain uncompromising. Three songs spotlight her talents: "How Bold," an energetic, angry response to a casual sexual encounter, "In the Face," a love song set in the midst of war in Central America, and "Just a Plain and Simple Love Song," a gentle testament to the rewards of commitment in relationship. *Don't Hold Back* is personal, upbeat, and charged with en-

Earth Mother Lullabies: Volumes I and II © Earth Mother Productions, Inc., 1987.

ergy, but definitely not for the faint of heart. AO

Redwood Records, 1987, Pop/rock. Available from Redwood Records (LP or cassette $9.98 ppd., CD $14.98 ppd.).

EARTH MOTHER LULLABIES FROM AROUND THE WORLD: VOLUMES I & II

PAMALA BALLINGHAM

Lullabies are songs of peace, embodying our deepest hopes and dreams for our children. On the two volumes of *Earth Mother Lullabies*, Pamala Ballingham has gathered a collection of ancient, timeless lullabies that express the thread of human hope and longing lying within us all, regardless of the era or culture in which we live. Soothing vocals, harp, flute, and guitar will relax children and adults alike. On Volume I, songs from Latin American, Russian, Ethiopian, Jewish, Icelandic, and Appalachian traditions convey spiritual contentment and gentle, nurturing love to the sleeping child. Volume II continues to carry us through culture and time with ten beautiful melodies from South Africa, the Isle of Man, the Americas, Sweden, Slovakia, and the world's oldest piece of music, "Hymn to a Moongoddess" (1400 B.C.), translated from an ancient cuneiform tablet found in Ugarit near the Mediterranean Sea. Pamala's vocals are especially soothing and rhythmic on this beautiful and enchanting song from the very cradle of Western civilization. *Earth Mother Lullabies from Around the World* will evoke a tender heart—whether parent with child, lover with lover, or self with Self. PW

Earth Mother Productions, 1987, Children. Available from The Gaia Catalogue Company, (cassette $11.98 each ppd.). For wholesale inquiries contact Earth Mother Productions, Inc., P.O. Box 43204-W, Tucson, AZ 85733, (602) 575-5114.

FEEL SOMETHING DRAWING ME ON
SWEET HONEY IN THE ROCK

This collection of sacred songs, drawn from Christian, gospel, and African traditions, unabashedly inspires hope, celebration, and joy within the listener. Under the guiding spirit of Sweet Honey's founder, Bernice Johnson Reagon, the personal artistic stamp of the individual women members shines through each arrangement. The recording includes two songs of West African origin, "When I Die Tomorrow" and "Meyango." The arrangement of "Meyango" by member Aisha Kahlil, a student of African song and dance, is indicative of traditional African women's choral song style and uses the sounds of feet moving in a traditional African dance pattern. PW

Flying Fish Records, 1985, Gospel. Available from Flying Fish Records (LP or cassette $8.98 ppd.).

FIRE IN THE RAIN
HOLLY NEAR

Even though Holly Near's music is not specifically related to women's spirituality, her music has had a profound spiritual effect on many people. Since the mid-seventies she has, through her singing, songwriting, and political activism, been a leading spokeswoman for progressive beliefs and actions for social change. One of the founding mothers of women's music, Holly Near, as a sister and an artist, continues to inspire hope, vision, affirmation of womanstrength, courage, commitment, deep love, and faith in our political visions. *Fire in the Rain* is a lyrically rich blend of some of Holly's most well-known love songs and forceful political ballads, including "Foolish Notion," "Voices," "Ain't No Where You Can Run," "Wrap the Sun Around You," "Golden Thread," and "Once or Twice." Sparkling with tight arrangements,

polished harmonies, and emotive delivery, Holly is joined on vocals and instrumentations by friends Cris Williamson, Nancy Vogl, Vickie Randle and June Millington. A personal favorite of mine. PW

Redwood Records, 1981, Pop. Available from Redwood Records (LP or cassette $9.98 ppd.).

FIRELIGHT
DEBBIE FIER

Firelight is a New Age album that offers audiences a different look at the talents of jazz musician Debbie Fier. The completely instrumental work highlights Fier's more introspective side as a composer. It offers a well-balanced blend of comfortable moods and arrangements that are highlighted by Fier's strong keyboard technique. She is backed by understated percussion (much of which she plays herself), strings (played on synthesizer by Mary Watkins), and soothing woodwind arrangements. AL

Ladyslipper Records, 1985, Jazz/New Age. Available from Ladyslipper (LP or cassette $9.95 ppd.).

GIVE YOURSELF TO LOVE
KATE WOLF

Kate Wolf's original songs are a reflection of her spiritual search as a woman in the eighties and the Earth-honoring social movements of the last two decades. Her folksinging has a softness around the edges that speaks of the strength of a woman. This double LP, recorded live, is a compilation of well-known folk favorites and some of Kate's originals. The title cut is an admonition to make love our greatest teacher, while "Medicine Wheel" is an American Indian invocation of the four directions. Also includes "Peaceful Easy Feeling," "Who Knows Where the Time Goes," and a live version of "Redtail Hawk." NVS

Kaleidoscope Records, 1983, Country/folk. Available from The Gaia Catalogue Company (double LP or cassette $15.45 ppd.).

GOLD IN CALIFORNIA
KATE WOLF

Gold in California is a double recording, a retrospective of Kate Wolf's music from 1975–1985. This compilation captures the very best of Kate's prolific career before her death from leukemia in December 1986. For those who have never heard Kate's music before, *Gold in California* is the best place to begin. Kate's deep, soothing voice emanates straight from the soul, and her words evoke stark, peaceful images of rural life and intimacy between friends and lovers. *Gold in California* emphasizes Kate's later work. These are complex songs that tell of a contemporary woman's spiritual quest, evoke the wisdom of Native American shamanism, and invite communion with Nature as a source of spiritual sustenance. I hope *Gold in California* will encourage those who don't know Kate's work to explore the rich legacy of music she left behind, for this woman's talent is destined to become legendary. As she sings to us in "Brother Warrior": "At this time when the earth is waking / to the dawn of another age, / I tell you there is no reason to be afraid. / We are crying for a vision / that all living things can share / And Those Who Care are with us everywhere." AO/ PW

Kaleidoscope Records, 1986, Folk. Available from The Gaia Catalogue Company (double LP or cassette $15.45 ppd.).

Kate Wolf. Photo © Art Rogers, Point Reyes, 1984.

REMEMBERING KATE WOLF
JANUARY 27, 1942–DECEMBER 10, 1986

BROOKE MEDICINE EAGLE

I sit here today looking out over the beauty of Mother Earth, listening to Kate Wolf's wonderful voice on tape and giving thanks for her in my life. My mind wanders to a time when I was feeling like a lost soul and she welcomed me to her home, giving me her beautiful studio in the tall redwoods as my home for a time of healing and renewal.

We had been like sisters since the first time she contacted me personally, asking me to perform her wedding ceremony to this wonderful man, Terry. Although I couldn't participate in that happy occasion, we touched over the airways frequently from then on, sharing the joys and challenges of our similar pasts and presents—the fun of country music, the beauty of our Native American ancestral ways, our commitment to a good life for all Earth's children, and life "on the road." In the mail one day I received a tape of many of her new songs, with the title in her handwriting, *Songs for the Eagle's Flight.* I loved the music, of course, and thought it was the latest album title. Only later did I discover that it was something she had put together just for my travels down the road—for *this* Eagle's flight—another gifting from her generous heart! So it was a special joy when we came together in the "golden rolling hills of California" those few precious weeks at her studio. We decided upon an exchange: I needed coaching on putting the words of my poetry to music, and Kate wanted to work on her body. We wrote a song together and played music for each other, giving me the beginning of what I needed. And I gave Kate lessons in Feldenkrais and taught her an ancient art called Chinese Wands that would help her keep fit and relaxed on the road. During this time she spoke of her experience of "never having come completely into her physical body," never having *really* committed to being here as a physical being. We talked of her need to make that commitment clearly and strongly for her own well-being although she did not seem ready to do that then. Again, when we spoke after her discovery of the leukemia, she knew that same issue was present in more urgent form. As Kate wrote and sung, "In China and a woman's heart, there are places no one knows." And from that place in her heart, her choice was to move on from this life into what my people sometimes call "the summer country"—to another step on her special path of growth and love.

As I think back on her life—of her filling our lives with song, of the benefits she continually gave for Native American causes, and the commitment of her life as a give-away of beauty to All-Her-Relations— I feel blessed that Kate chose to stay with us for the wonderful years that she did. For one who was not totally committed to this form of life, she gave more than many of us who will be around for a long while. Although I know we miss her, I also know that when I close my eyes and touch the larger Circle, I can hear one angel still singing out to us the Medicine Wheel Song of Life. Wherever we are, let us sing out harmony to that same joyful song!

Brooke Medicine Eagle, native Earthkeeper, healer, poet, and songwriter, wrote this remembrance of her spiritual sister, folksinger Kate Wolf, in March 1987 from Sky Lodge, Montana, where Brooke currently lives.

Sweet Honey in the Rock. Courtesy of Flying Fish Records and Roadworks.

GOOD NEWS
SWEET HONEY IN THE ROCK

Good News, recorded live at a Sweet Honey concert in Washington, D.C., features one of the finest, most breathtaking pieces of sound improvisation on record! "Breaths" is a prayer to the ancestors, a circular sharing of female voice-wisdom, an invocation to the spirits of Earth-things: "Listen more often to things, than to deeds,'tis the ancestors' birth when the fire's voice is heard . . . those who have died have never never left, the dead are not under the Earth . . . they are in the groaning woods . . . they are in the moaning rocks . . . the dead have a pact with the living . . . they are in the waiting child, they are with us in the home . . .'tis the ancestors' birth in the voice of the water. . . ." Includes "Echo," "Biko," and "On Children" (from the poem by Kahlil Gibran). PW

Flying Fish Records, 1981, Gospel. Available from Flying Fish Records (LP or cassette $8.98 ppd.).

HAWKS AND HERONS
LORRAINE DUISIT

This album may not strictly belong in a list of women's spiritual music, but the feeling for the Earth demonstrated by this member of the West Virginia group Trapezoid is extremely deep and her music moves me. Expanding on her renowned Appalachian style, Lorraine Duisit makes her first foray into a lyrical jazz style. Her light soprano voice is not what we normally associate with jazz, but it is perfect for this album of introspective acoustic music. "Wild Bird in a Purple Plum" sets my heart to dancing, and both "Forgive the Cactus" and "Redwood Evergreen" convey the beauty of life in its many manifestations. NVS

Flying Fish Records, 1983, Folk/traditional. Available from Flying Fish Records (LP only, $8.98 ppd.).

HEALING MUSIC

JOANNA BROUK

Healing Music appeals to an ancient female place within each of us, the source of our power to heal. Joanna Brouk's work incorporates the character of silence as a major element of the musical healing experience. Used by many people in the healing professions, this recording guides the listener in an awareness of the silence within, making it ideal for massage, birthing, visualization, lovemaking, rituals. Side 1 consists of all-original piano and synthesizer arrangements; side 2 consists of flute improvisations. Aptly titled, *Healing Music* is soothing and deeply healing. PW

Hummingbird Records, 1981, Meditative/New Age. Available from The Gaia Catalogue Company (cassette $11.50 ppd.).

IN SEARCH OF OUR NATIVE ROOTS

THE CIRCLE

A singing tape of Native American chants with drum and guitar accompaniment by The Circle, a group of women and men who have done ritual together for ten years. Many of these songs are well-known favorites of ritual groups, spiritual circles, and political actions around the world. These chants are sung in a way that enables the listener to easily learn them and to teach them to others. Spiritually uplifting, they're an excellent resource for group work, morning prayer, children's circles. Includes "I Am a Circle," "We All Fly Like Eagles," "The Earth is Our Mother," "I Love the People," "Wearing My Long-Winged Feathers," and "Yani Yoni," a song sung by midwives to birthing women. PW

Acoustic Medicine Productions, 1980, Ritual/chant. Available from Acoustic Medicine Productions, P.O. Box 1082-WS, Ojai, CA 93023 (cassette $9 ppd.).

INVOCATION/ BETWEEN THE WORLDS

HOLLY TANNEN

Holly Tannen mesmerizes with the sweet sound of her dulcimer and her strong folk voice. Besides being an accomplished musician, she is also a dedicated folklorist who spent five years living in the British Isles researching the Pagan ceremonial origins of traditional music. Her lyrics, often tinged with wry humor, celebrate the blessedness of Earth and the magical life. With the exception of a single guitar accompaniment on "Cutty Wren" and vocal harmonies on "King Orfeo" and "All Among the Barley," *Invocation* (Kicking Mule, 1983) is a wonderful offering of Holly and her dulcimer alone. Especially moving is "Spirits," the chilling a cappella invocation of the four directions by a Witch condemned to the fire. *Between the Worlds* (Gold Leaf, 1985) brings together two streams of Holly's musical style. The recording is filled with folk ballads about the everyday lives of women

and men as well as songs that evoke images of the sacred and the Otherworld domain of Nature spirits. One song, "Through All the World Below," can best be described as a benediction to the Earth—a mystical, sensual song of praise to the Mother. NVS/PW

Folk/traditional. Available from Holly Tannen, P.O. Box 7012, Berkeley, CA 94707 (cassette $10 ppd.).

Cover artwork
© Linda Ware,
1984.

INVOCATION TO ISIS: ORIGINAL HARP AND FLUTE MUSIC

MELISSA MORGAN AND DIANE CLARKE

A rare blend of feminine sounds and feelings, *Invocation to Isis* transmits the delight of two women creating beautiful spiritual music together. Melissa's harp with Diana's flute plus the additional embellishment of serendipity—a baby's laughter, crickets, Tibetan bells, gently lapping ocean waves—evoke magical moods and elfin, playful feelings. The compositions ("Initiation," "Madonna," "Diana," "Gypsy," "Isis") have been collaboratively written and invoke the symbols and inner visions of women's spiritual journeying. PW

Melissa Morgan, 1984, Meditative/New Age. Available from The Gaia Catalogue Company (cassette only, $11.50 ppd.).

LIFELINE

RONNIE GILBERT AND HOLLY NEAR

Lifeline is one of two live recordings made by Ronnie and Holly of their three-year musical collaboration, and what a glorious achievement! Ronnie Gilbert, who had kept a low profile since The Weavers made their indelible mark on American folk history in the fifties, gracefully augments Holly's magnanimous stage presence. The blending of their voices, one alto and one soprano, creates a harmony rich with vibrato and feeling. Highlights of the recording are a duet of the hymnlike "Hay Una Mujer," tributes to Harriet Tubman, Stephen Biko, and Sacco and Vanzetti, and an updated version of "No More Genocide." The tone of *Lifeline* is reverent and celebratory; the songs are timely, uplifting, and resound with a profound sense of people's history; Ronnie and Holly, great performers respectively, sound stupendous together. What more could you ask for? AO

Redwood Records, 1983, Fold/pop. Available from Redwood Records (LP or cassette $9.98 ppd.).

LIVE FROM THE VERY FRONT ROW

BETSY ROSE

Betsy Rose sings from the heart— not necessarily about strictly spiritual subjects. Playing a great gospel/ jazz piano and a very good folk guitar, Betsy has a rich voice that speaks to the "Love at the Core" of our lives as women. She is a dynamic per-

former and a warm, compassionate person, both of which are amply demonstrated here. Listening to this live performance moved me to tears, the healing tears of self-knowledge and self-love. NVS

Redwood Records, 1984, Pop-jazz. Available from Redwood Records (LP or cassette $9.98 ppd.).

MARY LOU'S MASS

MARY LOU WILLIAMS

Mary Lou Williams was truly a jazz great. Like her career, *Mary Lou's Mass* spans the entire history of Black music from old-time spirituals to gospel to bebop to rock music, and even includes a very difficult avant-

LUMIÈRE

CRIS WILLIAMSON

A delightful science fantasy fable written, narrated, and sung by Cris Williamson. X-Ray Ted and his dog Sirius meet up with some real stars (and I don't mean the Hollywood variety) and eventually save them from a black hole. Ted and Sirius are led to "enlightenment" by his mentor, Glory. Many surprises await the big and little children who discover this record. It has great sound effects and seven rather lightweight songs by Cris. Comes with a beautiful full-color book illustrated by Viido Polikarpus. NVS

Pacific Cascade Records, 1982, Children. Available from Pacific Cascade Records, 47534 McKenzie Hwy., Vida, OR 97488-9707 (LP or cassette $10.98 ppd.).

garde choral piece. It is a celebration of the joy and pain of life using the traditional elements of the mass ("Kyrie," "Gloria," etc.) in English translation, plus several sections that are more reminiscent of Afro-American culture: "Praise the Lord," "Old Time Spiritual," "People in Trouble." A powerful piece of music. NVS

Mary, 1975, Jazz/liturgical. Available from Ladyslipper (LP only, $9.70 ppd.).

MEG AND CRIS AT CARNEGIE HALL
MEG CHRISTIAN AND CRIS WILLIAMSON

Imagine the surprise of New York music critics when Meg Christian and Cris Williamson, two "unknowns," packed Carnegie Hall in 1982 and brought the house down! This momentous event, commemorating Olivia Records' tenth anniversary, was made into a two-record set for all of us who weren't there to treasure the memory. Meg and Cris, backed up by Linda Tillery and Vicki Randle, are in glorious voice on this collection. The recording contains old-time favorites from each of their performing careers as well as spirit-filled duets. What makes this recording so very special is the warmth and magic that binds these two gifted women together musically and spiritually. Listening to Cris and Meg at Carnegie Hall, it's hard not to let the song of the soul fill your life. AO

Olivia Records, 1983, Pop/rock. Available from Olivia Records (LP or cassette $11.50 ppd.).

MICHIGAN LIVE '85
MICHIGAN WOMYN'S MUSIC FESTIVAL

Michigan Live '85 captures the fervor and the magic that makes women's music festivals the landmark events that they are in the lives of so many

women. This two-record set includes live performances by Kay Gardner, DEUCE, Chévère, Ferron, Rhiannon, Linda Tillery, Holly Near, Casselberry-Dupreé, Ronnie Gilbert, Barbara Higbie, Lucy Blue Tremblay, and Teresa Trull. Every genre of music is represented, from reggae to classical piano, from folk to modern jazz, proving once again that women's music defies categorizing. Especially worth hearing are duets between Holly Near and Rhiannon, Ferron and Lucy Blue Tremblay, and Barbara Higbie and Teresa Trull. A celebration of the many talents in women's music! AO

August Night, 1986. Available from Horizon Distribution, P.O. Box 85, Cambridge, MA 02140, (617) 661-0554 (double LP or cassette $16.73 ppd.).

MOODS AND RITUALS: MEDITATIONS FOR SOLO FLUTES
KAY GARDNER

The flute has an inherently tranquil and healing sound, especially when played by a musician as talented as Kay Gardner. On this recording, Kay has applied her research into the healing power of music to create four long meditative improvisations for solo flute. In four distinct modes (or scales), each improvisation is played on a different type of flute, yet each is calming in its own way. In the last and longest piece, "Soul Flight," Kay

uses an echoplex, which plays back what the musician has just played, and thus creates the effect of a flute duet (or trio or quartet or . . .). A beautiful album. NVS

Even Keel Records, 1980, Meditative/New Age. Available from Ladyslipper (LP or cassette $9.95 ppd.).

MOONCIRCLES
KAY GARDNER

Kay Gardner's first recording, *Mooncircles*, is an eclectic combination of relaxed instrumental jazz, Beethoven (a flute improvisation of "Moonlight Sonata"), and feminist/Goddess songs ("Touching Souls," "Inner Mood II") sung by Kay. On "Lunamuse" Kay's exquisite flute playing teams up with the equally marvelous guitar work of Meg Christian. Other instruments include violins, viola, cello, piano, and a variety of percussion. NVS

Urana Records, 1975, Meditative/New Age. Available from Ladyslipper (LP or cassette $9.95 ppd.).

MOTHER'S SPIRITUAL
LAURA NYRO

On *Mother's Spiritual*, the inimitable Laura Nyro has created an album of woman/Nature-centered songs using the rock-ballad style she's best known for. The songs on this album inspire women in their daily struggles—as working mothers and as women working for peace and for equality. She affirms the Goddess in each one of us, especially on such cuts as "A Wilderness," "Trees of the Ages," "Sophia (Goddess of Wisdom Serene)," and "Mother's Spiritual," the title piece, a poignantly reverent song in honor of her mother. *Mother's Spiritual* deserves recognition as the first feminist recording on a major record label. PW

Columbia Records, 1984, Pop-folk. This recording is out of circulation. Look for it in used record stores.

SPIRITUALITY IN A FEMINIST WORLD

LAURA NYRO

Laura Nyro is a singer, composer, and pioneer in the field of contemporary music. Mother's Spiritual, *her most recent recording, released on the Columbia label, is one of the strongest statements on spirituality and feminism to come out of a major recording company. In this article, excerpted from a story she wrote for* Woman of Power *magazine, Laura reveals her passion for Nature and her inspiration as a woman artist rooted in Goddess spirituality.*

Do I consider myself a spiritual woman? Maybe I should say I'm a spirited woman. If you mention the word spirituality—I may think "boring and corrupt." If you say feminist spirituality or green spirituality—I'm interested and I trust it as heartfelt toward the planet. The music of *Mother's Spiritual* refers to my spirit and to the spirit of life—all of life—including sexuality, religion, and romance. The personal meaning spirituality has to me is in many ways the reverse of the world's meaning which teaches that light is good—dark is bad; male is leadership—female is not; god above—devil below. It's all disconnected. After you cast off these notions about yourself and life, you find that spirituality is about joy, connection and nature. As a kind of wild earthy woman I sometimes feel more in common with the trees around my house than with the society I live in.

I always saw songwriting as part of the mysteries; like a natural force or something romantic in nature. It could be the way the spring wind wraps around you or stirs something inside of you or an incident of joy or pain. From these experiences I would feel inspired to write music. As I'm working, elemental principles like harmony and dissonance, structure and variation, are important. I've always experienced the beginning of a song as coming from the wild—and inside of that wildness is a music intelligence. Formwise, my songs that are influenced by tree environments follow the energies of outreaching branches; whereas my city songs bounce off walls, streets and sky-scrapers rhythmically and emotionally.

For me, work, nature and spirituality are inseparable. A pattern on a wall that contains light, dark and movement can teach music. On some level, as I write a song it's just a song. But I'm also defining who I am—as a woman—and at the moment—and at the same time I'm connecting with my wild romantic home—the moon and the stars.

When I was writing the music for *Mother's Spiritual*, I felt so close to nature. The trees were this tangible reality of peaceful co-existence. I wrote a green love song called "Trees of the Ages" and also "Talk to a Greentree"—which is about talking to some higher spirit when you feel trapped in a draining situation. Along with the music, I was also raising a small child. So my spirituality became very elfin. I could feel the spirit of nature and elves, and I'll always feel that anytime I'm around the trees.

Certain primal experiences in my life—like birth and death—led me lyrically to a song I wrote called "Late for Love." After writing the song I realized that it was made up of all questions—with some new answers. That song carries my spirituality—not a religion that's handed to you—but a personal meaning.

One of my memories is of the house my mother built. In my early twenties, I made a lot of fast money when my music became known. I gave some money to my mother to find herself some land and build a house of her own. Eventually, she designed and built a beautiful country nest for her family. I remember the downstairs had an eat-in kitchen with red dishes, a living room with high cathedral windows looking out on the trees, and the bedrooms were up an open stair-case. Well, my mother had this window in her bedroom that she designed; it had no glass, just light wood shutters that opened on the inside of the house. It had a view of the kitchen and living room below, and the kids' rooms on the side. Sometimes she'd look out for a minute in the morning or evening; she seemed to be looking at her people and her things and at a home she built and loved. The spirit of that window never really left me. She died unexpectedly a year after she built the house. She was forty-eight. After that, I clearly knew what was and wasn't gray in the world.

Sometimes spirituality dreams into the mystic, the mysteries, into birth, death and nature and matters of the heart. If feminist politics gives you a framework for a decent world to live in, then feminist spirituality fills it in and enriches it. Other than a faith that you get from your own meaningful life experience, Goddess is the only lusty joyful spirituality I know of that empowers feminism. Goddess, who is the colors of the earth, trees, moon and stars, transcends race and age and reflects all. A spirituality that is in harmony with the cycles of your life, that teaches you to love the cycles of your life, is inspiration in a feminist world.

From *Woman of Power* magazine, Issue Two: "Envisioning a Feminist World," Summer 1985 (see listing on pg. 127)

Spirit Spiral
© Jennifer Badger Sultan, 1986. Oil on canvas, 36" × 36".

MUSIC FOR THE MASS BY NUN COMPOSERS

ISABELLA LEONARDA AND HILDEGARD OF BINGEN

Isabella Leonarda's "Missa Prima" (first mass) is a beautiful example of seventeenth-century Italian sacred music. Its composer was a nun who seems to have been intensely devoted to the Virgin Mary, since almost all of her music carries a double dedication, one to the Virgin as well as the more usual dedication to a highly placed living person. Her mass is Baroque music of fluid beauty. This album also contains a "Kyrie" by Hildegard of Bingen, an eleventh-century abbess from Germany, with an all-woman chorus. The album insert contains an article about music in Italian convents, detailing the musical achievements of women composers who were members of religious orders. NVS

Leonarda Productions, 1982, Classical/liturgical. Available from Leonarda Productions, Inc., P.O. Box 124, Radio City Station, New York, NY 10101 (LP only, $10.95 ppd.).

WOMEN COMPOSERS: A NEW AND REVOLUTIONARY BEAUTY

NANCY FIERRO

When most of us think of nuns, our image is of women committed to lives of service. This is certainly true of Nancy Fierro. What makes her unique, however, is that most of those whom she serves are no longer living. Her work involves uncovering the music of women composers long buried by patriarchal culture. She recorded one of the first compilations of women's music (Premier Recorded Performances of Keyboard Works by Women, Avant 1012). A member of the Sisters of St. Joseph of Carondelet, pianist Nancy Fierro combines performing, lecturing, and teaching with an internal pursuit of the spiritual dimensions of her life.

I was six years old and taking piano lessons. I loved to play music from my favorite piano book which was filled with pictures of the masters. Photos and drawings sparked my imagination about the great composers of the past. But even at six, I remember thinking as I saw page after page of bearded men, "Why aren't any women here?" I buried the question until years later when I encountered a remarkable piano piece by a contemporary Polish composer, Grazyna Bacewicz. Her music surfaced my childhood question and started me on a serious search for women composers of the past and present. The names of these women are rarely to be found in the text of music histories; rather, they are hidden in footnotes and appendices. Along with other musicians and researchers, I looked for manuscripts and scores in libraries, private collections, and stores selling out-of-print music. Unlike the music of their male counterparts, women's music has had no widespread publication.

As the scattered information is woven into a whole historical fabric, we discover that women have been active as composers and instrumentalists since the Egyptian era in 2500 B.C. Many of these composers have been forgotten beyond their lifetimes—some never taken seriously, still others thwarted by a society that excluded them from its traditional institutions of musical training and education. For the most part, women of the past lived and worked in cultures which did not value their involvement in music.

This societal attitude can be summarized in the words Abraham Mendelssohn spoke to his daughter, Fanny, when she expressed a desire to work seriously in the field of music: "Prepare more earnestly and eagerly for your real calling, the only calling of a young woman—I mean the state of a housewife." Fanny's grandfather reinforced this admonition with one of his own: "Moderate learning becomes a lady, but not scholarship." Fanny had received the same musical education from her mother as that given her famous brother, Felix. At thirteen, she surprised her father by playing Bach's 24 Preludes and Fugues from memory as a birthday gift. Even her brother Felix acknowledged her the better pianist. Yet her father never accorded her the travel expense he gave to her brother. Her works were not permitted submission for publication until years later. She could play in public only occasionally for charity benefits. In letters written to a friend, Fanny expresses her frustration at the lack of support for her musical ambitions: "If nobody ever offers an opinion, or takes the slightest interest in one's production, one loses in time not only all pleasure in them, but all power of judging their value." She later observes dolefully, "Not a soul dances to my piping."

Throughout history, women generally experienced grave restrictions in opportunities for artistic development. Taking these limits into account, it is surprising that women wrote music at all. Yet some women reached prominence in their own lifetimes. On what, then, did their creative musicianship depend? As research continues to unmask the stories and reclaim the music of women composers, it is becoming evident that the women who have made vital contributions have one thing in common: they lived in a particular context which stimulated and supported creativity. Whenever creative channels are open to women, they can be found among the significant contributors to their culture. Evidence exists, for example, that women who lived the monastic lifestyle in the medieval period received extensive training and experience in sacred music. One of the tasks of the abbess was to provide hymns, songs and canticles for her nuns to use during the liturgical seasons.

Abbess Hildegard of Bingen, a mystic, visionary and author of scientific works, achieved a notable work in her "Symphony of the Harmony of the Heavenly Revelations," a collection of seventy-seven liturgical songs for which she wrote both music and text, arranged according to subject matter. Hildegard claims she received her artistic ideas from Divine revelation and that her songs express Divine mysteries in musical form. Some music scholars consider her *Ordo Vir-*

tutum an important step in the development of musical drama. Gratifying balance between spontaneous melody and skillful variation techniques characterizes her music. Her own awareness of feminine creativity reveals itself in her texts about women saints. These consistently proclaim the radiant and charismatic ministry of women.

A multitude of creative women in music stand out in the span of the centuries. As interest in the cultural contributions of women rises, the faces of these women emerge from the shadows of history and their music echoes in recital halls everywhere. Both in the United States and Europe, women's music has attracted major attention. In the last fifteen years a fanfare of reprints, publications and recordings of women's music heralds a "Period of Reclamation."

As musicians, and as women, we build toward a future in which society will cherish creative potential in all people. That day will free into the world new and revolutionary beauty.

This article first appeared in *Creation* magazine, January/February 1986 (see listing on page 118). Nancy Fierro's cassette recording of piano works by women, *The Romance of Women's Music*, is available from Carondelet Productions, 11999 Chalon Rd., Los Angeles, CA 90049 ($10 ppd.).

MUSIC OF THE ROLLING WORLD
RUTH BARRETT AND CYNTIA SMITH

Barrett and Smith's second recording, *Music of the Rolling World*, includes love songs, legends ("Unicorns," "Faerie's Love Song"), songs of women's lives ("The Broomfield Hill," "The Weaver and the Factory Girl"), and invocations of the cyclic nature of Mother Earth, all in the Celtic folk style of the British Isles. As with their other recordings, this album is exquisitely produced and features the traditional instruments of Britain: the dulcimer, psaltery, harp, cello, and violin. NVS

Kicking Mule Records, 1982, Folk/ traditional. Available from Aeolus Music, 4111 Lincoln Blvd. #211, Marina del Rey, CA 90292, (213) 851-3201, (LP or cassette $10 ppd.).

NEW GOODBYES, OLD HELLOS
CLAUDIA SCHMIDT

A wonderful recording of traditional folk and original compositions from a spirited, thoughtful Midwestern woman's perspective. Claudia Schmidt sings complex, lyric poetry while accompanying herself on pianolin, dulcimer, and guitar. Claudia's clear, soaring voice, resonant with gospel influence, will stay with you long after the music stops. A written review can't begin to describe Claudia's energizing talent or her charisma as a performer. Music lovers are urged to find out for themselves. AO

Flying Fish Records, 1983, Folk. Available from Flying Fish Records (LP or cassette $8.98 ppd.).

NEW MUSIC FOR THE ELECTRONIC AND RECORDED MEDIA
VARIOUS ARTISTS

Several of the pieces on this anthology are intended for healing, meditative purposes. Annea Lockwood's "World Rhythms" is a powerful recording of real-life sounds accompanied by a large gong struck infrequently. Megan Roberts's "I Could Sit Here All Day" has the driving, drumming energy of an African ritual punctuated by the wailing of two male voices. And Ruth Anderson's "Points" has a wonderfully relaxing and healing effect on the listener. Even Laurie Spiegel's "Appalachian Grove" and Johanna Beyer's "Music of the Spheres," although not specifically written to induce deeper states of consciousness, would be appropriate for trance work. This album of recorded and electronic music also contains two short cuts by Laurie Anderson. NVS

Pauline Oliveros, 1977, Ritual/new music. Available from Pauline Oliveros Publications, P.O. Box 1456, Canal St. Station, New York, NY 10013, (212) 219-0615.

ONE FINE DAY/TAKE THE POWER
KAY WEAVER

One Fine Day and *Take the Power* are noteworthy both for Kay Weaver's polished, bluesy style and dynamite voice, plus the fact that the title songs are spiritually inspired feminist music videos (see listings on pages 251 and 254)! A mega-talented singer, songwriter, musician, and filmmaker, Kay makes music that celebrates women's contributions to culture. She invites women to assume roles of leadership and responsibility in the world and to "take the power" for the survival of the planet. Songs like "No Turning Back," "Lay Your Burden Down," and both of the title cuts attest to Kay's faith in a feminist future. When life gets you down, turn to Kay Weaver for hope and renewal. AO

Circe Records, 1984/1987, Pop. Available from Circe Records, 256 S. Robertson Blvd., Beverly Hills, CA 90211 (LP or cassette $10 each ppd.).

THE PATIENCE OF LOVE
CATHERINE MADSEN

Catherine Madsen writes beautiful vocal music in a medieval folk style, using woman-identified, feminist lyrics ("My skin, my bones, my heretic heart / Are my authority"). Although Catherine's musicianship is not al-

ways of professional quality, the music itself carries us with it. Includes "Kore," "The Unwilling Bride," and "Allu Mari Mi Portati," the hymn of Italian women during the fifteenth and seventeenth centuries who marched to their death in the sea rather than face the flame for their Witchcraft. NVS

Wormwood Productions, 1982, Folk/ traditional. Available from Wormwood Productions, Box 6167, East Lansing, MI 48826 (LP or cassette $10 ppd.).

The Patience of Love
CATHERINE MADSEN
with The Greater Lansing Spinsters Guild

THE POWER OF MY LOVE FOR YOU
SUSAN SAVELL

"Keep simple ceremonies / Follow the quest / Bring crystals and flowers To the Sea Mother's Breast / The Earth is in ruin / She calls for attention / Lay your hands on Her body / And release all the tensions of hate and neglect / Balance, balance, balance the energies of life with love!" *(Susan Savell, "Simple Ceremonies").*

Susan Savell is the minister of The Peace Church in Portland, Maine, a spiritual community open to women, men, and children that offers services in Judeo-Christian, Native

American, meditation, and feminist traditions. For fifteen years, in her careers, both as an ordained minister and a performing artist, Susan has been integrating feminine images of sacred reality into her art and ministry. *The Power of My Love for You*, her long-awaited first recording, is a musical feast. From the Native American drumbeats invoking our powers to heal the Earth to lyrics addressing the tender concerns of our everyday lives, Susan's richly-timbered voice inspires and empowers us to live from our hearts and to carry on our vision of a world of peace and social justice. Drawing on a wide range of musical genres—pop, rock, blues, gospel, and jazz—*The Power of My Love for You* features Mary Watkins on piano, Rhiannon and Linda Tillery on supporting vocals, and a talented chorus of backup singers and musicians. "Simple Ceremonies" is just one of the many songs you will want to play over and over and over again on this recording. Highly recommended! PW

For information on The Peace Church and booking inquiries for Susan's spiritual healing workshops and concerts write: Heartlight House Music, P.O. Box 253, Biddeford Pool, ME 04006, or call (207) 282-0752. Available through Ladyslipper (LP or cassette $10 ppd.).

Courtesy of Heartlight House Music. Cover photo by Irene Young, cover design by Laura Parker, 1986.

Cover artwork
Green Tara
© Lisa Thiel,
1986.

PRAYERS FOR THE PLANET
LISA THIEL

Prayers for the Planet, the second recording of original "channeled songs" by Lisa Thiel, awakens the heart at the core of Womanspirit. These songs to the Goddess are not just listened to but experienced in the body. Blending symbols and myths of the Sacred Feminine from both Eastern and Western Indian spiritual traditions, Lisa's music is a unique synthesis of ancestral memory and contemporary women's spirituality. I am aware of no other musical recording that offers such a wealth of women's myths in song. From the East: "White Tara Prayer," "Green Tara Prayer," "Song to Inanna," "Lotus Goddess." From the West: "Rainbow Woman," "Cornmother Chant," "Song to the Grandmothers." *Prayers for the Planet* is dedicated "to the healing of our selves, so that we may begin to heal each other, and the Earth who is our Mother." PW

Sacred Dreams Productions, 1986,

Ritual/chants. Available from The Gaia Catalogue Company (cassette only, $11.50 ppd.). Wholesale inquiries welcome.

QUARTET FOR BRASS, MOMENTI, MISSA BREVIS
VIVIAN FINE

Vivian Fine is an excellent composer who has been winning awards for the past twenty years. Her *Missa Brevis* is a "personal version of the Mass," according to the composer. Employing a shifting tonal center, nine of the mass's ten movements contrast the exquisitely close, plaintive harmonies of the mezzo-soprano soloist (on four separate tracks of tape) with the dark tones of the four cellos. In contrast, the "Lacrymosa" uses only the high tones of the cellos in ululations reminiscent of the weeping implied by the title. This is ritual music with an unexaggerated but definite sense of drama. The "Dies Irae," for instance, abstracts the most salient qualities of the same movement from Berlioz's *Requiem for the Dead* and compresses them into a more modern but nevertheless just-as-affecting version. NVS

Composers Recordings, Inc., 1982, Ritual music/classical. Available from Composers Recordings, Inc., 170 W. 74th St., New York, NY 10023 (LP only, $9.98 ppd.).

RITUAL SONGS
EMILY MARIENTHAL, JANE DE JONGHE, TERRI KOSMICKI, AND JENI SHRAISHUHN

A special collection of familiar chant songs that celebrate birth, life, womanhood, and the greatness within each of us. Sung in simple yet powerful harmonies by four women of the Colorado Midwives Association (CMA), the tape was created to be used for ceremonies and gatherings as well as private meditations, strengthening, and healing. Fourteen songs in all, many well known from women's spirituality circles, include: "Listen to My Heartsong," "I Am the Circle," "Earth, Water, Fire, Air," "May the Blessing of God Rest Upon You." Proceeds benefit CMA, a non-profit organization dedicated to providing better birth experiences through home birth services. PW

Ritual Songs, 1983, Ritual/chants. Available from Ritual Songs, Salina Star Route—Gold Hill, Boulder, CO 80302 (cassette only, $9.50 ppd.).

SEAPEACE
GEORGIA KELLY

A soothing, meditational recording using Eastern and Western musical idioms (ragas, Greek modes) by New Age harpist and composer Georgia Kelly. *Seapeace* is Georgia's original recording on her own label, Heru Records, which she founded in order to create and distribute music that has a healing effect on the mind, body, and spirit. Her music provides the mind with a welcome respite from the ever-present sounds and actions of our daily lives. The blend of harp and electronic violin in *Seapeace* creates a tidal ebb-and-flow spaciousness in which it is easy to lose oneself. Includes "Nilapadmam (Blue Lotus)," "Chinese Sunrise," and "Aeolian Temple Music," based on an ancient Greek mode. NVS

Heru Productions, 1978, Meditative/ New Age. Available from Heru Pro- *ductions, 845 Via de la Paz, Suite 454, Pacific Palisades, CA 90272 (LP or cassette $11.98 ppd.).*

SECRETS FROM THE STONE
JUDITH PINTAR

For anyone who fell under the spell of *The Mists of Avalon* this tape is the perfect accompaniment. Judith Pintar is a superb harpist and a professional storyteller who has apprenticed herself to an Ojibwe medicine woman/storyteller. Pintar skillfully combines her training in both these areas on this recording of all-original music. *Secrets of the Stone* is a blend of Celtic, traditional, and New Age sounds, written and played as a musical tale. Song titles include "Secrets from the Stone," "In Defense of Guinevierre," "Dialogue between the Sun and Moon," and "Songs From the Four Winds." A storybook, *The Tale of Guinevierre*, accompanies each LP and is available by special request with purchase of cassette from the publisher. PW

Sona Gaia Productions, 1984, Folk/ New Age. Available from The Gaia Catalogue Company (LP or cassette $12.50 ppd., CD $18.45 ppd.).

SIGNATURE/DATURA/SUSAN
SUSAN OSBORNE

Susan Osborne is one of today's finest female vocalists. Susan's music, sung with every part of her being, is soulful, earthy, and evocative of the deep feelings and energies we tend to submerge in the course of our everyday lives. I first heard Susan Osborne perform in San Francisco's Grace Cathedral several years ago as lead vocalist with the Paul Winter Consort. When she sang the opening lines to "Mystery," a wave of spiritual energy swept through the cathedral. In a moment of intense feeling—love, compassion, gratitude—we collectively experienced the Great Mystery and Grace of Life. Susan is a priestess who heals through sound; her music is informed by a passionate commitment to the sacredness of life and a grounding in New Age vision. *Signature* (Lifeline Recordings, 1983), a collection of jazz, blues, pop, and gospel music, captures the strength and power of Susan's magnificent voice. This is not background music—the lyrics and arrangements are passionate, inspiring, emotional. (*Note*: Some songs use Christian symbols and masculine pronouns for deity.) *Datura* (Datura Recordings, 1984), an a cappella recording, is named after the sacred plant used in Eastern and Western shamanic rituals. Songchants include "Lay Down Your Bur-

den," "Grand Canyon Chant," the Quaker hymn "How Can I Keep From Singing?" "Morning Has Broken," and a thirty-minute truly amazing rendition of "Amazing Grace." Susan's latest recording, *Susan* (Living Music, 1987), includes nine original songs recorded live with members of the Paul Winter Consort. PW

Pop/spiritual. Available from The Gaia Catalogue Company or directly from the artist % Datura Recordings, P.O. Box 848, Eastsound, WA 98245 (all recordings LP or cassette $11.50 ppd., Susan also on CD $16.45 ppd.).

SKIES ABLAZE
LINDA HIRSCHHORN

Drawing on themes of peace, female heraism, personal freedom, and her Jewish heritage, Linda Hirschhorn's original music and songs emphasize personal/spiritual growth and social action. Songs include "The Overturning," dedicated to the people of Nicaragua, "Circle Chant," a popular song of the disarmament movement in the United States and Europe, and "Women of Belau." In the traditional clan structure of Belau, a matriarchy in the Micronesian Islands, women have the power to appoint and revoke the leadership and to determine the disposition of lands. Belau regards land and water as holy and is the only republic with a nuclear-free constitution. On four separate occasions the United States has attempted to have the people overturn their constitution. This song invites us to "hearken to the women of Belau . . . spreading ancient wisdom here and now." PW

Courtesy of Oyster Records. Cover photo by Irene Young, cover artwork by Carol Ehrlich, 1984.

Oyster Albums, 1985, Folk/pop. Available from Oyster Albums, P.O. Box 3929, Berkeley, CA 94703 (cassette $9.50 ppd.).

SO GLAD I'M HERE
BESSIE JONES

Bessie Jones is considered one of the best living singers of black folk spirituals. Her music evokes the "Gullah" culture of the Georgia Sea Islands, a unique Afro-American culture that developed almost completely independently from white influence. Her reputation is well deserved. On this live recording, she sings with other hand-clapping, foot-stomping Georgia Sea Islands singers in a beautiful strong voice that overflows with spirit. Includes traditional Georgia Sea Islands songs and games, many descended from slavery times. NVS

Rounder Records, 1975, Folk/traditional. Available from Rounder Records, 1 Camp St., Cambridge, MA 02140 (LP or cassette $8 ppd.).

SONGS OF THE GODDESS
CINDEE GRACE AND BAND

Goddess music in a variety of styles—folk, jazz, rock—with a delightful dose of good humor! Cindee sings of the many facets of feminist spirituality with lyrics that get to the heart of women's religion: "But if it's only 'God the Father,' I just can't relate New Age to me / I want something matriarchal, not so patriarchal to embrace / So as I realize myself, I won't leave out half the human race." Lyric sheet is included with each cassette, along with a money-back guarantee, rare in the music industry. If you're not satisfied for any reason, return the tape for a full refund! Songs include "Aphrodite," "Space Child," "The Great Mother," "Perfect Lover," "Source-Heiress." PW

Grace & Goddess, Unlimited, 1983.

Available from Grace & Goddess, Un-limited, P.O. Box 4367, Boulder, CO 80306 (cassette only, $9 ppd.).

SONGS OF THE SPIRIT: MEDICINE SONGS OF THE EAST AND WEST
LISA THIEL

Medicine songs are channeled from the spirit to awaken the consciousness of the listener, to heal the body and soul, and to inspire our true selves to become manifest. "Songs of the Spirit," a collection of channeled songs from Eastern and Western spiritual traditions, is a recording of superb musical quality and content. The songs are imaginative, inclusive of the sacred male principle, and representative of the joy, depth, and life-affirming values being expressed in women's spiritual music today. The tape begins with a prayer to White Buffalo Woman for vision, grace, and peace. In Western Indian traditions, Buffalo Woman taught the people to sing the sacred songs so that they might never forget the divinity within them. The lyrics of all songs are simple enough to be easily learned so you can sing along with divine abandon! PW

Sacred Dreams Productions, 1984, Ritual/chant. Available from The Gaia Catalogue Company (cassette only, $11.50 ppd.). Wholesale inquiries welcome.

Cover artwork
White Buffalo Woman © Lisa Thiel, 1984.

SPIRITSONG
MARY WATKINS

Spiritsong is an impressionistic collection of seven original piano compositions that strongly reflect the classical and jazz training of Mary Watkins. The selections are quiet and reflective musical environments, and the energy and spirit is unmistakably Watkins. She moves from a bluesy mood to a lilting one to a gospel feeling without skipping a beat or jarring your ear. She makes tricky technical passages sound effortless and can give the simplest of phrases a timeless and dramatic quality. *Spiritsong* has the double-edged ability to be the perfect mood and background music as well as an exciting and musically challenging listening experience. The arrangements are intelligent, the technique brilliant, and the musical message is clear. AL

Redwood Records, 1985, Jazz/New Age. Available from Redwood Records (LP or cassette $9.98 ppd.).

STABAT MATER
JULIA PERRY

One of the most haunting pieces of contemporary religious music, Julia Perry's *Stabat Mater* was composed for contralto and symphony orchestra in 1951. Appropriately, this description of the sorrows of the Virgin Mary at the cross was dedicated to Perry's mother. The intertwining or echoing of the powerful contralto voice with one or more of the string lines gives this work much of its poignancy. NVS

Composers Recordings, Inc., 1972, Classical/liturgical. Available from Composers Recordings, Inc., 170 W. 74th St., New York, NY 10023 (LP only, $9.98 ppd.).

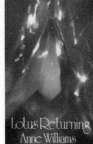

SUMMER ROSE, LOTUS RETURNING, VIOLET IN SPRING
ANNE WILLIAMS

Anne Williams is a superb harpist who performs all-original compositions on Irish, Celtic, and concert harps, with the additional embellishments of autoharp, dulcimer, bamboo flutes, cello, Tibetan bells, and soothing vocals. *Summer Rose* (1983), dedicated to "the child in all of us that yearns to dance for joy," evokes the memory of angels, devas, garden goddesses, and magical beings so alive in the child's imagination. *Lotus Returning* (1982) features original songs celebrating the joy of remembering ancient woman-wisdom. Rippling harp music and angelic vocals guide the listener into a state of spacious peace and meditative calm. *Violets in Spring* (1985) features folk harps played in ancient modes, accompanied by flute, ocarina, tablas, Tibetan bowls, and soundings (wordless vocals). Anne's instrumentation and vocals on this recording are supported by the Motherpeace Choir, a gathering of musical friends from the central Arizona desert community of Sedona. The haunting modes and melodies have a deepening effect on the body/mind, reflecting the spiritual intent with which the music was created. Each of these recordings is highly recommended for guided meditation, massage, dance or movement classes, and for rocking restless children to sleep. PW

Earthsong Productions, Meditative/ New Age. Available from Earthsong Productions, P.O. Box 780, Sedona, AZ 86336 (cassette only, $10 ppd. each).

SYMBOLS OF HOPI
JILL MCMANUS

Symbols of Hopi is a unique cross-fertilization of two musical forces with roots in American soil. Jill McManus blends modern jazz and American Indian songs on this rare and captivating recording. Jill has adapted to jazz four pieces composed by Hopi song-poets for traditional ceremonies and added three of her own pieces inspired by visits to New Mexico and Arizona. While many of the Hopi ceremonies are outwardly focused on bringing rain and crops,

they also have an inward focus on rebirth, renewal, and right actions in the service of life. It is this spirit that imbues the musical compositions on *Symbols of Hopi*. Titles include "Corn Dance," "Cloud Blessing," "All the Earth to Bloom," "Inner Spirit Dance," and "From the Four Directions." PW

Concord Records, 1984, Jazz/ritual. Available from Concord Records, P.O. Box 845, Concord, CA 94522 (LP or cassette $9.98 ppd.).

TAKE A LOOK AT MY PEOPLE
JANE SAPP

Jane Sapp is a dynamic pianist and gospel singer in the tradition of Sweet Honey in the Rock. On this recording, Jane delivers original and traditional material with an emphasis on social justice issues such as civil rights, single motherhood, and human dignity. Also included are jazzy torch ballads, blues, lullabies, and freedom songs. Serious music collectors will value this album for its treatment of gospel spirituals, a rich chapter of Afro-American history. AO

Flying Fish Records, 1983, Gospel. Available from Flying Fish Records (LP only, $8.98 ppd.).

TESTIMONY
SHADOWS ON A DIME
FERRON

A facile guitarist and literate poet, Ferron writes passionate, complex songs with understated themes of

women's struggles, juxtaposed with images of the artist as spiritual traveler and healer. *Testimony* is the more introspective of the two recordings. The title song is a haunting, chantlike affirmation of women's contributions to creating a better world: "By our lives be we spirit / By our hearts be we women / By our eyes be we open / By our hands be we whole. . . ." Two cuts, "Belly Bowl" and "Misty Mountain," are both rich with mystic imagery and evocative, upbeat tempos, while "Ain't Life a Brook" and "Louise" take a wry, uncompromising look at romantic love in relationships. With the exception of the title song, *Shadows on a Dime* is a less personal, more experimental collection of songs. Images of Nature permeate the lyrics. The title song is a mesmerizing piece of musical poetry that reveals the artist's relentless questioning as a mystical traveler, her poignant memories of an impoverished working-class childhood, and her lucid vision of Nature as an artistic and spiritual catalyst. AO

Lucy Records, 1974/1976, Folk/rock. Available from Ladyslipper (LP or cassette $9.70 ppd. each).

TOTEM
GABRIELLE ROTH AND THE MIRRORS

Find a large, carpeted room and get ready to move! *Totem* features a band of talented musicians who weave percussion, synthesizer, and ethnic instrumentation into tribal rhythms for the body and soul. The musical sounds of *Totem*—earthy, sensual, playful—invite you to move from inertia to ecstasy, to liberate the free-flowing Wise One Within with roots in the Earth and power in the heart. A musical feast from Gabrielle Roth, the queen of spiritual rock, *Totem* is the best dance tape I know of and one of the best-selling tapes in our catalogue and bookstore! When you've had your fill of New Age music that leaves you hanging in outer space, turn on *Totem* for an in-the-body experience. PW

The Moving Center, 1986, Ritual/dance. Available from The Gaia Catalogue Company (cassette only, $11.50 ppd.). Wholesale inquiries welcome.

TRANSFORMATIONS
BETH YORK

New Age jazz dedicated to the Goddess Within, *Transformations* is a healing album by music therapist Beth York and the New Women's Chamber Ensemble (oboe, English horn, alto sax, flute, synthesizer, bass, percussion, piano, guitar, and harp). Unlike some New Age music, which is meant solely for meditational purposes, *Transformations* has many moods. Includes "Time and Again" and "Dolphina," a dance piece. AL

Ladyslipper Records, 1985, Meditative/New Age. Available from Ladyslipper (LP or cassette $9.95 ppd.).

TURNING IT OVER
FROM THE HEART
MEG CHRISTIAN

Meg Christian is one of the founding mothers of women's music. Her recording career began with the classic *I Know You Know*, which launched Olivia Records, the first national music company devoted to the development of women in the recording arts. Throughout Meg's career, her music has been characterized by a gentle honesty, a sense of humor, and a vulnerable expression of her spiritual journey. On *Turning It Over*, Meg shares her experiences as a recovering alcoholic. Far from being melancholy, it is a recording filled with heartfelt ballads, soothing instrumentals, personal reflections, and joy. This album has influenced an enormous number of people seeking comfort and strength on the road to recovery from addictive patterns. *From the Heart*, Meg's latest, takes the listener on another stage of her spiritual journey, siddha yoga. It is a recording of shared intimacy, poignancy, laughter, and self-recognition. PW

Olivia Records, 1981/1984, Pop. Available from Olivia Records (LP or cassette $11.50 ppd. each).

TWO HANDS HOLD THE EARTH
SARAH PIRTLE

Two Hands Hold the Earth is a joyous musical celebration of all creatures of this precious planet. Sarah accompanies herself on guitar and banjo in a sweet and melodic voice. When she sings of whales, furry animals, dancing stars, and children of all nations, her enthusiasm is contagious. Songs, most of which are "sing-along-able," affirm the wisdom and natural harmony of the Earth and teach children the values of cultural and ecological diversity. Recommended by both the American Library Association and the Children's Creative Response to Conflict Program. PW

A Gentle Wind, 1985, Children. Available from A Gentle Wind, P.O. Box 3103, Albany, NY 12203 (cassette only, $7.95 ppd.). An eight-page guide booklet with song lyrics and home and classroom activity suggestions is available free from the artist. Send a SASE to: Sarah Pirtle, % Arts Resources for Cooperation, 54 Thayer Rd., Greenfield, MA 01301. A Gentle Wind is the producer of many fine musical recordings that teach children the values of caring for each other and the planet. A free catalogue is available upon request.

Cover artwork © Jill Person, A Gentle Wind, 1985.

WE ALL COME FROM THE GODDESS
TORI REA, MOLLY SCOTT, AND SARAH BENSON

We All Come from the Goddess is a tapestry of songs, chants, and invocations to the Goddess. Recorded in sacred places in the south of France, the music has a shamanic, trancelike quality that moves through ancient hollows of the body. Instrumentation includes drums, flute, wind chimes, Tibetan bells, rattles, dulcimer, voice, guitar, crickets, sound improvisation. Extensive liner notes describing the process of creating music in caves enables the listened to Journey with the artists. PW

Medicine Song Productions, 1986, Ritual. Available from Medicine Song Productions, 156 Sullivan St. #19, New York, NY 10012 (cassette only, $12.50 ppd.).

WE ARE ALL ONE PLANET
MOLLY SCOTT

Molly Scott's long-awaited second release is a richly voiced collection of original songs that reflect her artistry as composer and singer in the world of classical music, musical theater, and popular folksongs. The title song has become an anthem in the peace and ecology movements. Molly's songwriting reflects ecofeminist spiritual themes: "Song to the Seagull" is a song from Earth Mother to Bird Mother, "Engie's Waltz" is a poem/song to a ninety-year-old friend, "Seasons in Between" is about cycles of birth and death, and "Boy Child," with David Darling of the Paul Winter Consort, is a searing meditation on children and war. Instrumentation includes voice, piano, guitar, cello, dulcimer, flute, clarinet, Irish harp, bass, sax, percussion, and chorus. NVS

Sumitra Productions, 1984, Folk/New Age. Available from Sumitra Productions, Inc., Box U, Charlemont, MA 01339 (cassette $10.98 ppd.).

TUNING: THE POWER OF SOUND AND SONG

MOLLY SCOTT

Molly Scott, composer, singer, and poet, has an extensive background in the performing arts and has focused her music and teaching work on issues of personal and planetary healing, disarmament, and peace. An ecofeminist and environmental activist, she creates music that "illuminates our connection with the Earth and each other."

I am a musician—a composer and singer, a practitioner of the art of sound. Wondering at the power of music to affect me and the people for whom I sing, I began to investigate the nature of sound, the history of sound healing, the psychology of music. As a composer, I explored different forms of music, working with the feeling of different tones, textures, and intervals. As an inquiring human being, involved in spiritual practice and my own quest for understanding, I began to perceive, as so many of us have, that the threads of different knowledge systems are reaching toward each other in a webbed synthesis, confirming the truth of what Aldous Huxley called "The Perennial Philosophy": we are indeed all One, made of the same stuff, energy in constant change and motion. Flashes of insight come from many directions: Neuro-physiology, nonlinear dynamics, psycho-acoustics, psycho-biology—all confirm that we are part of the same pulsing, vibrational soup, infinitely diverse, yet connected in interdependent systems of pattern, order and process.

What happens to us, to this body/mind/spirit instrument, when we sing? The act of singing generates a concentrated "charge" in the psycho-physical system, resulting in more efficient use of the brain, better concentration, and higher states of awareness and receptivity. The deepened rhythmic breathing that singing requires, coupled with the higher acoustical frequencies which delineate song from speech, act to release physical and emotional stress by slowing and stabilizing the heartbeat and increasing the amount of oxygen in the bloodflow to the brain. The higher (more rapid and subtle) musical frequencies such as those generated by traditional forms of chanting (Hindu, Gregorian, Buddhist, Native American) create highly concentrated

Molly Scott. Photo
by Lionel
Delevingne, 1987.

stimuli to the brain, opening resources of energy and vision not available to ordinary consciousness. Singing is like an internal massage, cleansing and vitalizing the system. In religious communities that include chanting as part of a daily regimen, it has been observed that people need fewer hours of sleep and lighter diet when they chant regularly.

The act of singing is an act of consciousness change. You cannot sing and stay depressed. "Singing the blues" changes your color scheme, raising you from the condition of pain that sparked the song to begin with. Song is a next step from wound to healing. To know this is in itself a powerful tool for working with yourself and others through sound and music. When we sing we are tuning ourselves as instruments to a higher energy field. We attune the frequencies of our bodies through the sounds we make in the same way that we tune the strings of our instruments.

Music can draw on those deep resources of hope and strength common to us all—which are often, in these anxious days, beyond our conscious reach. We can speak, sound, and sing not to bandage pain, but to speak to the truth of what we all know: We are not so fragile as we fear. Our music is a testimony to our strength-in-connection. And this can give us hope in a complex and often fearsome world. We are not islands in isolation; we are open systems, instruments of energy. When we open to the flow of the web's energy, the web's music, we are part of the current of life, the real music of the spheres.

This article is reprinted from *The New Holistic Health Handbook*, edited by Shepherd Bliss, Edward Bauman, Lorin Piper, Armand San Brint, Pamela Amelia Wright, Stephen Greene Press, 1985.

WHO FEELS IT KNOWS IT
RITA MARLEY

Traditional Rastafarian music for the brethren and sistren from a talented daughter of Zion. This album includes many songs in praise of Jah as well as the customary Rasta emphasis on love and peace. Titles include "One Draw," "Good Morning Jah," and "That's the Way." Great backup musicians make this an exciting reggae recording. NVS

Shanachie Records, 1981, Reggae. Available from Shanachie Records, Dalebrook Park, Department R, Ho-Ho-Kus, NJ 07423 (LP or cassette $8.40 ppd., CD $16.40 ppd.).

WORKING WONDERS
JUDY MOWATT

Judy Mowatt's latest release has many more songs that deal with the Black diaspora than her previous album, plus many more songs for dancing. She stands firm in her commitment to Black women on such songs as "Hush Baby Mother," a song about the single motherhood of an abandoned teen, the title song, "Working Wonders," and "Lovemaking," a tune sung by a "gentle woman" to a man who seems to be having second thoughts. NVS

Shanachie Records, 1985, Reggae. Available from Shanachie Records, Dalebrook Park, Department R, Ho-Ho-Kus, NJ 07423 (LP or cassette $8.40 ppd., CD $16.40 ppd.).

Rita Marley.
Courtesy of
Shanachie
Records.

WHERE

WE

GATHER:

ORGANIZATIONAL

RESOURCES

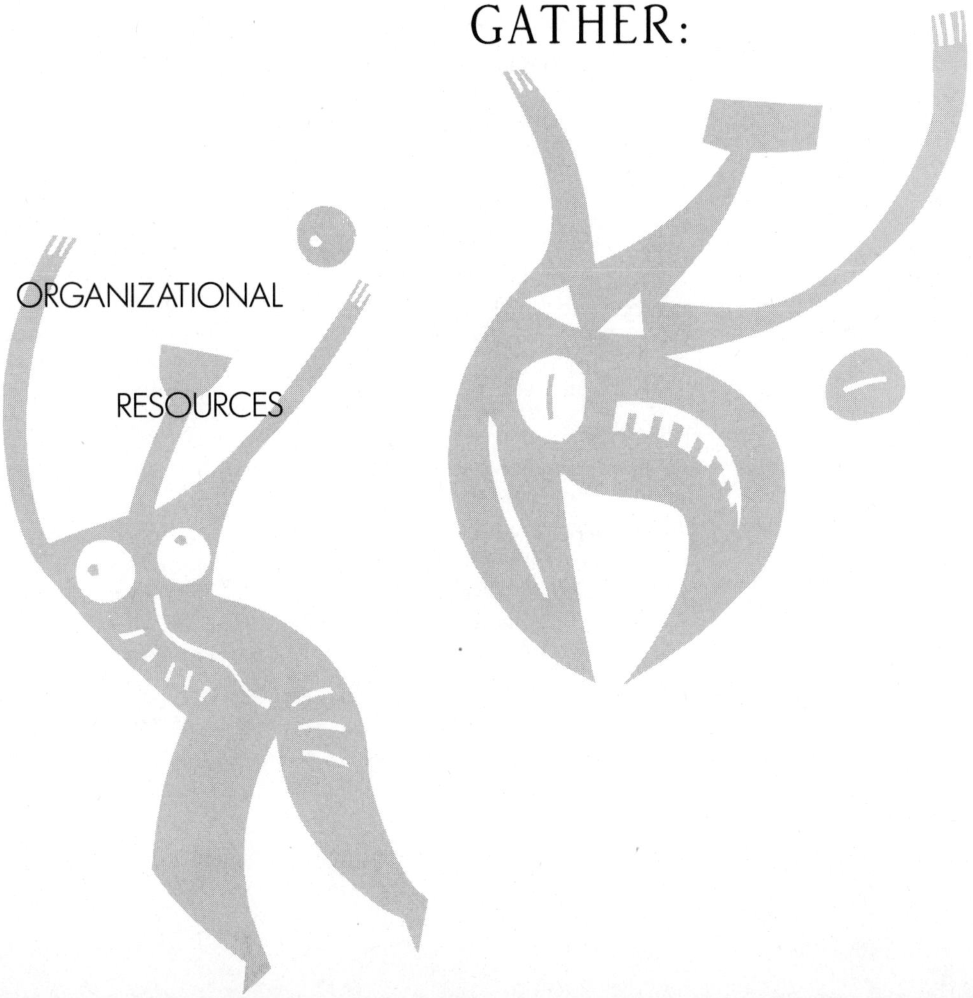

**THE WOMANSPIRIT
SOURCEBOOK**

ORGANIZATIONAL

RESOURCES

AL-ANON FAMILY GROUP HEADQUARTERS

Al-Anon is for families and friends of alcoholics. Many women, long-time sufferers of co-dependent behavioral patterns, have made enormous changes in their lives as a result of the support received at Al-Anon meetings. Based on the same principles as Alcoholics Anonymous (AA), Al-Anon uses the twelve-step program, has ongoing free meetings open to everyone (including women-only and gay groups), and offers many publications and educational materials upon request. Al-Anon sponsors the Alateen and Adult Children of Alcoholics programs. Look in the phone book or in the Personals section of the newspaper under Al-Anon Family Groups. If there is no listing, call the nearest office of Alcoholics Anonymous.

Al-Anon Family Group Headquarters, P.O. Box 682, Midtown Station, New York, NY 10018-0862, (212) 302-7240.

ALCOHOLICS ANONYMOUS WORLD SERVICES

Alcoholics Anonymous (AA) is an international peer-support program with over one million members worldwide. The primary purpose of AA members is to stay sober and to support other alcoholics in achieving sobriety. Nearly every telephone directory in the country has a listing for local AA groups. An estimated seventy-four thousand groups (including women-only and gay groups) meet regularly, sharing their stories and offering each other love, hope, and strength to maintain sobriety. There are no dues or fees; the only membership requirement is a desire to stop drinking. Call for directory of local meetings, to obtain free literature, or simply to talk to someone in the program.

Alcoholics Anonymous World Services, P.O. Box 459, Grand Central Station, New York, NY 10163, (212) 686-1100.

THIRSTING FOR GOD

———

THE STORY OF RACHEL V.

After some time passed in AA, I was able to hear the phrase "God, *as I understand him,*" a phrase added to the Third Step so that anyone and everyone could find a way to connect with a power greater than herself or himself. After three years, I noticed that there's a chapter in the Big Book, "We Agnostics." I read that I could be an agnostic and still have a spiritual experience. I didn't have to go back to the God of my childhood. "The Realm of the Spirit is all-inclusive. . . . When we speak to you of God . . . we mean your own conception of God" (*Alcoholics Anonymous,* pp. 46–47).

Gradually my morning meditations shifted from zazen, an emptying of the mind, into a dialogue with a higher power. It took a long time to admit that what I was doing was praying. I wasn't a Christian. I was horrified. Now I can laugh at that.

In meetings now I say that I'm promiscuous with God. I call on everyone: the Blessed Mother, the Lord Buddha, God the Father, Jesus Christ, Tara, the Holy Ghost, my Grandmother, Inanna, Kuan Yin, Isis, Ishtar, Kali, Sophia, the Shekhina, anybody and everybody. I need all the help I can get. I'm sure that God understands. My life is evidence.

I've begun to let myself look at my Christian roots again. I've found medieval Christian mystics who addressed God as "Mother," like Julian of Norwich, Hildegard of Bingen. I've found the Black Madonna, a Catholic remnant of the pre-Christian worship of the Great Mother Goddess. Looking for the female side of God is a way of coming to peace with myself as a woman, finding the female body which I thought so terrible, inhabitable by God.

Getting sober has meant getting in there and looking into the dark places. That's been a Fourth Step for me. I'm in the middle of doing it a second time. The longer I'm sober, the more nooks and crannies I see I have. Little dark corners, twists. A labyrinth. I call doing the Fourth Step "eating the darkness." In the Fifth Step, I found out that even darkness is good. Sobriety doesn't change having good days and bad days. It's just that now I can have a bad day and remember that it'll change before I know it. Today I think God keeps my life on the edge so I'll pay attention. . . .

Alcoholism is full of irony. Never before have I understood so fully what mystics of all traditions have been trying to tell us: there is no separation between body and soul, mind and matter. Alcoholism has taught me this through my own experience. It is a physical disease for which the only known recovery is a spiritual transformation. On one level alcoholism is a hunger for spirit, for God. . . . My disease was a distortion of my search for God. We are all hungry for God. It's no accident that alcohol is also referred to as "spirits." What I hungered for, thirsted for is God and for whatever reason, biochemical, genetic, emotional, I used to look for that spirit in the bottle or through a drug. What I wanted is communion, our common union, and that's what I found through the help of AA.

From Rachel V., *A Woman Like You: Life Stories of Women Recovering from Alcoholism and Addiction*, Harper & Row, 1985.

AMARGI CENTER

The name Amargi derived from an ancient Sumerian grassroots political movement. It means both return to the Mother and freedom. The Amargi Center is dedicated to the practice of women's spirituality. Activities include seasonal rituals, meditation retreats, rites of passage, slide presentations, and weekend intensives in the philosophy, practice, and transformative power of the Feminine. Send SASE for descriptive brochure.

Amargi Center, % Joan Iten Sutherland, director, P.O. Box 894, Pt. Reyes Station, CA 94956, (415) 663-8821.

Logo of Amargi Center by Joan Iten Sutherland, 1981. Drawn from photographs of an ancient symbol, the bundled sheaves of the Sumerian Goddess Inanna.

CONTEMPLATIVE ACTIVISM

JOAN ITEN SUTHERLAND

Joan Iten Sutherland, creator of Amargi Center, is currently writing a book on contemplative traditions and women. As a writer, scholar, teacher, and ritualist, she brings together her study of Asian philosophy and zazen (Zen meditation) practice with the exploration of a new thealogy arising out of women's spirituality.

I light two candles on the altar, offer a stick of incense. Sitting on my meditation cushion in the gesture of presence, I follow my breath. The ego's constant chatter fades, allowing the wisdom of the body to emerge. As awareness joins breath in my pelvic cradle, my whole body breathes, in and out, until the distinction between in and out begins to drop away. I find the center and rest there.

Later, I take a call on the rape and battering hotline. The woman is very upset, having a hard time speaking. We breathe together, and she can begin her story. I listen with my heart and respond from the still center of the morning's meditation.

Contemplative activism is a radical way of being in the world, in the original sense of the word: "of the root." Meditative practice allows us to rediscover our essential self, where we are truly present in any situation, a sensitive participant in each moment. We find that the response that arises naturally from that participation is compassion. Contemplative activism is our life's inhale and exhale, ebb and flow, waxing and waning, as the practices of still awareness and compassionate movement create together the form of our being in the world.

The pelvic cradle is a woman's physical and spiritual center of gravity. When the breath moves in and out of our body, from world to pelvic cradle and back to world, our awareness flows with it, in a channel that passes through our heart. We feel what comes in; if we stay open we are deeply moved by the joys and sorrows, the great tenderness of life. When the breath is exhaled, if we are open, it is warmed by the compassion in our hearts, and the gift is returned. So too with our actions, arising from the stillness at the center, moving through the heart's chambers, flowing out from open palms.

Compassion means "together feeling," letting membranes dissolve between self and other. It is the realization that there is only one body that is wounded, and it is mine; only one struggle that is successful, and that is mine, too. Most difficult of all, if we truly believe in the essential oneness of the world, then there is no separation between the atomic bomb and myself. It becomes my responsibility to discover the ways in which this is so, and to begin practicing what Deena

Matrika: A Birthing Amulet © Lynn Pollock Marsh, 1985. Bronze sculpture 1-3/4". Photo by Lorraine Capparell. Matrika, A Birthing Amulet available for purchase from the artist: Lynn Pollock Marsh, 804 Bryant St., Palo Alto, CA 94301.

"Matrika is a sculpted image of the Great Mother holding the World together at its innermost core. She is a helper to channel our connections to the wisdom, mystery, and strength of the Maternal Ground. . . . The patriarchal principle is 'Thou shalt,' or 'Thou shalt not.' The Goddess says, 'You may, perhaps; play, discover, find out for yourself.' She is my mentor" (Lynn Pollock Marsh).

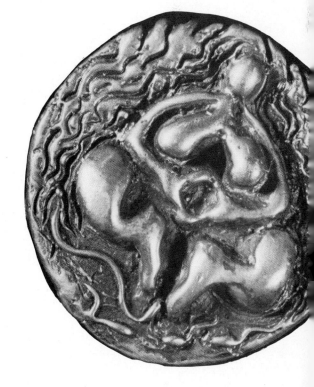

Metzger calls "personal disarmament."

This kind of political awareness can be debilitating if the flow of energy is all one way, from personality self to world. Too many dedicated and caring people have burned out, feeling eaten alive by their work. Centering in our pelvic cradle allows us to connect with a transpersonal source of energy, so that we become conduits rather than generators. At the same time, this center can be expansive enough to take in the sorrows and frustrations we receive, composting them into material useful to the growth of our own practice.

While contemplation may be largely a solitary experience, we can support each other in our practices. When our circle meets, we experience the power and peace of women meditating together, creating a loving vessel to contain the cycles of transformation in individual and community. At the end each of us dedicates the energy we have generated together to another person, a cause, or a dream.

One contemplative activist sets out on a peace march across the country; another teaches self-defense to women and children; a third goes down to the harbor and buys up all the live bait, releasing them back into the sea. With joyful spirits, we blockade weapons labs, alter offensive billboards, live in intentional communities, go to Nicaragua to help bring in the coffee harvest. What should you do? Sit down. Invite your mind to be quiet for awhile. Follow your breath. Listen to your heart: it already knows.

A MEDITATION PRACTICE

It is a very powerful practice to connect with the center of creativity, strength, and passion in our pelvic cradle. Try this: Sit in a comfortable position with your back straight. Close your eyes and imagine a light glowing in front of you. Bring the light up over the top of your head and then let it fall slowly through your body, bringing your awareness with it. Pause to let it join with your breath as it comes in and out through your nose, runs up and down your windpipe, as your lungs fill and empty, your belly rises and falls. Then let it settle down into your pelvic cradle, until it finds the place where breath begins. Feel it there as a full moon glowing between the horns of your pelvis. Let the moon go translucent, your breath washing through it like a tide.

Make a time to do this each day, and consciously return here as often as you can in the midst of your activities. This is your center; become aware of the difference when you are acting from this place. When you feel yourself thrown off center, take a moment to come back here. And when you're with other women, imagine the full moon glowing in them; let that connection be the cradle of your relationship.

ANNA'S PRAYER: SPIRITUAL GROWTH FOR WOMEN

When Jesus was presented at the temple as an infant, he was received by two holy people: Simeon, a devout and righteous religious man and the prophetess Anna. Simeon's prayer is recorded in the Bible; Anna's is not. In recognition of women's spirituality as a dynamic source of inspiration and strength for contemporary women, Bobbi Henderson and Paula Vella founded Anna's Prayer. Activities include interfaith retreats, workshops, and special programs designed to meet the spiritual/religious needs of women within the community.

Anna's Prayer, % Bobbie Henderson and Paula Vella, P.O. Box 700953, Tulsa, OK 74170, (918) 258-9020.

AT THE FOOT OF THE MOUNTAIN

At the Foot of the Mountain is a theater of action, transformation, celebration, and hope where women of many races, classes, ages, and cultures create the magic that makes theater a catalyst for social change. The hallmark of their work are plays they name "ritual drama," a contact improv between performers and audience. Scripted during the rehearsal process and created collaboratively by writer/directors and performers, ritual drama is structured to incorporate audience testimony into key moments of the production. The boldness of the themes (women and addiction, nuclear madness and the denial of death) and the interaction between performers and audience often leads to a communal bond and a spiritual healing rarely experienced in theater. At the Foot of the Mountain honors women's feelings, nurtures women's values, and empowers audiences to participate in the creation of a just and joyous world. Though the company is based in Minneapolis, touring is a regular part of its performance life. The company has been sponsored by universities, churches, community centers, prisons, theaters, and grassroots organizations. The company has been commissioned to create solstice and equinox ceremonies, rituals for political events such as the "Take Back the Night" march, and performances to honor births, deaths, and menarches. Write for touring schedule and information on performances, ritual services, ongoing classes, workshops, and summer training programs.

Phyllis Jane Rose, artistic director; Nayo-Barbara Watkins, managing director; Kay Bolstad, tour director, At the Foot of the Mountain, 2000 S. 5th St., Minneapolis, MN 55454, (612) 375-9487.

Logo designed by
Leslie Bowman,
1985.

AWEHAI CENTER FOR HEALING AND TRANSFORMATION

Awehai is named for an Iroquois earth goddess who, as she was plunging through a dark abyss, held onto life so passionately that she created a new world—Earth. Awehai offers a variety of services designed to facilitate the personal transformation process as well as the collective transformation of our world. All of Awehai's work reflects the central theme of reclaiming the transforming power of the feminine principle in ourselves and in the world we create. The intuitive arts—myth, astrology, visualization, tarot, ritual—are the tools used to reclaim the power of the Goddess. Yana Breeze, co-director of Awehai, is a feminist priestess and workshop facilitator.

Awehai Center, % Yana Breeze and Raven, co-directors, 230 SW 3rd St., Suite 200, Corvallis, OR 97333, (503) 758-0330.

BLACK WOMEN IN CHURCH AND SOCIETY

A research and resource center on the campus of the Interdenominational Theological Center, this group is concerned with the problems of Black women in church and society, primarily Black churches but also Black women in white churches. Leadership development and training are provided through conferences, continuing education courses, and special seminars designed to develop women's spiritual and material resources. The center collects data on Black women in religion and offers a directory (1984) of Black women in ministry.

Black Women in Church and Society, % Jacquelyn Grant, director, 671 Beckwith St., SW, Atlanta, GA 30314, (404) 527-7741.

CALIFORNIA SCHOOL OF HERBAL STUDIES

Rosemary Gladstar, founder of the California School of Herbal Studies (CSHS), envisioned a school without walls in a peaceful country setting where the ancient wisdom of herbs could be learned anew. The school is now recognized as one of the nation's leading centers of herbal education. Courses focus on many aspects of herbal studies, ranging from plant identification, wild crafting, and ceremony and ritual to plant preparation and medicinal uses. Located on a beautiful eighty-acre ranch, school facilities include an herb garden, a lab and drying room, a spring-fed swimming pond, a sweat lodge, and an extensive library. Each year the school sponsors a women's spirituality and herbal retreat in the Mendocino Woodlands, bringing together women herbal students and practitioners from around the country to learn and celebrate with one another. Send a SASE to receive current catalogue.

California School of Herbal Studies, P.O. Box 39, Forestville, CA 95436, (707) 887-7457.

CENTER FOR CHRISTIAN FEMINIST MINISTRIES

A resource center for women and men exploring areas of convergence and divergence between Christianity and feminism, the Center for Christian Feminist Ministries (CCFM) offers quarterly ritual celebrations, a drop-in resource library, lectures by well-known women religious leaders, a feminist "base community," ongoing support groups, retreats, an annual conference in feminist theology, and women-centered counseling and ministry services. CCFM plays an active role in the Women-Church movement both locally and nationally. A monthly newsletter of activities, resources, and occasional articles is available for a suggested

Hands © Lorraine Capparell, 1982. Ceramic sculpture, 30″ × 60″ in diameter. Photo by Lars Speyer.

"The creative spark was struck three years ago. Since then I have been bringing life to an image that appeared fully realized in a dream: Twenty pair of hands emerge from an outer pentagon. Five torsos—handbuilt—revolve in the inner circle, frozen in the Tai Chi movement 'pushing forward,' also known as the I Ching hexagram "Li" or flame. To this end the colors range from deep purple to white, with shades of flame red and golden yellow as the transition between earth and sky. The work reflects my feelings about women and strength and unity, as well as mirroring facets of myself. With the help and support from many— 'lending a hand'— comes one. From a dream, reality" (Lorraine Capparell). For more information about the artist's work, see page 215.

donation of $5-$10 annually.

Center for Christian Feminist Ministries, % Jan B. Anderson, M.Div., director, 4135 Bagley Ave. N., Seattle, WA 98103, (206) 547-3374.

CENTER FOR TRANSFORMATIONAL ARTS

The Center for Transformational Arts is a women's networking and support organization that offers workshops and retreats in the state of Utah open to all women. Emphasis is given to developing women's natural healing abilities, connecting to the Earth's energies and one's own inner healer, and using healing as a spiritual path. Ongoing programs include full moon rituals, tarot study groups, and seasonal spiritual retreats on the solstices and equinoxes. Focus is on cross-cultural Goddess spirituality, planetary healing, and Native American practices. Write to be placed on the events mailing list.

Center for Transformational Arts, % Shirley Schnirel, 515 Crestview Dr., Summit Park, UT 84060, (801) 649-9531.

CENTER FOR WOMEN AND RELIGION

Founded in 1970, the Center for Women and Religion (CWR) of the Graduate Theological Union in Berkeley is the oldest center for women in theological education and the only women's center sponsored by ten theological institutions. Beginning with a small number of dedicated students and women in transition in the Bay Area, the CWR has expanded to become a national and international network of members committed to mutual support and education in feminist theology. The CWR's work includes curriculum development, conferences, retreats, newsletter publication, faculty support and development, and the CWR House, an "intimate place that offers a sense of belonging" for women and men seeking a quiet place for reflection or a community of sister/fellow questers. The services of a licensed counselor are available through the CWR. Membership ($18 students; $30 individuals; $50 institutions) includes a subscription to the annual *Journal of Women and Religion*, membership newsletter, invitations to conferences and programs, and national and international networking mailings.

Center for Women and Religion, 2400 Ridge Rd., Berkeley, CA 94709, (415) 649-2490.

CIRCLE

Circle is a nonprofit Wiccan resource center serving people worldwide interested in nature religions, ancient and modern Pagan cultures, consciousness exploration, holistic healing, Goddess worship, Wiccan ways, ecofeminism, shamanism, and magical arts. Circle, begun in 1974 and located at Circle Sanctuary, a 200-acre sacred Nature preserve and herb farm in the rolling hills of southwestern Wisconsin, offers a wide range of networking services, edu-

Selena Fox, High Priestess of Circle Sanctuary. Photo by Lynnie Johnson, 1986. Courtesy of the National Film Board of Canada.

cational activities, public gatherings, ministry services, and publications. Of particular interest to women is the work of Circle founder and high priestess Selena Fox. Each summer a School for Priestesses directed by Selena is held at Circle. The week's workshops, chanting circles, meditations, discussions, rituals, and other learning opportunities are oriented toward helping participants develop themselves as leaders of ongoing spiritual groups and special occasion group ceremonies. Write for further information on the School for Priestesses and other Circle activities.

Circle, % Selena Fox, co-director, P.O. Box 219, Mount Horeb, WI 53572, (608) 924-2216.

CIRCLE OF ARADIA

Circle of Aradia is a woman's circle offering full moon and seasonal rituals, classes, and workshops. Skills are taught in the theory and practice of Goddess religion and its use in fueling the goals of the feminist movement both personally and globally. Activities are experientially based on developing woman-identified symbols to reprogram our psyches and to reclaim, protect, and embrace the sacredness of life. Ritual, trance, guided meditations, and discussion are used to develop and channel woman-power and self-healing. Circle of Aradia also publishes *Diana's Arrow*, a newsletter of fem-

inist Witchcraft; audio tapes; and written publications. For information on products and a schedule of Circle of Aradia classes, send a legal-size SASE.

Circle of Aradia, % Felicity Artemis Flowers and Ruth Barrett (Rhiannon), 4111 Lincoln Blvd. #211, Marina del Rey, CA 90292, (213) 306-7316.

CIRCLES OF EXCHANGE

Circles of Exchange are small kinship networks of women sharing their spirituality through "round robin" letter exchanges around the country. The five to seven women in each group send and receive an ever-changing packet of womenwords: letters, poems, stories, photocopies of articles, drawings, photographs. Each Circle begins with the coordinator and when the packet has made one cycle she removes her first offering and sends it round once again for the second offering. Thus the circles are like the moon cycle—ever changing but ever returning. Circles of Exchange are free of charge. Send SASE for information. Newsletter available for nominal charge to members.

Circles of Exchange, % Nan Hawthorne, coordinator, 4807 - 50th Ave. South, Seattle, WA 98118.

COALITION ON WOMEN AND RELIGION

The Coalition on Women and Religion is a network of women from various religious traditions who endeavor to support one another in their spiritual questing and to promote the equality of women in all areas of religious life. The Coalition publishes a variety of books of interest to religious women: *The Women's Bible*, by Elizabeth Cady Stanton, the *Study Guide to the Women's Bible, The Word for Us*, an inclusive language version of the Gospels of John and Mark and the Epistles to the Romans and Galatians by Joann Haugerud, and a book of cartoons designed to "prick the balloon of religiosity." Membership in the coalition ($12 annually) includes a subscription to *The Flame*, a quarterly journal filled with feminist religious resources, book reviews, events announcements, and feature articles.

Coalition on Women and Religion, 4759–15th Ave., N.E., Seattle, WA 98105, (206) 525-1213.

COVENANT OF THE GODDESS

The Covenant of the Goddess (COG) was founded in 1975 to increase cooperation among Witches, and to secure for Witches and covens the legal protection enjoyed by members of other religions. It is a federation of covens and solitaires of various traditions, who share in the worship of the Goddess and the Old Gods and subscribe to a common code of ethics. COG publishes a newsletter; issues ministerial credentials to qualified persons; sponsors a national festival each summer; and encourages regional and national networking. For a sample newsletter send $2; for additional information on COG send legal-size SASE.

Covenant of the Goddess, P.O. Box 1226, Berkeley, CA 94704.

DARKMOON CIRCLE

The Darkmoon Circle is a group of women who work together to rediscover and interpret the ancient mysteries of the Goddess to meet modern needs. The first Darkmoon Circle took place in 1977 when a group of women gathered for a menarche (coming-of-age) ritual in honor of a young woman seeking a more positive introduction to menstruation. They discovered in their young friend's request an opportunity to create woman-honoring rituals for themselves and their daughters. The group decided to meet regularly to explore the spiritual reality of the Goddess and the growing sense of community they experienced in learning and worshiping together. At present, the Darkmoon Circle meets twice a month, at the new and full moons. Its focus is the Goddess in her manifestations as Maiden, Mother, Wisewoman, and as she is revealed within every woman. Meetings, open to new women visitors, include workshop/rituals in honor of a goddess of a specific culture, practice in psychic skills, ceremonies of transition, healing rituals, chanting, and dance. The Liturgy of the Lady, a formal worship service honoring the Goddess, is presented on the last Sunday evening of each month. The Liturgy is available in book form. Send $9.95 plus appropriate sales tax to MZB Productions, Box 72, Berkeley, CA 94701.

For information on Darkmoon Circle *write: Diana L. Paxson, P.O. Box 5521 Berkeley, CA 94705, (415) 658-6033.*

DELPHOS WILDERNESS SANCTUARY

Delphos is a dream waiting to be born. It is the dream of the womb-space, of creativity, giving birth to ourselves, to a new people. It is the dream of sanctuary: a place where the holy lives, where we come to be in the presence of the sacred. It is a place to breed truth; to listen, long and longer to the voices of the Earth and the voices of our souls and the voices of each other, to listen within forever and speak and move and act. Naming this sacred place Delphos (womb, dolphin, delve) indicates that it belongs to the depths: here transformation is sought by going down and within, by allowing birth to happen. The name came in a dream, conceived as a retreat space whose power lies in sacred lesbian consciousness—whatever that may be. The beginnings of Delphos have been in groups and weekend-long retreats, for lesbians and mixed groups, whose forms have been meditation, laughter, music, stillness, dance, drumming, and ritual. For more information on Delphos workshops and retreats, call or send a SASE.

Delphos, % Janet "Cedar" Spring, founder, 3046–15th Ave. S., Minneapolis, MN 55407, (612) 721-4653.

DHAMMA DENA

Dhamma Dena is a Vipassana retreat center located near Joshua Tree in the high desert of southern California. Over the years it has grown from a few vacation cabins to a comfortable complex of remodeled buildings including an enlarged meditation hall built through the generous labors and dana of Ruth Denison and her students. This process is an integral part of Dhamma Dena and has allowed it to grow very naturally as the needs demand. There are often po-sitions for Vipassana students to stay as managers, builders, and/or cooks. Write or call for information regarding group, private, or work retreats.

Dhamma Dena, % Ruth Denison, founder, Star Rt. #1 Box 250, Joshua Tree, CA 92252, (619) 362-4815.

Logo design by
Cedar Spring.

LIONESS OF THE DESERT: AN INTERVIEW WITH RUTH DENISON

BY BARBARA GATES

Ruth Denison is a Vipassana meditation teacher. She was born in eastern Europe and lived there during the hardships of the Second World War. She later studied under the guidance of the Burmese master U Bha Khin and several Japanese masters. Since 1974 she has taught at the Insight Meditation Society (IMS) in Barre, Massachusetts (see listing on page 185), throughout the United States and Europe, and at the Dhamma Dena Desert Meditation Center, of which she is the founder. I have allowed Ruth's European accent and expressive syntax to speak directly to you.

BG *I've heard that one of your students has named you the Lioness of the Desert. When you teach your courses in the high desert, what feline qualities do you express? Are you ferocious?*

RD I am uncompromising in developing your awareness. I can be so permitting, so loving, and so kind of playful, but I will never forget that my function is to activate the forces within you which are suitable for developing mindfulness, which will bring you to detachment, which will bring you to see the aspect of impermanence, of suffering, of anatta. And I can be ruthless.

BG *Ruthless Ruth. Another namesake.*

RD My teacher, U Bha Khin, called me *Root*. In Burmese they don't have the "th" sound, so as in Germany, my name is pronounced Root, not Ruth. He would say, "Root, become rootless," that is to become boundless in your love, and in your nonattachment. Then, "Ruth, become *Ruthless*." And I have. I can be all rosy-posy, attend to that which needs cradling, but I never forget to respond to that which needs a knife to cut, that which needs sharp teeth. Sometimes I am the clown, sometimes a lion, sometimes a shoulder patting mama, sometimes the sister, sometimes the brother, whatever is appropriate for the situation.

BG *When you began teaching Vipassana courses, you developed your own approach which involved attention to the movement of the body. How did this approach evolve?*

RD I was working with Charlotte Selver in sensory awareness at the end of the '50s, before I came to Vipassana. Charlotte never mentioned spirituality. She just showed you that the body was alive. When I first came to my teacher, he taught me to observe my sensations. I said, "That's not what I came for. I do that since a long time." But then suddenly what I knew became deeper. I gave up my innate suspicion of the new and I understood the connection to all things.

BG How did you depart from the tradition that you studied?

RD I still haven't departed. I still teach what my teacher taught. My approach is more from the wholeness of the being. I consider all aspects, and that, in turn, is very much in alignment with what the Buddha says. He gives us four foundations of mindfulness to practice. The first foundation is mindfulness of the body, sensations, the breath, movement and posture. My teacher said, "When you sit, when you take a shower, when you are eating you are to be mindful," but his formal training focused only on observing the bodily sensations in sitting position. In my approach I use the bodily movement; sometimes it's just standing; sometimes it's lifting the cooking pot. This is the first foundation of mindfulness, darling.

BG Could you give an example of how you work?

RD You are lifting the arm. (Slowly she lifts her arm.) I invite you to notice the sensations flowing. The sensations, through movement, become more exhilarated and the mind goes naturally where there's lots happening. The mind has a connection to the sensation level, is now there, is a little finer, has a little confidence, knows there is sensation—doesn't need to grasp for it. You are then more sure of the object, which is sensation. Now you sit still. You take the arm down and continue noticing the sensations. Now you become aware of the subtler form of life or awareness. This can lead to yet finer perceptions of your own awareness. You are experiencing delight. Through delight (one of the factors of enlightenment) you will also strengthen your attention.

This way you come more easily into the second foundation of mindfulness. You will notice the pleasantness or the unpleasantness of sensations. Then you will also see the third foundation is arising. You are aware of the knowing. Finally you will get a sudden right-connection of the mind's right-observation. You will at that moment have noticed the object and noticed your attention. This the real Vipassana mind that has the power of a total unloosening of knots, a release of tensions throughout the entire body. You have a high appreciation of the body, high delight without attachment. But you know that you are not the body. That moment sets the mind into freedom.

BG Through your training can you help students develop new habits which really translate into their lives when they leave retreats?

RD You remember, yes, we were lifting, we were bending. When you sweep, when you drive, when you cook, you are more skillful at practicing awareness. So you train the mind to the good habit of being present and then it is your property. Also, you discover your feet. You discover how your pelvis carries you. You train the mind in such a way it sees the bad habits and sees the good ones. Then when the occasion arises, and it arises from moment to moment, life presents itself from moment to moment, you will always see to it that you have a good posture, that your body serves you right.

But that is just one aspect. The higher implication of the experience is that your mind gains a purity. You take it away from its own willful moving into irrelevant subjects and objects. It stops its compulsion to create its own world, to create its own emotion unnecessarily. You are developing through your mindfulness to the body a very pure mind. . . . You are developing the ability of the mind which is able, when an emotion comes, when a thought comes, to meet it and witness it in the pure state. The body is a beautiful base. It is a *foundation*, that means a big thing, a *foundation*, you see?

BG Particularly here in California, where the "cult of the body" is flourishing, isn't there a danger that a student will experience your course as a "Body Workshop"?

RD The "cult of the body" has its danger, but also its tremendous advantage. Jump into the hot tub. Jump into the swimming pool. Jump into . . . you develop kinesthetic sense with deep participation in it for feeling good and for relaxation, which has its value. Many people are so locked up and so sunk in their depressions and negative emotions that they need first to feel and to identify. You cannot take the identification away until you establish a healthy ego first. Then you can come and start Vipassana. You cannot start Vipassana—putting the mind in the position where it is just observing and knowing—it's too much—with a morbid mind.

BG You are well known in the sangha not only for the work you do with awareness through movement, but also for the work you do with women. In recent years, along with the emancipation of women in the social and political realms, more and more women are teaching the Dharma, and a number of teachers are offering courses particularly for women. Why do you teach women's courses?

RD I like our work together. I feel a great pioneering spirit in the women's hearts; they are tremendously dedicated to transforming traditional forms.

BG Have you found that the pressures in our society on women to conform to a "feminine image" lead to certain repeating ways of suffering?

RD There is a subtle, not spoken demand about how a woman should be: she should be gentle; she should be loving. We have that as conditioning in our minds. Then we find out that we are just the opposite, too—robust, we are tough; we are also hating. Then we find ourselves in conflict. We begin to hate ourselves or to hate some-

"I feel a great pioneering spirit in the women's hearts. They are tremendously dedicated to transforming traditional forms and patterns of experiencing their lives into new ones more appropriate to our time and condition." (Ruth Dennison, founder, Dhamma Dena).

"Pioneering Spirit."
Photograph by
Dhamma Dena
(on behalf of one
of its students).

one else. Mostly we hate ourselves, you see.

(Michele McDonald joins the conversation briefly. She is about to teach a course called "Women and Spirituality" at IMS in Barre. She poses the following two questions.)

MM In the women's courses, how do you work with the nonseparating mind, the deeper mind, the absolute, where there is no man and no woman? And how do you work with the anger of women against men?

RD On several levels. I make it very much known from the beginning that we are a women's course in order to find out about our womanhood, but not in the sense that we are women versus men, only for the investigation of our deeper selves, as we happen to be women. I bring their attention back again and again to the body according to the first foundation of mindfulness. As the attention stabilizes, the mind becomes quiet. This allows for sharper awareness of things as they really are, namely sensations—hard, soft, pleasant, unpleasant—which are always changing. The cognition of this lets the concept of woman dissolve; the mind is in harmony and can eventually let go of the identification with *me* or being a woman separated. This awareness then opens the door so we can become the human beings we really want to be.

MM How do you handle the sense of victim or powerlessness that women tend to bring to . . .

RD . . . the dominating. You begin to see more because the mind, through the practice of using the body as mindfulness, becomes more perceptive to what we think we are, to what society asks of us, to our hidden conditioned ideas and to our own mental motives, to our mental creations and projections and accusations. In a very habitual way, we need objects to hang it on when we are suffering. I will gradually lead them through the first foundation of mindfulness, through the second, the feelings, pleasant and unpleasant, in the mind and in the body. We wake up to all the impulses, to desire, to craving, to the need to have an object to blame it on, to inferiority complexes, or superiority, to the instinct to fight, to put others down, to be righteous. The mind becomes very flexible, very open and allows us to experience the Goddess within us. Not as something special or superior, but just as our natural state. Everyone is the Goddess. We express this in a beautiful song: "Blessed are we. Freedom are we. We are the infinite, Without beginning, Without any end. All this we are. Blessed are we. Freedom are we. We are the infinite. Within Ourselves. All this we are." We chant this. This is practicing directly.

BG I have one last topic. You seem to love to play the heretic. Remember on Easter, in your movement session you instructed us to put our arms out and be Christ on the cross. It provoked us to take a look. . . .

RD That's right. It is coming, however, not just to provoke. Being nailed on the cross is a tremendous deep event for us. Christ got nailed on the cross because he was misunderstood. At the end he said, "Forgive them for they do not know what they are doing." That means there was a lack of mindfulness. He had tremendous compassion. He was to his little self dying. So when I say, "Be on a cross and die," I am saying grow and die to your little self; be gracious like Christ.

BG Yes, but at the same time, we all laughed. You were making a serious point (which most of us unfortunately missed), and you also were making light.

RD It was evoking a bit of joy for you. By that too, it was a statement of the cross. It expressed samsara and also the higher awakened mind. So when we played the cross it was a joke—to experience the profound and the profane together. They meet at the edge. There was a kind of laugh in it because we saw the absurdity; a meeting of worlds, really. At that moment, everyone laughed and was happy.

At that moment there was much more openness for what we were doing. And at that moment I immediately said, "Celebrate." You got it at the same time, a little thought about our culture, about Easter. We were there. It was a relearning. I just don't say these statements, what you call provoking, out of whims. They come to invite you.

BG You call attention to the cosmic joke.

RD It's more calling your attention to your own little devil. It is for freeing the mind.

This interview is reprinted from *Inquiring Mind: A Journal of the Vipassana Community*, Winter 1984 (see listing on page 121).

Listening to the Elders © Leav Bolender, 1985.

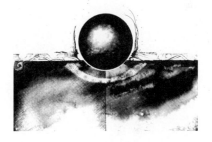

"Listening to the Elders *evolved from my travels throughout the American Southwest while guiding a spiritual pilgrimage and Vision Quest with twelve beloved friends. During a visit with the elders at Hotevilla in the Land of the Hopi, I listened to the prophesies as told by the Grandfathers. These teachings touched me deeply, and confirmed my commitment to pursue a Medicine Path of heeding the wisdom of the ancients, as well as preserving their sacred sites from the onslaught of technocracy."* From the notecard line Earth Imagery Series. Available from The Gaia Catalogue Company or by writing directly to the artist % Earth Rites, Inc., 1265 S. Steele St., Denver, CO 80210.

EARTH NATION

Earth Nation was founded in 1977 by Carol Bridges "based on a vision of an eternally bountiful planet giving forth her gifts to people of all nations." Workshops, ceremonies, and study programs rooted in Native American and New Age practices are open to women and men who wish to deepen their relationship with the Earth in the context of an extended community. Ceremonies are held to celebrate the seasons and to ritualize significant life passages such as the birth of a child. Ongoing classes in women's spirituality, called "The Four Powers," focus on thought, sexuality, time, and money as symbols of the greater powers of focused direction, the creative force, daily worship, and Earth fertility. Send a SASE for a schedule of activities.

Earth Nation, % Carol Bridges, director, P.O. Box 158, Nashville, IN 47448, (812) 988-6285.

EARTH RITES, INC.

Recognizing a need for meaningful rites of passage in a world undergoing rapid cultural changes, Earth Rites offers vision quests for women and men. Courses ranging from wilderness vision quests to urban "Transition Workshops" focus on the joy and power resulting from truly accepting the process of change in our lives. Programs are designed to assist

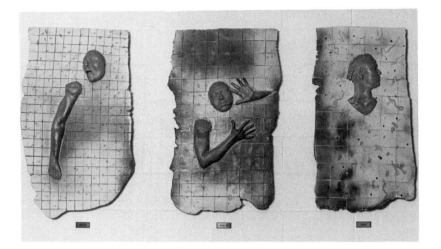

*Despair/Shelter/
Hope © MaryAnn
Fariello, 1985.*

*"The anti-violence
triptych* Despair/
Shelter/Hope
*commissioned by the
city of Nashville has
provoked an intense
dialogue extending
beyond the usual
parameters of the art
community. This has
created an
awareness of the
issue made more
evident by its
installation in a
prominent place
outside of the
courtroom. By
providing a visual
picture of a woman
experiencing
transition from
despair to self-
protection to the*

*beginnings of self-
esteem, I hope to
encourage women
who are taking the
first steps to change
their situation. Like
my Amazon
installation, The
Triptych on behalf
of the Women's
Emergency Shelter
represents the
enduring strength of
the female self, the
Amazon within us
all"* (MaryAnn
Fariello, 2311 Grove
Avenue, Richmond,
VA 23220-4413).

participants in shedding old skins
and giving birth to a new self born
of courage, commitment, and heart.
Specialized vision quests for women
and men recovering from addictive
patterns are scheduled. Leav Bolender, co-founder of Earth Rites, is
an artist whose popular notecard line
the Earth Imagery Series evolved out
of her vision questing work in the
wilderness.

*Earth Rites, Inc. ℅ Leav Bolender
and Ron Pevny, co-directors, 1265 S.
Steele St., Denver, CO 80210, (303)
777-2348.*

Ecumenical Women's Center

Since 1972 the Ecumenical Women's
Center (EWC) has functioned as a
ministry and educational resource
center for lay and religious women.
EWC offers education and advocacy
in feminist spirituality, serves as a
referral center for women in crisis,
and maintains a Prison Ministry Data
Base on resources for incarcerated
women and ex-offenders. EWC publishes a newsletter (ten issues for $10
a year) with articles of interest to
feminist women of faith, and offers
for sale EWC publications: inclusive
language liturgies, nonsexist hymns,
educational packets, and original
feminist songbooks. Membership,
subscription and resource information is available upon request. Send

a legal-size SASE.

*Ecumenical Women's Center, ℅ Liz
Okayama, director, 5253 N. Kenmore
Ave., Chicago, IL 60640, (312) 728-
1850.*

Elizabeth House

An ecumenical house of prayer
founded as a place where women can
experience self-healing and bonding
in sisterhood with other women. Retreats, spiritual guidance, and programs are designed to heal the alienation and estrangement between
people and to serve as a model for
ways of self-healing in community.

*Elizabeth House, ℅ Claire Wolter-
storff, director, 1309 Sherman St.,
S.E., Grand Rapids, MI 49506, (616)
458-0806.*

Eugene Center for Personal Education and the Healing Arts

Eugene Center is a multidisciplinary
institute of educators who share a
commitment to ending the suffering
born out of ignorance. The staff of
thirteen offers a wide range of psy-
chotherapeutic, spiritual, and educational services: meditation and visualization courses, therapy, women's
studies, men's studies, intuition
training, astrology, bodywork thera-
pies, and wilderness vision treks.
Networking and referrals with religious and political groups on a local,
national, and international level is an
essential part of the center's work. A
traditional women's sweat, Singing
Moon Lodge, is part of an ongoing
women's circle that meets each
month for ritual, study, and nurturance of women's spirituality. Write
or call for brochure and program list.

*Eugene Center, ℅ Norma Cordell,
executive director, 1309 Williamette,
Eugene, OR 97401, (503) 344-0178.*

EVANGELICAL WOMEN'S CAUCUS, INTERNATIONAL

Evangelical Women's Caucus (EWC) is an international organization of feminist Christian women and men who believe that the Bible, when properly understood, supports the fundamental equality of the sexes. Local chapters function as support and educational groups, holding seminars, retreats, and all-day workshops. The caucus attempts to move beyond issues of personal freedom to a broader involvement in social justice issues such as increased military buildup, racism, impoverishment of women, and human rights. EWC participates in interfaith dialogues with women of other traditions. *Update*, the EWC newsletter, contains articles, reports on events, book reviews, and "Herstory," a column of members' joys and struggles as biblical feminists. Membership is $30 annually.

Evangelical Women's Caucus, 1357 Washington St., West Newton, MA 02165, (617) 527-3560.

FAITH AT WORK: WOMEN'S MINISTRY

Faith at Work sponsors "Women's Events" throughout the country for renewal and encouragement of ministry women, ordained and nonordained. "Women's Events" include both verbal and nonverbal processes, journal time, prayer, silence, movement, biblical reflection, resource sharing, and discussion of spirituality and sexuality, women's power, and turning points in a woman's life. A schedule of regional "Women's Events" is available upon request.

Women's Events, % Marjory Zoet Bankson, 11065 Little Patuxent Pkwy., Columbia, MD 21044.

FEMINIST SPIRITUAL COMMUNITY

Members and friends of the Feminist Spiritual Community meet on Mon-day nights at the Portland Friends Meeting House to explore dimensions of peace, justice, healing, and feminist spirituality. Ritual, feminine imagery, and story are central to the life of the community. The four directions, the ocean, the winds, trees, and rivers, as well as Jewish, Christian, Eastern, and Third World religions play an important role at gatherings. Members are encouraged to share an event or process in their own life so that celebration, comfort, and private support may be given. Twice yearly retreats are held to deepen commitment to community and feminist spirituality. Projects include a speakers series on feminist spirituality and social justice, courses, workshops, and resources for developing a wider community. Call or write for program schedule and resources.

Feminist Spiritual Community, P.O. Box 3771, 9 Deering St., Portland, ME 04104, (207) 773-2294.

THE GODDESS AND THE CREATIVE PROCESS

PATRICIA REIS

Patricia Reis has an M.E.A. in sculpture from UCLA and an M.A. in depth psychology from the Human Relations Institute, Santa Barbara, California. She has taught courses on women and spirituality and has published articles on mythology, the Goddess, and the female psyche. She is dedicated to working with the creative process of the feminine psyche and has a private practice of therapeia for women. She lives with her husband on Flying Pond in central Maine.

"The icons of old are the codings of tomorrow. And tomorrow holds the promise of recovery of forgotten wisdom."

—Jean Houston

From earliest times, there has existed in the human imagination a creatrix, a Great Goddess who brought forth all living things. Her images and imaged stories are reminders of an ancient female gnosis— a special knowledge about the profound intricacies woven into the cosmic pattern of life, death, and rebirth. It is very important for modern women who are consciously engaged with their own creativity to have some awareness of this ancient Goddess-Creatrix. In order to create from our depths as women, we must find, somewhere in our psyches, an image of a creatrix, a creator in female form. It is helpful for us to know that in our human history there was a primordial Goddess-Creatrix. How she developed through time, what her stories

Pierced Relief
© C. Regina
Kelley, 1980.
Maple wood
sculpture, 1' high.

and images were is important because her history and development is intimately linked with our own. Her story is ours and in the process of experiencing our own creativity we, consciously or unconsciously, reenact her mysteries.

The ancient images of the Great Goddess give evidence that our early ancestors understood the inherent sacrality of the feminine mysteries. The tremendous potency of this imagery is demonstrated by the conservative continuity of these symbols through time. The prehistoric female figures with their sacred signs and symbols persisted in the religious and mystic imagination of our ancestors from Paleolithic times. For more than twenty thousand years they continued to be expressed. During the Neolithic era of Old Europe (6500–3500 B.C.) the symbol system of the Great Goddess not only remained intact but her images flourished. They became increasingly more refined and articulated by the high cultures of that era. This was signified by a tremendous flowering of artistic creativity surrounding the depictions of the Great Goddess in her many aspects.

According to archaeologist Marija Gimbutas, the indigenous peoples who inhabited Old Europe during the Neolithic period were agriculturalists; peaceful, without evidence of weapons of war. They were theacratic: their political structure was based on religious worship of the Great Goddess in her many manifestations. This is evidenced by the more than thirty thousand female images, signs, and symbols that have been found throughout Old Europe. As in the imagery from the Paleolithic era, each image depicted some part of her story, telling us of a highly refined and sophisticated culture and a rich mythical imagery complete with cult and ritual.

What do these images of the Great Goddess from prehistory tell us as modern women about the process of creation? What new/old ideas may be sparked by exploring these images? What may we learn by listening to the Goddess's unspoken language of signs and symbols? How do we undertake a journey to this ancient, ancestral Great Goddess to be initiated into her wisdom? How can we remember her? The answers to these questions are to be found by exploring the mysteries surrounding the Great Goddess and in our own deepest experiences of female creativity. What follows comes from my experience of the way these personal and collective poles of human consciousness inform each other.

In 1978, as a thirty-eight-year-old woman in a master of fine arts graduate program, I suffered a profound rupture in the fabric of my being. I had been seriously making art for eight years. I had been engaged in a process called "surface design" working with dyes on silk. The decision to enter graduate school was a commitment to deepening myself as an artist. At the time, I was obsessed by images of the grid. In my work, I made grids and then attempted to break them down and dissolve them. I was impelled by a desire to "get beyond the grid," to penetrate the surface, to reach the deeper structures that I suspected were behind the imprisoning grid.

In the summer, after one year in graduate school, my own structures were being dramatically torn apart by forces that I could not name. I could no longer "make art." The thin thread of meaning that connected me to my surface images had been cut; the carefully knit structures of my life were unraveling at a speed faster than I could keep up with. This process of unmaking left me with feelings of a terrifying fragmentation and a deep emptiness. I walked on the beach every day. That vast oceanic space somehow both reflected and held my falling-apart self. I was burning with questions about the meaning of making images, my spiritual nature, and myself as a woman. These were questions I had never asked before; they had never even occurred to me.

In the attempt to keep myself together and to fill this seemingly endless and profoundly dark emptiness, I began to read. One day in the UCLA library, as the same questions were throbbing in my head, I came upon pictures of the Venus of Willendorf and other female figurines from the Paleolithic era. My body became electrified. I began to realize that this was the beginning of an answer. These objects held a haunting mystery filled with sacredness. They were saying something about a time when those three aspects, art making, femaleness, and the sacred, which felt so sundered in me, were once unified.

The awareness that I was seeing an image of a female creator painfully brought home to me that my image of a creator had always been male, and that my inner artist was also decidedly male. Slowly, my profound lack of female groundedness was made clear. But with these goddesses from the Paleolithic, from 30,000 B.C., I was ignited. I spent the rest of the summer devouring books and decided to take a leave of absence from school and go to Europe on a quest for the Great Goddess. It was to be a search for my artistic and spiritual heritage as a woman and a profound experience of the creative process at work within my own being.

I spent days in museums looking at these tiny, seemingly insignificant figures. I sought out the Paleolithic caves of central France. I crawled in the cool, dark womb/tombs of prehistoric Brittany—sitting like a seed-stone in the center of the earth waiting to be reborn. I had no idea at the time what I was doing or what was happening to me. All I could do was follow the inner necessity.

In the years that followed the trip, the process of destructuring continued. My studio resembled an archaeological dig filled with strange, fragmented artifacts. My images were ones of death and decay. At one point my studio was filled with "bones" and "skeletons." I called them the "grandmas." They were at once comical and filled with immense grief and sorrow. I was digging up my dead. Still, I had no conscious knowledge of what I was doing; only on a deep instinctive level did I sense that this process was absolutely vital for my survival. I began to work laboriously with fragmented clay images made from casts and molds of my own body, which I would then subject to the purifying and hardening fires of the kiln. The images of fragmented female body parts looked like pieces unearthed from an archaic dig.

Finally, driven by a desperate desire to make whole images, I began to conceive of a large three-dimensional sculptural piece. There were eventually nine 8-foot-tall "presences" that seemed to grow up out of the ground. I called them the "Ancient Ones" or privately, the "Mamas." They were very phallic in shape, which seemed strange to me, and yet they were fully female in feeling. The making of them was hugely satisfying. I felt that I was creating them while they were creating me. The process was one of loving labor and I had endless energy and patience for the making of them. I installed them in a gallery with sonorous vibrational music and they took on a life of their own. Another installation gave me the opportunity to do a perfor-mance/enactment with them. And I knew that it was time to give them a voice. What follows is what the "Ancient Ones" said to me:

From the beginning,

We have been with you.

We are the ancient ones

And we remember.

We remember the time when there was only love,

The time when all breathing was one.

We remember the seed of your being

Planted in the belly of the vast black night.

We remember the red cave of deep slumber,

The time of forgetting,

The sound of your breath and the pulse of your heart.

We remember the force of your longing for life,

The cries of your birth—bringing you forth.

We are the ancient ones

And we have waited   and watched.

You say that you cannot remember that time

That you have no memory of us.

You say that you cannot hear our voices

That our touch no longer moves you.

You say there can be no return

That something has been lost,

That there is only   silence.

We say the time of waiting is over.

We say the silence has been broken.

We say there can be no forgetting now.

We say   listen.

We are the bones of your grandmothers' grandmothers.

We have returned now

We say you cannot forget us now

We say we are with you

And that you are us.

Remember, Remember.

It took me four years to go through the whole process of destructuring, death, inner seeding, fruition, and renewal. One very important aspect of this time has to do with the fact that I removed myself completely from the whole outer arena of the "male world." In order to accomplish my own second birth, so to speak, I had consciously to separate myself from the world of men. It was this deliberate process of pulling in, or creating my own female matrix, that helped me to find my own inner powers, my own feminine ground. I doubt that I could have accomplished this in any other way.

Now eight years later, I find that these experiences were a profound initiation into the mysteries of the creative process and have resulted in my current life's work, the labor of making connections between the images of archaeology, myth, the female psyche, and the creative process. I continue to immerse myself deeply in the study and research of these female images from the Paleolithic and Neolithic eras. I am struck by the stunning synchronicity that these Great Goddess images are literally coming to light in the past one hundred years as the feminine is attempting a return to the consciousness of our Western culture. I am convinced that they hold a message of forgotten wisdom.

Patricia Reis with her sculpture *Ancient Ones.* Photo by Martha Walford, 1982.

FREEHAND

Freehand is a unique educational institution that formalizes a working community of women artists and writers into a collaborative learning experience for personal and social change. The seven-month intensive program is aimed at establishing habits of work, health, and attitude at the intuitive pace that familiarity with geography, community, and one's change in their midst can provide. Each year's program is based on the talents and needs of that year's students yet adheres to a conceptual foundation: concentration in the use of bodywork, movement, drawing, and dreamwork to stimulate, enrich, and heal the imagination; opportunity for response to and criticism of work in progress; making conscious our relationship to racism, classism, health, pleasure, power, and vision; and active celebration, healing circles, readings, exhibitions, and performances. Work/study scholarships for financial aid are available; two are designed specifically for women of color. Write for full descriptive literature and admissions requirements.

Freehand, % Olga Broumas, Marian Roth, and Rita Speicher, founders and directors, P.O. Box 806, Provincetown, MA 02657, (617) 487-3579.

FULL CIRCLE WORKSHOPS, INC.

"A woman is the full circle. Within her is the power to create, nurture and transform. A woman knows that nothing can be born without darkness and nothing can come to fruition without light. Let us call upon woman's voice and woman's heart to guide us through this age of planetary transformation" (Diane Mariechild).

Combining twenty-five years in counseling, education, and ritual making, Diane Mariechild and Shuli Goodman have created Full Circle Workshops for personal and social transformation. Both Diane and Shuli are psychospiritual counselors who bring ancient womanwisdom to Buddhist and native American practices. Workshops, lectures, and consultations are offered throughout the United States, Canada, and Europe. The goal is to help each participant develop and deepen the qualities of compassion, strength, and balance and bring to the world the joy of celebration and the sustaining power of inner peace. For bookings and information on the activities of Full Circle, call or write.

Full Circle, % Diane Mariechild, M.A., and Shuli Goodman, M.A., RFD #3, Amherst, MA 01002, (413) 259-1657.

GRAILVILLE

Grailville is an international conference and retreat center located on 350 acres of rolling farmland in southwest Ohio. It is operated by the Grail, an international movement of Christian women dedicated to a world vision of community, wholeness, and holiness in which women have an active influence in shaping direction. Grailville's programs include international and cross-cultural seminars, ecumenical gatherings, educational conferences, and retreats for groups and individuals. Time for meditation, solitude, group sharing, and enjoyment of the beautiful rural grounds is fostered in an atmosphere of unpressured reflection and spiritual communion alone or with others. Grailville facilities include an art and bookshop and a large garden and solar greenhouse where ongoing explorations in ecologically sound methods of food and energy production are conducted. A calendar of programs is available upon request.

Grailville, 9320 Bannonville Rd., Loveland, OH 45140, (513) 683-2340.

WOMANKIND

JONNIE VANCE

I am the eldest of six females—a woman-power family. I grew up in the Methodist church with strong heart ties to the rituals of the Catholic church. Even the insipid ministers I suffered as a youth did not cause me to lose my passion for the Word, the rituals, or the songs.

My Goddess shapes, my Womankind figures, are an expression of my desire to honor the completeness of God. I am a Christian in the institutional church who adores the Father and the Mother. These words from a hymn to Inanna:

My Lady, the Amazement of the Land, the Lone Star

The Brave One who appears first in the heavens—

All the lands fear her . . .

They make offerings to her . . .

They purify the earth for my Lady.

They celebrate her in song . . .

and these from the Psalms:

Sing for joy to God all the earth . . .

Roar sea, and every creature in you;

Sing, earth, and all who live on you!

Clap your hands, you rivers;

You hills, sing together with joy before God.

bring me equal delight.

I have seen visions and I have a deep mystical faith. I learned about feminism in the institutional church, as well as social action, communication skills, massage, healing, and meditation. I hold and cherish what I have received from the Church and I know there is so much more beyond.

The seed of my feminism sprouted when I heard the song to Atalanta on the record *Free to Be You and Me*. Our stories don't have to be as always; they can be different. In reading books such as Merlin Stone's *When God Was a Woman* and *Sarah the Priestess* by Sevina Teubal, I began to know what had been left out of our roots: the completeness of our story—or God. In addition to the anger and sadness I feel at the deep wound, I also feel a physical pain of surprise—surprise that I have always known Her. As I have always known Him.

One of my most powerful dreams, from which I awoke sobbing and which brings tears whenever I think of it, has a wounded figure, a woman's body and a lion's head. She is wounded and bleeding—but She is not dead.

Womankind (1)
Keeper of the Hearth (2)
Warrior (3)
Turban Woman
© Jonnie Vance, 1986. Cloth images available from the artist: Jonnie Vance, 740 Noe St., San Francisco, CA 94114.

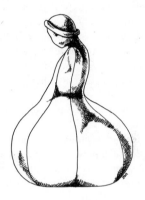

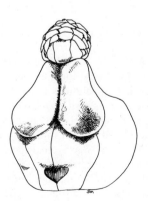

The Great Round Vision Quests

American Indian lore teaches us that the Sacred Hoop of Life is the relatedness of all beings. The plant, mineral, animal, and human kingdoms are all connected, interdependent, unique, equal. In modern times, the Sacred Hoop lies broken because the humans have forgotten their place in the circle of equals and have built hierarchies instead. The Great Round Vision Quests offer individuals the opportunity to step into their own place in the Sacred Hoop. This is self-healing, Earth-healing process on the deepest level. Great Round Vision Quests programs are open to women and men and involve clarification of intention, Medicine teachings, dancing, singing, ceremony, vision-seeking, and the evolution of personal life myths. Questors return to the "small round" of their everyday life able to draw on the power of visions they have received and to transform the world in healing ways. To receive a brochure send a legal-size SASE.

Great Round Vision Quest, % Sedonia Cahill, founder, P.O. Box 201, Bodega, CA 94922, (707) 874-2736.

Green Politics: Committees of Correspondence National Clearinghouse

Committees of Correspondence (C of C) is the largest Green political organization in the United States, with local affiliate groups and regional contact persons in nearly every part of the country. Green Politics is an Earth-based politics of wisdom and compassion. It starts with the recognition that all aspects of our lives are profoundly interconnected and that finding solutions to our current systemic crisis will involve profound transformation of our institutions, values, and ways of thinking. Green politics interweaves ecological wisdom, decentralization of economic and political power wherever practical, personal and social responsibility, postpatriarchal consciousness, global security, and community self-determination within the context of respect for diversity of heritage and religion. It advocates nonviolent action, a cooperative world order, and sustainable future focus. Like other Green movements around the world, the local committees of the Committees of Correspondence operate both inside and outside of electoral politics. Gender balance and ethnic/racial inclusiveness are core operating principles. For the name of the Green group contact person in your community send a SASE.

Committees Correspondence P.O. Box 30208, Kansas City, MO 64112.

Healing Through the Arts

Healing Through the Arts was founded to promote research into the application of art for healing the mind, body, and spirit. Current and future projects include the musical recording and mandala art of *A Rainbow Path* (music by Kay Gardner, art by Gina Halpern—see listing on page 135), a three-day conference on alcohol and the arts, retreats and public lectures, concerts, gallery showings, theater, and multimedia events.

Healing Through the Arts, % Kay Gardner and Gina Halpern, P.O. Box 399, Stonington, ME 04681, (207) 867-5076.

A Rainbow Path: The Belly Chakra Mandala © Gina Halpern, 1984. Acrylic painting, 10″ × 10″. From A Rainbow Path, a collection of eight mandalas for meditation and healing. Photo by Margaret E. Kauffman for Healing Through the Arts. For information on the creation of personal mandalas for use in healing, meditation, birthing, and rituals contact: Gina Halpern % Healing Through the Arts, P.O. Box 399, Stonington, ME 04681.

"Every traditional culture and religion has used the mandala image to raise the spirit and focus the viewer toward greater personal harmony and peace. The mandalas of A Rainbow Path are drawn from rich and varied sources: Celtic, Tibetan, Hindu, Sufi, personal and contemporary, as well as a wealth of information on the significant uses of color for healing. Each painting was created to center in, and then to draw up, moving first into an experience of depth and then moving us up visually and, hopefully, emotionally, physically, spiritually, loving and balancing all the elements. In the process of this work I have been learning that all pains can be tempered in this fire of transformation and that in the light of these flames all becomes truly visible and radiant. By understanding and nurturing the broken pieces, by reclaiming the lost parts of ourselves and embracing them, and by entering into harmony with all the elements of our being, we can establish balance in our bodies, on the earth, in the universe" (Gina Halpern).

THE HERMITAGE: ECUMENICAL RETREAT CENTER

The Hermitage is an ecumenical retreat center dedicated to the spiritual, emotional, intellectual, physical, and professional formation of persons of every age, persuasion, and circumstance. The programming focus of the organization is sensitive to the needs of women and their particular requirements for daytime workshops and child care provisions. Programs specifically address women's spirituality and women's bodies as they relate to the cycles of life, creative family living for single parents and couples, and power as it relates to women and physical weight. Program schedule available upon request.

The Hermitage, 3650 E. 46th St., Indianapolis, IN 46205, (317) 545-0742.

HYGIEIA COLLEGE CORRESPONDENCE COURSE IN WOMANCRAFT AND LAY MIDWIFERY

Hygieia College was founded by Jeannine Parvati Baker to heal birth in our culture. Jeannine is an activist in the spiritual midwifery and women's self-health movement. Hygieia College offers a unique home-study correspondence course designed as a maiutic (in the manner of a midwife) experience. The program enables a woman to study at a pace best suited to meet her personal and family needs. The ten-lesson course provides in-depth study on subjects such as herbalism, sexuality, mythology, conscious conception, dreams, lotus birth, chants, and soundings. A personal evaluative dialogue is included with each lesson. Tuition: $250 for all ten lessons or $30 for each individual lesson. Sample lesson (#1 "The Innerview")

Jeannine Parvati Baker. Photo by Kris Wilcox, 1986.

is available for $20. Inquiries welcomed for Hygieia College and for information on Jeannine's "Book of the Moon Club." Send a legal-size SASE.

Hygieia College, % Jeannine Parvati Baker, P.O. Box 398, Monroe, UT 84754, (801) 527-3738.

IMMACULATE HEART COLLEGE CENTER

Immaculate Heart College Center offers a master of arts program in feminist spirituality. *Feminist spirituality* refers to the movement for full social, political, moral, and religious equality for all women and men. Although theology forms the core of the curriculum, spirituality is understood to include every dimension of human life, not only methods of prayer and the development of virtue. The faculty is composed of a small core group and visiting professors from around the world who are leading feminist scholars in their respective fields. The program is designed for working women: courses take place in the evenings and on weekends. Students may enroll in the graduate

program, certificate program, or audit courses for personal/spiritual enrichment. Write for brochure and description of current course offerings.

Immaculate Heart College Center, % Dr. Pat Reif, director, Suite 2021, 10951 W. Pico Blvd., Los Angeles, CA 90064, (213) 470-2293.

INSIGHT MEDITATION SOCIETY

Insight Meditation Society (IMS), a retreat center set on eighty wooded acres in central Massachusetts, provides a secluded environment for the intensive practice of insight or Vipassana meditation, the moment-to-moment investigation of the mind-body process through calm and focused awareness. Vipassana retreats are available on a daily, weekly, and monthly basis for beginning and experienced meditators. Silence and a daily sitting schedule are maintained at all times. In addition to teacher-led retreats from ten days to three months, the society is open all year for individual retreats and long-term meditation practice. Each fall a women's spirituality retreat is offered to provide women the opportunity to explore meditative practice together. Dharma talks and discussion groups enable participants to investigate, develop, and express their spiritual vision. Write or call for schedule of retreats. Tapes of dharma talks from previous retreats are available from Dharma Seed Library (See listing on page 237).

Insight Meditation Society, Pleasant St., Barre, MA 01005, (617) 355-4378.

INSTITUTE IN CULTURE AND CREATION SPIRITUALITY

The Institute in Culture and Creation Spirituality (ICCS) is a center for the study, exploration, celebration, and experience of Western creation-centered spiritual traditions. Creation spirituality reveres the sacredness and goodness of creation and celebrates every creature as a mirror image of the divine. Creation spirituality integrates the wisdom of Nature and the teachings of prophets and mystics of the West, such as Hildegard of Bingen and Meister Eckhart, with today's scientific understanding of the emerging universe. Master of Arts degrees or certificates are offered in three programs: Culture and Creation Spirituality, Geo-Justice and Creation Spirituality, and Psychology and Creation Spirituality. Friends of Creation Spirituality is a nonprofit organization established to support the aims of ICCS and the spread of creation-centered spirituality. Information about the M.A. and certificate programs is available from ICCS.

ICCS at Holy Names College, 3500 Mountain Blvd., Oakland, CA 94619, (415) 436-1046. Information about weekend workshops, lecture tours, and summer programs is available from Friends of Creation Spirituality, P.O. Box 19216, Oakland, CA 94611.

INTERHELP

"Suffering—whether from loss or change—is part of human life. Because the suffering we face today exists in a linear system that appears to have no end, it is particularly difficult. When we return suffering to its place in the natural cycle of birth-growth-decline-death-rebirth, its function returns to our lives. We can look forward to renewal" (Chellis Glendinning, co-founder of Interhelp and author of **Waking up in the Nuclear Age**—*see listing on page 98).*

Logo by Mara Loft, 1984.

Interhelp is a nonpartisan global network founded on the conviction that our painful feelings are a healthy response and a sign of deep caring for the planet and that achieving a healthy planet demands more than politics alone. Heart, spirit, feelings, visions, and our deepest inner responses need to be awakened if we are to move beyond powerlessness and numbness into effective action. Interhelp activities include "despair and empowerment" workshops, local support networks, community gatherings, training intensives, and programs for schools, churches, parent groups, and private organizations.

Resources include regional and international gatherings, international contacts and offices, a network newsletter, a manual for starting a nuclear support group, a speakers bureau; and consultation services to individuals and groups. Membership in Interhelp is free and open to all. Subscription to the bimonthly newsletter is $20 annually.

Interhelp, Inc., US Network Resource Office, Rae Atira-Soncia P.O. Box 8895, Madison, WI 53708-8895, (608) 231-1219.

SWEAT LODGE CEREMONIES FOR WOMEN

PORTIA CORNELL

Portia Cornell is a practicing psychotherapist who draws her skills and powers from the rural environment in which she lives. She is a member of Interhelp, an international network that supports those who believe that the maintenance of a healthy planet demands the deepest response of one's heart and spirit to the world.

Since 1980, women have gathered on the full moon every month in a secluded meadow in western Connecticut to practice Earth healing, using the form of the Sweat Lodge. Based on Native American tradition, the Sweat Lodge is historically a religious ceremony for purification, performed before a difficult feat, battle, or festival. It cleanses and prepares one physically, emotionally and spiritually. This wholistic threefold nature has drawn contemporary women to the Sweat Lodge ceremony.

The Sweat Lodge is a hut made of saplings stuck in the ground and bent over to form 13 ribs, with a door open to the east, to the rising sun. The shape of the Lodge is a dome—representing both the womb of the earth, and the back of the turtle. In Native American tradition North America is known as Turtle Island. Before the Sweat, rocks are heated in fire, then placed in a hole in the Earth in the middle of the Sweat Lodge floor. The frame is covered with blankets to contain the heat. We prepare for the Sweat by meditating, fasting, drumming, smudging (cleansing with sage and cedar smoke).

We enter the doorway of the Sweat and invoke the powers of the four cardinal directions. We give thanks for the elements. We breathe deeply in the soft moist dark. We feel the heat on our flesh and the smell of our bodies. Sitting solemnly in sacred circle and flanked on both sides by sisters, we are guided to confront the terminal dangers of our times.

The Sweat is done in four rounds. The first round is a spitting out of angers, resentments, grudges, and fears that hold us back from realizing our power. We go deeper into our own feelings as we hear others speak their truth. The second round is that of visioning, where images and sounds, from nature or one's personal experience, serve as beacons upon which to build dreams and hopes.

The third round is that of asking assistance, from a higher being or guide or goddess, from persons in one's own life or from an Earth force like the wind. Ancestors and those whom we love are often called in at this time. Hearing the prayers of those whom we have never met before brings us closer together. We sing lullabies to one another. We cry together and hold one another. And in the last round we express our appreciation for each other and what we have shared, sensing the delicate and tender preciousness of life. Gathering the power shared in the Sweat, we extend it in ripples to family and friends, then outward to the Earth herself and the Universe. It is a relief when the Lodge door is thrown open and the first woman emerges with a whoop into the night air, fresh as a newborn babe.

We close the Sweat Lodge ceremony with a give-away, a Native American tradition. Each woman has brought something meaningful to her, to give away to someone who has touched her deeply during the Sweat. This ceremony expresses that we really possess nothing, that everything passes through us, even our own lives.

"It is good medicine to sit upon the Earth Mother," we say. It is good to spend an evening naked under the full moon, sweating from our bodies, pouring our sweat and tears back into the Earth. The Sweat Lodges performed by women in Connecticut are political statements, and an opportunity to tell our stories of living in the nuclear age. As each woman speaks, the myth that is articulated is the collective story of the group and of the hurts and struggles of the Earth Mother. The myth resides in the emotions and in the physical expression of sitting down upon the Earth as an act of personal and planetary purification.

We have been asked how we feel about borrowing from a ceremony that is sacred to Native Americans. We have respect and gratitude to Native Americans for showing us a form that works so well. We feel drawn to using the sacred rites of Turtle Island to heal her of the havoc she is wreaking worldwide. We hope it offends no one that we use this form to empower us to continue our work of healing the Earth Mother.

Some people ask why we only do these circles with women. We had considered inviting some of our brothers who were sensitively asking to come. However, so many women wanted Sweats that it developed into a tradition. This may not be so much an oversight, as a response to a voice from the Earth for women to sit in Sacred Council.

For many women, alienated from traditional churches because of their sexism, it is a welcome relief to at last find a spiritual home for themselves. It is something we have been waiting for for a long time. You might call it post-Christian ritual. It is good to have a "moveable church."

Perhaps this is a ritual purification we are doing in preparation for a battle. Living in the nuclear age, it is hard to imagine what the battle might be like. Perhaps the battle is already being waged in each of us, and our cries are the cries from the ongoing wars upon the Earth.

"Thank you, all my relations," we say as we exit from the Sweat into the moonlit night. We are thanking all life forms, the departed as well. We have been honored to touch our commonality and we pray that seven generations will come after us to know the same.

This article was previously printed in the *Interhelp Newsletter* and the *Women Outdoors Bulletin*.

Spiral Prayer Bowl © Jonda W Friel, 1985. Gourd with sand, brass, shells, fossils, and feathers, 5" × 3-1/2". Photo by Carolyn Brown. Ceremonial bowls, masks, rattles, pouches, and jewelry available for sale from the artist: Jonda W. Friel, P.O. Box 1141, Tahoe City, CA 95730.

Logo by Pat Runo, 1985.

INTERNATIONAL SOCIETY FOR RELIGION AND ANIMAL RIGHTS

Joan Beth Clair believes that reverence for other forms of life is a buried religious tradition. After earning a divinity degree from the Graduate Theological Union, where she found little religious support for animal rights, she founded the International Society for Religion and Animal Rights (ISRAR), with the immediate goal of changing the public's perception of animals as objects for experimentation and manipulation. Each year ISRAR holds a memorial service for animals in a traditional religious site to create "sacred space" for more than one form of life. One liturgical service created by Clair in honor of her dog Wind-of-Fire included prayers for coyotes, wolves, seals, pigs, monkeys, and "all other animals who are victims of human injustice." An agape meal, a sacrament of communion for all of creation, was shared by both animal and human participants. ISRAR develops liturgies inclusive of all forms of life; makes these liturgies available for worship services; provides a list of lay and ordained religious willing to conduct inclusive services; and provides a speaker's bureau and audiovisual materials to religious and other concerned groups to address animal rights from a religious perspective. Membership ($5–$35) includes an annual subscription to the newsletter, *Anima/L.*

Joan Beth Clair (Newman), M.Div., founder and director, 1798 Scenic Ave. (Box 543), Berkeley, CA 94709, (415) 841-7744.

INTERNATIONAL WOMEN'S STUDIES INSTITUTE

The International Women's Studies Institute is an educational organization dedicated to the study of women's lives from a cross-cultural perspective. Summer programs in Greece, Israel, Kenya, Thailand, and Italy, as well as a semester program in the Mediterranean, bring together women of all ages, backgrounds, and nationalities. Each program matches fifteen to twenty individuals with faculty from the United States and the host countries. Courses treat the themes of women in development, women's spirituality, women's literature, women in community, and other cultural, social, and political issues relevant to each culture. The Institute combines programs in women's studies with a unique international live-in community experience. Classes are small and provide for exchange between scholars, students, professionals, artists, and activists. Write for a brochure.

International Women's Studies, % Judith Mings, director, 1230 Grant Ave., Box 601, San Francisco, CA 94133, (415) 931-6973.

RITUALS WITH APHRODITE

CAROL P. CHRIST

Carol P. Christ has been active in the feminist, peace, and Goddess movements. She is co-chair of the Women and Religion Section of the American Academy of Religion and is Professor of Women's Studies and Religious Studies at San Jose State University. She is the author of Diving Deep and Surfacing *and* Laughter of Aphrodite, *co-editor of* Womanspirit Rising, *and is currently working on* Womanspirit Rising, Volume II. *Her spiritual home is the island of Lesbos, where she spends a great deal of time writing and making rituals.*

In my class at the Aegean Women's Studies Institute in Lesbos we read my book *Diving Deep and Surfacing* in conjunction with Christine Downing's *The Goddess*. We write in our journals about our experiences of nothingness, awakening, insight, and naming, and about our relation to Downing's visions of the Greek goddesses. We share what we have written in groups of two and three. Our classes are held in the sunlight in view of the Aegean Sea below us. An atmosphere of openness, intimacy, and trust develops.

After writing about our experiences of nothingness, Alexis and I share our stories of being left by men we had loved too much. We speak of how we had felt whole, alive, sexual, creative, and then empty, devastated. A few days later we discuss Downing's chapter on Aphrodite in class. Downing writes of Aphrodite as goddess not simply of love and beauty, but as cosmic life force. Aphrodite is associated especially with that aspect of the life force that we know as the transformative power of intense sexual connection. Downing mentions that Aphrodite's temples often stood at places of transformation: on cliffs where mists rise from the sea, on marshy ground where sea and dry land meet. She writes that Aphrodite is often imaged rising on the sea from a shell, that she is known as the Golden One because she prefers the sunlight. Downing also mentions Aphrodite's laughter.

After we write in our journals about Aphrodite, Alexis and I speak of going to Aphrodite's temple on Lesbos to reclaim our sexuality. The tensions builds within each of us until we know that we must go.

While wandering through town agitatedly, waiting for the time we had agreed to meet to go to the temple, I suddenly realize why temples to other deities are often in the vicinity of a major temple on a site. I realize that we must make offerings to other goddesses before we can approach Aphrodite. We must approach her free of distraction. Objects begin to beckon to me from shop windows: a bottle opener picturing Priapus with an enormous erection, another with an owl, a postcard of a Greek woman weaving, golden worry beads, and finally the white gauze dress woven with golden threads and golden shawl I had admired the night before. I would go to Aphrodite's temple in white, symbolizing my desire to be initiated into her mysteries. I would wear the golden shawl to honor her goldenness and my own. When I meet Alexis at my friend Axiothea's tourist shop, she is wearing the white dress she found in Athens. We bedeck ourselves in golden bronze necklaces and buy a handmade pottery pitcher and bowl, white with rose and indigo flowers. Alexis decides that she too must wear a golden shawl.

Our last stop is the grocery shop where we find red wine and golden retsina, golden biscuit cookies, milk and honey, yogurt. On impulse we each pick out a pair of double shells, Alexis's yellow, mine pink, which will become one of the central symbols of our ritual. We ask for directions to the temple but all we learn is that we must turn down a small unmarked road some kilometers from the next town. Someone writes the words *Naos Aphrodite* on a scrap of paper in Greek letters.

The temple is at the end of a farm road in marshy ground within sight of an enormous womblike bay. Despite its proximity to a farm with goats and turkeys, the temple itself, which is surrounded by barbed wire and unmarked, appears deserted. We have arrived during the afternoon nap time. We are alone. The temple is small, and though none of its columns still stand, its light grey stone floor is clearly exposed, and fragments of columns are strewn about the site. Two trees grow at the center of the temple, and the crumbling walls of a tiny Byzantine church built over the rear part of the temple are visible. The freshly whitewashed altar in the ruins of the church and

Alexis between trees. Photo by Carol P. Christ, 1982.

a couple of dusty icons and oil lamps indicate it is still used.

Our excitement builds as we scramble over barbed-wire fence and find ourselves standing amidst thorns and thistles in what must have been the temple's forecourt. We begin to take things out of our bags. We haven't planned much, but we have spoken about the altars we will make outside the temple. We fill the flowered pitcher with red wine and the bowl with water. We set the rest of the wine and the food aside. We put our offerings into the bowl.

I begin. On an exposed flat rock, I set a postcard of a Greek woman weaving, and golden worry beads. This is my altar to Hestia, goddess of hearth and home. I speak to Hestia, telling her how honored I am to live in her realm, continuing the traditions of home-making I have learned from my mother and grandmothers, a bond I share with women across the ages. Though I also work outside the home, I affirm my connection to Hestia. I spend a good deal of my time working in my home and in my garden. But I also speak to Hestia of how much she demands. I tell her that when I wake on a weekend morning thinking of what needs to be done, rather than thinking of my husband, she asks too much. I pour out libations to her, begging her to leave me time to worship Aphrodite. She seems very thirsty, and Alexis has to stop me before I pour out a whole pitcherful of wine. My second altar is to Athene. On it I place the owl, Athene's sacred animal. For me, as for Christine Downing, Athene symbolizes my intellectual self, my ability to move into the world of men, like the patriarchal Athene, as well as my ability to draw upon the wisdom of night, the realm of the prepatriarchal Athene. I tell Athene I am honored to live in her realm, proud of my academic credentials and training, proud also to remember the wisdom of my mother. But I remind her that she too can be a demanding goddess. As I pour out red wine offerings to her, I plead with her to leave me time and space for Aphrodite.

Alexis's altar is to Demeter and Persephone. She arranges the black scarf of Demeter's mourning and green worry beads for Persephone on a small rise. She pours out her story to the Mother, telling Demeter of the loss of her beloved daughter, of a husband who threatened to take her children where she would never see them again if she sued for custody. She shares with Demeter her joy at learning that her daughter soon would be returning to live with her after many years of separation. Finally she tells Demeter her fear that her Persephone would try to destroy her relationship with her lover. She offers libations at the altar.

And then we are ready to enter the temple. We are excited and apprehensive, ready to meet Aphrodite. We do not know what that will mean. We gather the retsina and food and our shells, pouring the last of the red wine and water into the pitcher. We pause at the threshold of the temple, and I begin to pour out the water and wine. All of a sudden I hear what I can only describe as the laughter of

Aphrodite, from Trajan's fountain. Ephesus museum. Photo by Carol P. Christ, 1981.

Spiral and first altar within Aphrodite's temple. Photo by Alexis Masters, 1982.

Carol at the threshold of the temple. Photo by Alexis Masters, 1982.

Aphrodite. The sound may be in my mind but it is clear as a bell. I hear Aphrodite saying through her golden laughter, "Whoever told you that you could know sexual ecstasy without pain?" And then she begins to laugh again, saying, "What can you do but laugh?" I begin to laugh with her. I laugh with joy and pain. Alexis laughs too.

We step into the temple. She is everywhere. We find womblike spirals and vaginal roses carved in stone. We start to make an altar on one of the broken columns, but I feel myself drawn to the space between the two trees, at the center of the temple. I go to the spot, remove my shoes and my dress. I sit between the trees opening my body to the midday sun, wearing only my golden shawl, which reflects rays of golden light. I anoint my body with milk and honey, saying to myself, surely this is the land flowing with milk and honey. I pour milk and honey into the rose-colored shells, which open and close like my own. The sun warms and transforms my body. Though Alexis is standing nearby, I am alone with the Goddess in her sacred space. I feel myself opening. I become Aphrodite.

After Alexis has performed her own ritual in the space between the trees, we sit together eating from our shells, drinking retsina, and sharing stories. We speak of our first lovers, and our current lovers, and many in between. When we finish, we each fill one of our shells with milk and honey and leave it for the Goddess. We pour out a libation of retsina and toss Priapus into the air. A bit of milk and yogurt is left and we offer it on the whitewashed altar with a prayer that Greek women also reclaim their connections to Aphrodite.

We pack our things and make our way past the goats and turkeys and small farms along the dirt road that leads us back to the main road. We walk a long way down the road before a German tourist bus picks us up and brings us back to our town.

We are glowing, and when we tell our story, three women ask us to take them to the temple. When we return, Alexis and I know that we have become priestesses of Aphrodite. One of the women is a virgin. We begin to understand what it means for women to initiate other women into the mysteries of sexuality. Our rites are sensual, not sexual: each woman discovers that her sexuality is her own. We all give the virgin lots of advice, much of it contradictory. Some time later, I take another woman to the temple. This time I lose my watch. It is a small price to pay.

JEWISH WOMEN'S RESOURCE CENTER

The Jewish Women's Resource Center (JWRC) was founded in 1977 to document and advance the modern Jewish women's movement. Women looking for a supportive community, parents wishing to celebrate the birth of a daughter, and professors preparing course syllabi on Jewish women's spirituality have all benefited from the resource center's facilities. Center services include networking and referrals, library facilities, seminars, celebrations, and study and support groups. Popular materials available from the JWRC include a birth ceremonies guide, egalitarian *ketubot* (marriage contracts), a guide to Rosh Hodesh (new moon) ceremonies, and feminist nonsexist Passover Haggadoth.

Jewish Women's Resource Center, 9 E. 69th St., New York, NY 10021, (212) 535-5900.

JEWISH WOMEN'S RESOURCE LIBRARY

The Jewish Women's Resource Library, a project of the Los Angeles section of the National Council of Jewish Women, is both a resource center and a circulating library of books and unpublished materials on Jewish women. The library contains the West Coast's most comprehensive collection of publications for, by, and about Jewish women. It also offers a wide range of educational programs that appeal to a wide and varied audience. Past programs have included an exhibit of women's Judaic crafts, Jewish storytelling, life cycle ceremonies, and book discussion groups.

Jewish Women's Resource Library, 543 N. Fairfax Ave., Los Angeles, CA 90036, (213) 651-2930.

LORETTO SPIRITUALITY NETWORK

Loretto Spirituality Network is an ecumenical networking group that offers an environment in which women and men may share dialogue, ritual, and prayer. Liturgy and symbol are drawn from a Christian/feminist perspective, though all paths are honored. The network is a center for feminist resources in music, theology, and spirituality. Women Church West, the regional section of the national Women-Church movement, is a vital part of its networking activities. Public prayer gatherings, consisting of ritual, music, and celebration, are held each week at the network house.

Loretto Spirituality Network, 529 Pomona Ave., Albany, CA 94706, (415) 525-4174.

MADRE: A PROJECT OF WOMEN'S PEACE NETWORK

In 1983 the Mothers of Heroes and Martyrs in Nicaragua asked a small group of visiting women from the United States to "please urge the women of your country to support us. Please use your strength . . . to stop the killing of our children." Madre was formed and since 1983 has grown into a powerful, wide-reaching network of women who know each other through their work, their children's schools or day care centers, through churches or synagogues. Madre connects the problems women face every day in this country with the struggles of women in Central America and the Caribbean. For example, the Twinning Program pairs local day care centers in the United States with child care centers in Nicaragua for joint educational and fund-raising work. As of March 1987, Madre had sent $450,000 in supplies and services to the women and children of Nicaragua. Madre also has ongoing programs in support of the women and children of El Salvador, focusing on women's health and child care.

Members of Madre ($10 annual membership fee) receive the Madre newsletter and mailings on Madre projects and activities.

Madre, 853 Broadway, Room 301, New York, NY 10003, (213) 777-6470.

MANY VOICES: A NEW AGE CENTER

Many Voices is a women-owned business and teaching center for women and men with special emphasis on women's spirituality, healing, and self-development. Programs feature out-of-town and local speakers/ teachers on many traditions within the women's spirituality and new age movements. A central clearinghouse for information on women's spirituality within the Twin Cities community, Many Voices publishes a monthly newsletter that lists classes, workshops, events, and other news of interest.

Many Voices, % Anahid Sarkissian and Johanna der Boer, 889 Grand Ave., St. Paul, MN 55105, (612) 224-0374.

MEDICINE WHEEL CENTER

The Medicine Wheel Center is the home of Pan's Forest Herb Company. The vision for the use of the land grew from the work of Lorien as a practicing herbalist, midwife, and spiritual journeyer. Herbal Intensives train participants in growing and gathering techniques, the nutritional use of herbs, herbs for childbirth and children, text resources, and intuitive diagnostic techniques. Retreats and vision quest assistance are available through the center.

Medicine Wheel Center, % Lorien, 411 Ravens Rd., Port Townsend, WA 98368, (206) 385-6524.

MINISTRY OF LIGHT: WOMEN'S SPIRITUALITY GROUP

The Ministry of Light was founded to provide counseling services to lesbian and gay people, their families and friends, and to educate schools, churches, and synagogues in the area of human sexuality, homophobia, and AIDS. Within the Ministry, the Women's Spirituality Group provides a place where women of a variety of sexual preferences share faith and religious experiences. Meetings combine learning and intellectual stimulation with sharing and interpersonal communication. Ritual—Christian, Jewish, Buddhist, Pagan—establishes an atmosphere of acceptance that allows each participant to change and grow spiritually and emotionally. The group meets twice a month in each other's homes.

Ministry of Light, % Rev. Jane Adams Spahr, 240 Tiburon Blvd., Tiburon, CA 94920, (415) 457-1155.

MOTHERHEARTH

Motherhearth is a group of women who meet as a coven and follow a positive path blending Wiccan, American Indian, Goddess, and other traditions meaningful to circle members' spiritual growth. Its primary purpose is to explore women's spiritual heritage and to revive Goddess mysteries, rituals, and healing knowledge. Motherhearth celebrates the eight holidays of the Wheel of the Year following the moon cycles and harvest holidays. Once a month, Motherhearth sponsors a community discussion group as a forum for study and sharing of information on women's spiritual and healing traditions. Circle members also meet among themselves for in-depth study and work in the healing arts.

Motherhearth, % Spider, 111 Branch St., Pittsburgh, PA 15215.

Logo by Spider.

NATIONAL ASSEMBLY OF RELIGIOUS WOMEN

National Assembly of Religious Women (NARW) is an organization of women of faith—women religious and laywomen—committed to the prophetic task of raising feminist awareness within the Roman Catholic tradition. NARW's membership acts collectively to build a world of peace with justice, responding critically and immediately from a faith context in the public forum. Through training events, workshops, national conferences, coalition building, and program resources, NARW provides a way for women to share lived experiences, do theology across lines of economic, cultural, and religious diversity, and envision possibilities and strategies for change. *Probe*, the national bimonthly publication of NARW, educates, challenges, and activates its members to do justice. Annual $20 membership includes a subscription to *Probe*.

National Assembly of Religious Women, % Judy Vaughan, CSJ, and Kathy Osberger, coordinators, 1307 S. Wabash, Room 206, Chicago, IL 60605, (312) 663-1980.

NATIONAL WOMEN'S MAILING LIST

Since 1981, the National Women's Mailing List (NWML) has been linking individual women with grassroots women's organizations that share their feminist concerns. In signing up with NWML, you choose from a long list of interest area categories. NWML is then able to supply feminist groups that are planning actions, events, publications, etc., with mailing lists of interested women. Lists can be made up that contain the names of feminists in a particular state or region in order to advertise local gatherings, retreats, conferences. NWML maintains a mailing list of women's spiritual or religious organizations that runs the gamut from feminist caucuses within traditional religions to Goddess-centered groups. For information on how to sign up to receive mail or how to obtain NWML mailing lists, send a SASE to NWML or call.

National Women's Mailing List, % Jill Lippitt, director, P.O. Box 68, Jenner, CA 95450, (707) 632-5763.

NATIONAL WOMEN'S STUDIES ASSOCIATION

The National Women's Studies Association (NWSA) was founded in 1977 to further the social, political, and professional development of women's studies at every educational level and in every educational setting. Members consist of individuals, academic and community-based programs, projects, and groups involved in feminist education. NWSA works to eliminate not only sexism, but racism, anti-Semitism, heterosexism, and oppression based on age, class, religion, ethnicity, disability, and national origins, as well as other barriers to human liberation inherent in the social structure. NWSA sponsors an annual national conference, regional conferences, graduate schol-

arships, and a prize for the best manuscript in women's studies. Members receive the quarterly journal *NWSA Perspectives*, discount subscriptions to feminist journals, a national college directory of women's studies programs, and affiliation with regional chapters.

National Women's Studies Association, University of Maryland, College Park, MD 20742, (301) 454-3757.

THE MIKVEH CEREMONY—
CONNECTING BLACK AND JEWISH WOMEN

———

E. M. BRONER

There are impurities of the body. They are wounds that leak pus, running sores, scabs, dandruff, herpes, that which is a fungus upon the skin.

But that which builds life is holy and all matters relating to it are natural and joyful.

It is in the nature of society to border us, to mark our maps carefully, to warn us of tempestuous winds at the four corners of the flat earth.

It is in the nature of women to know the earth is round; the earth is her mother breathing, filled with healing herbs, with telling signs.

It is in the nature of society to make woman's intelligence concern itself with the state of her menses rather than with the state of the world.

There are impurities that must be cleansed from the soul: the impurity of separation from another woman, the impurity of suspicion of another color, the impurity of superiority over another religion.

At this point I must speak of this Mikveh Ceremony, presented to the hundreds of academicians attending the National Women's Studies meeting at Ohio State University, 1983.

This was to be a bridging ceremony connecting the disaffection that had occurred between two major groups in the women's movement, the Blacks and the Jews.

We had suffered too much in the split between the various camps of the women's movement. Our efforts were disconnected. Our actions at cross-purposes. It was time to try to touch fingertips, at least, if we were not yet ready to embrace.

Those of us on the program at Ohio State University, June of 1983, that 100 degrees day, were nervous. The NWSA and Ohio State University had added funding from the National Endowment for the Humanities to bring in leading writers. Each night, at the large auditorium on campus, a Black or Chicana writer shared the platform with a white author. The plenary session was to be on "Racism and Anti-Semitism." We were facing one another at last.

I was the first reader. Sharing the platform with me was a Black poet whose poetry we considered blatantly anti-Semitic. Even when her new poetry was read in Lebanon, it seemed to us, also in the throes of that terrible conflict about that war, another setting for her earlier anti-Semitism. Could I reach this poet? Could I move the audience? Did I have the necessary engineering skills to build a bridge?

The Jewish women in the audience sat close to the stage to send out their energy and courage. Some, like Judith Arcana, the author, wore amulets to call down special powers upon me. I felt the tone of the following meetings would depend on the direction of this initial presentation.

I ascended the podium and placed my yarmulke on my head. I wanted them to know I meant business. I described the ritual of the Mikveh.

I. ENCOUNTERING THE IMPURITY

We sit in a circle, averting our eyes from one another, as the menstruating woman is not supposed to look directly, nor is she supposed to gaze upon husband or water or food. We avert our eyes to allow each of us our own privacy.

We sit widely spaced and lower our head and chin into our neck. We speak to the deepest, angriest, most hidden part of ourselves.

One of us speaks. She may say something like this:

We are here to raise issues, to face down lies, to give account of our history, to be our own chronicle, and to hope that we are not talking to ourselves but through ourselves to the group.

II. RELATING OUR HISTORIES

Each, looking at herself, tells her history as a woman of color, a woman of another accent, another tongue, a woman of a different body, a woman of keen hearing, a woman not able to hear, a woman of religion, a firm atheist, a woman with no sense of belonging and a woman in context of family, a woman who loves men, a woman who loves women, a woman orphaned, a woman solitary, a woman celibate, a woman who celebrates, a woman who mourns, a woman under siege and a woman attacking.

We call ourselves the names we have been called.

We speak of our terror of the Other.

We name our metaphors of that terror.

A Black woman might think of White as a skeleton, a shroud, a ghost, a descending cloud, gleaming teeth in a skull, blinding sight.

A White woman might think of women of color, of Black, as coal, a tunnel without light, a deep hole, a cloak that hides, charred remains, the cellar, a pit, the unknown.

Christian women may think of the Jew as being stiff-necked, unreasonable, aggressive, materialistic, clannish, tribal, exclusive, physically unlovely, physically sexual, people of patriarchy and woman bound, radical women, people of cowardice, people who aggress against their peaceful neighbors, people who go sheep-like to their destruction, people of vengeance, people who assimilate and forget, people who live their lives in the past; people who control the world through international connections; people who withdraw from the world into the provincial, parochial; the rich Jew, the Jew in the slums of the lower East Side; the Jew with pushcart; the Jew as international Banker.

The Jew may view the Christian as the Crusade, as Richard the Lion-Hearted herding the Jews of Jerusalem into their wooden synagogue and setting it aflame. The Christian is the Inquisition. The Christian imposes the costume on the Jew of the horned hat, the yellow star. The Christian is the howling horde, the Russian pogrom. The Christian controls the economy. The Christian is the military and that will ultimately be used against the Jew. The Christian would sacrifice the Jew here and in Israel. The Christian would recognize the Jew only to convert her.

III. CURSING

We call one another names, terrible, hurting, piercing names. We shout, we point the finger of accusation.

If we are Arab sisters, we speak of the terror of the military and the differently religious state in our midst.

If we are Israeli, we speak of the giant across the border who would stamp us out.

If we are Black, we speak of the Jew as woman of privilege.

If we are Jews, we speak of the Black as the betrayer.

IV. CONNECTIONS

We must speak of that which connects us.

If we are Egyptian or Arabic, we speak of the pain of theocratic law, family law, of losing house, child and self in divorce. In the House of Israel we speak much the same, of the shame of the "get," the divorce and of our losses of custody and self-respect.

When we speak of our shames, we blame one another less. When we speak of our connections, we can move closer in this wide-gapped circle.

We as women of color speak of the night and of violence against us.

We women of white skin also speak of the terror of assault, of our faces, white like street lamps, inviting attack.

V. EXCHANGING AND CHANGING OURSELVES

We protect one another. We cover another's hands. We look deeply within the eyes of our sisters for therein lie hidden lives and truths.

We weep for one another and become alike in the shape of the tear.

We say:

If I hurt you, forgive me.

If I continue to hurt you, inform me.

If I have touched you, return the touch.

If I have separated from you, call out to me.

If I have forgotten you, remind me.

If you or I are anonymous, name us.

We say words that are pejorative names for ourselves. We write those words on strips of paper, strike a match to them.

We vow not to use terms that denigrate, reduce, humiliate. We vow to invent new words of honor, dignity, new psalms to sweeten our tongues. We write psalms of difference, of the rainbow of women.

We become one another.

The Jew wears the Christian's ring or blouse, rises, walks in the Christian's shoes and tells the Christian's history with sympathy and new insight.

The Christian wears the garment of the Jew, walking in her shoes, slipping or cramped, to tell of being a Jewish woman.

The woman of white skin exchanges apparel with the woman of color. The woman who is white speaks as a Black, of the household, church, of fears, of pride. The woman who is white names Black woman heroes. The woman who is white fills her mouth with the speech of the Black woman, colors her tongue with the beauty of the words of the Spanish woman.

The woman of color speaks of her perception of the white woman. Is she someone far away and dimly seen? Can she ever be someone close?

VI. SONG OF PURIFICATION: IMMERSION

We need a mikveh, a baptismal font, a swimming pool to say these words.

Our Mother, who created us

from a single drop of blood

from Her holy womb,

Our Mother who gave us this

design of body,

these protected parts,

this internal architecture,

Our Mother who enabled us

to cunningly feed and nourish,

to be the cavern of life,

we act with Your strength,

and in Your dignity,

each of us different in her faith,

her coloring and her shape,

each of us alike in our structure.

Oh, Mother, rejoice with us

in this meeting of your daughters!

We bless each woman as she enters the water.

We say that water is what all women share,

water of amniotic fluid, water of rivers where clothes were washed, water of cleaning and cooking.

We say, at the edge of the pool:

We are part of the body of women,

of earth and water.

May we survive at sea, on land,

in shallow straits or over our heads.

May we rescue one another

in deep water.

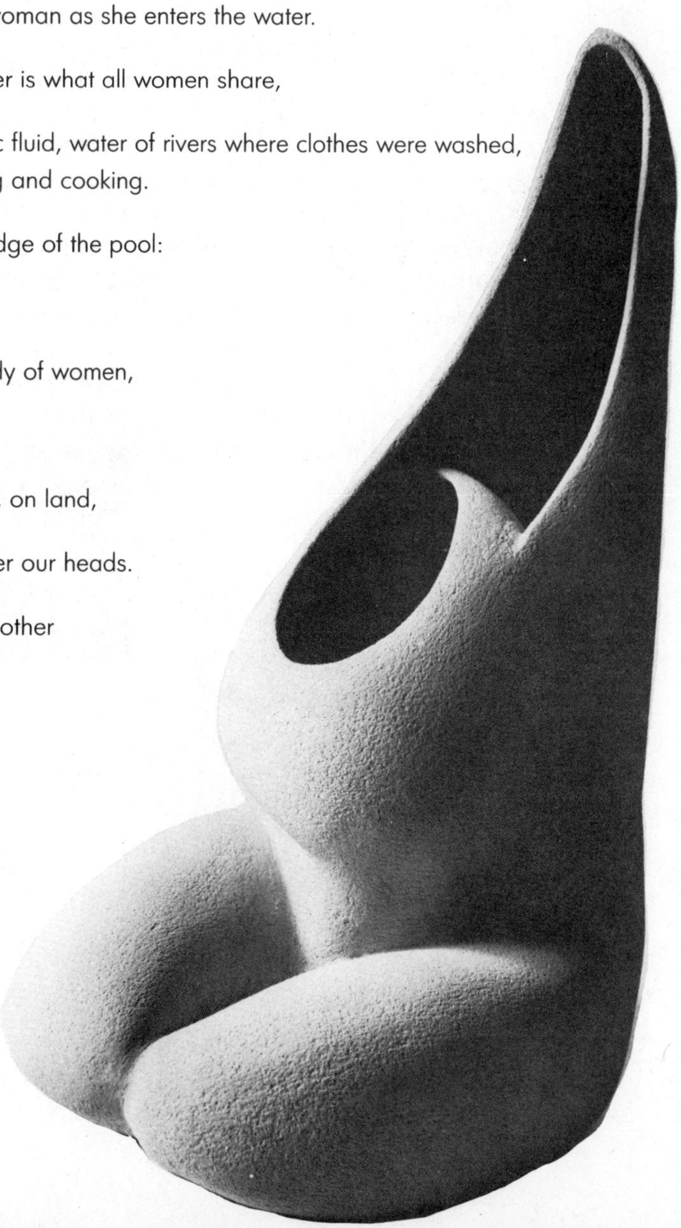

Woman © Tania Kravath, 1986. Clay sculpture, 22″ × 12″. Photo by Yonah, 1986.

We swim together, splash, laugh, hold onto the sides of the pool to tell water tales or earthy tales. We leave the water. We towel-dry one another. We see ourselves replicated and we sing:

The eyes of your breasts look upon mine.

The eye of your navel faces inward and outward.

Your arms are extensions of yourself.

Your body is my twin.

Your back will not be turned against me.

Your lids will not close when they encounter me.

Your legs will not stride away from me.

I dry your forehead, nose, cheeks and chin.

I know that I am within you.

We hold one another in a circle, colorful bodies on a mound of grass, on carpeting, on sand. We hold onto that ring of women, that magical ring of connection.

From E. M. Broner, work in progress: "Perilous Journey." To contact the author write: E. M. Broner, 40 W. 22nd St. #7A, New York, NY 10010.

"Birthing and nurturing my children teaches me why I make art and what there is to make art about. But, I learned about the Spirit side of painting from my Dreams and from our Mother Earth. I paint in our kitchen at home in Tuba City, Arizona in Dineh' Nation. We live on the mesa

Dreaming a Crystal Path © Charleen Touchette, 1984. Acrylic on canvas, 36" × 48". Photos by Barry Paisner.

above Echo Cliffs with Navajo Mountains to the north, the Inscription House Ruins to the east, the sacred San Francisco Peaks to the south and Grey Mountain to the west, with "beauty all around." My 'studio' is always filled with my sons and the neighborhood children painting at a crowded easel" (Charleen Touchette, P.O. Box 5188, Santa Fe, N.M. 87502 (505) 982-0803

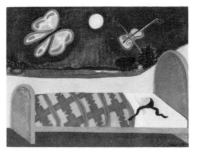

Listening to the Dancing © Charleen Touchette, 1985. Pastel on paper 22" × 30".

Reindeer Woman Vision © Charleen Touchette, 1985. Casein, watercolor on paper, 22" × 30".

NORTHWEST INDIAN WOMEN'S CIRCLE

Northwest Indian Women's Circle (NWIWC) is a nonprofit grassroots organization of Indian women involved in projects, activities, and ceremonies that address the special needs of Indian women and their families. In Indian culture women traditionally occupy a respected and honored position as the central figure in the family structure. Indian tradition provides a firm foundation for the tasks of the Women's Circle: development of women's inner being, the healing and uniting of Indian communities, public education, and the protection of Indian children, dignity, rights, land, and resources. NWIWC functions as a vital communications network for dissemination of information and resources on a local, regional, national, and international level, and is the organizational center of the Indigenous Indian Women's Network, an organization of native women from North America and the Pacific islands. A Friend of the Circle supporting membership ($25) includes a subscription to the newsletter *Moccasin Line*, regular bulletins and alerts on news of interest to the Indian people, and invitations to public ceremonies. Circle founders are available for speaking and lecturing. A slide show of projects within Indian country is available to the public.

Northwest Indian Women's Circle, % Janet and Barbara McCloud, P.O. Box 8279, Tacoma, WA 98408.

THE OJAI FOUNDATION

The Ojai Foundation is an educational retreat center and residential community in the upper Ojai Valley, north of Los Angeles. Founded in 1927 by Dr. Annie Besant, it is based on forty acres of protected semiwilderness land once inhabited by the Chumash Indians. For the last seven years, under the direction of Joan Halifax, the Foundation has served as an educational sanctuary for teachers and friends from many spiritual traditions, scholarly disciplines, and artistic pathways who come together for innovative programs, ceremonies, and spiritual renewal. Many programs are held in Council, a unique learning environment in which all participants—including faculty and staff—live, work, study, and practice together. The Ojai Foundation program brochure is available upon request. A $5 mailing list contribution is kindly requested.

The Ojai Foundation, P.O. Box 1620, Ojai, CA 93023, (805) 646-8343.

OUR LADY OF THE WOODS NATIONAL WICCAN MINISTRY AND RESOURCE CENTER

Our Lady of the Woods is dedicated to the service of the Lady and the Lord through teaching and healing in the Wiccan tradition. The long-term goal is to create Ardantane, a Wiccan residential seminary, and Singing Willow Healing Center. There are five other branches to its ministry. Singing Willow Counseling Services offers guidance in health and healing. Eldertree provides seminars and workshops on Wiccan, Paganism, magick, and psychic development. The Coven of Our Lady of the Woods emphasizes teaching and healing, and is open to both women and men. Moonstone Publications and Nine Candles Artisan's Bench together publish a mail-order catalog of Pagan-oriented goodies such as calligraphed posters, embroidered emblems, a children's activity book, and other publications on magick and the Craft. *Priest/ess* is the quarterly newsletter of Our Lady of the Woods and focuses on the seminary/healing center project: a donation of $13 or more (check payable to O.L.W.) puts you on the mailing list.

"Find many teachers. Go to classes,

workshops, and seminars. Hang out with Sufi's, Mormons, and Iroquois. Compare and contrast. Read a thousand books, ask a million questions, let your curiosity run free. Meditate, recall past lives, travel all over, lie in the grass and listen to crickets. Never stop learning, on subways and horses, in ancient tombs or childbed, behind a podium or in the bathtub. Learn in your head and in your gut, with your eyes and tongue and feet, that which is in words and that which can never find words to express it" *(Amber K).*

Our Lady of the Woods, % Amber K.; P.O. Box 176, Blue Mounds, WI 53517, (608) 437-3669.

PEACEWORK ALTERNATIVES

Peacework Alternatives is a national organization that provides educational, spiritual, psychological, and economic counseling to people employed in the defense industry who wish to leave that kind of work. It provides resource material and support services to workers in the arms race—assembly line workers, technicians, engineers, scientists—who are grappling with moral, ethical, and practical concerns about their work. Peacework Alternatives was founded by a Catholic nun, Julie Driscoll. Under her direction, the organization raises consciousness about nuclear madness and supports a wide range of concerned workers, without judging or condemning anyone. Peacework Alternatives is funded by donations from individuals, local organizations, national religious organizations, and concerned groups and foundations.

Peacework Alternatives, % Sister Julie Driscoll, director, 3940 Poplar Level Rd., Louisville, KY 40213

RECLAIMING: A CENTER FOR FEMINIST RELIGION

Reclaiming, a collective of San Francisco Bay Area women and men, works to unify spirituality and politics, a vision rooted in the religion and magic of the Goddess as Immanent Life Force. Reclaiming offers a week-long summer intensive, ongoing classes, day-long workshops, and public rituals, and publishes a quarterly newsletter (sample issue $2). Reclaiming's programs are designed to strengthen our bodies, energy, intuition, and minds, both as individuals and as community, to voice our concerns about the world in which we live, and to bring forth a vision of a new culture. Starhawk is a member of the Reclaiming collective. A chant tape of ritual music, featuring twenty songs often used in reclaiming rituals, is available for $10 ppd. A Reclaiming workbook is currently being developed. Send legal-size SASE with all inquiries.

Reclaiming, P.O. Box 14404, San Francisco, CA 94114, (415) 849-0877 (Events Line).

RE-FORMED CONGREGATION OF THE GODDESS

The Re-formed Congregation of the Goddess (RCG) is an international womyn's religion that provides the benefits and recognition of organized religion to its members. Its purpose is to foster positive spiritual growth among all persons, particularly womyn. RCG provides a spiritual, ethical, and social structure that is essential to validating womyn's

experience. Application for membership in RCG is generated by signing the Affirmation of Womyn's Spirituality. Send a SASE to receive a brochure listing membership benefits and services, including information on RCG's regional and international activities, conferences, trainings, and retreats for both individuals and groups.

Re-formed Congregation of the Goddess, Box 6021, Madison, WI 53716, (608) 838-8629.

Old friends are just like creatures from dreams. Painting title is a quotation from Dale Loves Sophie to Death by Robb Forman Dew. Oil painting © Sudie Rakusin, 1984. Photo by Beth Karbe, 1984.

RESOURCE CENTER FOR WOMEN AND MINISTRY IN THE SOUTH

Nestled in an old stone house called Avalon Center, the Resource Center is an ecumenical professional and spiritual support network and gathering center for women in ministry and feminist women and men of faith. The center hosts conferences, retreats, and workshops, and assists religious institutions in developing programs that address women's needs. A bimonthly newsletter,

South of the Garden ($12 per year), includes a calendar of local and national events, job listings, mail-order books, and articles on women, religion, economics, and the South.

Resource Center for Women and Ministry in the South, % Rev. Jeanette Stokes, director, P.O. Box 1365, Greensboro, NC 27402, (919) 272-0844.

SISTERHOOD OF THE GODDESS

Sisterhood of the Goddess is a feminist spirituality group for Wiccan and Pagan women. Activities include creative ritual, celebration with music and dance, healing, study, and discussion. The Sisterhood encourages dialogue and exchange with women of other spiritual paths. The founder, Lady Isadora is a feminist Goddess-oriented songwriter and performer whose musical recordings *The Witching Hour* and *The Queen of Earth and Sky* are major works of music in the neo-Pagan community. Artists with a spiritual orientation who wish to network on ideas and projects are invited to write or call.

Sisterhood of the Goddess, % Lady Isadora, P.O. Box 2483, Des Moines, IA 50311, (515) 274-1480.

SISTERHOOD PROJECT: CENTER FOR SOVIET-AMERICAN DIALOGUE

The Sisterhood Project grew out of a 1985 trip to the Soviet Union when several Soviet and American women established a deep personal connection with each other and were inspired to use this contact as an instrument of peace and friendship between their countries. Soviet and American "sisters" hostess each other in their respective countries and create projects to increase understanding and trust. Sisterhood Certificates are exchanged between the women as a symbol of their commitment to share their lives and cultures and to be available in an exchange of visits. The Sisterhood Project offers networking on Soviet-American citizen diplomacy.

Sisterhood Project, % Anne Stine, coordinator, 3 Hillcrest Ave., Larkspur, CA 94939, (415) 461-7336.

SISTERSPIRIT: WOMEN SHARING SPIRITUALITY

Sisterspirit was formed in December 1985 to create a place where women from different spiritual paths and traditions could celebrate their spirituality, build bridges between their divisions, and seek the common ground we share. Celebrations are held every other Sunday, and on alternate Sundays Sisterspirit discussions take place on themes of interest to women. Write or call for schedule of celebrations.

Sisterspirit, % Frodo Okulam, P.O. Box 9246, Portland, OR 97207, (503) 282-8615.

SOUTHWEST EARTH FESTIVAL ASSOCIATION

Southwest Earth Festival Association (SEFA) sponsors Goddess and Wiccan oriented activities in New Mexico. Membership is open to women and men. Referrals to affiliated women-only groups can be made. Annual public gatherings include Beltane, Winter Solstice, and the Enchanted Mountain Gathering, a four-day festival in the mountains of New Mexico.

Southwest Earth Festivals Association, P.O. Box 26414, Albuquerque, NM 87125.

Spiderwoman Ensemble, New York City, performing *Three Up, Three Down.* Photo by Lynne Cowan, 1986.

SPIDERWOMAN THEATRE WORKSHOP INC.

The New York-based theater company Spiderwoman Ensemble is made up of three Cuna (Central American)-Rappahanock Indian sisters, Lisa Mayo, Gloria Miguel, and Muriel Miguel. The group is named after the Hopi goddess of creation, Spiderwoman or Spider Grandmother Woman. The first to create designs and to teach Her people to weave, Spiderwoman always wove a flaw into the design to allow Her spirit to find its way out and be free. In Hopi tradition, Spiderwoman has prophetic insight into the future, speaks all languages, and by nature of being a spider is ever-present to give aid and to guide Her people through crisis and change. The women of Spiderwoman Ensemble do, in fact, create designs and weave their performance stories with words and movement, a method they call storyweaving. "We work onstage as an ensemble, basing our productions on life experiences. We translate our personal stories, dreams, and images into movement, and redefine them into the essential threads of human experience. In seeking out, exploring, and weaving our patterns, we reflect the human tapestry, the Web of our common humanity. Finding, loving, and transcending our own flaws, as in the flaw in the Goddess tapestry, provides the means for our spirits to find their way out and be free." Using everyday experiences, the themes are rehearsed, improvised, thought over, transformed, and reworked among the group prior to staging. Dreams, images, rituals, and political issues are integrated into the weave. By representing all areas of womanhood in their productions—lesbians, heterosexuals, older women, younger women, mothers, daughters, and granddaughters—Spiderwoman Ensemble expresses the diversity within the Web of Life, the connecting theme in each of their productions. (Contributed by Patricia C. Camarena from an article that originally appeared in *Woman of Power* magazine, Fall 1986.)

Spiderwomen Theatre Workshops, 77-7th Ave., Eight S., New York, NY 11011, (212) 243-6209.

SUNRAY MEDITATION SOCIETY

The Sunray Meditation Society is an international spiritual society dedicated to planetary peace. The Sunray teachings are rooted in Native American Earth wisdom shared in accordance with the Elders' guidance. Dhyani Ywahoo, Sunray's spiritual director, is a member of the Etawa Band of the Eastern Tsalagi (Cherokee) Nation and caretaker of the Ywahoo lineage. Trained by her

grandparents, she is the twenty-seventh generation to carry the ancestral wisdom of the Ywahoo lineage. Native Elders of the Cherokee Nation (and other indigenous peoples) have requested that sacred teachings be disseminated in our era, to ease the suffering of the Earth and her people and to empower transformation and renewal for all the family of life. Sunray offers a program of spiritual trainings and meditation circles throughout the United States and Canada. The Peacekeeper Training, a contemporary program of personal and planetary education and training rooted in Native American wisdom, includes sitting and moving meditations, community dream practices, chanting, quartz crystal healing studies, and Tibetan Buddhist principles. For information on Peacekeeper Training and regional Meditation Circles, contact the Sunray Meditation Society.

Sunray Meditation Society, % Dhyani Ywahoo, spiritual director, P.O. Box 308, Bristol, VT 05443, (802) 453-4610.

TAPESTRY: A WOMEN'S MEETINGHOUSE

Tapestry is a women's religious educational organization focusing on new ways for women to be together spiritually and religiously. Programs, open to all women, include worship groups called In-Gatherings, one-day workshops, and study groups on issues related to feminist theology and women's spirituality. Music, art, literature, poetry, mythology, and ritual are the pathways taken to rediscover the strength, beauty, and power of the Goddess within each of us. A newsletter of announcements, poetry, and stories focusing on challenges and opportunities for women in activating their spiritual/religious powers is available upon request.

Tapestry, % Alicia Forsey, P.O. Box 138, 2124 Kittredge St., Berkeley, CA 94709, (415) 845-6232.

TEMENOS

Built over the healing mineral waters and rock foundations of a nineteenth-century spa, Temenos connects ancient lore with present and future concerns for our planet. *Temenos* is a Greek word signifying sacred space; it describes the sanctuary surrounding the temple or altar, a place where, in ancient Greece, dreams were listened to and initiatory rites enacted. Carl Jung refers to temenos as a private space deep within the psyche where soul making takes place. Temenos, a primitive woodland retreat and workshop center in western Massachusetts, offers a daily practice of attending to and nurturing the inward temenos. Daily life reflects the convergence of Buddhist and Quaker practice: shared silence and physical work, active nonviolence in conflict resolution, closeness to Earth and the elements. The facilities include a lodge with space for sacred dance, ritual celebrations, and workshops, and a library on world religions, mythology, women's studies, and nonviolence. Temenos workshops take place May through October. The facilities are available for sojourners seeking total solitude, shared meals, worship, and conversation. Write for schedule of programs.

Temenos, P.O. Box 84A, Star Rte., Shutesbury, MA 01072.

THROUGH THE FLOWER

Dedicated to art that honors women's experience, Through the Flower "midwifed" the making of both *The Dinner Party* and *The Birth Project* of Judy Chicago. *The Birth Project*, an extension of the artistic process developed by Chicago in *The Dinner Party*, features painting, drawing, and needlework honoring birth and creation: the birth of the universe, our planet, and the family of humankind. Through the Flower serves as a clearinghouse for information on the status of both exhibitions (*The*

Dinner Party is currently in storage in England), offers art images on poster and paper of *The Birth Project*, and welcomes visitors to its working studio located in the Bay Area of northern California. For information on sponsoring *The Birth Project* in your community or organization and a current touring schedule, send a legal-size SASE.

Through The Flower, % Mary Ross Taylor, executive director, P.O. Box 834, Benicia, CA 94510, (707) 746-0398.

Guided by the Goddess from Judy Chicago's *The Birth Project* © Judy Chicago, 1983. Airbrush/embroidery, 54" × 107". Needlework by Marjorie Smith. Photo by Michele Maier.

TRANSFORMATIONAL ARTS INSTITUTE

The Transformational Arts Institute offers residential workshops on the dark feminine, one of the most powerful forces emerging in our culture. The dark feminine teaches us to reconnect with Earth and eros and to reclaim parts of ourselves too often lost in the pursuit of perfection, achievement, and masculine values. Ongoing groups with an emphasis on women's rituals, myths, and symbols are offered through the Institute.

Transformational Art Institute, % Nancee Redmond, associate director, 1380 Pacific St., Redlands, CA 92373, (714) 792-1940.

TWIN CITIES WOMEN'S MINYAN

The Twin Cities Women's Minyan offers a supportive community for Jewish women who wish to integrate personal spiritual expression within a Jewish tradition. Minyan members encourage each other to learn and share skills such as reading from the Torah, learning Hebrew songs, and transgendering God(dess) stories in search of alternatives to exclusively male God-imagery. Shabbat services are held once a month, rotating in members' homes and followed by potluck lunch. The Minyan has sponsored feminist Passover Seders, Rosh Hashanah services, and Rosh Hodesh rituals. Send a SASE to receive a calendar of events.

Twin Cities Women's Minyan, % Jackie Urbanovic, 2207 21st Ave. S., Minneapolis, MN 55404, (612) 724-7101.

WISE WOMAN CENTER

The Wise Woman Center exists to draw together the threads of our lost heritage as healing women of power and knowledge, where the Goddess is alive and green Witches grow. Located on forty-eight acres of rocky Catskill ground, the center is the physical base of the life and work of Susun Weed, herbalist and author of *The Wise Woman Herbal for the Childbearing Year*. Wise Woman Center is a teaching center where ordinary people can learn how to heal and maintain spiritual/physical health using common plants (weeds), compassionate intuition, Earth wisdom, and simple rituals. This is the healing tradition of Wise Woman, the oldest healing tradition on Earth. The center offers herbal healing intensives for women, apprenticeships in the Wise Woman tradition, daylong workshops open to men and women, self-healing retreats for women, private instruction with Susun Weed, and weed walks for adults and children. Complete descriptive brochure available on request.

Wise Woman Center, % Susun S. Weed, P.O. Box 64, Woodstock, NY 12498, (914) 246-8081.

Photo by Emily Whitewolf.

REFLECTIONS OF A CATHOLIC OR PAGAN? MEXICAN-AMERICAN WOMAN

PATRICIA C. CAMARENA (RAVEN)

A woman wearing a peasant skirt that flounces with her every movement, her long hair cascading onto the banister, descends the stairs. She is carrying a child with bold, alert eyes. He carries in his tiny hand a big, wooden rattle that is round and almost the size of his head. My mind flashes to the Madonna and Child that I've often seen pictured on my mother's holy cards. The child in these pictures carries a small world globe in his hand. It, too, is as big as his head. And I remember: Madonna and Christ Child, Goddess and son, are one and the same in Mexican tradition. Rather than denying our cultural past—the truth of our Pagan ancestors—we have incorporated it into the traditional Catholic/Christian belief system of today. The ancient beliefs are in disguise. Both Pagan and Catholic systems coexist in Mexican life, as do many other *seemingly* noncompatible practices.

One of these practices is that of herbal medicine, often considered to be linked with paganism. As a child, I was taken to healers and treated with herbs. Red ribbons and prayers to the Virgen de Guadalupe ridded me of the demons or *cosas* (things) that were ailing me. I wore a copper bracelet for a heart murmur. Yet my parents and grandparents did not discredit the benefit of medical doctors. Both prayers and medicine, doctors and healers, were acknowledged.

As a child, I was plagued by asthma. My grandmother solicited a woman to make a replica of the habit worn by Saint Theresa. I had a wool habit to wear in the winter, a cotton habit for summer. She invoked Saint Theresa, promising her that I would wear the habit in her honor for a year if she, being the patron saint of respiratory illness, would cure me. Today, the entire action taken by my grandmother seems to me very Pagan in nature. It is similar to the practice of invoking the Goddess ritualistically, taking aspects of Her into oneself and serving Her as priestesses have done in ancient times. I was

Virgen de Guadalupe, the modern day counterpart of the Aztec Goddess Tonasti. Photo © M. Camerena, 1986.

to pray to Saint Theresa often, to surrender myself to her care alone, and to believe in her ability to cure me. This practice is considered sacrilegious in traditional Catholicism, which does not allow a saint to have so much power.

Again, when I was a child, I remember having a pain in one of my eyes. My grandmother lit a cigarette and blew smoke into my eye after murmuring a prayer. In *Secrets of the Mind-Altering Plants of Mexico*, Richard Heffern cites this as a healing practice called *soblando*, or blowing. I have also seen this documented in some Wiccan herbal healing books and in books on Native American traditions.

Until very recently, I have been confused about childhood experiences having to do with this strange mixture of old and new worlds. Yet, however particular to Mexican culture this combination had seemed to me before, I have recently noted the integration of Pagan practices with Christian thought in many other cultures. What is unique to Mexico is its secretiveness about Pagan practice. In general, it is a devoutly Catholic country. The mention of Witchcraft is bound to elicit direct challenges as to its existence. Yet in the villages there are healers (*curanderas*), tarot card readers, midwives, charms to be purchased, trees of life for sale, and much talk about premonitions, ghosts, and evil spirits.

My first tarot card reading took place in my hometown near Chicago. The tarot reader had an altar in her bedroom filled with stones, jewelry, pictures of various saints, and a huge rosary that hung around a picture of the Virgen de Guadalupe. She shuffled the cards, said a prayer, and then proceeded with the reading. Nothing was ever said about her invocations except that she had also invoked an angel and that I was to pay attention to my own guardian angel after the reading. Still, I felt a dimension of secretiveness in her invocation of the Christian deities for a Pagan purpose.

The Virgen de Guadalupe is the most venerated female figure in all of Mexico. She holds a magnitude of power unmatched by any saint or even the Christ figure. Much has been written recently about the phenomenon of the Virgin. It is now commonly believed that the Aztec goddess Tonasti was replaced by Guadalupe, who has merely taken over Tonasti's reign under a different title. All Her power remains. In recent years, with the reemergence of Goddess movements, the Virgin has become more of a public figure. There exist a wealth of practices such as those I have described, most of which, although commonly practiced, are kept very secret by people in Mexican villages and in the United States. I attribute this secretiveness to fear of persecution. Mexico has witnessed a high degree of religious persecution from the days of the Spanish invasions and the massacre of the indigenous people for the purpose of converting the populace. Yet through all this, many of the ancient practices have survived and continue to be passed on in families through an ongoing oral tradition.

This article is lovingly dedicated to my grandmother, Cirila Camarena, who contributed much to my present interests in Pagan practices.

WOMANCENTER AT PLAINVILLE

Womancenter is an ecumenical retreat center located in a large old house thirty-five miles south of Boston on forty acres of land. Founded by Dominican sister Chris Loughlin and feminist singer/songwriter Carolyn McDade, Womancenter offers programs, centered in the arts, for the evolving of a women's perspective of justice and community. One of the strongest aspects of the work is music. Three music tapes of peace and justice songs written by staff member Carolyn McDade are available: *This Tough Spun Web*, *Rain Upon Dry Land*, and *We Come with Our Voices*. Funds from the sale of the tapes supports the ongoing justice work of Womancenter. Each tape comes with an accompanying songbook, useful for rooting the songs in one's own experience. Midweek, the center is open to women seeking an overnight retreat house for reflective solitude or quiet work space. Call or write for program schedule, tape prices, and overnight retreat rates.

Womencenter, % Chris Loughlin, O.P., and Carolyn McDade, co-creators, 76 Everett Skinner Rd., Plainville, MA 02762, (617) 699-7167.

WOMANEARTH FEMINIST PEACE INSTITUTE

WomanEarth Feminist Peace Institute was initiated in 1985 by Starhawk and Ynestra King to bridge the insights of academic feminism and the wisdom of our experience. WomanEarth programs bring together a multiracial, multicultural, international diversity of women committed to creating/refining intellectual, emotional, political, cultural, and life-supporting tools of transformation. Long-term focus areas include feminist thought and culture, spirituality, common differences, ecology, and peace action studies (organizing for peace, international relations, conflict resolution, nonviolence, strategies for so-

cial change). Programs include *WomanEarth Review*, Pacific Women's Tour, weekend workshops, biannual international conferences, and plans for a traveling institute. WomanEarth Feminist Peace Institute has a strong commitment to parity between women of color and white women in all areas of our organization and activities, considering this a most powerful way to put our lives where our mouths are. Send a SASE for further information.

WomanEarth, % Rachel Bagby and Gwyn Kirk, coordinators, P.O. Box 2374, Stanford, CA 94309, (415) 327-2919.

WOMANFEST SEASONAL CELEBRATIONS

Womanfest celebrates the four seasons with feminist ritual, storytelling, and workshops on women's spirituality practices and issues. Celebrations are open to all women. Attention is given to creating a place where diversity is savored and women's experience is affirmed. Child care is available. Write or call for upcoming events.

Womanfest, % Clarita Bourque, 4123 Woodland Dr., New Orleans, LA 70114, (504) 394-8500.

WOMANFLIGHT: A CENTER FOR FEMINIST SPIRITUALITY

Womanflight was founded in 1986 to help women and men examine their lives from a spiritual perspective. Courses and workshops provide opportunities for dialogue among women of different traditions, to create awareness of divergent viewpoints, to celebrate common ground, to explore her-story in religion from the past, to imagine the future, to create new rituals and express personal faith in the present. Womanflight speakers are available to address issues concerning women's spiritual liberation. Tuition is based on a sliding scale according to in-

come. Send a SASE for current course schedule and newsletter.

Womanflight, % Mary Faulkner and Margaret L. Meggs, co-founders, P.O. Box 60131, Nashville, TN 37206, (615) 225-1225.

WOMANSHINE

WomanShine began as a single performance for the Woman's Touch Bookstore. The company quickly grew out of the need in the Midwest for performance and theater opportunities that honored women's cultural contributions and global concerns. The belief that the Earth and physical life are sacred—the principle of the Great Goddess—inspires and informs the work of WomanShine. Since 1977 they have worked with women of all ages and ethnic backgrounds to produce original theater such as *Woman's Word*, a collage of women's writings that celebrates creativity, work, relationships, and spirituality; and *Eleanor*, a reminiscence of Eleanor Roosevelt drawn from her own writings in which she discusses her personal growth and her work for peace. In addition to stage productions, WomanShine offers a series of experiential workshops that explore issues involving religion, theology, and practical spirituality. Write for touring schedule and for information on bringing WomanShine to your community, educational facility, or organization.

WomanShine, % Sid Reger, manager, and Nancy Brooks, director, 1600 N. Willis, #200, Bloomington, IN 47401, (812) 339-9498.

WOMANSPACE

Womanspace is an interfaith centering place for women, founded to provide women with the tools and support to make a significant contribution in the creation of a more human, connected, and spiritual new Earth. Womanspace provides resources to promote and affirm each woman's search for self-awareness and self-esteem: counseling, support groups, wellness forums, referral services, interfaith retreats, and a library of more than thirteen hundred books, slides, and tapes. "Leadershops" help women sharpen their leadership skills and improve leadership abilities. Seminars and workshops probing issues in spirituality, psychology, sociology, and the arts allow participants to deepen their insights and touch the life sources that run deep and clear within them. The *Web*, a bimonthly newsletter, details current activities and programs. Subscription/membership $15 per year.

Womanspace,% Dorothy Bock, SSSF, and Elaine Hirschenberger, SSSF, co-directors, 3333 Maria Linden Dr., Rockford, IL 61111, (815) 877-0118.

WOMEN-CHURCH CONVERGENCE

Women-Church Convergence is a coalition of women's groups and organizations concerned with justice for women and united in common cause by their work for the recognition, empowerment, and development of women as church. Convergence meets several times a year and sees as its immediate goal an understanding and analysis of the power structure affecting women's lives; economic, political, sexual, and spiritual. The intent is not only to analyze the structures but also to develop strategies that are proactive rather than reactive; to develop leadership training; to reach out to grassroots groups of women. Write for information on Women-Church groups within your geographical area.

Women-Church Convergence, % Laurie Michalowski, 1020 S. Wabash, Room 401, Chicago, IL 60605, (312) 427-4351.

WOMEN IN CONSTANT CREATIVE ACTION (WICCA)

Women in Constant Creative Action (WICCA) is a network of small local groups called Wings who meet for supportive spiritual growth and metaphysical learning. Coming together for celebrations and rituals each month enables members to connect with other women who honor the Goddess within. Working, playing, and studying together provides the community/extended family that is missing for so many in our mobile society. The newsletter *On Wings* contains book reviews, a calendar of events, and engaging articles on practices and themes related to women's spirituality. (Available to nonmembers for $16 a year.) WICCA sponsors the annual Festival of Women's Spirituality, enabling women to leave the patriarchal world behind and experience a matrifocal society. Send a SASE for additional information.

WICCA, % Norma Joyce, P.O. Box 201, Monmouth, OR 97361, (503) 838-6095.

WOMEN IN SPIRITUAL EDUCATION (WISE)

WISE is an organization dedicated to the rediscovery and development of the spiritual strength attributed to the Earth, women, and the feminine. "Heart of the Goddess" workshops, Womanspirit Initiation training pro-

Hallie Iglehart Austen (left) and Karen Vogel (right). Photo by Marcelina Martin, 1986.

grams, seasonal rituals, audiovisual presentations, and private consultations are offered throughout the country. WISE programs have emerged as an integration of the Womanspirit work of Hallie Iglehart Austen and the Motherpeace work of Karen Vogel. Drawing on cultural traditions that honor our ancient women's wisdom, their work provides tools for adapting these traditions to a spirituality that combines power with love and is relevant to our everyday lives. Send a legal-size SASE for a schedule of current programs and products available through WISE.

WISE, % Hallie Iglehart Austen and Karen Vogel, co-directors, P.O. Box 697, Pt. Reyes, CA 94956, (415) 663-8280.

WOMEN'S ACTION FOR NUCLEAR DISARMAMENT (WAND)

Because "Children Ask the World of Us," pediatrician and mother Dr. Helen Caldicott founded Women's Action for Nuclear Disarmament (WAND) in 1980. Today WAND is a national membership organization of women and men working to halt and reverse the nuclear arms race. WAND affiliates are groups of WAND members who have joined together to educate their communities about the nuclear weapons issue and to work for legislation in support of nuclear disarmament. Affiliates, formed as community-based organizations, receive WAND's monthly *Update*—a packet of current information on nuclear weapons issues. WAND PAC (Political Action Committee) supports electoral candidates who are committed to ending the nuclear arms race. Call or write for WAND membership information. An excellent resource bulletin entitled *What You Can Do Right Now to End the Nuclear Arms Race* is available upon request.

WAND, P.O. Box 153, New Town Branch, Boston, MA 02258, (617) 643-6740.

WOMEN'S ALLIANCE

Women's Alliance is a nonprofit corporation founded to nurture the development of feminine spirituality as a worldview and as a spiritual and political movement. Each year Women's Alliance produces a summer solstice camp, "Her Voice, Our Voices," a gathering of two hundred women and twenty facilitators representing a diverse range of spiritual, religious, and political perspectives. Ritual, dance, the arts, song, visualization, storytelling, and dialogue are the means by which feminine vision is deepened and explored during the week-long camp. The focus of "Her Voice, Our Voices" is to encourage participants to integrate feminine values into their careers, family life, and in the world. (See "Her Voice, Our Voices" videotape listing on page 245.) Women's Alliance also produces weekend, daylong, and quarterly programs. $35 annual membership includes a subscription to the Women's Alliance newsletter with news of public events sponsored by the alliance.

Women's Alliance, % Charlotte Kelly, director, P.O. Box 1882, Nevada City, CA 95959, (916) 477-1064.

WOMEN'S ALLIANCE FOR THEOLOGY, ETHICS, AND RITUAL (WATER)

Based in the Washington, D.C., metropolitan area, WATER uses women's insights and skills to work for structural change toward a more just society. WATER trains women

to be active theological agents, gathering women and men together to address key ethical issues and to create new rituals from religious traditions. Activities include ecumenical workshops, lectures, and liturgies. WATER works with sister base groups in Argentina and Chile, sharing insights and experience between Latin American and American women. This network, called Women Crossing Worlds, is creating a new feminist model of mission. Write for schedule of programs and list of WATER Resources.

WATER, % Mary E. Hunt and Diann Neu, directors, 8035 13th St., Suites 1 & 3, Silver Spring, MD 20910, (301) 589-2509.

WOMEN'S INSTITUTE FOR CONTINUING JEWISH EDUCATION

The Women's Institute for Continuing Jewish Education is an adult education and resource center offering innovative courses expressly designed for and about Jewish women, underscoring their active role in Jewish history and religion. Institute courses are designed to enable women to take an active role in shaping Judaism for the sake of making a better Jewish community for everyone. Students are encouraged to become the directors of their own educational experience. This goal is furthered through creation of midrash and ceremonies, creative services, and the publication of books that serve to educate Jewish women about themselves and the roles they might play in their collective history-making. Learners at the Institute have published four texts, including a women's Shabbat service prayerbook and a women's Passover Haggadah. A complete list of institute books and courses is available upon request.

Women's Institute for Continuing Jewish Education, % Dr. Irene Fine, director, 4079 54th St., San Diego, CA 92105, (619) 442-2666.

Song of the
Jewish Feminine Lineage:
The Story of Lilith and Eve

Rabbi Lynn Gottlieb

Lynn Gottlieb is a rabbi, storyteller, ritualist, and poet. She first began working as a rabbi in 1973 in the deaf community of New York City. She has traveled extensively telling tales and making ceremony with people of all faiths and all ages. She currently serves Congregation Nahalat Shalom, which was founded in Albuquerque, New Mexico, in 1983.

I was born Jewish and I grew up in a Jewish family. It's been very special in my life to have a tradition that's part of my family and my blood ancestors. Being Jewish, you feel five thousand years flowing in your veins. The stories, the holidays, and the life-style that comes with being Jewish has been a fairly positive experience in my life. And being Jewish, too, has brought me into contact with early ancestors, Abraham and Sarah, and the ancient women, Miriam and Deborah. Although Judaism has been part of the patriarchal world, these women still spoke to me when I was growing up: women of long ago who were related to me, and who sang about God.

In rabbinic school you learn a lot about the men, Rabbi this, Rabbi that, you hear tales about the male rabbis, and the laws that you study apply to men. At times it seems like God was mostly talking to men. Not until 1972, when I came into contact with the feminist movement and the questions that feminism brought, was I able to reevaluate my tradition from a women's perspective. The storytelling that I'm doing today is because feminism asks the questions: What is the history of your ancestors? What of women's experience? What was the women's story?

These are the stories of my female ancestors and male ancestors and these are the generations of my grandmothers, the old-time ladies. Their stories are told generation after generation, and I would like to share their stories with you. Now the first tale is the story of the very first woman created. You probably think this woman was Eve, but the truth of the matter is that her name was Lilith, and this story is a very old story. Lilith is associated with the Sumerian goddess

Inanna, but Jewish women have a special way of telling her tale and it goes like this:

In the beginning the Spirit of Life created the whole world and on the sixth day spun out man and spun out woman from the dust of the ground and the light of the Spirit, and no sooner were they awake than Adam looked at Lilith and said, "Lilith, I shall lie above you and you shall lie below me," and Lilith said, "Adam, no! We were both created from the dust of the ground and we're both equal and I shall not lie below you," and they started fighting back and forth and back and forth and neither one of them would listen to each other and finally Lilith said, "Adam, is this your final word?" and he said, "Yes it is, Lilith," and she said, "In that case, yelp, yelp, yelp, yelp, yelp," and she uttered the name of the ineffable and she flew off and she came and she sat by the Red Sea. Now this is the sea of transformations, the sea that opened for my ancestors and brought us into the wilderness, out of slavery. This is the same sea that drowned the soldiers of violence. Well, there she sat, Lilith, fiery-night-woman, and she wouldn't go back to the garden. Well, Adam was pretty angry and he started yelling at God and he said, "God, what kind of a woman did you make me anyway? She wouldn't be on the bottom and now she's left! What are you gonna do about that, God?" And God didn't want to deal with it so God said, "I think I'll create some bureaucrats," so God created three angels and said, "You go talk to Lilith and tell her to come back," so these angels flew over to the Red Sea and they said, "Come on Lilith, come on back. It's not gonna be so bad, a little cooking, a little cleaning, a little child bearing but don't worry, Adam will protect you." Well, I guess that kind of protection Lilith didn't need, so she didn't go back. She just sat there. Then the angels started getting nasty and they said, "Look Lilith, if you don't come back to the Garden right away, you're going to give birth to one thousand demons and watch them die and you're going to have to go get other children and kill them for your own. So you better come back now," and still Lilith didn't come back.

Well, in our tradition, Lilith turned out to be the wife of the trickster, Satan, and she is, kind of, but when Jewish women discovered her collectively and Lilith's story was told, she redeemed us. For Jewish women live under the patriarchy. Our mythic structure is patriarchy. Lilith represented the old-time religion, the old-time woman who said, "No, I am not going to be a second-class citizen in life." And so, for those of us who are beginning to define our second-class citizenship within our heritage, Lilith was the first woman to stand up for her rights. But her path was rather demonic (yelp) and women were afraid of Lilith. It was said that Lilith would come and kill your unborn children and so women tied little red ribbons about the bedpost, putting up the names of certain angels so that Lilith, powerful demon that she is, would not come. You had to make your peace with Lilith at the

time of birth. My grandmother still remembers tying those ribbons about the bed.

We sing Lilith's story today as women in a different way. Jewish women started asking the question, "Ok, you have Lilith, fiery-night-woman, and you have the second woman, Eve, Hava, life-bearing-woman. And they're both associated with the Garden. What would happen if Lilith and Hava would meet? Can we bring their stories together?" And that was a way out of a certain kind of feminine isolation. So we looked in our tradition to see if there was a conversation recorded between Hava and Lilith. And there is not one. But that didn't depress us. It's sad. We wish there were more words of the women recorded, but in Jewish tradition it says that you receive the Torah, the guidance, the revelation, the communication with the Spirit in two modes: one is through the written word, the Torah, and the other is through the oral. And the oral, in our tradition, is huge. The oral tradition is our dreams. The oral tradition is the real life-touching experience that we have with the Spirit talking in us, in our lives. And it is that which, when we come back to the written, makes it alive. This is the story that Judith Plaskow first told of what happened when Lilith and Hava got together.

Well, the Spirit of Life looked down on Adam; he was standing in the Garden by himself, stewing, and there was Lilith, sitting by the Red Sea. She wasn't coming back. And so, the Spirit of Life said, "It is time to make new creation. Once again, keep this moving along." So the Spirit of Life took from the soul of woman and the soul of man and began, like a potter, making a being from the Earth. Kneading and kneading, kneading and kneading, thousands of generations. Then the Great Spirit took those beings, and Elohim separated them, and Adonai blew into them the Breath of Life (whhhh), put them down on the ground, waited to see what was gonna happen. And it's recorded that this is what happened. It just so happened that the woman landed on her knees. The man landed standing. Both of them were very beautiful. They were woven from light made from the Earth. The man opened his eyes. He was standing there gleaming and the angels, even they thought that he was God, and they started singing, "Kadosh, kadosh, kadosh." And so, it's no wonder that when the woman opened her eyes and saw Adam standing there gleaming, handsome and beautiful, she said, "Oh my God." And he kind of liked the way that sounded. And he said, "Yes, sweetheart, that's right. And these are the rules of the Garden." And he started showing her around the Garden telling her what she could do, telling her what she couldn't do, what she could and couldn't eat, and how he wanted things done. She, being a very nice woman said, "Yes, dear, all right." So in the middle of the Garden is a tree. It is the tree of light. And within that tree, there is another tree. It is the tree of knowledge of all things. Both of them were very drawn to that tree. And they looked at it and stared at it, and Adam said to Eve (though they were just then man and woman), "I don't think we better eat this. I don't think you should even go near that. In fact, if you touch that tree, you're gonna die. So don't touch it, you understand. Don't go near the tree." "Yes, dear." Well, a little later on, she found herself near the tree, lookin' at that tree, and as she was lookin' at that tree, sssssssssssssssssssssssssssss "Hi," said the snake. In those days they walked, of course. The snake walks right up to her and says, "Hello, what's new?" and the woman says, "What's that?" and the snake says, "I'm sent by the Mother of Light, a snake shedding skins, teaching you how to shed the old and embrace the new," and the snake said, "Look at the tree," and the woman looked at the tree, and the snake said, "What do you see?" and the woman looked at the tree, and she saw the tree was beautiful, and she saw the tree was good to eat, and she saw the tree was good to make one wise, so she reached out, but she remembered what Adam said. The snake laid down on the grass and it grew very still. She watched that snake for a thousand years, still in the grass, and then after a time, the snake began moving. It shed its skin. She held the skin up and she said, "That's a pretty good trick—how did you do that?" That snake crawled over to the tree, wrapped itself around, took a bite of the fruit, slithered away. The woman went up to the tree, took a bite of the fruit, and at that moment, it says in our tradition, that woman saw the angel of death standing there like a fiery-night-woman and she was afraid. And those wings of fire wrapped themselves around her and embraced her and she opened her eyes, standing before fiery-night-woman, and she was still afraid. And then the tree wrapped itself around her and she found herself standing in the center of the tree for a thousand years until she felt the rivers flowing inside her, until she felt the Earth growing inside her, until she felt new life moving inside her, she felt new life in her womb, opening, growing, and she began laboring with that life, laboring with that life, new life inside her, coming through her into the world. Hallelujah, hallelujah, Hava, life-bearing-woman. And when the man saw her standing by the tree, he was amazed, and he said, "Hava, you are mother of all things." And she knew what it meant to be a woman. And that night she lit a fire, a sacred flame, and she said on the seventh day, we put down all our work, this is our sacred time and on this day we remember, we remember the power of creation, the power of giving light. To this we light a flame, this we remember, and this is what my ancestors called Shabbat, the day of rest, which is the day made sacred by the women who light the fires of holy time and make a space to remember.

So you can see that what's happening for Jewish women is what's happening for many women. We are finding women's power, the feminine, and bringing it to life again in our own heritage. What's exciting for Jewish women is that it is possible to make whole the heritage in our time. We don't have to shed it because it carries the patriarchal. The feminine remembers times and spaces that are not oppressive and that can liberate us. This is the tale of our people.

This article is excerpted from a presentation given by Rabbi Gottlieb at the Ojai Foundation during the November 1985 Council of the Feminine Fire.

Woman Breaking Bread. Announcement for 29-minute radio documentary on the explosive issue of priesthood for Catholic women, "The Power and the Spirit," produced by Anne Bohlen and Celeste Wesson. Photo by Richard Rashke, 1985.

WOMEN'S INTERNATIONAL LEAGUE FOR PEACE AND FREEDOM

Women's International League for Peace and Freedom (WILPF) was founded in 1915 during the First World War when 1,136 women from twelve countries met in The Hague to seek an end to the war. Two of WILPF's founders, Jane Addams and Emily Greene Balch, were awarded Nobel Peace Prizes for their work. Recognizing the multiple causes of war, WILPF maintains a multifaceted approach to peace and disarmament, redefining national security to include housing, food, medical care, education, child care, racial harmony, and peaceful relationships with other countries. Currently, local branches are working on a Comprehensive Test Ban and a women's federal budget designed to meet human and social needs at home. Membership ($25 regular, $5 student or low income) includes subscription to *Peace and Freedom*, the newsletter of WILPF. Subscription to WILPF's Political Action/Legislative Alert network is available for $10.

WILPF, 1213 Race St., Philadelphia, PA 19107, (215) 563-7110.

WOMEN'S ORDINATION CONFERENCE

Women's Ordination Conference (WOC) is an international grassroots movement of women and men, secular and religious, committed to working for the ordination of Roman Catholic women to a "renewed priestly ministry," that is, a transformed church. WOC lobbys with bishops and theologians for removal of gender as a criterion for priestly ministry, participates in the international Women-Church movement, is a co-founding organization of the Catholic-based Women-Church Convergence, and conducts workshops, seminars, and national conferences within the Catholic feminist community. WOC members are persons from various religions and denominations who support WOC ecumenically. Membership ($20 annually) includes subscription to *New Women, New Church*, a bimonthly newspaper of activities related to women's ordination and other social justice issues within the Catholic church and society.

WOC, % Ruth Fitzpatrick, P.O. Box 2693, Fairfax, VA 22031, (703) 255-1428.

WOMEN'S QUEST

Women's Quest was founded to provide spiritual nourishment and a supportive community for carrying women's spiritual visions into the world. Questing circles, which meet in member's homes, provide a place where each woman's questing is supported in an ongoing way in communion with other women. While circles vary in content, there are common elements in the process: opening and closing rituals, meditations for healing and inspiration, spiritual journeys shared and held without judgment, and the free expression of play and creativity. Women's Quest can present a questing circle in your community, which includes a training session for those who would become circle facilitators. Participants become seed members for local ongoing circles. For information, send a legal-size SASE.

Women's Quest, % Sandra Lewis, coordinator, 79 Pixley St., San Francisco, CA 94123, (415) 567-3882.

The Three Ages of Women: Maiden, Mother, Crone © Lorraine S. Capparell, 1986. Ceramic sculptural columns. Photo by Lars Speyer. To inquire about installation of *The Three Ages of Women* and other commissioned work available from the artist write: Lorraine S. Capparell, 698 Kendall Ave., Palo Alto, CA 94306.

"*The Three Ages of Women* is a group of columnar figures representing the Maiden (or virgin) the Matron (or full womanhood), and the Crone (the wise old woman). These are architectural pieces. I see the two 6' columns, the Maiden and the Matron, as a gate to a circle of five 8' Crone columns, creating a sanctuary for contemplation of the ever-changing constancy that is our life" (Lorraine S. Capparell).

WOMEN'S RETREAT

Women's Retreat is offered as a low-cost retreat for women of all ages and traditions who seek a turning-within time away from the pressures of day-to-day life. Workshops are experiential and generally include movement, discussion of personal and planetary concerns, journal writing, art, yoga, tai chi. The retreat setting is a two-hundred acre preserve; plenty of free time is given during workshops for exploration of the landscape, both inner and outer. Women's comfort and pleasure is the focus of weekend workshops. Work scholarships are available.

Women's Retreat, % Manuela Schreiner, 849 Drake St., Cambria, CA 93428, (805) 927-4137.

WOMEN'S THEOLOGICAL CENTER

Women's Theological Center (WTC) is an ecumenical, multiracial center where women gather for study, action, reflection, and celebration of issues of faith and social justice from a women's perspective. Besides a nine-month program of theological and ministerial studies, WTC offers year-round workshops, conferences, and Womanspirit rituals. Programs (both formal and informal) are open to all women regardless of educational, economic, or religious backgrounds. Requests for admissions information, membership, networking, and schedule of activities welcomed.

Women's Theological Center, % Nancy Richardson and Adele Smith-Penniman, co-directors, 400 The Fenway, Boston, MA 02115, (617) 277-1330.

WOODSWOMEN

The goal of Woodswomen is to foster leadership and a spirit of adventure with women in the wilderness. Spiritual work on the trips is usually private, though formal ritual around the moon, stones, and sacred places may occur. Besides a complete program of wilderness trips available to the public, Woodswomen offers a membership program. Members receive a directory of national and regional women's wilderness programs, discounts to the Woodswomen General Store (a mail-order service for outdoor supplies), and a subscription to the newsletter *Woodswomen News*, filled with stories from women's trips, articles on outdoor leadership, book reviews, and information on women's history, natural history, and environmental issues.

Woodswomen, 2550 Pillsbury Ave. S., Minneapolis, MN 55404, (612) 870-8291.

JOURNEY

TO THE

SOURCE:

TEACHING AND

MEDITATION TAPES

**THE WOMANSPIRIT
SOURCEBOOK**

A U D I O - T A P E

R E S O U R C E S

THE BOOK OF HAGS
DEENA METZGER

The Book of Hags, an audio tape novel in the form of a play, asks searing questions: why do so many women have cancer, why now, and why so young? It was developed to explore the interior world of women as they confront their lives, relationships, community, history, and modern myth. Like much of the best recent fiction, *The Book of Hags* abandons utilities of time, space, and character in order to better grasp the unities of body, brain, and imagination. "Somewhere on an island, on a rocky coast, a woman is writing, alone." Characters emerge as she writes: "The writer, Diana. The old woman, Alma. Myself, yourself, all of us." Voices weave, overlap, fade in and out of music, cry out alone in a relentless examination and confrontation with the subtle, unacknowledged murders: "Death by hunger, death by cancer, death by madness. And there is resistance. And there is memory. And there are survivors."

Deena Metzger, healer-poet, who healed herself of cancer, wrote in *Tree*, "Quiet kills, cancer comes from silence." *The Book of Hags* is about speaking, naming, crying our minds—and healing ourselves! KA

1977. Available from Deena Metzger, P.O. Box 186, Topanga, CA 90290, (213) 455-1089 (two cassettes $15 ppd.).

BROOKE MEDICINE EAGLE TEACHING TAPES

Like many of the wisest teachers, Brooke Medicine Eagle speaks in a down-to-earth style frequently laced with humor. Her personality comes across vividly as she shares aspects of her life and her many visions, including those of Rainbow Woman and the "medicine eagle" from whom she took her name. Brooke's tapes are filled with practical suggestions for strengthening our bodies and hearts and for aligning our energies in harmony with the Earth. Each of these tapes are highly recommended.

Healing Through Ritual Actions: Teaches ways to reprogram your nervous system and to clear the path for spiritual growth in your everyday life. Ways to act out metaphors such as "leapin off the edge," "going for it," "dropping burdens," and "getting to the heart of the matter" are explained. (1986)

For My People: An outstanding singing and drumming tape features songs written by Brooke and friends. Includes "Buffalo Woman is Calling," "Altar Song of the Ancients," "Wolf Chant," and ten others. These chants are evocative, celebratory, and full of Earth imagery.

Visioning (two-tape set): Includes practical advice for letting go of ex-

Tree © Deena Metzger. Poster, 17" × 24", black and white. Photo by Hella Hammid. Poster design by Sheila Levrant de Brettville. Available for $11.50 ppd. (California residents add appropriate sales tax) from: Tree, P.O. Box 186, Topanga, CA 90290.

pectations, balancing nurturing and aggressive tendencies, freeing one-self from the artificial, and traditional Indian teachings such as the Medicine Way, vision quest, and the symbolism of the four directions. (1984)

Singing Joy to the Earth: Includes Native American songs and chants, a rendition of Kate Wolf's beautiful song to the spirits of the four directions, and Brooke's "Song of Active Waiting." This last is a great stress-reducer, whether you are waiting for a vision on a mountaintop or standing in line at the supermarket. Since Brooke sings most of the songs four times, there is plenty of time to learn each song. A musical "Best of Brooke," highly recommended for new and old students alike.

Moon Time: Focuses on the spritual aspects of moon (menstrual) time and how women can reclaim the lost ways of women's unique power. Addresses menopause, the grandmother Lodge and ways we can use the moon cycle for strengthening our connection to the Earth. (1987)

Moon Lodge: Teaches ways to create a women's place for retreat and visioning during the menstrual cycle. Practical advice for creating a Lodge; activities for group harmony; ceremonies for girls entering menarche and women beginning menopause; songs, dances, and spirtual actions to connect with the wisdom of the ancient grandmothers. (1987) LY/PW

Available from The Gaia Catalogue Company (Visioning, two-tape set $21.50 ppd.; All others $11.50 ppd. per tape) For wholesale inquires write:

Singing Joy to the Earth
Brooke Medicine Eagle

Brooke Medicine Eagle, % Harmony Network, P.O. Box 9725, Berkeley, CA 94709. See page 232 for Brooke Medicine Eagle article.

THE CAULDRON OF THOTH
A JOURNEY OF EMPOWERMENT
NICKI SCULLY
MUSIC BY JOHN SERGEANT

I'm one of 135 people lying on the floor in the dark, eyes closed, ears open, listening. There's music. Rhythmical. Eletronic. Music that makes pictures flicker behind my eyelids. And then there's a voice-engaging, rich, setting the scene for a guided fantasy, a safe trip to visit the Goddess, an adventure into imaginary realms. I stoke the fire of my heart, stir the water of my Cauldron, and—hsss! I'm face to face with Thoth, Nicki's guide, (and now mine) to the secret deep cave of the crone. *"The Cauldron is ... cup of the Tarot, the grail of the Christians, and a ting of the Chinese. It is the soup pot of every nurturing mother. It is the vessel of our being and it contains the whole of the collective consciousness."* "The Cauldron of Thoth" is rich with a satisfying mix of musical and mental moods for imagining yourself as Goddess and friend of Goddesses. (Reviewed by Susan Weed, director of Wise Woman Center, see listing p. 205.)

1987. Available from The Gaia Catalogue Company or directly from the artist, Nicki Scully, P.O. Box 5025, Eugene, OR 97405, (503) 484-1099 ($14 ppd.).

CELEBRATIONS
RUTH MOUNTAINGROVE

New Woman Press specializes in tapes, songbooks, and poetry for women about women's experiences. Ruth Mountaingrove is a co-founder of *WomanSpirit* magazine (see listing on page 128). New Woman carries Ruth's recordings and publications

including: *Celebrations: Songs for Solstices and Equinoxes, Menarche, and Menopause* (60 min., $7 ppd.); New Woman also carries the work of feminist artists Carolyn McDade, Susan Arrow, Laverne Reed, Cris Carol, Connie McKinnon, Urashan, and Zana. PW

Send a SASE for title list to New Woman Press, 2575 Alliance Rd., 16-B, Arcata, OR 95521.

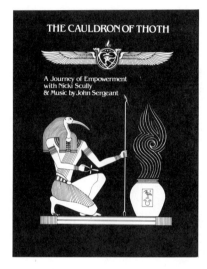
THE CAULDRON OF THOTH
A Journey of Empowerment with Nicki Scully & Music by John Sergeant

CREATIVE VISUALIZATION
SHAKTI GAWAIN

Shakti Gawain, author of *Creative Visualization* and *Living in the Light* (see listing on page 48), teaches practical techniques for expanding the possibilities in our lives and in the world. Exercises to help the body relax deeply, affirmations of love, health, and abundance, and exercises to practice experiencing a state of wholeness. The tape is down-to-earth and well-grounded in the creative visualization techniques that Shakti has been teaching for the past fifteen years. KHA

1980. Available from The Gaia Catalogue Company ($12.50 ppd.) and selected stores.

Rhiannon. Photo by Irene Young, 1987.

FINDING YOUR VOICE/ LOOSEN UP AND IMPROVISE
RHIANNON

Jazz singer and improvisational storyteller Rhiannon combines her years of experience as a teacher and performer (known to many as the lead singer of Alive!) in these two innovative and inspiring tapes. With a relaxed and encouraging touch, Rhiannon shares her wisdom of the power that resides in the voice. As we develop our voices, our self-expression expands, our hearts open, and old pains begin to heal. If you think you can't sing, if you want to fine tune your style, or if you just want to develop your voice, these tapes provide tools and techniques for both beginners and advanced students. *Finding Your Voice* teaches you how to discover the songs of your soul through physical music warm-up, breathing exercises, and simple duets. *Loosen Up and Improvise* uses guided physical stretching, breathing, sighing, rhythmic duets, and call and response. PW

1987. Information on tapes, private sessions, workshops, and performance bookings available upon request from Rhiannon Music, 1334 Carlton St., Berkeley, CA 94702, (415) 841-2672 ($10 ppd. each tape).

ILLUMINATING THE UNWRITTEN SCROLL: A CONFERENCE ON WOMEN'S SPIRITUALITY AND JEWISH TRADITION

In November 1984, over five hundred people gathered in Los Angeles for the first public conference to focus exclusively on Jewish women's spirituality. Panels and workshops ad-dressed a wide variety of topics. Audio tapes covering keynote addresses and panel presentations are available for purchase. They represent a range of perspectives with regard to religious background and orientation as well as feminist experience. Tapes available for purchase include: "Spiritual Journeys" (Beu Greenberg, Deena Metzger, Ruth Weisberg), "Women's Experience of God" (Rachel Adler, Ellen Umansky), "Women's Prayer and Women's Praying" (Lawrence Hoffman, Marcia Falk), and "Sanctifying Women's Lives through Ritual" (Barbara Myerhoff, Esther Broner.) TDS

1984. Available from Infomedix: Educational Resources and Services, 12800 Garden Grove Blvd., Suite F, Garden Grove, CA 92643, (714) 530-3454 ($6 per tape, plus $1 postage for first tape, 50¢ for each additional tape).

ILLUMINATING THE UNWRITTEN SCROLL: A CONFERENCE ON WOMEN'S SPIRITUALITY AND JEWISH TRADITION

CANTOR JANET BIEBER

We gathered from all walks of spirituality to hear our mothers speak, in person, through others, and in our own voices. From Blu Greenberg, a woman born and raised in the Orthodox tradition, to Deena Metzger, who has come back to her Judaism through her own search, we are creating a past through shreds of collected memory, and envisioning a future that redefines our roles in our culture, religion, and life paths.

For some of the women, it took this gathering to awaken the desire to find new places in our culture. For others who have already blazed a trail for themselves, this conference was a place to find camaraderie and the nurturing that comes from knowing that one is not alone. Yes, there are others who feel excluded because God is largely referred to in the masculine, because our protagonists are mostly men, and because all our *tefilot* (prayers) are written from a male point of view.

Where is our story? Between the lines.

We spent two days together, exploring such diverse subjects as "Mechitza: A View from the Other Side," and "The Goddess as Symbol of a New Feminist Holistic Consciousness: Explorations and Meditations." We told stories of our mothers, grandmothers, maiden aunts, and legendary ancestors. Nearly everyone remembered a *bubbe* (grandmother) lighting Shabbos candles . . . the silence of the moment just before she struck the match . . . the torchlike brightness of the flame.

"Blessed is the match, consumed in the kindling flame."

Her dark face, mostly covered with a scarf, illuminated by the tiny fire.

"Blessed is the flame that burns in the secret places of the heart."

Baruch ata Adonai,

Blessed are you, Source of the Universe.

At the closing session, we made symbolic Torah scrolls, inscribed with names of women important in our lives, and significant spiritual moments from our own experiences. Esther Broner, author and creator of ritual relevant to women's lives, helped us created a new Havdalah (post-Shabbat ceremony), as we left our spiritual togetherness and dispersed to our private destinations.

There is a momentum building in Jewish women's lives. It isn't an easy time. Change, evolution, never is. We are searching for our rightful place in the context of our religion, culture, and heritage.

We want to carry out our callings. We want to sing with our God-given voices, hearts, bodies, and souls. Horizontal exactitudes, such as rabbinic law, must be balanced by vertical, timeless truths, such as the equality of each living soul before God. Without this, we as a people are in danger of being cut off from our roots, the very wellspring of our life.

May God grant us the power and vision to achieve the balance. Amen.

Cantor Janet Bieber belongs to Temple Beth Ami, West Covina, California. The article first appeared in *"Lillith"*, the Jewish Women's Magazine.

INNER DANCE TAPES

DIANE MARIECHILD WITH SHULI GOODMAN MUSIC BY KAY GARDNER, ADRIENNE TORF, JULIA HAYES AND NARUDAFINA PILI ABENA

At long last, meditation tapes based on the writings and teachings of Diane Mariechild! Diane is a psychospiritual counselor and ritualist who brings a woman's perspective to Buddhist and Native American spritual traditions. The four inspirational *Inner Dance Tapes* contain guided meditations set to music, which guide the listener through the healing process. *Inner Dance 1* offers peaceful solutions for transforming a chaotic world. "The Earth and Sky Meditation" lays the foundation for a personal spritual practice, encouraging you to root deeply in the Earth while gently opening your heart. The meditations on *Inner Dance 2*, "Healing the Hurt Child" and "The Forgiveness," provide a supportive and safe environment to practice loving kindness and forgiveness with those you love. *Inner Dance 3* fires the energy of transformation. "Lovers and Warriors Talk and Meditation" leads the listener on a journey to the wholeness of our many selves. This tape encourages the integration of the lover (compassion) and the warrior (action) energies. *Inner Dance 4* contains body movement exercises based on the flow of Earth and Sky energy and it's manifestation in the body. Each of the *Inner Dance Tapes* can be enjoyed alone, in group meditations, and as a companion to the book *Inner Dance* (see listing page 36).   PW

1987. Available from The Gaia Catalogue Company ($12.45 ppd. per tape). Wholesale orders write: Aquila Tapes, RFD #3, Amherst, MA 01002, (413) 259-1657. A free catalogue available upon request.

INNER SOUND AND VOICE
JILL PURCE

Jill Purce, author of *The Mystic Spiral* (Thames & Hudson, 1974), conducts "Inner Sound and Voice" workshops around the world to teach techniques for making contact with deeper levels of self through overtone chanting, an ancient mystical sound technique created by changing the vocal cavity to produce chords of simultaneous notes octaves apart. This tape features a British radio broadcast interview with Jill on the spiritual effects of sound on the psyche, followed by solo and group overtone chanting. The chanting on the tape has a powerful healing and restorative effect on the listener. PW

For workshop and tape ordering information, write Jill Purce, 20 Willow Rd., Hampstead, London NW3, England ($12.75 ppd.).

INNER WOMAN TAPES:
MOON PRIESTESS, MOON RITUAL
INITIATION INTO THE MYSTERIES
OF THE GODDESS
INNER SANCTUARY
DENISE LINN

Denise Linn spent three years in a Zen monastery, after which she trained with a Hawaiian kahuna (shaman). Part Cherokee Indian, she draws on her experience in the study and practice of Eastern religions and indigenous cultures on her tape series *Inner Woman*. And no doubt

about it—these are excellent tapes! There is much poetry and magic in Denise's voice, and the meditation landscapes are rich and detailed. Each tape features a body of teachings on side 1; side 2 contains a guided meditation-visualization that deepens the teachings found on side 1. *Moon Priestess, Moon Ritual* describes the importance of the moon in women's lives, nature's cycles, dreams, intuitions, the feminine power principle, the White Goddess. *Initiation into the Mysteries of the Goddess* covers Goddess mythology, feminine rites of passage, death of the old self, rebirth, integration, the dark of Kali, the Veiled Isis, the power of the female. *Inner Sanctuary* has the listener create an inner retreat for spiritual renewal and self-healing, visualize a safe place for nourishment and regeneration, develop inner calm. PW

1983. Available from The Gaia Catalogue Company ($12.50 ppd. per tape).

MAGICAL JOURNEYS
SELENA FOX

Selena Fox is a shamanic psychotherapist, Wiccan priestess, and founder of Circle Sanctuary, an international Pagan resource center (see listing on page 168). On *Magical Journeys* she eases the listener into a relaxed state of consciousness, then embarks on a shamanic healing journey into the mind. Side 1, "The Five Elements," offers an attune-

ment to earth, air, fire, water. Side 2, "The Magic Cauldron," is a vision quest into past, present, and future possibilities. KHA

1981. Available from Circle, Box 219, Mt. Horeb, WI 53572 ($9 ppd.).

MEDICINE WOMAN
LYNN V. ANDREWS

On these two one-hour audio cassettes, Lynn Andrews tells the dramatic story of her personal experiences of Native American magic and her life-transforming apprenticeship with Agnes Whistling Elk. With its roots in Native American oral tradition, *Medicine Woman* belongs to the spoken world. In vivid language and a powerful voice, Andrews relates the story of her search for self-discovery from Beverly Hills to the Canadian wilderness, with an exciting background of Native American music by R. Carlos Nakai.

1987. Available from Harper & Row ($16.45 ppd.).

MENSTRUAL MYTHS AND MYSTERIES
REV. ARIADNE WEAVER, PH.D.

One of this world's most miraculous and taken-for-granted events is the wonder that women "can bleed and not die, can change in cycles even as the moon cycles, in deep rhythms and harmony with Nature." Ariadne Weaver, historian of religions and Wiccan priestess, addresses the long-suppressed wisdom and the sacramental nature of the bleeding act. Side 1 includes material about approaching menstruation in a sacred way. Side 2 offers some specific suggestions for creating a menstrual ritual, either for a younger woman's first moon or for any older woman who has not been properly initiated into the mystery of the menstrual cycle. Also included on the tape is a reading from the narrative "Coming of Age in the Apache Way," several very singable menstruation songs, and

readings by poet Ellen Bass. PW

1984. Available from Welcome Home, 484 Lake Park, Suite 260, Oakland, CA 94610, (415) 837-4536 ($10 ppd.).

MOTHER WIT TAPES

DIANE MARIECHILD

Derived from the ever-popular book by the same title (see listing page 64), the *Mother Wit Tapes* can be used alone or as a companion to the book. On *Mother Wit* the "Self-Healing Meditation" acts as a self-healing guide to relax and release pain and tension in the body and heart; the "Inner Wisdom Meditation" offers gentle, nuturing imagery that opens the listener to the source of wisdom within. On *Mother Wit For Children of All Ages* the child is welcomed to the planet Earth and invited to journey to a mystical place, to relax, to enjoy, to imagine. These tapes are superbly produced by Shuli Goodman with magical musical accompaniment by Kay Gardner, Adrienne Torf, Julia Haines and Nurudafina Pili Abena. PW

1987. Available from The Gaia Catalogue Company ($12.45 ea. ppd.). Wholesale orders write: Aquila Tapes, RFD #3, Amherst, MA 01002, (413) 259-1657. A free catalogue available upon request.

RAINBOW WARRIOR MEDITATION

DIANE MARIECHILD

Spirals of light, pillar of light. Seated within the light. Breathing in, breathing out, certain of the light.

Within you resides a warrior, a warrior of the light, a warrior of the rainbow. She is a powerful woman, she is a woman of power. She expresses her power in unique and wonderful ways. She is a wise woman. She is a woman who is wise. She is a strong woman. She is a woman who is strong. She is an intuitive woman. She is a woman who is intuitive. She is a woman who is prepared to meet the challenges of this time. She is a woman of strong, clear will. She is a woman of clear intention. She is a mindful woman. She is a woman, awake. Within you is a warrior, a woman of light.

The warrior is a woman of peace. She is able to turn aside anger, transforming it into compassionate action. The warrior is a woman whose heart is filled with compassion. She sees the suffering and encompasses it. The warrior is a woman of clear action. She can act with lightning speed. She can act with great circumspection. The warrior realizes the unity of all life. The warrior walks within the sacred circle of life. The warrior walks the path of balance. The warrior is a woman walking. The warrior is a peaceful woman walking. She is walking the path of the rainbow, the path to our deepest wisdom, the wisdom of the heart.

Hear the beat of your heart. Hear the beat of a drum. Let the drumbeat of your heart carry you to the warrior. You are traveling on a road of light, traveling on a road to the sea. Traveling on a rainbow road. Here along the rainbow path you will meet the rainbow warrior, the clear thinking, clear acting, compassionate being who wields a sword of light. You will know her well. She is a being who has made a commitment to the light by serving the light within herself and within all beings.

You see the warrior now. And you walk with this warrior woman

until you come to the place of the sacred fire. Here the fire of trans-mutation is built. You dig the pit. Place the stones, lay the sticks. Light the fire. Let the smoke be an offering that the flame, the light, be clear within you. As you hear the crackling sound of the fire and watch the smoke curling in the air you can cast into that fire any doubt or fear. This is the fire of transformation. Here you can drop the shroud of your pain. Here you have the opportunity to drop any patterns or habits that have obstructed the clear light of mind. You make the courageous choice to let go of the pain and hurt of the past. And as you release your pain you realize that this fire of trans-formation always burns within you. Within your center burns a sacred fire in which you can dispel any thoughts of separation or scarcity. Now the fire has burned down. You and the warrior woman leave together. You leave the ashes and walk to the edge of the stream. In this stream you wash away any remaining guilt or pain. The water, a stream of forgiveness, washes over you. As it streams down your back, as you bathe in the water, you forgive yourself. You wash away that which needs to be washed away. Forgive yourself for not meeting needs and expectations of self and others. Forgive yourself for errors of the past, for that which was left undone. In this moment be washed free.

From Diane Mariechild, *Crystal Visions*, Crossing Press, 1985 (see listing on page 15).

MOTHERPEACE CASSETTES
VICKI NOBLE

From its conception, the Mother-peace Round Tarot was designed to heal and reawaken the denied femi-nine aspect of the divine (see listing on page 259). The deck was brought into being during sessions when Vicki Noble and her partner Karen Vogel were in deep trance states. In Vicki Noble's book *Motherpeace: A Way to the Goddess through Myth, Art, and Tarot* (see listing on page 66), the entire seventy-eight card system is linked image by image with the sacred ways of ancient Goddess-worshiping matriarchal cultures. The Motherpeace Cassettes guide the stu-dent of Motherpeace into a deeper understanding of the cards: their meanings, the presence they trans-mit, the meaning of reversals. Be-cause it is possible to work with and look at the cards while simulta-neously taking in the spoken infor-

mation on the tapes, these lessons provide an immediacy that can't be received from a book. The Mother-peace Tarot deck, books, and taped lessons provide a powerful system for delving into the almost-lost realm where women and men can know and trust their feminine power and use it in the world for positive change.

Matriarchal Herstory: On this tape Vicki Noble rekindles our mem-ory and pride in women's rich God-dess-worshiping herstory and cul-ture. Taped live at a lecture, this tape documents the ways recorded his-tory, a male-dominated profession, has consistently misinterpreted ar-tifacts and icons from highly evolved Goddess civilizations, then weaves this teaching into the story of the cre-ation of the Motherpeace tarot deck when she and her partner, Karen Vo-gel, set out to learn how and why the Mother-led societies were usurped by sun-worshiping patriarchal cultures.

Major Arcana: The Major Ar-cana are the first twenty-two cards in any tarot deck. They run from the Fool (#0) through the World (#21) and represent stages in the evolution of the soul. Vicki gives an in-depth interpretation of each Major's essen-tial quality, then shows how this quality is altered when it comes up reversed.

Minor Arcana: The Minor Ar-cana, in the tarot refers to our actions in everyday life. In the Motherpeace system, these cards are divided into four suits: discs, cups, wands, and swords, corresponding to the ele-ments of earth, water, fire, and air, respectively. Besides elaborating on the meanings of these forty cards, Vicki discusses how the tarot func-tions as an oracle, an honest friend, a personal therapist. She teaches several ways Motherpeace can be used to repattern and transform the psyche, and gives directions for a rit-ual using the Motherpeace images.

Elemental Personalities: Un-like the Major Arcana, which rep-resent "larger-than-life" forces, the People cards (known as the court cards in traditional card decks) can

The Warrior Mother © Rohmana Harris d'Arezzo. Ink on paper. One of a continuing series of archtypal drawings, the "Goddess Series," each of which has been reproduced in a limited edition, signed and numbered by the artist. For more information write: Rohmana Harris d'Arezzo, 66 Summit Ave., Mill Valley, CA 94941.

be related to on a personal or individual level. On this tape Vicki gives detailed explanations of the elemental qualities of each card, clarifies the relationships between different combinations of People cards, and teaches how to read reversed and tilted cards.

Chakras: Offers a complete lesson on the location, essential qualities, and function of each of the seven energy centers in the body, the chakras. After presenting the chakra teachings, Vicki leads the listener into experiencing and working with each energy center so as to disconnect from habitual tendencies that limit our full unfolding, with the immediate effect of both eliminating harmful psychic patterns and helping the listener feel good, physically. KHA

1986. All tapes are available from The Gaia Catalogue Company ($11.25 ea. ppd. or 5 tape set for $50 ppd.) or from selected bookstores.

CHAKRAS
Meditation and Healing with Motherpeace; How to Clear Energy Centers and Break Negative Agreements
by **VICKI NOBLE**

On each 60-minute tape, Vicki Noble uses what she calls "sacred play" to lead you through explanations, exercises and meditations for deepened interpretations in reading the Tarot.

THE PATH OF A SHAMAN
GABRIELLE ROTH

"The path of a shaman is a dancing path, an inner journey always moving back to zero, the still point, back to a visionary, illuminated state of consciousness. It is a path for edge-walkers, dreamstalkers, jive-talkers who prowl the outskirts of the American Dream."

Gabrielle Roth, dancer, choreographer, and founder of the Moving Center in New York City, describes the way of the twentieth-century shaman-healer, she who embodies ancient, sacred wisdom while remaining fully present to the dance of present-time reality. With the lyric intonations of preacher, magician, enchantress, Gabrielle challenges the "edge-walking woman" to trail-blaze through her own depths, back to that inner frontier where wholeness is found, where the courage that comes with clear vision is restored. This tape incorporates the spoken word, poetry, and a rock-and-roll finale. Not recommended for use while driving or rocking babies to sleep. KHA

1986. Available from The Gaia Catalogue Company ($12.50 ppd.).

GABRIELLE ROTH
THE PATH OF A SHAMAN

Judgment,
Healing the Earth.
Motherpeace
Tarot © Vicki
Noble and Karen
Vogel, 1981.

PRAY THE BODY,
FREE THE SOUL

GABRIELLE ROTH

Gabrielle Roth is a dynamic artist, teacher, choreographer, and healer whose work is on the leading edge of experimental dance theater. As artistic director of the American Ritual Theater in New York City, she unites art and healing in the context of theater, the one art form inclusive of all others. Gabrielle is honest, soulful, bold, and at home in the shaman's world of opposites and constant change. She spoke the following thoughts to me during one of her workshops at Westerbeke Ranch in Sonoma, California.

—Patrice Wynne

Several years after I had been teaching dance, people began to ask if they could train with me. I realized that in order to communicate what I was doing I would have to observe the process more consciously. I discovered I wasn't as Zen as I thought, that I have a method to my madness. In fact it was below my mind. I began to see that there were rhythm patterns that I consistently used and that in fact they fell into an order that was directly from life. I experienced these patterns when I had my baby, when I made love, when I created a piece of art. These rhythms were the rhythms of life, the rhythms of being. The electrical magnetic currents that are flowing in our bodies right this second are flowing in these rhythms.

Gabrielle Roth.
Photo © Robert
Ansell, 1980.

Working with the rhythms catalyzed my work with the emotions. My way to work with emotions is to celebrate them, to dance them, to move them, to paint them, to sing them, to write them into poems. I began to see the connection between our emotions and the sexual cycles and how afraid we are of our sexuality. Just as we repress all of our emotional energies, we repress our physical energies and in that way we lose a vital source of feminine wisdom.

Women are the teachers of the body but women have stopped performing that function. We're mother, mistress, and madonna. Men separated those entities. The mistress was Mary Magdalene; the madonna was the Virgin Mary; and the mother was everybody else, Mensch. Never should those three meet in the body! Keep them separate whatever you do, because all three energies would be way too powerful! As women we got stuck in the mother without realizing the mistress and the madonna within us. Whatever we do should be emphasizing and nourishing and bringing to full value those three archetypes. That is the feminine power.

You separate the spirit from the body, boom, you make the neurosis. Religion essentially has created neurosis just like medical technology has created *candida*. You cannot separate God from the body, you cannot. God is in the body of each of us! We have to take back the religion into our own power zone. The movements of life are sacred, our relationships are sacred. Giving birth to children is the most profound religious act. There is no unit more sacred than the family unit.

The five aspects of the self are the body, the heart, the mind, the soul, and the spirit. These are governed by three other aspects, the mother, the father, and the child. That is the sacred trinity. When those three are in unity, then you have the God and Goddess within. Our bodies contain both the mothering, nurturing, feminine, permissive energy, as well as the masculine, authoritative, line-drawing energy. Just as the mother draws circles, the father draws lines. Both must be drawn. Those two energies are the aspects that create the child, the spirit that we all are. The child spirit is our divinity. Spirit is androgynous in that it is equally male and female. It is such an absolute balance point that it is neither one nor the other.

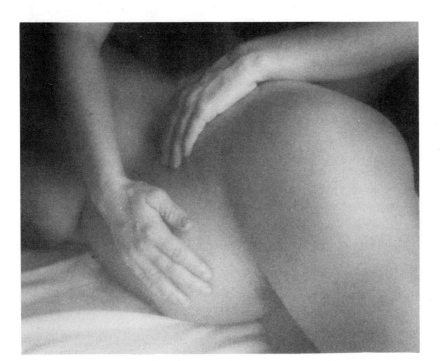

A Touch of Love © Kathleen Thormod Carr, photographer, 1986. *A Touch of Love* and other images of pregnant women, birth, infants, and children are available from the artist: Kathleen Thormod Carr, P.O. Box 519, Big Sur, CA 93920.

It is the task of the spiritual warrior to cultivate what I call tribal individualism. Our children must be taught pride and responsibility to the tribe, as well as to oneself. This is my problem with education. Education creates mediocre, nice, normal, neutral, neurotic people. It is not serving the individualism in each child in any respect. I would have all young girls study belly dancing between the ages of ten and fifteen. And I would have all males of the same age study African-type dancing. Dancing gives the child an opportunity to experience the power, divinity, and sacred energies contained in the body.

You can learn from other cultures, but you can't become them. You can go to a foreign culture to study dance with a shaman but it probably won't change your life because the shaman develops these teachings for his or her own culture. Our major task as warriors is to free the body to experience the power and profundity of our own being, *being* being a verb. The problem with *god* and *goddess* is that they are nouns. For me *god* has to be a verb, it has to be motion, it has to be dynamic.

Spirit is as simple as breath. Most of us are holding our breath most of the time. The toes aren't breathing. The fingertips aren't breathing. The earlobes aren't breathing. To really awaken, we have to allow ourselves to breathe fully and deeply. The fastest way to still the mind is to move the body. The fastest way to allow the body to take over, to have a revolution of spirit, is to breathe. Breathing allows you to move through the blocks and the barriers that are holding you back. When a body is fully breathed and totally relaxed, that's power. And you can see it, you can smell it, you can feel it. It is absolutely obvious.

Gabrielle Roth conducts Ritual Theater classes and dance workshops around the country. For booking information and schedule of classes, write: The Moving Center, P.O. Box 271, Cooper Station, New York, New York 10276, (212) 505-7928.

THE POWER AND THE SPIRIT
ANNE BOHLEN AND CELESTE WESSON, PRODUCERS

Aired on National Public Radio, *The Power and the Spirit* is a powerful, in-depth radio documentary on the rising movement by Roman Catholic women to seek ordination to the priesthood and the controversy this movement has created within the Roman Catholic church. The tape presents the historical context for the issue of women's ordination; features interviews with activists within the Women-Church movement; includes coverage of the "Ordination Reconsidered" convocation in St. Louis; reports on the church's position and bishops' response to the movement; interviews Catholic women opposed to ordination of women. A baptism of an infant child and a communion service provide glimpses into the distinctive nature of Women-Church ritual and worship services. PW

1985. Power and the Spirit Radio Project, 1503 Crittenden St. N.W., Washington, DC 20011, (202) 829-0619 ($10 ppd.).

A CALL FOR WOMEN'S ORDINATION

In 1979, Pope John Paul II came to the United States and visited six cities. In Washington, he spoke to a group of two thousand nuns. The sister who greeted him was the head of the Sisters of Mercy, Teresa Kane. With a round sweet face and silver hair, wearing a business suit, not a habit, she was the only woman except for the President's wife who had a chance to address the Pope publicly. Millions of people saw her on television that night. She stood before him, under the vaulted ceiling of the Shrine of the Immaculate Conception.

Sister Teresa Kane: "As I share this privileged moment with you, your Holiness, I urge you to be mindful of the intense suffering and pain which is part of the life of many women in the United States. As women we have heard the powerful messages of our church. Our contemplation leads us to state that the church in its struggle to be faithful to its call for reverence and dignity for all persons must respond by providing the possibility of women as persons being included in all ministries of our church."

The Pope did not respond to her unprecedented public confrontation. Later, he reaffirmed the ban on women priests. Since then, he has warned American bishops not to encourage women's ordination.

From Anne Bohlen and Celeste Wesson, The Power and the Spirit Radio Project, 1985.

just imagine...

women priests

Just Imagine, Women Priests. Free brush logo and Just Imagine lettering contributed by Corita Kent for the "Ordination Reconsidered Conference" poster in St. Louis, MO, October 1985. Women Priests lettering added at the conference by Sharon McMullin.

PRACTICAL WISDOM I AND II
LYNN ANDREWS

On these studio-taped interviews, Lynn Andrews addresses the suppression of female wisdom in our patrilineal world, presenting practical guidelines for restoring and empowering the feminine in our everyday lives. Her answers to audience questions are sometimes startling, often thought-provoking, and her stories enchant as they teach. KHA

1985. Available from Channel Light Productions, P.O. Box 480086, Los Angeles, CA 90048 (two-tape set, $21.50 ppd./CA residents $22.74 ppd.).

REBIRTH OF THE GODDESS: A TALK ON WITCHCRAFT, FEMINISM, AND SOCIAL CHANGE
STARHAWK

The Goddess, as Starhawk brings her to life in this dynamic discussion of spirituality, sexuality, and personal power, is not a static image, but an ecstatic movement, ever changing, fluid, all-inclusive. In this talk, given at the University of Wisconsin in 1981, Starhawk presents an extensive overview of the history and intent of the Old Religion of the Goddess, and shares elements of her spiritual-political journey that eventually led her to become a Witch. KHA

1981. Available from The Gaia Catalogue Company ($11.25 ppd.).

RETURN OF THE GODDESS
MERLIN STONE
CANADIAN BROADCASTING CORPORATION

Merlin Stone is the author of *When God Was a Woman* (see listing on page 99) and *Ancient Mirrors of Womanhood* (see listing on page 5). A sculptor and art historian, she is one of the leading spokeswomen in the emerging Goddess spirituality movement. "Return of the Goddess" was originally aired on Canadian Broadcasting Corporation affiliates as four one-hour radio programs. The series, which was conceived, edited, and narrated by Merlin Stone, consists of interviews, readings, and music by feminists concerned with the emergence of women's spirituality and/or the reclamation of the Goddess in their work. "Return of the Goddess" is available as a four-tape set only: Program 1, "The Goddess in Contemporary Women's Music and Arts"; Program 2, "The Goddess in Contemporary Women's Literature, Performance, and Psychology"; Program 3, "The Goddess in Contemporary Women's History, Theology, and Religion"; Program 4, "The Goddess in Contemporary Women's Politics." PW

1986. Available from CBC Enterprises Audio Products, Box 6440, Station A, Montreal, Quebec H3C 3L4 Canada ($27.75 U.S. per set or $32.70 Canadian per set).

THE SACRED ART OF PREGNANCY
SURIA LESS

"What can be more profound than becoming co-creative with the Divine Being?" Suria Less, Sufi teacher and lay midwife, teaches the art of conscious conception—establishing a relationship with the spirit of the unborn child before and during pregnancy. She explains how the mother-to-be, alone or with her mate, can create an attunement with the incoming soul by means of certain spiritual practices. She discusses and interprets concerns of pregnancy such as miscarriage and abortion, cesarean births, symptoms such as disturbing dreams, and the effects of the pregnancy on the father's spiritual life. This tape contains quality material covering an area about which there is little previously recorded material on tape. KHA

1986. Omega Press, P.O. Box 574, Lebanon Springs, NY 12114, (518) 794-8181 ($9.95 ppd.).

TREAD LIGHTLY UPON THE EARTH THE WISDOM OF THE SOUL
DIANA KECK, M.A.

Diana Keck is a psychotherapist in Boulder, Colorado, and on the faculty of Boulder College. She lectures widely on the healing benefits of guided imagery for adults and children. Modern medical and scientific research are now confirming what has been known intuitively by wise healers throughout the ages: visualizing healing symbols and images, while in a state of deep relaxation, fosters physical, emotional, and spiritual well-being. *Tread Lightly* is one of a series of twenty guided imagery tapes available from Diana Keck. Side 1 contains powerful imagery exploring the Indian Medicine Wheel and the connected nature of reality. This side is especially useful in group meditation. Side 2 is a journey in consciousness to the center of the self. Diana's training in meditation and dreamwork, and her skill in the use of mental images combine to invoke healing and wisdom from deep within. A free catalogue of additional tapes for adults and children including stress reduction, freedom from pain, healing, changing habit patterns, spiritual growth, self-improvement, and creative mothering is available upon request. Highly recommended. PW

1986. Available from Mountain Spirit Tapes, Inc., 616 Poplar, Boulder, CO 80302, (303) 449-8412 ($11.45 ppd.).

VISUALIZATION AND AIDS
MARGO ADAIR AND LYNN JOHNSON, MUSIC BY STEFAN DASHO

Recognizing the need for tools to help gay men and the worried well live amidst the AIDS epidemic, the San Francisco Shanti Project has co-produced these visualization tapes with Margo Adair, author of *Working Inside Out—Tools for Change* (Wingbow Press, 1984). Two sets of audio cassettes are available; each set comes with a booklet explaining the process of visualization and offering specific guidelines for using the tapes. *For People with AIDS*—four meditations: "Envisioning a Healthy Immune System," "Healing and Treatment Choices," "Respite: Enlightening the Heart and Relieving Pain," "Wise Self: Courage to Keep Up the Fight and/or Let Go" (two-cassette set w/instruction booklet $14.15 ppd./CA residents $14.98). *"For the Worried Well*—two meditations: "Envisioning a Healthy Immune System" and "Cultivating Wellness in Your Life" (cassette w/ instruction booklet $9.90 ppd./CA residents $10.45). PW

Make checks payable to Tapping Deeper Resources, and send to Tools for Change, P.O. Box 14141, San Francisco, CA 94114, or call (415) 861-6838.

THAT THE PEOPLE MAY LIVE

BROOKE MEDICINE EAGLE, CHALÍSE

"It is the dawning of the night upon Bear Butte. I look down across a lake below and in the far distant twilight see the tiny lights of Rapid City in the Black Hills. I lie very peacefully. Then beside me there comes a woman, older than I am, yet not really an old woman. She is dressed very simply in white buckskin. Now the little clouds that cover the moon move off, and as they move away, the moonlight shining upon her dress creates a flurry of rainbows, so I see that her dress is beaded with crystal beads, hundreds of tiny crystal beads. The slightest movement she makes sends little flurries of rainbows around me in the darkening twilight.

"She says to me that the Earth is in trouble, that the land is in trouble—that here on this land, this Turtle Island, this North American land, what needs to happen is a balancing. She says that the thrusting, aggressive, analytic, intellectual, building, making-it-happen energy has very much overbalanced the feminine, receptive, allowing, surrendering energy. She speaks to me as a woman, and I am to carry this message to women specifically. And not only women need to become strong in this way; we all need to become this—men and women alike."

—Vision of Rainbow Woman by Brook Medicine Eagle, Chalíse

Rainbow Woman's vision was given to Brooke more than ten years ago, yet its prophetic message continues to have relevance in our lives today. Brooke Medicine Eagle, Chalíse, is an Earthkeeper, a healer, poet, and songwriter. She was born and grew up her early years on the Crow Reservation in Montana, her home state where she has recently returned to live. Brooke is currently dedicated to a four-year public ceremonial cycle that will align the consciousness of peoples around the globe and whose purpose is to move us gracefully into a golden new time of harmony and peace on Mother Earth.

I spoke with Brooke at Dominican College in San Rafael, California. As we sat under a great and spacious oak tree that protected us from the afternoon sun, Brooke braided two strands of buffalo hair. At the end of our time together she offered me the braided strands

with a prayer, "May the message of Rainbow Woman reach into the hearts and minds of people everywhere."

—Patrice Wynne

In my vision of Rainbow Woman she said very directly to me that we must raise the feminine energy into balance on Mother Earth. She gave those simple words to me then and I've been learning the deeper meaning and implications of her message during all the years since.

Much knowledge of the feminine, especially the women's traditions, was lost and confused in the shattering of our cultures. (In fact, it has been broken for most women, not only native women.) The few native grandmothers who still held it associated themselves in hoops to keep it strong. Since Indian spiritual practice was illegal, they held the vision and the wisdom in their wombs. And as we become ready now to know and practice the ancient truthful ways, it is being released to us through our grandmothers in body and in spirit.

At this present time, when we are unrolling an incredible new future, the most useful information comes through each of us who learns to use her moon time (menstrual time) for stilling herself and calling vision. Conversely, for each of us who does not use her moon time well, much is lost, including the respect of others for her bleeding time. Among our people, the most prophetic dreams and visions were often brought to the people through the Moon Lodges. So begin now to honor and use your moon time well. Come together in small hoops (optimally of eight women) and create for yourselves a Moon Lodge—a communal women's retreat and meditation room—for the beauty, for the quiet, for the visions that will guide us and our families at this crucial time. Create a place where you can retreat and nurture yourselves. Seek vision for a radiant, harmonious life for your children and the children of seven generations. Pray, "Not for myself alone, Great Spirit, Mother Earth, do I ask this vision, but that all the peoples may live."

Women are stepping forward as teachers, the ones who say not "How much?" but "How well?" and "How can we be of service to Mother Earth at this time?" To be feminine is the most yin of all tasks and, at the same time, we are being asked to teach and to lead the world, which is a very yang thing to do. It's like the roots of this beautiful tree, which couldn't grow tall into the sky (the masculine) if it were not equally rooted deep in the gentle, renewing, nurturing Earth—the feminine. So we must be able to find quiet and receptive ways, and the Moon Lodge is a simple and powerful way to do this.

I've been gathering with a small circle of women of Asian, black, English, and American descent. We are very active, powerful women who have accomplished things like going through medical school, Ph.D. programs, directing organizations, creating businesses, etc. In order to succeed in that way we often had to push ourselves and

Menarche, © Sasha McInnes, 1986. Woven tapestry of handspun/dyed wool and silk, various dyes including menstrual blood, 8' × 8'. Photo by Jeff Carroll.

do it alone. Now, like many women today, we're recognizing that we can soften our tone, and together model a new way of using our power as women. Our vibration is changing from a loud Tchk-TchkTchk, to a soft Aaahhhhhhhmmmmmm, a harmonious hum that is gentle, like a lullaby. It reminds me of a lovely saying from the Samurai tradition, "A woman is strong in her discipline and gentle in her teaching."

Here on Turtle Island, Buffalo Woman is one of our most powerful models of the gentle nurturing spirit of the feminine. Sometimes buffalos are thought of as big and aggressive, and thus you might wonder how buffalo can be the symbol of the feminine. Remember that the buffalo provided everything for the people—hides for lodges, meat for food, bone implements for tools—nurturing us in more ways than any other thing. Nurturing power holds all things in balance so that the people may live harmonious lives. Females were given the charge of nurturing and renewing the people, and as we chose to come into female bodies, we chose to have the responsibility of creation, nurturing, and renewing. As women we need to be very clear that our nurturing and creating energy is in harmony with the Great Web of Life.

The women's spirituality movement is an inexorable movement. It is happening. We can either drag our feet or help the feminine move easily and gracefully back into our experience. One of the functions of a circle of women is to deepen our relationship with Mother Earth and Father Spirit, to make through ourselves the connection between heaven and earth, to listen and pray there. Our prayers reverberate across the land, changing the very molecular structure of all things. Women of spirit praying together are setting a new tone in the nervous system of humanity. Our very cells are being restructured.

Part of the restructuring will be a reaching out and connecting in a good way with other people so that we can become fully functioning children of Mother Earth in the great circle of life. Our lives were more devastated than we realize by the breakdown of clan and family connectedness. We're not often around our brothers and sisters; we're not around our cousins, our grandmothers. Yet now is the time to practice the understanding that the woman next door is our sister, and her children are our children, and the old woman down the street is the grandmother our children will have. We have the beautiful opportunity to build at a much deeper level, a rainbow clan of peoples.

We learn cooperation when we come together in circles. We learn to strengthen ourselves and become clearer channels. Then we can step out from those circles into our families as mothers who influence our growing children, as women who require a nurturing life-style and nurturing relationship with our mates. The focus is to retreat and be quiet, to soften and resonate, to harmonize and listen in service, so that we can take what we learn back out to the world in a balanced way.

One of the things we must begin to know deep in our wombs is that our true mother is in fact Mother Earth; she gave us our very bodies, our physical selves. She is a feminine being with arms big enough to take in a town, a whole city, a state, an entire planet and all the peoples upon it. If each of us has a loving, open, gentle relationship with her, then our world is a very different place.

We came to Earth as absolutely loving beings. That is our basic nature. And all we want is to have a joyful life together—a peaceful, harmonious, laughter-filled, beauty-filled, song-filled kind of life together. And it *is* coming. The feminine energy, Buffalo Woman's energy, is very strong in many of our hearts at this time. Buffalo Woman is willing to shine out through each of us who quiet ourselves and call.

I have spoken.

To receive information on Brooke Medicine Eagle's workshops, public ceremonies, and trainings, write: Sky Lodge, P.O. Box 1682, Helena, MT 59624, or call (406) 442-8196. Audio cassette tapes of Brooke's teachings can be ordered from The Gaia Catalogue Company. See page 219 for a complete description of audio tapes.

Brooke Medicine Eagle, Chalise. Photo by Scout Lee Gunn, 1984.

SHED TEARS

Lisa Yount

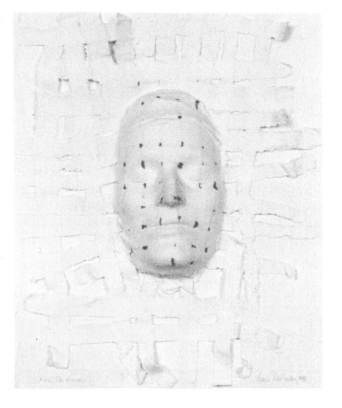

Shed

tears

in chunks.

Shed tears

like pieces of skin.

These tears are monolithic.

They *SHOULD* go Thunk.

They have been held within

long enough to grow

into works of art,

solid and carefully carved.

All the maps of our journeys are here

in their picture—puzzle locks,

their soft silver skin

scaled like a butterfly's wing.

Shed tears like bark,

the leper's beautiful scars

that must come off

before the healing can begin.

Kari, The Weaver
© Viki Ford-Boskey, 1986.
Handmade paper.
"My goals in both my artistic and spiritual counseling work are one and the same: to touch the exalted self of a human being so that she comes to know that her life is divine, that every action that she takes and words she speaks can be channeled from the God-center within herself" (Viki Ford-Boskey, 1301 West Hill St., Champaign, IL 61821).

From Lisa Yount, *Stones and Bones*, Half-a-Lump Press, 1986. For ordering information, see Lisa's biography on page 273.

WOMEN IN RELIGION
SURIA LESS

Suria Less, Sufi teacher and retreat guide, invokes and honors women guides from Hindu, Muslim, Buddhist, and Christian religious traditions. Some of these women are mythical, others are saints who have lived in our time. As each of these women is introduced we are also invited to attune to her—to take in and resonate that essence that she embodies. Suria's soothing, trustworthy voice guides us, stirring those qualities represented by these women— qualities such as compassion, innate beauty, conscience, the will for planetary survival, and the "glance that triggers unfoldment." This inner communion is both informative and transformative. KHA

1986. Available from Omega Press, P.O. Box 574, Lebanon Springs, NY 12114, (518) 794-8181 ($9.95 ppd.).

WOMEN POET SERIES
VARIOUS ARTISTS

The creative works of contemporary women poets are available on recorded tape through the Watershed Foundation. In these times when our cultural imagination is greatly in need of spiritual vitality, Watershed preserves the prophetic, provocative, and courageous voices of women poets reading their own works. The Women Poet series includes Ai ("Nothing but Color," 1981), Audre Lorde ("Shorelines," 1984), Carolyn Kizer ("An Ear to the Earth," 1977), H.D. ("Helen in Egypt," 1981), Muriel Rukeyser ("Just Before the Gates," 1975), Denise Levertov ("The Acolyte," 1985), May Sarton ("My Sisters, O My Sisters," 1984), Olga Broumas ("If I Yes," 1980), Joy Harjo ("Furious Light," 1986), Marge Piercy ("At the Core," 1976), Ntozake Shange ("I Live in Music," 1984), June Jordan/Bernice Reagon ("For Somebody to Start Singing,"

1979) and Adrienne Rich ("Tracking the Contradictions: Poems 1980–1986," 1986). PW

Catalogue available from the Watershed Foundation, P.O. Box 50145, Washington, DC 20004, (202) 722-9105 (cassette tapes $9.95 ppd. each).

WOMEN, POWER, BODY, AND SPIRIT
PATRICIA SUN

Patricia Sun, a well-known New Age teacher and healer, speaks on the unresolved fears that are passed from generation to generation and that intensify in intimate relationships, often leading to great suffering. These panic states live in our body chemistry and are released when we commit ourselves to facing the truth of our condition. This lively discussion focuses on how not to "match energies"—that is, how to disconnect psychically from the pull of others' fearfulness—with emphasis on healing the interactions between women and men, parents and children. Encouraging, startling, and wise. KHA

1985. Available from Patricia Sun, P.O. Box 7065, Berkeley, CA 94707, (415) 524-5795 ($21 ppd. for two-tape set).

WOMEN'S SPIRITUALITY
CHRISTINA FELDMAN

The Insight Meditation Society of Barre, Massachusetts, offered its first retreat focusing on women's spirituality in August of 1984. The five days were guided by Vipassana teachers Christina Feldman and Michele McDonald and so profoundly touched the hearts of the participants that IMS responded by making the retreat a part of their yearly schedule. This tape is representative of the fresh and women-side experience of the dharma that emerged during the retreat. The groundwork is laid for participants to discover their own spirituality as

women and to question the traditional forms of Buddhist practice that may inhibit women's spiritual expression.

Available from Dharma Seed Tape Library, 106 Jackson Hill Rd., Leverett, MA 01054 ($6.50 ppd.).

WOMANSPIRIT MEDITATION TAPE
HALLIE IGLEHART AUSTEN, WITH MUSIC BY GEORGIA KELLY

"We must bring back the power of women's wisdom. This strength is not a power over anything else, but a force emanating from deep within each of us, radiating out into the world and connecting and interacting with each other, creating a new definition of strength."

Hallie Iglehart Austen is the author of *Womanspirit: A Guide to Women's Wisdom* (see listing on page 105) and a pioneer in the women's spirituality movement. On this tape, rich in imagery and tools for relaxation, Hallie's practical approach to women's spirituality is combined with the spacious, cascading sounds of harpist Georgia Kelly. Side 1, "Exploring Our Heritage," guides the listener on a matrilineal journey through time to contact our inner Wise Woman. Side 2, "Living in Harmony," is a guided meditation/visualization for harmonizing our inner rhythms with the cycles of the Earth, sun, and moon, an essential spiritual practice for keeping our roots intact and our womanspirit in a state of well-being. PW

1983. Available through The Gaia Catalogue Company ($11.25 ppd.) and selected bookstores. For wholesale inquires write: WISE, P.O. Box 697, Pt. Reyes Station, CA 94956.

THE

LIGHT

WITHIN

US:

FILM AND VIDEO

RESOURCES

**THE WOMANSPIRIT
SOURCEBOOK**

VIDEO · TAPE

RESOURCES

Photo
© Catherine
Busch, 1986.

BEHIND THE VEIL: NUNS

NATIONAL FILM BOARD OF CANADA/ STUDIO D, PRODUCER

Behind the Veil: Nuns is the first film ever to record from a global perspective the turbulent history and remarkable achievements of nuns, from pre-Christian Celtic communities to the radical sisters of the 1980s. In Part 1, filmed in Ireland, Canada, the United States and Italy, nuns talk freely about religious life and voice their feelings about love and sexuality. The film explores the roots and effects of the denigration of religious women, from Christ's female followers to Pope Joan in the eighth century to present-day Church misogyny. Part 2 reviews the periods in history when women religious held leadership positions: the Celtic religions of the pre-Christian era and the medieval period of the Great Abbesses. These religious women of the Middle Ages performed liturgical rites and founded monastic centers of scholarship, medicine, and the arts. As the film closes, today's active nuns challenge the Church to redefine spirituality and global politics. For sale/rental as color film or video. Spanish language version available.

Wombat Productions, dist., 1985, Part 1 64 mins., Part 2 66 mins. Write or call the distributor for availability: Wombat Productions, 250 W. 57th St., Suite 916, New York, NY 10019, (212) 315-2502.

THE BURNING TIMES

SUSAN C. GRIFFITH, PRODUCER AND DIRECTOR

Through interviews, historical stills, performance, and narration, *The Burning Times* commemorates the burning of women as Witches in medieval Europe and explores several key principles of Witchcraft as practiced by contemporary feminists. The video features a choreographed dance performed to "The Burning Times," music written and recorded by Charlie Murphy. Can be used as a valuable springboard for discussion and further study of Witchcraft, women's history, and feminist spirituality. The film stands apart as one of the only films on the subject of Witchcraft. Available for sale only (½″ VHS; no rentals) for $30 (postage included).

Stella Nova Media Productions, dist. 1985, 15 mins. Make checks payable to Susan C. Griffith, Stella Nova Media Productions, P.O. Box 472, Somerville, MA 02144.

CREATIVITY AS PRAYER: ART AS MEDITATION

INSTITUTE IN CULTURE AND CREATION SPIRITUALITY

Art is one of the most basic centering experiences available to each of us for entering into relationship with the sacred. When we turn our attention to creation—in all its myriad forms—we awaken our senses and can more easily experience the sheer wonder of our aliveness. On this color video, filmed at the Institute in Culture and Creation Spirituality, students and instructors (including Starhawk, Sister José Hobday, and Luisa Teish) participate in art forms ranging from African dance and Native American circles to clay, massage, computer art, clowning, and ritual making. The video ends with a discussion of the theological implications of art-as-meditation within the creation-centered tradition.

Friends of Creation Spirituality, dist., 1986, 43 mins. Available for purchase ($79) from Friends of Creation Spir-

From the film *Emerging Goddesses.* Photo by Joan Delaney Grant, 1987.

ituality, P.O. Box 19216, Oakland, CA 94619, (415) 253-1192.

EMERGING GODDESSES

JOAN DELANEY GRANT, PRODUCER AND DIRECTOR

Emerging Goddesses is a color video production that depicts aspects of the feminine—mythically, religiously, culturally, and artistically. The progression of the images brings the audience from ancient through modern times. A series of instrumental and vocal compositions by such contemporary artists as Cris Williamson and Sweet Honey in the Rock accompany the images. The presentation is designed to evoke a deep emotional and spiritual connectedness among women of all ages, races, and beliefs, and to elicit from both women and men a new relationship to and awareness of the feminine archetype throughout time and cultures. The production has been used extensively as an educational resource throughout the country at churches, conferences, women's spiritual groups, fund raisers, celebrations. Audiovisual slide presentation also available.

Consciousness Connections, dist., 1987, 26 mins. Contact the producer for booking inquiries and video purchase: Consciousness Connections, 621 Maryland Ave., N.E., Washington, DC 20002, (202) 543-9306.

THE GODDESS SERIES ... I: A MULTIMEDIA SLIDE PRESENTATION

ASUNGI

"Because I am a ritualist, I seek to create a visual testament of the journeys, the goals, the hopes, dreams and realities of wimmin/Africane. As a womanist, Africanist, I seek to represent wimmin's herstory: the rainbow, stretching proudly across the face of history, a visual monument of her ultimate triumph over the often immobilizing confrontations with social constriction. I create visual

praise songs that keep us flowing positively on." *The Goddess Series . . . I* is a color multimedia slide documythology of the life and process of ritual artist Asungi and her search to create positive female imagery of the black wimmin's experience. Asungi, whose work has been exhibited across the country and in *Woman of Power* magazine, provides an interior view of her creative process, a direct experience of the Goddess within. The artist is available for lecture/discussion. Asungi's art, says Doris Davenport, author of *Eat Thunder and Drink Rain*, "is healthy—like fresh air in a smoggy city. Essential—like collards and black-eyed peas. Visionary—like all black women have the potential to be. And necessary—because it frees, it frees, it frees."

Asungi Productions, dist., 1986, 35 mins. For information, write Asungi Productions, Mary Alice Bailey/business associate, P.O. Box 875527 Term. Annex, Los Angeles, CA 90087-0627, (213) 235-2189.

"Yoruba Goddess, Mother of the River, Sister of the Sea, Yemeye. Ochun is a very well-known and important Orisha among the Yoruba peoples. She would be Venus in Western culture, for She is the Goddess of love, creative arts, gold and all things beautiful. She's represented here as a mermaid, glowing in the silver light of the Moon, also a symbol for femininity. . . . This pastel painting is part of a series titled "Amazons," in honor of Black wimmin', because I needed to see strong, self-contained and focused Black wimmin', so I reached into our tales, myths, goddesses, and other spiritual realities and thus created this series as my visual song, in praise of the wonders of the feminine spirits I found there" (Asungi).

Ochun's Praise Song II, © Asungi Productions, 1982. Pastel painting, 23" × 32".

"*This Goddess came to me out of a great struggle. I had envisioned another concept and another Goddess. But She was determined to remain—veiled and very insistent upon Her being. I finally saw Her and knew she was Isis Veiled. The veil represents a reserve of power, mystery—is She smiling—serious? Only Her eyes reveal Her real emotions. The moon (also*

representing Selene of Greek mythology and Yemeya of Yoruba mythology) is Her symbol for She is the Goddess of the Ultimate Feminine Principle. She is the Cosmic Mother, thus the galaxy is Her hair. Her hands on Her hips come from black mythology of a stance that tells one She is equally

Isis Veiled
© Asungi Productions, 1982. Pastel painting, 23″ × 32″.

open and guarded. The orchid represents the feminine principle of rebirth. She wears a naval guard to protect Her cosmic ties with the universe. As Isis Veiled She is the destroyer. As Isis Unveiled She is the Creator. Her total spirit is the full circle of life and nature, which must destroy (change) to recreate (rebirth)" (Asungi).

Vision Birthing
© Linda A. Lee Howe, 1985. Tempera. 16″ × 20″. Available for sale by the artist in poster and postcards. Write: Linda A. Lee Howe, 214 Wayne Avenue, Narberth, PA 19072, (215) 664-3703.

HEART OF THE GODDESS: VISIONS OF THE SACRED FEMININE

HALLIE IGLEHART AUSTEN, KAREN VOGEL, PRODUCERS

"When I first saw sacred images of women and goddesses, I felt a vast range of emotions: awe, peace, grace and an indescribable power," says Hallie Iglehart Austen, who, with the aid of Karen Vogel, primary artist for the Motherpeace Round Tarot, has created *Heart of the Goddess: Visions of the Sacred Feminine*. The color slide show is designed to awaken in both women and men the memory of feminine and female power, wisdom, and creativity. The images, drawn from cultures throughout time and around the world, portray women's central and influential position as birth givers, artisans, healers, and priestesses. Seeing this art is a powerful meditation on the Goddess as the ageless symbol of women's wisdom and powers of creation. *Heart of the Goddess* actively and directly affects women's and girls' self-esteem. For all viewers, the show reorders our sense of women's abilities, as well as possibilities for all of human society and our life on a peaceful planet. The producers are available for presentations and workshops.

Women in Spiritual Education, dist., 1985, 60–90 mins. For further information write: Women in Spiritual Education (WISE), P.O. Box 697, Pt. Reyes Station, CA 94956, or call (415) 663-8280.

OSHUN'S TEACHING: SPIRITUAL ART IS A POWER THAT HEALS

KAREN VOGEL

Several years ago I spent months carving a life-size image of the goddess Oshun. Since the carving was out of ironwood, which is a very hard wood, I had a lot of time to think about art in general, and mine in particular.

When I finished Oshun, someone asked to buy her to put on a patio. I declined as I felt that Oshun was more than a garden decoration.

A short while later I heard a story that clarified my feeling about Oshun's place in the world. The story was about a church that had a statue of Mary. People would meditate on her image and eventually see Mary cry. The result was a profound opening of people's hearts.

Photo by Karen Vogel of shamanic doll

That story reminded me that there is a difference between art that is decorative (or a conversation piece), and art that is sacred, healing, or shamanic. The difference isn't always obvious, but I would say that if an artist is transformed by the process of creating, then her art has healing or sacred energy. I believe we have healing experiences when we make art because using our hands gets us out of linear, left-brain activity and into the right brain, where we have access to altered states.

When I create art I feel myself link up with spirits and bring them into my work for healing purposes. As a result, my art becomes alive with these spirits and their stories. This is true for many women creating women's spirituality art today. Not only is our art healing on a personal level, but our work also expands and heals the female across time and space. When we bring forth images of the Goddess, as well as other art that is infused with female archetypes and inspired by the inner world of visions, dreams, and myths, we are giving form to the sacred feminine—which is the wisdom and love we carry in our bodies and spirits.

Karen Vogel has a degree in anthropology and a background in women's studies, primitive art, and shamanism. She was the primary artist and the first publisher of the Motherpeace Round Tarot deck. She currently teaches workshops throughout the country on sacred play and healing through art. For workshop brochure and Motherpeace Tarot consultations, write: Karen Vogel, P.O. Box 697, Pt. Reyes, CA 94956, or call (415) 663-8280.

HER VOICE, OUR VOICES

CHARLOTTE KELLY, PRODUCER

Her Voice, Our Voices documents participation of one hundred women in a celebration of the summer solstice at a yearly camp in the Sierra Nevada foothills. From the early morning Sun Dance, a greeting to the rising sun, to the masked dance of the setting sun, these women use the ancient tools of ritual, dance, mask, and celebration to connect with the Earth's cycles and their inner rhythms. The color video includes interviews with Barbara Marx Hubbard, Joanna Macy, Dr. Jean Shinoda Bolen, Brooke Medicine Eagle, and Hallie Iglehart Austen speaking on women's spirituality and its role in personal and global healing. Excellent resource for women's groups and university classes.

Women's Alliance, dist., 1985, 25 mins. Inquiries welcomed for sale or rental: Women's Alliance, P.O. Box 1882, Nevada City, CA 95959, (916) 477-1064.

OUR LIFE AS GAIA

JOANNA ROGERS MACY

Joanna Rogers Macy, Ph.D., is a scholar of world religions, systems theory, and social change. She teaches at the California Institute of Integral Studies and travels widely in the United States and abroad, speaking on the interface between spiritual awakening and work for peace and justice. She co-founded Interhelp, an international network focusing on the psychological and spiritual dimensions of the planetary crisis and is active in the Sarvodaya community development movement in South Asia, based on Gandhian principles. She has authored Despair and Personal Power in the Nuclear Age *and* Dharma and Development. *A Buddhist meditator in the Vipassana tradition, she is a wise and compassionate teacher. This article is adapted from a talk she gave at the Women's Alliance summer solstice camp, 1986.*

Come back with me into a story we all share, a story whose rhythm beats in us still. The story belongs to each of us and to all of us, like the beat of this drum, like the heartbeat of our living universe.

There is science now to construct the story of the journey we have made on this Earth, the story that connects us with all beings. There is also great yearning and great need to own that story—to break out of our isolation as persons and as a species and recover through that story our larger identity. The challenge to do that now, and burst out of the separate prison cells of our contrivings, is perhaps the most wonderful aspect of being alive today.

Right now on our planet we need to remember that story—to harvest it and taste it. For we are in a hard time, a fearful time. And it is the knowledge of the bigger story that is going to carry us through. It can give us the courage, it can give us the strength, it can give us the hilarity to dance our people into a world of sanity. Let us remember it together.

With the heartbeat of the drum we hear the rhythm that underlies all our days and doings. Throughout our sleeping and rising, through all our working and loving, our heart has been beating steady, steady. That steady sturdy inner sound has accompanied us all the way. And so it can take us back now, back through our lives, back through our childhood, back before our birth. In our mother's womb there was that same sound, that same beat, as we floated there in the fluid right under her heart.

Let that beat take us back farther still. Let's go back, back far beyond our conception in this body, back to the first splitting and spinning of the stars. As scientists measure now, it is fifteen billion years ago we manifested. Being mostly male, the scientists call it the Big Bang.

There we were, careening out through space and time, creating space and time. Slowly, with the speed of light, in vast curls of flame and darkness, we reached for form. We were then great swirls of clouds of gas and dancing particles—can you imagine you remember? And the particles, as they circled in the dance, desired each other and formed atoms. It is the same desire for form that beats now in this drum and in our hearts.

Ten billion years later, one of the more beautiful swirls of that swirling mass split off from its blazing sun—the sun we feel now on our faces—and became the form we know best. And our lifetime as Gaia began.

Touch our Earth, touch Gaia.
Touch Gaia again by touching your face; that is Gaia, too.
Touch Gaia again by touching your sister; that is Gaia, too.

In this very planet-time of ours, Gaia is becoming aware of herself, she is finding out who she is. How rich she is in the multitudinous and exquisite forms she takes.

Let us imagine that her life—*our* life as our planet—could be condensed into twenty-four hours, beginning at midnight. Until five o'clock the following afternoon all her adventures are geological. All was volcanic flamings and steaming rains washing over the shifting bones of the continents into shifting seas—and only at five o'clock comes organic life.

To the heartbeat of life in you and this drum, you too, right now, can shift a bit—shift free from identifying solely with your latest form, middle-class American female. The fire of those early volcanoes, the strength of those tectonic plates, is in us still. And it may well be, if things continue the way they are going, that we will all return for a spell to nonorganic life. We'd be radioactive for quite a while, but we are built to endure.

For now and in these very bodies of ours, we carry traces of Gaia's story as organic life. We were aquatic first, as we remember in our mother's womb, growing vestigial gills and fins. The salt from those early seas flows still in our sweat and tears. And the age of the dinosaurs we carry with us, too, in our reptilian brain, situated so conveniently at the end of our spinal column. Complex organic life

Joanna Rogers
Macy. Photo by
Kathe Kokolias,
1985.

Camp Baptism
© Kathleen
Kokolias, 1985.
Camp images
available for sale
as prints and
postcards.
Contact the artist:
Kathe Kokolias,
Professional
Photographer,
5722 Huntington
Ave., Richmond
Annex, CA
94804.

was learning to protect itself and it is all right there in our neurological system, in the rush of instinct to flee or fight.

And when did we appear as mammals? In those twenty-four hours of Gaia's life, it was at 11:30 P.M.! And when did we become human? One second to midnight.

Now let us take that second to midnight that is our story as humans and reckon that, in turn, as twenty-four hours. Let's look back through the twenty-four hours that we have been humans.

Beginning at midnight and until two o'clock in the afternoon, we live in small groups in Africa. Can you imagine you remember? We feel pretty vulnerable; we haven't the speed of the other critters, or their claws or fangs or natural armor. But we have our remarkable hands, opposable thumbs to help shape tools and weapons, and we have in our throats and frontal lobes the capacity for speech. Grunts and shouts turn into language as we collaborate in strategies and rituals. Those days and nights on the verge of the forests, as we weave baskets and stories around our fires, represent the biggest hunk of our human experience.

Then in small bands we begin branching out. We move out across the face of Gaia; we learn to face the cold and hunt the mammoth and name the trees of the Northern forests, the flowers and seasons of the tundra. We know it is Gaia by whom we live and we carve her in awe and fear and gratitude, giving her our breasts and hips. When we settle into agriculture, when we begin domesticating animals and fencing off our croplands and deciding they could be owned as private property, when we build great cities with granaries and temples and observatories to chart the stars, the time is 11:58. Two minutes to midnight.

At 11:59 comes a time of quickening change: we want to chart the stars within as well as those we see in the skies; we want to seek the authority of inner experience. To free the questing mind we set it apart from Gaia. We make conjectures and rules and heroes to help us chart our freedoms to think and act. The great religions of our planet-time arise. At six seconds to midnight comes a man called the Buddha and shortly after another called Jesus of Nazareth.

What now shapes our world—our industrial society with its bombs and bulldozers—has taken place in the last few microseconds of the day we have known as humans.

Yet those few microseconds bring us right to the brink of time. And each of us knows that. Each of us, at some level of our awareness, knows that we are doing ourselves in—that Gaia herself, our self, is in danger. And at some level of your consciousness that is why you are here. Oh yes, you may think you are here to heal yourselves on the personal level and find your power in terms of your individual lives. True enough. But we are also here because we know our planet is in danger and all life on it could go—like that! And we fear that that knowledge might drive us insane if we let it in.

Much of the time it is hard to believe that we have come to this—to such an apocalyptic moment. Even I, who spend most of my waking hours working in some relation or other to nuclear weapons, have trouble believing that nuclear weapons exist. After the millions of years of life on Earth, after the millennia of our civilizations, after Ishtar and Shakespeare and Gandhi and Dorothy Day, I find it hard to credit the fact that we are deliberately manufacturing and deploying these weapons, poising them on hair-trigger alert, knowing they could go off on a computer malfunction . . .

So we are now at a point unlike any other in our story. I suspect that we have, in some way, chosen to be here at this culminating chapter or turning point. We have opted to be alive when the stakes are high, to test everything we have ever learned about intercon-nectedness, about courage—to test it now when Gaia is ailing and her children are ill. We are alive right now when it could be curtains for conscious life on this beautiful, silvery blue water planet hanging there like a jewel in space. Our foremothers and forefathers faced nothing quite like this, because every generation before us took it for granted that life would continue. Each lived with that tacit assumption. Personal death, wars, plagues were ever encompassed in that larger assurance that life would continue. That assurance is lost now and we, sisters, are alive at the time of that great loss. It is not the loss of the future. It is the loss of the certainty that there will be a future. It affects everyone, whether they work in the Pentagon or the peace movement. And the toll that it takes has barely begun to be measured.

In so-called primitive societies rites of passage are held for ado-lescents, because it is in adolescence that the fact of personal death or mortality is integrated into the personality. The individual goes through the prescribed ordeal of the initiation rite in order to integrate that knowledge, so that he or she can assume the rights and responsibilities of adulthood. That is what we are doing right now on the collective level, in this planet-time. We are confronting and integrating into our awareness our collective mortality as a species. We must do that so that we can wake up and assume the rights and responsibilities of planetary adulthood—so that we can grow up! That is, in a sense, what we are doing here.

When you go out from here, please keep listening to the drumbeat. You will hear it in your heart. And as you hear it, remember that it is the heartbeat of the universe as well, and of Gaia your planet and your larger self.

When you return to your communities, organize to say no to the machinery of death and yes to life, remember your true identity. Remember your story, our story. Clothe yourself in your true authority. You speak not only as yourself or for yourself. You were not born yesterday. You have been through many dyings and know in your heartbeat and bones the precarious, exquisite balance of life. Out of that knowledge you can speak and act. You will speak and act with the courage and endurance that has been yours through the long, beautiful eons of your life story as Gaia.

gration of spirituality, ceremony, and art into everyday life. As Hopi land use and ceremonial roles are passed down from mothers to daughters, the feminine values of growing and nurturing life are respected. The film focuses on how corn, the central symbol of the Hopi, is used to mark the major transitions in a life cycle and is the inspiration in every art form: song, dance, weaving, pottery, painting. The Hopi's philosophy of living in balance and harmony with Nature is a model for the Western world of an environmental ethic in action.

New Day Films, dist., 1983, 58 mins. Color, 16-mm film. Available from New Day Films, 22 Riverview Dr., Wayne, NJ 07470, (212) 477-4604 (rental $100; purchase, film, $850; video $650). Write or call for price and availability. Note: Hopi: Songs of the Fourth World—A Resource

HOLY TERROR

VICTORIA SCHULTZ, WRITER/ PRODUCER/DIRECTOR

Holy Terror is a thought-provoking documentary that examines the emerging political activism of the religious New Right, focusing in particular on their antiabortion efforts, and explores the nature of their impact on American political life. The film provides a revealing inside look at the movement and its philosophy as expressed by its leaders—including TV evangelist Pat Robertson, antichoice author Joseph Scheidler, antichoice activist John Ryan, U.S. Senator Jesse Helms, and numerous antichoice ministers—as well as by its rank-and-file activists. These interviews are combined with scenes filmed at antiabortion conventions and strategy planning sessions; as well as picket lines and demonstrations designed to harass and intimidate doctors, abortion counselors, and women patients. *Holy Terror* explores numerous controversial issues and shows the broader political sig-

nificance of this new movement that blends religious fervor with well-financed political activism. *Holy Terror* makes clear that the growing coalition of the religious New Right and the political New Right has a long-range political agenda that extends far beyond the abortion issue. Color, 16-mm film and all video formats.

The Cinema Guild, dist., 1987, 58 mins. Available from The Cinema Guild, 1697 Broadway, New York, NY 10019, (212) 246-5522 (rental $100; purchase, 16-mm, $895; video, $595).

HOPI: SONGS OF THE FOURTH WORLD

PAT FERRERO, PRODUCER

Hopi: Songs of the Fourth World is a compelling study of the matriarchal and Earth-based spiritual values of the Hopi people. Amidst beautiful images of Hopi land and life, a variety of Hopi—farmer, religious elder, grandmother, painter, potter, and weaver—speak about the inte-

Hopi Girls in Window by Edward S. Curtis. Rare books and manuscripts division of the New York Public Library, Astor, Lenox and Tilden Foundation. Postcard © Crossing Cards. Available for $1.00 by writing Crossing Press, Freedom, CA 95019.

Handbook *is a 32-page book beautifully illustrated with contemporary Hopi artwork (photography, drawings, pottery) and featuring essays that supplement the material presented in the film. Includes an excellent annotated bibliography. A complimentary copy of the handbook is provided with all film sales and rentals. Additional copies of the Hopi handbook are available for $6 each ppd. directly from the producer: Ferrero Films, 1259(A) Folsom St., San Francisco, CA 94103.*

JUDY CHICAGO: THE BIRTH PROJECT
VIVIAN KLEIMAN, DIRECTOR; FRANCES REID, CINEMATOGRAPHY

A beautifully photographed color video that documents the making of *The Birth Project*, the most recent work of feminist artist Judy Chicago, involving 150 needleworkers across the country in a collective art making process. On the video Judy discusses her goal of portraying through art an experience central to all women but remarkably absent from works of art in Western civilization. *The Birth Project* explores the theme of human birth as a metaphor for creation of the universe. Images reaching into the archetypal mind blend ancient birth motifs with the more realistic images of the pain and magic experienced by individual birthing women. The video includes collaborative dialogue between Judy and the needleworkers on the aesthetic issues and content of the project, interviews with Judy Chicago and needleworkers, works in progress, and close-ups of *The Birth Project* artwork. Sound track features contemporary music by Liz Story, Jill McManus, and the group Oregon. The video is ideal for birth centers, medical and educational facilities, study/ritual groups and conferences.

Vivian Kleiman Productions, dist., 1985, 20 mins. Available in VHS/Beta for sale or in VHS for rental from Vivian Kleiman Productions, 2600 Tenth St., Berkeley, CA 94710, (415) 549-1470.

LEGACY OF THE SPIRITS
KAREN KRAMER, PRODUCER AND DIRECTOR

Legacy of the Spirits is the first in-depth documentary of the African-born religion of Voudou, an Earth-based religious system and one of the few world religions to honor women's sacred powers. The film portrays the significant role of the mambo (priestess) in Voudou religion, who is honored equally with the houngan, or priest. One scene, filmed in a Manhattan park, shows a woman conducting a candle-lighting ritual around a large tree and setting out special foods and drinks to the gods. In another scene, accompanied by music, drumming, and dancing, four women are initiated by a mambo in a large house in Queens (this particular mambo has only women initiates in her household). Throughout the film women sing sacred songs to the ancestral deities. *Legacy of the Spirits* explains the theology of Voudou, the meaning of the rituals, the pantheon of spirits, possession, sacred drawings, the Catholic influence. Filmed entirely in the Caribbean community of New York City, the film portrays the beauty and wisdom of one of the world's most misunderstood and persecuted religions. A valuable resource for educators, it demythologizes Voudou and dispels the rumors surrounding its practice.

Erzuli Films, dist., 1985, 52 mins. Contact producer for price and availability: Karen Kramer, Erzuli Films, 22 Leroy St., New York, NY 10014, (212) 691-3470.

MADELEINE L'ENGLE: STAR·GAZER
MARTHA WHEELOCK, DIRECTOR

An inspiring portrait of the author of *A Wrinkle in Time* and many other books of spiritual quest. Madeleine shares her life, her experiences with the universe, her discoveries, her faith, and her profound insights into the cosmos.

"Voodoo Service in New York City: Possession of Carole Lewis," From the film *Legacy of the Spirits*, 1984. Photo by Chantal Regnault, 1984.

Ishtar Films, dist., 1987, 25 mins. Available as both color film and ¾" color video for sale or rental from Ishtar Films, Box 51, Patterson, NY 12563, (914) 878-3561.

"Taschlich Service," from the film *Miriam's Daughters Now*, 1986. Left to right: Deborah Wolf, Esther Broner, Lilly Rivlin. Photo by Marilynne Herbert, 1986.

MIRIAM'S DAUGHTERS NOW: JEWISH WOMEN'S NEW RITUALS

LILLY RIVLIN, PRODUCER/DIRECTOR/ WRITER

Miriam's Daughters Now documents the making of community among leading Jewish feminists: Esther Broner, Bella Abzug, Letty Cottin Pogrebin. These women, by celebrating new woman-honoring Jewish rituals, are creating a place for themselves within the tradition. Three rituals are featured: a feminist *taschlich* (a Jewish New Year ritual by the water), a feminist Seder, and a female naming ceremony. At the annual Seder, Jewish and non-Jewish women, mothers and daughters, sisters and friends read from a feminist Haggadah (the Jewish text for the Passover Seder) created by Esther Broner, author of *A Weave of Women*. Instead of the Passover Seder where the mother toils in the kitchen while the male head of the household holds forth, these women choose a theme each year relevant to the lives of

women, and all those gathered speak to the theme. At the *taschlich* ritual, which takes place on a Hudson River pier, the women address human suffering, hunger, and the injustices of our time. The female naming ritual was created by two rabbis, husband and wife, for their newborn daughter. The color video is provocative for all audiences as it portrays an intimate, interior view of women speaking about their lives and their visions of a just world.

El Ar Film Productions, dist., 1986, 29 mins. Available from El Ar Film Production, 463 West St., Suite 510 A, New York City, NY 10014 (purchase $24.95).

ONE FINE DAY

KAY WEAVER AND MARTHA WHEELOCK

One Fine Day, the only feminist music video on the home market, is an "unabashedly matriotic" tribute to "our anonymous and celebrated foremothers and sisters of spirit" (*Ms.*, January 1985). The video includes

Women's Suffrage March, New York City 1915. From *One Fine Day*. Used with permission of the Schlessinger Library, Radcliffe College.

nineteenth-century daguerreotypes of some of our favorite heroines as well as color film footage of contemporary pioneers such as Sally Ride, Geraldine Ferraro, Martina Navritalova, and the Women's Peace Encampment of Greenham Common, England.

Ishtar Films, dist., 1984, 6 mins. Available from Ishtar Films, P.O. Box 51, Patterson, NY 12563, (914) 878-3561 (purchase, ½" VHS or Beta $39.95, ¾" videotape $100; 16-mm film $125; rental $35).

PORTRAITS OF PEACEMAKERS

MARYBETH WEBSTER, DIRECTOR

"We women must act. For people who look too long upon evil without opposing it go dead inside" (Agnes E. Meyer). When her grandson told her on his eleventh birthday that he didn't believe he'd get to grow up, Marybeth Webster quit her job, bought a camper, and took to the road on a thirty-seven state forty-four-thousand-mile peace pilgrimage. Her motto: Let's save the world and have fun doing it! which she took to mean: Use your talents to heal that which you care about passionately. *Portraits of Peacemakers* is the story of her journey and the planet-healing people she meets. Part 1 consists of interviews of "ordinary citizens" of all ages, classes, races, and religions; Part 2 is a portrait of twenty-three women whose peacework is grounded in a common theme of the connection between life, Nature, and spirit. These women reveal in their own words their motives and the intrinsic rewards for becoming active in planet-healing work. *Portraits of Peacemakers* provides role models to the inactive, warm affirmation to the already active, and courage to the despairing. Color slide/tape and video are available for sale or rental. Promotional materials and discussion guide are included. Preview copies are available for cost of postage.

Peaceworks, dist., 1986, Part 1 24 mins., Part 2 26 mins. Send legal-size SASE for descriptive brochure to Peaceworks, 11044 Weeping Willow Wy., Nevada City, CA 95959, or call (916) 477-6419.

POST SCRIPT
HELENE AYLON AND MYRIAM ABRAMOWICZ, PRODUCERS

Post Script is a thirty-minute color and black-and-white video with Hibakushas, survivors of the A-bomb who wrote their dreams and nightmares on pillowcases, in their own language, in their own homes. Visual and transformance artist Aylon and Belgium filmmaker Abramowicz co-produced this video on location in Japan. The video culminated a seven-year project by Aylon, who since 1978 has been doing public rituals around the world using the sac as a metaphor to evoke a reverence for the Earth and a healing of the spirit for those participating. Images of a river journey of two sacs en route to Hiroshima and Nagasaki appear and disappear within intimate conversations. The metaphor of the sac, beginning with liquid sacs that burst, to sand sacs, and later to stone sacs with Arab and Jewish women in Israel and Lebanon, is explained in the video. The producers are available for workshops and film presentations.

Helene Aylon, dist., 1987, 26 mins. For information, write: Helene Aylon, 55 Bethune St., #808 A, New York City, NY 10014, or call (212) 924-4133.

The Mountain Mother Between Horns of Consecration, Palace of Knossos, Crete, Greece. From the film, *The Presence of the Goddess* © Christy Baldwin, 1987.

THE PRESENCE OF THE GODDESS
CHRISTY BALDWIN, PRODUCER/DIRECTOR

An odyssey of the Goddess religion from its roots in the life and mind of the Paleolithic era to its many manifestations in the Neolithic, Minoan, Mycenaean, Greek, early Christian, and medieval ages, and the return of the Goddess as a psychospiritual vision of the universe as a living being. Important sites in Turkey, Greece, and the Aegean provide a sense of place to the many changing forms of the Goddess and her artifacts and attributes. Contemporary rituals created by Hallie Iglehart Austen and Diana Paxson draw on archetypal

Kamo River, Japan. Photo by Myriam Abramowicz, 1985.

themes relevant to the world today. Color. Available for sale or rental as 16-mm film ($750 purchase), ½″ VHS ($85 purchase) or ¾″ videotape. Reduced price for women's studies and educational endeavors: $700 purchase/$150 rental.

Balcoram Films, dist., 1986, 68 mins. Write to producer for brochure, preview charges, and distribution information: Balcoram Films, Christy Baldwin, 202 Meda Ln., Mill Valley, CA 94941, (415) 388-2576.

QUILTS IN WOMEN'S LIVES
PAT FERRERO

Quilts in Women's Lives presents a series of seven portraits of traditional quilt makers, among them a California Mennonite, a black Mississippian, and a Bulgarian immigrant. The film provides insights into the spiritual values of these women as they describe the inspiration for their artwork: family, tradition, the joy of the creative process, self-expression, the love of pattern making. They de-

Photo of Nora Lee Condra from the film *Quilts in Women's Lives.* Photo by Debra Heimerdinger, 1980.

scribe how quilt making has sprung from their daily lives, creating meaning and a sense of real identity.

New Day Films, dist., 1980, 28 mins. Available as color 16-mm film from New Day Films, 22 Riverview Dr., Wayne, NJ 07470, (212) 477-4604 (rental $50; purchase $450).

RIGHT OUT OF HISTORY
JOHANNA DEMETRAKAS, DIRECTOR; THOM TYSON, PRODUCER

For five years, feminist artist Judy Chicago worked with a community of four hundred artists, craftspeople, and researchers to create *The Dinner Party*, a monumental tribute to women of spirit and accomplishment throughout the ages—women whose names have been banished "Right Out of History." *Right Out of History* reveals the behind-the-scenes drama of this enormous undertaking—the meticulous research, the technical problems and financial pressures, and the amount of sheer physical labor involved in creating a symbolic history of women's achievements. The color film shows how Judy and the people who worked in her studio for months, even years, struggled to rescue the accomplishments of women from historical oblivion, and the traditional "feminine" arts of china painting and needlework from trivialization and obscurity. The film, says Judy Chicago, "is the only record of a community of primarily women trying to transform their experience into a work of art."

Phoenix Films, Inc., dist., 1980, 75 mins. Write or call for price and availability: Phoenix Films, Inc., 470 Park Ave. S., New York, NY 10016, (212) 684-5910.

SPEAKING OUR PEACE
BONNIE SHERR KLEIN AND TERRI NASH, DIRECTORS; NATIONAL FILM BOARD OF CANADA/STUDIO D, PRODUCER

Speaking Our Peace documents how women in Canada, Britain, Micronesia, and the Soviet Union have organized to reverse our collision course toward nuclear war. The color film opens with women demonstrating at the Greenham U.S. Air Force base, which now harbors thirty-two nuclear missiles; moves to the World War II memorial graves at Leningrad; and on to the Marshall Islands, site of early open-air nuclear testing. A Micronesian woman, a victim of living on contaminated islands, describes the tumors, cancer, and jellyfish babies being born in her country today as a result of the testing. The greatest part of the film is devoted to the Canadian women's peace movement. Women activists articulate their perspectives on peace: genuine peace means sharing resources equally. Granted no "extraordinary power" by our society, women in *Speaking Our Peace* are nonetheless organizing to "reconstitute the world." This is a provocative

documentary for classes and community programs. *Speaking Our Peace* reflects both directors' desires to address the real needs and concerns of women and is a progression from ideas explored in their earlier works. Terri Nash is best known as the director of the 1983 Academy Award winner *If You Love This Planet* and Bonnie Sherr Klein is best known as the director of *Not a Love Story: A Film about Pornography*, the internationally acclaimed documentary that examines pornography from the point of view of women. The filmmakers are available for speaking engagements. (Reviewed by Caryn McTighe Musil, national director, National Women's Studies Association.)

Bullfrog Films, dist., 1986, 55 mins. Available from Bullfrog Films, Oley, PA 19547, (800) 543-3764 (16-mm film purchase, $795; video purchase, $395, rental, $90 ppd.). (Reviewed by Caryn McTighe Musil, national director, National Women's Studies Association.)

"Woman in Market in Moscow, USSR," from the film *Speaking Our Peace*. Photo by Terri Nash, 1986.

TAKE THE POWER

MARTHA WHEELOCK AND KAY WEAVER, PRODUCERS

Take the Power is a music film/video that combines the matriarchal forces of our past with the varied roles of modern women. Says Martha Wheelock, founder of Ishtar Films and co-producer of *Take the Power*, "I wanted to create a film which would promote the knowledge of women's spiritual heritage, achieve a racial balance of images of women on screen, and honor the American and international working woman, the professional, the ground breaker, the one who by her daily life and her connection to the family of Woman-spirit moves us into a future of harmony, balance, and kinship with life." Film footage includes the Nairobi Conference, Simone de Beauvoir, Mother Teresa, and women of Asian, black, Chicana, and American Indian heritage.

Ishtar Films, dist., 1987, 7 mins. Available for individual and organizational purchase/rental on 16-mm film ($125/$35), ¾" video ($100 purchase) and VHS/Beta home video ($45) from Ishtar Films, P.O. Box 51, Patterson, NY 12563, (914) 878-3561.

Scene from *Take The Power*. Photo by Melissa Mosley, 1987.

WATER BABY: EXPERIENCES OF WATER BIRTH

KARIL DANIELS, PRODUCER/DIRECTOR

A color video documentary that portrays the positive experiences of American, French, and Soviet women who have chosen the water birth method, the most recent innovation in the gentle birth movement. The film conveys the reverent approach to birth of parents and doctors engaged in this process. The philosophies and approaches of the world's three leaders in the field of water birth are extensively explored: Guided by the principles of nonintervention, women at this center are encouraged to catch their own babies as they are born. During the film women describe their personal experiences of empowerment through the use of water birth. The video is intended for parents and health professionals concerned with advances in the field of gentle childbirth.

Point of View Productions, dist., 1986, 58 mins. For information on film availability, send a SASE to Point of View Productions, 2477 Folsom St., San Francisco, CA 94110, or call (415) 821-0435.

WOMAN TO WOMAN

JAN PHILLIPS, PRODUCER

Woman to Woman is a photographic journey into the heartland of the common woman. Eighty intimate color images of women from around the world are woven into a poetic portrait of strength and tenderness and synchronized to women's music. From the creased faces of the elders hunched over the campfire to the seeking eyes of the young gathering wood in the Himalayas, from the American rock singers to the Indian rock bearers, these images celebrate and affirm women's spiritual connection to life. Jan Phillips is a feminist artist and founding member of Syracuse Cultural Workers, a group of artists and activists working to create a culture responsive to the needs of the human family.

Syracuse Cultural Workers, dist., 1986, 7½ mins. Woman to Woman is available in both audio/slide show (rental $40/purchase $75) and ½" VHS or Beta video (rental $25/purchase $45). Write: Syracuse Cultural Workers, Box 6367, Syracuse, NY 13217, (315) 474-1132.

WOMEN—FOR AMERICA, FOR THE WORLD

VIVIENNE VERDON-ROE, PRODUCER

Winner of the 1987 Academy Award for best documentary short subject, *Women—For America, For the World* celebrates women in leadership who have the vision, courage, and determination to redefine the meaning of national and global security. The video consists of interviews with twenty-two prominent American women—Shirley Chisholm, Geraldine Ferraro, Rep. Patricia Schroeder, Randall Forsberg, Joanna Rogers Macy, Jean Shinoda Bolen, Ellen Goodman, Joanne Woodward, and others—speaking out with common sense and compassion for our health, educational, and economic needs in the face of the arms race and for the fundamental value of protecting and nurturing our most precious resource, the children. A training program, *Speaking Up and Speaking Out*, has been developed in conjunction with this film. It is designed to generate confidence in women who are concerned but who have been un-involved in peace work. In a sup-portive environment women are en-couraged to discover their wisdom, skills, and potential for creating a safer, saner world.

Educational Film and Video Project, dist., 1986, 28 mins. Educational Film and Video Project offers an ex-tensive collection of peace videos for sale or purchase, including Verdon-Roe's Academy Award nominee In the Nuclear Shadow: What Can the Chil-dren Tell Us? *Write or call for free catalog and schedule of women's training programs: Educational Film and Video Project, 1529 Josephine St., Berkeley, CA 94703, (415) 849-1649.*

WORLD OF LIGHT: A PORTRAIT OF MAY SARTON

MARITA SIMPSON AND MARTHA WHEELOCK, DIRECTORS

It is not surprising that Ishtar Films, an all-women filmmaking company, chose May Sarton as the subject of its first production. Sarton, who for the last fifty years has revealed her-self through her journals, poetry, and novels, has been a model of passion-ate commitment to the creative pro-cess for many contemporary women. *World of Light* is an in-depth look into Sarton's life, her environs, her courage, and the personality that sustains her creativity. The film ends with a reading of "Gestalt at Sixty," which Sarton has called her most personal and intimate poem. The color film images that form the back-drop to the reading take the viewer into every corner of Sarton's life.

Ishtar Films, dist., 1977, 30 mins. Available for sale or rental from Ishtar Films, P.O. Box 51, Patterson, NY 12563, (914) 878-3561 (16-mm film, rental $45/purchase $425; ¾" video, $300; home video, $69.95).

May Sarton from the film, *World of Light: A Portrait of May Sarton.* Photo by Kelly Wise.

WITH

WISDOM

INTO THE

FUTURE:

TAROT AND I CHING CARDS,

CALENDAR RESOURCES

**THE WOMANSPIRIT
SOURCEBOOK**

TAROT

RESOURCES

A POET'S TAROT

JESSE COUGAR

A Poet's Tarot are unique, two-sided cards—a deck and a book all in one! On one side are simple line drawings, portraying women of all shapes and sizes (including women who are physically challenged) living in harmony and enjoyment in the natural world. On the other side are koan-like poems that teach a heightened awareness of the universal truths in everyday life. A Poet's Tarot can be used to supplement and expand other tarot interpretations or to develop one's intuition using this ancient tool of divination. The cards can be colored in to deepen the spirit of play and learning. Each deck comes wrapped in pure silk. Choose from black, white, silver, and violet cards. PW

Tough Dove Books, 1986. Available from Tough Dove Books, P.O. Box 528, Little River, CA 95456 ($14 ppd.).

BARBARA G. WALKER TAROT

BARBARA G. WALKER

The Barbara G. Walker Tarot are printed in full color and retain the traditional tarot rectangular shape. The images are drawn from the rich history of matriarchal, Pagan, Christian, and Celtic mythologies that have been the primary source material for Barbara G. Walker's research as a feminist writer and his-

Isis

Daughters of the
Moon Tarot
© Ffiona Morgan,
1987.

Barbara G.
Walker Tarot
© Barbara G.
Walker, 1985.

torian. The companion book *Secrets of the Tarot: Origins, History, and Symbolism* (Harper & Row, 1984) was conceived prior to the cards. It is a comprehensive and intellectual study of the symbolism and mythology of the tarot. The cards are static in feeling, reflecting Barbara Walker's scholarly approach to the tarot, and present images of Caucasian women with perfectly shaped figures throughout the deck, a distraction to this reviewer. The Major Arcana contain traditional names and the court cards are named after ancient deities. Card titles are in five languages: English, French, German, Italian, and Spanish. Price includes 48-page instruction booklet. EF

Available in women's/selected bookstores ($12). Secrets of the Tarot is available from Harper & Row ($14.95 ppd.).

DAUGHTERS OF THE MOON TAROT
FFIONA MORGAN

From many women's visions, dreams, memories comes Daughters of the Moon Tarot, a stunningly beautiful tarot deck of women's ancient symbols. Goddesses, crones, Amazons, matriarchs, healers, lovers, priestesses, women of all shapes, sizes, races, abilities, and ages—every woman can find her image here. The cards are beautiful black-and-white pen-and-ink line drawings. By coloring them herself, the user is able to participate in the cre-

ation of her own tarot deck; thus, the cards become intensely personal. The 1987 edition of Daughters of the Moon was created collaboratively by many spiritual feminist artists and graphic designers, each of whom contributed to the whole. This deck eliminates traditional court cards and uses the female archetypes of Maiden, Mother, Crone instead. It also adds a fifth suit of ether, spirit. *Daughter of the Moon Tarot Book*, an illustrated guidebook essential to truly understanding the meaning of these cards, is included in the purchase price. Both the book and the deck can be purchased separately. EF

1987. Available from The Gaia Catalogue Company (deck and book $32 ppd.; deck alone, $22.50 ppd.; book alone, $11.50 ppd.).

MOTHERPEACE ROUND TAROT
VICKI NOBLE AND KAREN VOGEL

The full-color images of the Motherpeace Round Tarot draw on the mythology and art of thirty thousand years of shamanic and matriarchal cultures. Although following the basic tarot structure, the Motherpeace images were created to radiate the healing aspect of the tarot symbolism, providing a vision of hope and the possibility of transformation in one's own life and the world. Each of the seventy-eight cards is a gestalt or circle of symbols celebrating the life force and people's rituals. The

Three of Pentacles—Work: "Three pentacles suggested the number 15, long associated with the three Matronae (Mothers), or Triple Goddess worshiped in conjunction with Cernunnos (the Horned God) . . . the oldest myths said it was the Triple Goddess who first gave humanity a knowledge of the sacred runes. The heavenly father Odin himself knew nothing of writing and reading until he won this feminine knowledge by self-immolation. The Goddess who invented runes was the same Goddess who kept the divine apples of regeneration, with their inner pentacles. She made her consort Bragi a master of magical poetry by engraving her runes on his tongue. Like all mythologies, Norse mythologies called the alphabet a female invention." (Barbara G. Walker, Secrets of the Tarot, Harper & Row, 1984).

intensity of color combined with the powerful archetypal imagery of the Major Arcana are particularly useful as life-affirming meditative tools. Includes a 28-page instruction booklet. EF

1981. Available from The Gaia Catalogue Company ($27.45 ppd.) and at bookstores. For wholesale orders contact Karen Vogel, P.O. Box 697, Pt. Reyes, CA 94956.

Motherpeace
Round Tarot
© Vicki Noble
and Karen Vogel,
1981.

HOW THE MOTHERPEACE TAROT CARDS CAME TO BE

VICKI NOBLE

The Motherpeace tarot cards are different from ordinary tarot cards because they're round. That was something which crystallized only after the first drawing was made.

My friend Karen Vogel and I started exploring the amazing questions: What happened to make this world the way it is? More specifically, how did this great power imbalance happen? It couldn't be the human condition, that we were sure of. It's not a natural biological phenomenon that women are less important than men in the world—that just doesn't make any sense! And so we started searching.

Karen is an anthropologist and I'm a feminist historian. We spent about two years fully immersing ourselves in researching matriarchal cultures. We found that a matriarchal goddess-worshiping culture *always* preceded whatever male deity arose. In these cultures, cities grew up around women's activities: women acting as priestesses, bread baking taking place in the temple, women cultivating grain, settling communities, burying the dead, building communal houses and creating ceremonies. The mysteries of life were basic, like cooking, like transforming a food from a grain into a bread by means of fire.

We found that the place through which women lost their power was sexuality. Most of the rituals done in the early culture centers were fertility celebrations. Culturally, we think of sexuality as separate from and opposite to the sacred. But what we're dealing with in the earliest strata of culture is sacred sexuality. The early cultures are totally Earth-based, body-based religion. Because sacred knowledge is in the body, sacred sexual expression was connected to the cycle of the seasons, which, in fact, was connected to fertility cycles.

The lunar cycle is the first calendar in every culture. As a woman, you know that your fertility cycle is intimately linked to your sexuality cycle, not in whether you are sexual with someone, but in your vital energy. It's different when you are ovulating than when you are bleeding. In matriarchal cultures, the cycles of a woman's energy were collective knowledge. Imagine little girls today being taught early on about their powers and their sexual feelings and knowledge. These female sacred teachings eventually became hidden, for protection.

When the first Motherpeace image emerged it was a Shakti image, the six of wands. And we looked at it and said, "It's round." CLICK! "We're gonna make a round tarot deck!"

We divided the images and started drawing. Neither of us were artists, so it was very wonderful to have the images come through in a way that was playful, and not attached to ego. The pictures just flowed out of our hands! For a whole year. We went into deep trance every day and drew pictures. It was a totally ecstatic experience and I've never experienced anything quite like it before or since. We felt that these were little people who already existed in another place, who were just bursting through, and had a plan of their own. We were simply conduits for them. It was very unexpected.

We were conscious of wanting to make healing images, something that when you look at it, actually heals you. Even if you have to look at an image that's not so positive, it still can have a healing effect by bringing consciousness to your situation. On a real simple level, the magic of the Motherpeace deck occurs because the images are positive.

As you look at an image, another level of consciousness enters you and acts on you. If a deck of cards is healing, you are going to feel healed. If it's transformative, you may feel disturbed. What I really believe you can do with the cards is converse with the Goddess, the feminine aspect of divine energy. When you do that, in our culture, you're automatically healed, because, until recently, we have not had divine feminine energy coming through. So, all you need is just a little and you start to be transformed, to experience the world differently.

I think the return of the Goddess that's happening right now, that occult people call the manifestation of the feminine ray on the planet, means that we each have different tasks and ways of bringing it through, like the cards. We have to embody it, if we're women. And we have to surrender to it, if we're men. We both have different tasks, and they're often unknown to us.

Women do not know how to be feminine. We may think we have a corner on the market, since we were born with feminine bodies, but it's just as new to us as if we were men. We have to create the feminine. We have to feel into it, and try to get at what it actually is, aside from all the cultural pictures of the feminine which are distorting and distorted. And they are in us.

We're here, in the eighties, in America, and the Goddess is returning, and we're bringing Her through. And we're not going to bring Her through like Native Americans, and we're not going to bring Her through like ancient Sumerians, and we're not going to bring Her through like a Tantric priestess in the Middle Ages in India. We're here to bring Her through just as we are.

This article is excerpted from the *Motherpeace Cassettes, Matriarchal Herstory* (see listing on page 225). To contact Vicki Noble for Motherpeace workshops, and the Female Shamanic Training Program, send a SASE to Vicki Noble, P.O. Box 5544, Berkeley, CA 94705.

THEA'S TAROT
RUTH WEST

Thea's Tarot cards feature well-defined, high-contrast black-and-white images on quality glossy card stock. The uniqueness of this deck is in its consistent presentation of bold, solid female imagery. By renaming the court cards Mother, Daughter, Amazon, and Child, Thea's Tarot allows us to enter into relationship with the inner significance of these archetypes rather than placing their energy outside ourselves. This deck is particularly affirmative of familial relationships between women, as in the Ten of Cups, which depicts two women lovingly holding a child. Thea's Tarot comes with explanations for each card and an attractive box to protect and store the cards. EF

1984. Available from Medusa Graphics, 66 Dudleyville Rd., Leverett, MA 01054 ($16.50 ppd.).

TIGER AND DRAGON ORACLE I CHING CARDS
ROWENA PATTEE

The sixty-four cards in the Tiger and Dragon Oracle are designed for women and men seeking psychological and spiritual guidance based on an integration of the I Ching, Taoist yoga, and the universal wisdom found in archetypal patterns of change. In the Taoist system, the Tiger is the power of fire in the heart and the Dragon is the power of water in the abdomen and head. Asking a question is the first step in this harmonious guidance through change. A companion book, *Moving with Change: A Woman's Re-integration of the I Ching* (Routledge & Kegan Paul, 1986), is available at local bookstores or directly from the publisher. PW

1986. To order write: Golden Point Productions, P.O. Box 240, Mount Shasta, CA 96067 (cards $14 ppd., book $14 ppd.).

THE WOMANSPIRIT
SOURCEBOOK

C A L E N D A R

R E S O U R C E S

ART FOR PEACE CALENDAR
MAUI PEACE PRODUCTIONS

Andrea Smith's art reflects her faith in the unity of humanity and the possibility of world peace. At a World Peace Conference held in February of 1985 she met the president of the United Nations' University of Peace. Together they devised a way to use her art to generate peace in the minds of people. Says Andrea about her art: "My work is my message, and the message I want to get across is peace. I feel that the relationship we have with ourselves is the most important. . . . The paintings are universal messages about balancing the Earth and ourselves: about humanity blending in harmony, about states of consciousness and how those states create reality in our physical world. . . . My greatest desire is to help others find peace within themselves." Proceeds from the sale of the *Art for Peace Calendar* are contributed to the University of Peace.

Available from The Gaia Catalogue Company and Maui Peace Produc-

tions, 1590 Lokia Street, Lahaina, Maui Hawaii 96761, (808) 667-4377 ($8.95 ppd.)

CARRY IT ON PEACE CALENDAR
SYRACUSE CULTURAL WORKERS

Syracuse Cultural Workers (SCW) is a nonprofit organization dedicated to creating a climate of peace, social justice, and human liberation through cultural transformation. They publish and distribute calendars, posters, and cards by socially responsible artists whose works have a redemptive power. *Carry It On Peace Calendar*, the mainstay of their work, is a legend in our time. The calendar, published since 1970, celebrates cultural diversity with luminous artwork from around the world. Full-color reproductions of paintings, photographs, batik, fabric art, and mural art commemorate the peace movement, the struggle of working-class people, gay pride, women's spiritual wisdom, and the ongoing impulse toward creating a more just and humane society. Features lunar cycles, people's history dates, and a large networking list.

Available from Syracuse Cultural Workers, Box 6367, Syracuse, NY 13217, (315) 474-1132 ($10.70 ppd. per calendar; price break on multiple calendar orders).

CYCLES OF HARMONY PERSONAL MOON CALENDAR
JENNIFER SULLIVAN
SHANTIVANAM, HOUSE OF PRAYER

Cycles of Harmony is a simple calendar on which to daily chart your physical and emotional energies along with your moon time. The calendar can be personalized to chart whatever is of significance to you and to chart responses to the flow of your daily life. After several months you can easily observe your energy patterns in relation to the cycles of the moon. A small explanation card is included with the calendar. Printed on lightweight paper, it can be carried or posted on a wall. Size: 11″ × 17″.

Available from Cycles of Harmony, R.R. 1, Box 247, Easton, KS 66020, (913) 773-8255 ($5.95 ppd.).

EVER'WOMAN'S CALENDAR
CAROL CALVERT
MORNING GLORY COLLECTIVE

The female practice of observing and charting the menstrual cycle is as essential today as it was to our ancient foremothers. We walk in balance when we know our body's rhythms and make choices on the basis of that knowledge. *Ever'Woman's Calendar*, an 11″ × 17″ color poster/chart, provides a place to record your moon cycles, fertility patterns, and body rhythms. Includes herbal remedies, lunar lore, women's poetry, and art. Makes a wonderful gift for menarch (first menstruation) or for any woman seeking to reconnect with the wisdom of her body.

Available in bookstores or direct from the publisher: Morning Glory Collective, P.O. Box 1631, Tallahassee, FL 32302, (904) 222-7028 ($4.75 ppd.).

"Peace Within, Peace on Earth" © Andrea Smith, 1987. Full color 32″ × 25″ poster available from The Gaia Catalogue Company, $30 ppd.

LUNAR CALENDAR
NANCY PASSMORE, EDITOR/PUBLISHER

For the moon lover in us all, the annual *Lunar Calendar* offers a veritable Pandora's box of lunar treasures. This enchanting 32-page wall-hanging calendar depicts the thirteen lunations of the year as open spirals. In addition to containing splendid graphics, prose, and poetry by celebrated artists and writers, the *Lunar Calendar* notes all phases of the moon, rising and setting times, astronomical and astrological data, high earth festivals, and morning and evening stars, and includes an excellent bibliography, scholarly information, and complete instructions on how to use your calendar for maximum lunacy!

Luna Press. Available throughout the year from The Gaia Catalogue Company ($13.50 ppd.).

MOONDANCE: A WOMAN'S FERTILITY AWARENESS CALENDAR
TEXT BY RHONDA AKIN-DARNELL AND GINGER MITCHELL, R.N.; DRAWINGS BY MINISA CRUMBO

Moondance is a beautiful and informative new women's calendar that celebrates feminine cyclicity and fertility choices. Yet, more than a calendar, *Moondance* is a resource for women seeking the validation and empowerment of the feminine available to us when we deepen our understanding of our unique energy cycle. Each month features a personal fertility-tracking chart with space for notes and observations of your physiological cycle and PMS. It offers explanations of various methods of natural conception control such as calendar rhythm, symptothurmal method, lunaception, cosmic fertility method, oral contraception, and contraception devices. Exquisite line drawings by Native American artist Minisa Crumbo can be painted, colored, framed, and

The Triple Goddess © Linda Scharf, 1987. Pastels, full color, 11″ × 17″.

used for meditation.

Variena Publishing. Available from Variena Publishing, 3100 W. 71st Ave., Westminster, CO 80030, (303) 429-8888 ($13 ppd.).

WE'MOON ALMANAC
MUSAWA

An international, astrological lunar calendar as well as a datebook, *We'Moon Almanac* provides a way to track the ebb and flow of our lives from an Earth-loving, cross-cultural, Goddess-inspired we'moon perspective. You can schedule meetings, gatherings, and sacred time around the phases of the moon and your own bodily rhythms.

Available in women's bookstores, or from the publisher: Bréz Jayland, Mother Tongue Ink, 37010 Southeast Snuffin Rd., Estacada, OR 97023, (503) 630-7848 ($9.50 ppd.).

WHEEL OF THE YEAR CALENDAR
SUSAN BAYLIES

Wheel of the Year Calendar is a wheel mounted on heavy cardstock paper that rotates to show the phases of the lunar cycle. The calendar shows the ancient Pagan holidays and the

cross-quarter Sabbats: Candlemas, May Eve, Lammas, and Hollows Eve. A lunar phase card is mounted beneath the wheel. Available in green, blue, or red paper. Snake & Snake also produces the lunar phase card singly as a notecard that folds out to 8-½″ × 11″; it shows the moon's phases for every night of the year, new and full moon times, and astrological signs of the moon.

Snake & Snake Productions. Available from Snake & Snake Productions, Rt. 3, Box 165, Durham, NC 27713 (calendar, $5; lunar phase card, $1.50 ppd.).

"Featherwoman can be considered a self-portrait. I am shy to admit this, because she is someone I will have to grow into. Elegant, dignified, and serene, she has qualities I admire in strong Indian women. These qualities are shown to me by the elder women of my tribe who seem to only grow in beauty as they age." (Lillian Pitt, 11528 SE Lincoln St., Portland, OR 97216).

RITUAL FOR

THE GRANDMOTHER STICK

With ravens' wings,

brush the air.

Jonelle Maison

Place salt here

Name the Grandmothers!

and breadmeal.

Chant the deeds

Offer wine

of the Grandmothers!

to the Grandmothers

of the five directions.

As you circle

in the earth circle

Now as you begin the dance

match your heart to the drum

learned in dream

let your bracelets sound

the song you have brought

these words—

from the house of the Grandmothers.

let them enter you as fire,

as water.

It is your voice

in the song of women

that closes the circle.

You have washed

in the smoke of sweet herbs

put on your skin apron

As you dance

and tied the girdle, nine knots

praise the Grandmothers

as the Grandmothers have taught you.

who have taught you this.

Sweep the stone clean

Take your place in the circle,

with oak and cedar.

first and last.

Featherwoman
© Lillian Pitt,
1986. Raku, 18"
× 10" × 14".
Photo by Dennis
Maxwell.

**THE WOMANSPIRIT
SOURCEBOOK**

B O O K S T O R E S

The bookstores are alphabetized first by state, then by city.

Alaska Women's Bookstore
111 W. 9th
Anchorage, AK 99503

Lodestar Books
2020 11th Ave. S.
Birmingham, AL 35205

Aradia
116 W. Cottage
Flagstaff, AZ 86002

Humanspace Books, Inc.
1617 N. 32nd St., Suite 5
Phoenix, AZ 85008
(602) 220-4419

Antigone Books
403 E. 5th St.
Tucson, AZ 85705

Eucalyptus Books
1917 Maple St.
Bakersfield, CA 93304

The Gaia Catalogue Company
(catalogue $3.00)
1400 Shattuck Ave. #10
Shattuck Commons
Berkeley, CA 94709
(415) 548-4172

Gaia: Books, Music, Sacred Arts
1400 Shattuck Ave.,
Shattuck Commons
Berkeley, CA 94709
(415) 548-4172

Sisterspirit Bookstore
1173 Salerno Dr.
Campbell, CA 95008

The Pilgrim's Way Bookstore
P.O. Box 1944
Carmel, CA 93921
(408) 624-4955

Different Pages
2201 Park Ave.
Chico, CA 95928

Labrys Books
116 W. 2nd St. #2
Chico, CA 95926
(916) 894-2116

Valley Women
805 E. Olive Ave.
Fresno, CA 93728

A Different Drummer Bookshoppe
1027 N. Pacific Coast Highway #A
Laguna Beach, CA 92651

Sisterhood Bookstore
1351 Westwood Blvd.
Los Angeles, CA 90024

A Woman's Place
4015 Broadway
Oakland, CA 94611

Mama Bear's
6536 Telegraph Ave.
Oakland, CA 94609
(415) 428-9684

Stepping Stones
621 Hawthorne Ave.
Palo Alto, CA 94301

Page One
966 N. Lake Ave.
Pasadena, CA 91104

Lioness Books
2224 J St.
Sacramento, CA 95816

Old Wive's Tales
1009 Valencia St.
San Francisco, CA 94110

Sisterspirit
1040 Park Ave.
San Jose, CA 95126

ClaireLight
1110 Petaluma Hill Rd. #5
Santa Rosa, CA 95404
(707) 575-8879

Bread and Roses
13812 Ventura Blvd.
Sherman Oaks, CA 91423

Celebration
2209 W. Colorado Ave.
Colorado Springs, CO 80904
(303) 634-1855

Book Garden
2625 E. 12th Ave.
Denver, CO 80206

The Tattered Cover
2955 E. 1st Ave.
Denver, CO 80206

Golden Thread Booksellers
915 State St.
New Haven, CT 06511
(203) 777-7807

Bloodroot
85 Ferris St.
Bridgeport, CT 06605

Readers' Feast
529 Farmington Ave.
Hartford, CT 06105

Lammas Bookstore
321 7th St. S.E.
Washington, DC 20003

Lammas Bookstore #2
1426 21st St. N.W.
Washington, DC 20036

Lambda Rising Bookstore
1625 Connecticut Ave. N.W.
Washington, DC 20009

Rubyfruit Books
666–4 W. Tennessee St.
Tallahassee, FL 32304

Charis Books and More
419 Moreland Ave. N.E.
Atlanta, GA 30307

Woman's Word Bookstore
(lending library in YMCA)
1820 University Ave.
Honolulu, HI 96822

Book Peddlers
P.O. Box 2471
Des Moines, IA 50311

Women and Children First
1967 N. Halsted
Chicago, IL 60614

Wild Hags Literary Productions
(mail order)
2515 N. Prairie
Evanston, IL 60201

Dreams and Swords
116 N. Grant St.
Bloomington, IN 47401

Dreams and Swords
828 E. 64th St.
Indianapolis, IN 46220

Spinsters Books and Webbery
P.O. Box 1306
Lawrence, KS 66044

New Words Bookstore
186 Hampshire St.
Cambridge, MA 02139

Womonfyre Books
22 Center St.
Northampton, MA 01060

The Crystal Works
301 North St.
Pittsfield, MA 01201

Womancrafts Inc.
373 Commercial St.
Provincetown, MA 02657

31st Street Bookstore
425 E. 31st St.
Baltimore, MD 21218

Cover to Cover
7188 Cradlerock Wy.
Columbia, MD 21045

New Leaf Books
438 Main St.
Rockland, ME 04841

Crazy Wisdom
206 N. 4th Ave.
Ann Arbor, MI 48104

Pandora
226 W. Lovell
Kalamazoo, MI 49007

Motherwit Books and More
2011 E. Michigan Ave.
Lansing, MI 48912

Sapphire Books
P.O. Box 9063
Livonia, MI 48151

Amazon Bookstore
1612 Harmon Pl.
Minneapolis, MN 55403

Sun Sight Books
612 W. Lake St.
Minneapolis, MN 55408

Many Voices
889 Grand Ave.
St. Paul, MN 55105

Women's Eye
6165 Delmar Blvd.
St. Louis, MO 63112-1203

Common Woman Bookstore
1065 N. 33rd Street
Lincoln, NE 68503

Common Womyn
8 Prince St.
Concord, NH 03301

Herizon Books
P.O. Box 517
Convent Station, NJ 07961

Pandora Book Peddlers
68 W. Palisades Ave.
Englewood, NJ 07631

Full Circle
2205 Silver S.E.
Albuquerque, NM 87106

Emma: Women's Books and Gifts
168 Elmwood
Buffalo, NY 14201

Womankind Books (mail order)
5 Kivy St.
Huntington Station, NY 11746

Smedley's Bookshop
307 W. State St.
Ithaca, NY 14850

Oscar Wilde Memorial Bookshop
15 Christopher St.
New York, NY 10014

Silkwood Books
633 Monroe Ave.
Rochester, NY 14607

Alternatives Corner
374 Woodfield Rd.
West Hempstead, NY 11552

Crazy Ladies Bookstore
4112 Hamilton
Cincinnati, OH 45223

Six Steps Down, Inc.
1921 W. 25th St.
Cleveland, OH 44113

Fan the Flames
65 S. Fourth St.
Columbus, OH 43215

Iris Books
62 South Garfield St.
Dayton, OH 45403-2003

Herland Sister Resources, Inc.
1630 N.W. 19th
Oklahoma City, OK 73106

Mother Kali's Books
1070 Lawrence St.
Eugene, OR 97401

A Woman's Place
1431 NE Broadway
Portland, OR 97232

Giovanni's Room
345 S. 12th St.
Philadelphia, PA 19107

Gertrude Stein Memorial Bookshop
1003 E. Carson
Pittsburgh, PA 15203

Sign of Aquarius Studios
815 Copeland St.
Pittsburgh, PA 15232

Book Worm
1823 Murray Ave.
Pittsburgh, PA 15217

Book Women
324 E. 6th St.
Austin, TX 78701

Celebration
108 W. 43rd St.
Austin, TX 78751

Lucia's Garden
2213 Portsmouth
Houston, TX 77098
(713) 523-6494

Everyone's Books
71 Elliot St.
Brattleboro, VT 05301

Goddess Rising: Matriarchal
Wicce/Ritual Shop
4006 1st N.E.
Seattle, WA 98105
(206) 632-3829

A Room of One's Own
317 W. Johnson St.
Madison, WI 53703

Multi-Cultural Women's Market
(mail order)
2014 E. Lafayette Pl.
Milwaukee, WI 53202

Sojourner's Dial-A-Bookshop
1207 7th Ave.
Charleston, WV 25302

Sunrab Book Service
2705 5th Ave.
Huntington, WV 25702

Common Woman Books
8208 104th St.
Edmonton, Alberta, CN T6E4E6

Women's Bookstop
333 Main St. W.
Hamilton, Ontario, CN L8P1K1

Womansline Books
209 John St.
London, Ontario, CN N6A1N9

Montreal Women's Bookstore
4052 St. Urbain St.
Montreal, Quebec, CN H2W1V3

Ottawa Women's Bookstore
380 Elgin St.
Ottawa, Ontario, CN K2P1N1

Vancouver Woman's Bookstore
315 Cambie St.
Vancouver, British Columbia,
CN V6B2N4

The major portion of this list is provided courtesy of Feminist Bookstore News. Used with permission. For subscription information write: Feminist Bookstore News, 2120 Market St. #208, San Francisco, CA 94114. Tel: (415) 626-1556.

THE WOMANSPIRIT
SOURCEBOOK

C O N T R I B U T O R S

Kore Hayes Archer is a sign language interpreter, free-lance writer and mother. Her interests include improvisational theater, maskmaking and women's rituals. She lives in the hills outside Santa Cruz, California.

Asoka Bandarage, Ph.D., comes from a Sri Lankan Buddhist background. She is a scholar, teacher, and social change activist. Her publications include many articles, reviews, and two books: *Colonialism in Sri Lanka* (Mouton, 1983) and *Gender, Race and Class: A Global Perspective* (Zed Press, forthcoming). She was guest editor of the Women of Color issue of *Woman of Power* magazine (Fall 1986). She gives seminars and workshops on gender issues, race and ethnicity, Third World development, and the sociology of health and healing.

Gloria Bertonis, M.Ed., is a mother of six (including the editor of this book), grandmother of five, a psychological educator, a lecturer, counselor, and feminist researcher. She lives in Bucks County, Pennsylvania, with her daughter Holley.

Patricia Broughton is a free-lance writer, poet, and photographer. Her spirituality, originating in Christianity, finds expression these days in twelve-step programs, Connections with womyn, and Anne Wilson Schaef's "living process." She lives in Chicago with her two children.

Patricia C. Camarena (Raven) is a Mexican-American free-lance fiction and poetry writer and journalist. She was managing editor for the Woman of Color issue of *Woman of Power* magazine (Fall 1986). Her interests include the contemporary arts and the spiritual and magical practices of the Old Religions of various cultures. She believes that the connections of the web are stronger than the separations claimed to be reality.

Regina Falsetto is writer, an artist, a dancer, and the mother of a young son. In addition to writing children's stories and music, she is currently designing a lunar calendar, which combines her love of feminine spiritual images and knowledge and her commitment to healing through art.

Ellen Fishburn is an artist and ritualist living in the Bay Area with her husband Michael and their animals. She founded a notecard company, Fishburn Designs, with the intention "to reach large numbers of people with healing images." She is currently working on her own tarot deck out of a love for the power of images and the transformative wisdom of the tarot.

Adele Getty is a ceremonialist, consultant, and chanter whose songs have been recorded on *In Search of Our Native Roots*. Over the years she has worked with a variety of native teachers, and she leads rites-of-passage ceremonies as a way of deepening our relationship with the Earth. She lives in both London and Berkeley, teaching and lecturing on shamanism, sound healing, and the fate of the Earth.

Lynn Gottlieb is a storyteller, a mother of a young son, and a rabbi who lives in Albuquerque, New Mexico. She is currently working on a book entitled *Shekhinah Coming Home: A Feminist Revisioning of Judaism*.

Lish Hanhart is a Dutch free-lance journalist. For the last four years she has worked as a writer and field researcher in the international deep ecology movement and interspecies communication.

Virginia Hearn is a free-lance writer and editor living in Berkeley, California. An adjunct professor of communications at New College Berkeley, she also edits *Update*, national newsletter of the Evangelical Women's Caucus (EWC), and *Green Leaf*, newsletter of the Bay Area EWC.

Mara Lynn Keller holds a doctorate in philosophy from Yale University and is an associate professor of philosophy and women's studies at San Francisco State University. She has been active in the women's rights, civil rights, and peace movements since the 1960s, and is a practitioner of Rosen Method bodywork. Currently she is working on a book, *The Mysteries of Demeter and Persephone, Mother-Daughter Goddesses of Fertility, Sexuality, and Rebirth*.

Rebecca Kuiken is a writer, a Presbyterian minister, and executive director of the interreligious Council of Oakland, who seeks to weave faith and feminism in contemporary Christian spirituality. She lives in Oakland, California, with her husband and infant daughter. She is currently writing a book on women's stories of faith.

Andrea Lewis is a performer and writer who is currently trying to make ends meet in San Francisco. She has appeared with the San Francisco Opera, the Oakland and San Francisco Symphony Choruses, and in many of the popular music clubs of the Bay Area and her old hometown of Ann Arbor, Michigan. Her articles and reviews have been published in *Coming Up!* and *Plexus*, the West Coast Women's

Press, where she also worked as arts and entertainment editor for two years.

Alexis Masters is a writer and practicing professional astrologer in the San Francisco Bay Area. She has taught classes on astrology, meditation, and women's spiritual quest since 1976. In recent years, Alexis has traveled to Europe and the Aegean, where she has conducted research on the origins of mythology and religion. In *Aphrodite's Mysteries: The Path of Beauty, Grace, and Ecstasy* (a work in progress), Alexis explores the history of the Goddess and her relevance for contemporary women.

Amy O'Connor, a prodigious music collector, writes often about women's culture. She enjoys reading, jogging, and shouting back at TV news commentaries.

Diana L. Paxson is a writer and an ordained priestess of the Old Religion, whose novels, including *Bringsamen* and *White Mare, Red Stallion*, focus on the Goddess in past and present. She is a founder of the Darkmoon Circle, coordinator of the Fellowship of the Spiral Path, and author of *The Liturgy of the Lady* (MZB Productions, Berkeley, CA, 1987).

Arisika Razak is a single parent of a teenage son, who works as a midwife in an inner-city hospital in Oakland, California. She has been a student of the Earth-centered religious traditions of Africa, Europe, and northern Native American peoples since 1970. She is currently working with women to reclaim the sacredness of their bodies and their sexuality through dance.

T. Drorah Setel is currently working on her first book, *Making Our Own Way: Feminist Paths in Judaism*, an introductory study and action guide. She is a founding member of Benoyot Eysh, a Jewish feminist spirituality collective, and has been active in Rosh Hodesh groups and women's minyans. Setel lives in Los Angeles, where she is involved in a variety of Jewish, feminist, and Jewish feminist projects.

Carolyn Ray Shaffer is a professional writer and teacher whose work has appeared in *New Age Journal, Yoga Journal, Shaman's Drum, Plexus*, and *Commonweal*, and in Charlene Spretnak's anthology, *The Politics of Women's Spirituality*. She also coauthored *City Safaris: A Sierra Club Explorers' Guide to Urban Adventures for Grownups and Kids*. She is currently developing workshops designed to help women and men rediscover their natural spirituality.

Cedar Spring is a writer, healer, and ritualist living in Minnesota. Her work is in creating sacred human community, particularly the creative lesbian edge; she is in the process of creating a wilderness sanctuary/retreat space called Delphos. After years in feminist Wicce, by surprise she found herself involved with *zazen* as the way of awakening. She has two teenage daughters, and when they grow up will probably become a wandering monk.

Marilee Stark, Ph.D., is a psychologist, educator, writer, and mother committed to exploring and facilitating spiritual paths that reflect women's experiences. Her doctoral dissertation, "Maiden Voyage," is an examination of women's psychology and women's spiritual quest through an autobiographical account of her own journey. She is currently teaching women's psychology at the Rosebridge School of Integrative Psychology.

Joan Iten Sutherland is a writer, scholar, teacher, and ritualist who brings together her study of Asian philosophy and *zazen* (Zen meditation) practice with the exploration of a new thealogy arising out of women's spirituality. She is the creator of the Amargi Center and is currently writing a book on contemplative traditions and women.

Nancy Vedder-Shults is a free-lance writer and a scholar of women's music history and women's literature at the University of Wisconsin at Madison. She writes, "As an outgrowth of my feminism, the empowerment I find in the spirit of the Goddess within me is an ever-renewing fountain. To quote one of my favorite songs, 'filling up and spilling over, it's an endless waterfall.'" She has published a guide to women's music and is a founding member of Womansong, a feminist choir in Madison, Wisconsin.

Lisa Yount writes educational materials for children, science articles, poetry, and fantasy stories. Her poems have appeared in numerous magazines including *Anima, Womanspirit, Primavera*, and *Minnesota Review*. Her first book of poetry, *Stones and Bones*, is available from Half-a-Lump Press, 5642 San Jose Ave., Richmond Annex, CA 94804 ($5.95 ppd.). She lives in Richmond, California, with her husband and three cats.

ABOUT THE AUTHOR

Patrice Wynne has distinguished herself as a visionary activist, dedicated to restoring feminine and feminist spiritual values in today's world. Her spiritual path, an integration of Goddess, Buddhist and New Age traditions, provides the foundation for her work in the world. She is the owner of a mail-order catalogue company, The GAIA Catalogue Company, and a retail store in Berkeley, GAIA: Books, Music, Sacred Arts. A graduate of San Francisco State University, Womens Studies Department, with a degree in Women's Spirituality, she has worked as a corporate manager, a campus minister, a human rights spokesperson for Amnesty International, and as a staff member in residence at The Ojai Foundation. The Womanspirit Sourcebook draws on her life experiences and her committment to serve as a catalyst for a more compassionate, transformed world. She finds the strength to live out her dreams in loving, playful relationships with a community of friends and in doing work that nurtures and empowers herself and others. She lives in Berkeley with her partner, Eric, and her cat companion, Bonkers.

Photo by
Mark Johann

Index